A Death in Jerusalem

ALSO BY KATI MARTON

An American Woman
Wallenberg
The Polk Conspiracy

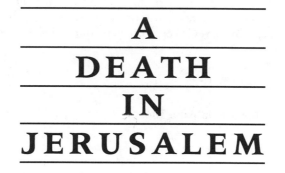

A
DEATH
IN
JERUSALEM

KATI MARTON

ARCADE PUBLISHING • NEW YORK

For my daughter Elizabeth Jennings
For my son Christopher Jennings

And for my mother and father,
Ilona and Endre Marton

FIRST ARCADE EDITION 1996

Illustration credits are on page 306.

Library of Congress Cataloging-in-Publication Data

   Marton, Kati.
      A death in Jerusalem / Kati Marton. —1st Arcade
   paperback ed.
         p.   cm.
      Previously published: 1st ed. New York: Pantheon Books,
      c1994.
      Includes bibliographical references and index.
      ISBN 1-55970-352-0
      1. Israel-Arab War, 1948–1949—Diplomatic history.
   2. Bernadotte, Folke, 1895–1948.   3. Loḥame ḥerut Yiśra 'el.
   4. Shamir, Itzak, 1915- .   5. Terrorism—Israel. I. Title
   DS126.92.M37   1996
   956.04'2—dc20   95-51833

Published in the United States by Arcade Publishing, Inc., New York,
by arrangement with Pantheon Books, a division of Random House
Distributed by Little, Brown and Company

10 9 8 7 6 5 4 3 2 1

Book design by Maura Fadden Rosenthal

RRD-VA

PRINTED IN THE UNITED STATES OF AMERICA

Contents

Introduction to the Arcade Edition

WHEN *A Death in Jerusalem* WAS PUBLISHED IN A HARDCOVER EDITION a year ago, I had no way to predict how tragically prophetic this story of the origins of Jewish extremism would become. But on Saturday, November 4, 1995, forty-seven years after the assassination of Count Folke Bernadotte, a Jewish zealot's gunfire again ripped through the body of a man of peace. Prime Minister Yitzhak Rabin had just finished addressing a rally in Tel Aviv. The seventy-three-year-old Rabin had exhorted his countrymen to follow him down the path of peace. "There are enemies of the peace process, and they try to hurt us," Rabin told his rapt audience. "But violence undermines democracy and must be denounced and isolated."

Moments later, a slight, dark figure closed in on the prime minister. Again the gunshots rang out. Again a man lay bleeding on a public square, and the flow could not be stanched. Again God's name was invoked by the killer. "I did this to stop the peace process," the assassin proclaimed. "We need to be coldhearted. . . . When you kill in war, it is an act that is allowed." Count Bernadotte's assassins might have chosen the same phrases to justify their crime forty-seven years ago. It would soon be apparent that Rabin's killer, like Bernadotte's, had more than divine inspiration supporting him. In the days to come the circle of conspirators widened to include more than half a dozen other members of a militant cell.

Like Count Folke Bernadotte's assassination, Rabin's murder was an impersonal crime, meant not so much to snuff out a life as to stop the peace process in its tracks. As in 1948, a struggle for the soul of Israel was at stake. Would the country be the province of absolutists, prepared for any act, no matter how violent, to preserve biblical Israel? Or would Israel's future be as a secular, pragmatic, democratic member of the family of nations? Now, as then, the gunman was part of an underground movement of zealots for whom Eretz Israel is God-given land, nonnegotiable.

For Amir and his fellow conspirators, Yitzhak Rabin was a traitor to Zion's cause. Rabin was prepared to trade land for peace. Amir, like Baruch Goldstein, who in 1994 gunned down Arab worshipers in the Hebron mosque, was a proponent of a messianic Judaism. Goldstein and Amir's spiritual roots converge with those who ambushed Bernadotte, the first United Nations Middle East peacemaker. Theirs is a righteous militancy that abides no debate. Amir, like Bernadotte's assassins, claims the Bible and the Torah as his manuals for nation building. Peace treaties hammered out by shuttle diplomats around internationally sponsored negotiating tables are the work of a *moser*, a betrayer of Jews. "A Jew who hands over Jewish land or wealth to an alien people," Rabbi Abraham Hecht, an Orthodox rabbi from New York, intoned during the last summer of Rabin's life, "is guilty of a sin worthy of the death penalty."

Yitzhak Rabin's willingness to make pragmatic choices for Israel's future — ceding ever more autonomy to the Palestinians, for the sake of peace — was betrayal in the zealots' eyes. Like Bernadotte's assassins, Amir and his conspirators were fanatics with a good aim. All had been trained in the military and then practiced their deadly craft in small, clandestine cells, blessed by rabbis who fueled their zeal.

In 1948, unlike today, Israel was a frail and very young state. Prime Minister David Ben Gurion was reluctant to tear at its fabric by energetically pursuing the mediator's killers. Within days of the crime, Ben Gurion knew who had hatched the conspiracy to kill Bernadotte. Putting the survival of his country ahead of punishing the killers, he struck a deal with them. Rejoin Israeli society, lead productive lives, and you may live as free men among us. The unwritten contract was respected by both sides. The killers kept their end, the prime minister his.

It is different today. Israel, though grief-stricken, is strong. The state today has the self-confidence to exact a fitting punishment for this crime. What is more, and in striking contrast to Bernadotte's assassination, Amir's bullets seem not to have shattered a peace process now too solidly entrenched. On the contrary, the assassination may have accelerated the process. On the first day following the end of the country's official mourning, acting prime minister Shimon Peres presided over the disengagement of Israeli troops from the town of Jenin, the northernmost Palestinian city in the West Bank. By day's end, Palestinian police were in full control of the city. But the deep wounds the assassin inflicted on Israel's collective psyche — a Jew capable of killing a fellow Jew in cold blood — will take far longer to heal.

A Death in Jerusalem traces the trajectory from the fiery rhetoric of early Zionist extremists Vladimir Jabotinsky and Abraham Stern (and by extension their spiritual heirs, Rabbi Meir Kahane and the militant rabbis who fueled Amir's rage) to the gunfire that felled both Folke Bernadotte and Yitzhak Rabin. The distance between rhetoric and gunfire is much shorter in a land soaked in the blood of the martyrs and villains of the world's three great religions than it is elsewhere. Yigal Amir, like Bernadotte's assassins in *A Death in Jerusalem,* acted with the calm of those convinced they are saving their people and land from the enemy. With the knowledge that God stands directly behind them, the assassins kill with impunity. In common with his deadly predecessors, Yigal Amir was ready to give his life for the cause of Eretz Israel. It is this willingness that makes fanatics on both sides of the Middle East divide the most dangerous barrier to peace in the most dangerous region in the world.

Kati Marton
November 15, 1995
New York City

Introduction to the Original Edition

ON FRIDAY, FEBRUARY 25, 1994, A BEARDED, UNIFORMED JEWISH SETTLER named Baruch Goldstein, armed with an automatic rifle, mowed down twenty-nine Muslim worshipers as they knelt in prayer in a Hebron mosque, the ancient Cave of the Patriarchs. The site of the massacre struck many with its bitter irony, for this cave is the one place on earth where both Jews and Muslims pray in the same building. Few places are so freighted with biblical and Koranic associations as the Cave of the Patriarchs, the burial site of Abraham and members of his family, sacred to both faiths.

By this mass killing on such holy ground, Baruch Goldstein intended to derail the Israeli-Palestinian peace process, begun on September 13, 1993, over a handshake on the White House lawn. That handshake between Yitzhak Rabin of Israel and Yasir Arafat of the Palestine Liberation Organization had offered remarkable hope that perhaps a way might be found to break the habits of hate that have paralyzed the Middle East for half a century.

Even as Rabin and Arafat took their tentative steps toward peace, powerful forces on both sides of the conflict fanned the flames of fanaticism in an effort to prevent progress. The fears held by many observers, that passion would once again overcome reason, and that another vicious cycle of terror and retribution would begin, were well founded.

The gunman, Baruch Goldstein, originally from Brooklyn, was only the most recent advocate of a brand of Jewish radicalism that opposes any compromise with the Palestinians. He was a follower of Rabbi Meir Kahane, a fiery zealot assassinated in Manhattan in 1991. But Kahane and Goldstein's ideological roots reach even farther back, to the charismatic and controversial figure of Vladimir Jabotinsky. A Russian-born writer and philosopher, Jabotinsky advocated a Jewish state on both sides of the Jordan River: Israel restored to its biblical proportions. Rabbi Kahane was first exposed to Jabotinsky's muscular Zionism as a member of his youth movement, Betar. But Kahane and his disciple Goldstein carried Jabotinsky's cry for Jewish rebirth to violent extremes that would have repelled their spiritual mentor.

Heavily armed settlers like Goldstein, clinging to settlements in the parched hills above Hebron, are not a new phenomenon in the life of the young state. Violence-prone zealots with the Bible and, on occasion, Jabotinsky's admonitions as their justification, have resorted to gunfire to block efforts at peace before. This is the story of the first attempt at reconciliation between Jews and Arabs, nearly fifty years ago. That effort also ended in bloodshed and the death of the mediator, Count Folke Bernadotte. Then, too, the gunmen were former disciples of Vladimir Jabotinsky. Their crime paid off: the 1948 mediation was derailed. Count Bernadotte's failed mediation and violent death is a prophetic tale.

*   *   *

Like Baruch Goldstein, zealots on both sides of the struggle can take a large measure of credit for the fact that peace in the Middle East has eluded half a century of effort by mediators ranging from Count Folke Bernadotte to Ralph Bunche, Henry Kissinger, Jimmy Carter, James Baker, and Warren Christopher. The peacemakers keep colliding with those for whom land is not negotiable. *Realpolitik* does not enter into the thinking of people whose point of reference is Abraham's biblical promise to the Hebrews that their land, Eretz Israel, shall stretch from the Nile to the Euphrates. For them, the Golan Heights and the West Bank are not just so many settlements, but part of their divinely fixed patrimony. And Palestinian extremists possessed of an equally fierce attachment to the same sliver of land have vowed to destroy any agreement that denies them any part of Palestine.

The first formal attempt to mediate the dispute began in the late spring of 1948 and was resolved in blood four months later. Jewish zealots gunned down a Swedish nobleman sent to the region by the United Nations to impose a peace neither side wanted. The assassins' motives were pure: to save Jerusalem, to save their vision of Israel. The four terrorists who ambushed Count Bernadotte — and those who dispatched them to do the deed — hated what the mediator stood for: the outside world encroaching on their bitterly earned independence. In their eyes Bernadotte threatened Israel's survival. Nor did they trust their own nation's leaders to remain true to the Zionist vision.

Bernadotte's assassins trusted no one but themselves. The Holocaust had taught them the lesson of self-reliance in a ruthless world. They believed they alone were fit to determine their country's future. Israel's leaders, the fabled pioneers revered by so many other Jews, were dismissed by Count Bernadotte's killers as cowards and compromisers, because of their apparent willingness to negotiate.

Thus, Bernadotte's assassination is also the story of the near destruction of a fragile new state, not only by the Arab armies massed on its borders, but also from a fratricidal conflict within her own borders. Jews struggled against Jews in a bitter contest for control of the future of their own country. Zionist maximalists insisted on an Israel of biblical proportions no matter what the cost. They saw as their enemies such internationally respected leaders as David Ben-Gurion and Golda Meir, who were willing to trim their dreams for their country to accommodate reality.

In 1994, as in 1948, Israel was threatened by clashing visions of the state being forged. Political and religious wounds were reopened as Israel turned over authority to Palestinians in Gaza and the West Bank — which many Israelis still call Judea and Samaria, their biblical names. Still engaged in the ongoing strife was the man who dispatched the death squad to ambush Bernadotte — Yitzhak Shamir. In April of 1994, Shamir urged Israeli soldiers to "disobey any command to remove Jews 'from the homeland' [the West

Bank] because that would be equivalent to an order to kill his parents."

Bernadotte's assassins and Shamir were members of Lehi, the Hebrew acronym for Fighters for the Freedom of Israel. More commonly known as the Stern Gang, after Avraham Stern, who founded the movement during the dark, wartime year of 1940, the underground army never numbered more than a few hundred. An independent Israel, free of any foreign presence, with Jerusalem as its sacred capital, was Stern and Lehi's goal. Lehi's method for achieving this dream was the traditional weapon of the powerless: individual terrorism, later to become, ironically, the hallmark of Israel's greatest enemy, the PLO. Obsessed by strength and independence, and trying to escape the Holocaust's shadow, Bernadotte's killers hoped to assert the victory of the Warrior Jew over the Victim Jew.

For the fledgling United Nations, Bernadotte's mediation between Arabs and Jews was its first crucible. The world body had been set up for the explicit purpose of peacefully resolving such conflicts among nations. A member of the Swedish royal family with a background as a humanitarian activist, Count Bernadotte had been chosen by the Security Council to mediate the world's most dangerously inflamed dispute. Bernadotte's mediation was stymied by more than just the extremists' refusal to negotiate the ownership of land they deemed nonnegotiable. His mission was seriously handicapped by a lack of real support from the United Nations' member states. In the 1990s the world body falters under the weight of a similar burden as its peacemakers and peacekeepers thread their way among ancient tribal enmities from the Middle East to Bosnia.

Recently, United Nations Secretary General Boutros Boutros-Ghali offered an insight into why Folke Bernadotte failed. Though not referring specifically to the Bernadotte Mission, the United Nations' first attempt at mediation and peacemaking, Boutros-Ghali might have been doing so. "Peacekeeping by itself cannot provide a permanent solution to a conflict. Only political negotiations can do that. . . . Peacekeeping success requires the cooperation of the parties, a clear and practicable mandate, the continuing support of the Security Council and adequate financial arrangements." Of the Secretary General's four minimum requirements for peacekeeping, Bernadotte could not count on a single one. What he had was a mandate from the General Assembly that stated, among other things, that he was "to take such measures as were necessary for the security and welfare of the population and promote a peaceful adjustment of the future situation of Palestine."

Drawn to the little-known and in many ways baffling story of Folke Bernadotte through my earlier work on his countryman Raoul Wallenberg, I found a vastly more complex tale than I had anticipated. In contrast to the morality tale pitting Adolf Eichmann's supreme evil against Wallenberg's luminous humanity, the story of Folke Bernadotte's ill-fated mediation and assassination defies the categories of absolutes. The lines between good and evil are often blurred in this chapter of Israel's history.

Reconstructing a decades-old murder at the intersection of diverse cultures and languages was made even more difficult because of the elusiveness of the man behind the crime. Until the recent publication of his memoirs, which obscure more than they illuminate about him, there was not a single English or Hebrew biography of the man who served as Israeli prime minister for longer than the country's revered patriarch, David Ben-Gurion. Yitzhak Shamir has good reason to shun the historian's scrutiny.

Fortunately, Shamir's former comrades from the underground were much less reticent than he himself. During the course of months of exhaustive conversations, one of these men, Baruch Nadel, provided me an illuminating journey into the mind of the zealot. Beginning with his remarkably vivid recollections of his youth spent under British rule in Palestine, the veteran Lehi fighter recounted the events leading up to Bernadotte's assassination with a passion the years have not cooled. Through Nadel and a handful of other surviving Lehi members, I began to fathom how otherwise decent men and women could kill in cold blood.

The line connecting the ambush of Count Bernadotte to Baruch Goldstein's mass killing at Hebron's Cave of the Patriarchs is all too tragically obvious. Both acts of violence had the same purpose: to thwart Israeli-Palestinian reconciliation. This book is in no way an apologia for atrocities committed in the name of some higher purpose. I hope, however, that it can help put in perspective the mad dance of violence in which Arabs and Jews have been locked for over half a century.

A Death in Jerusalem

JERUSALEM 1948

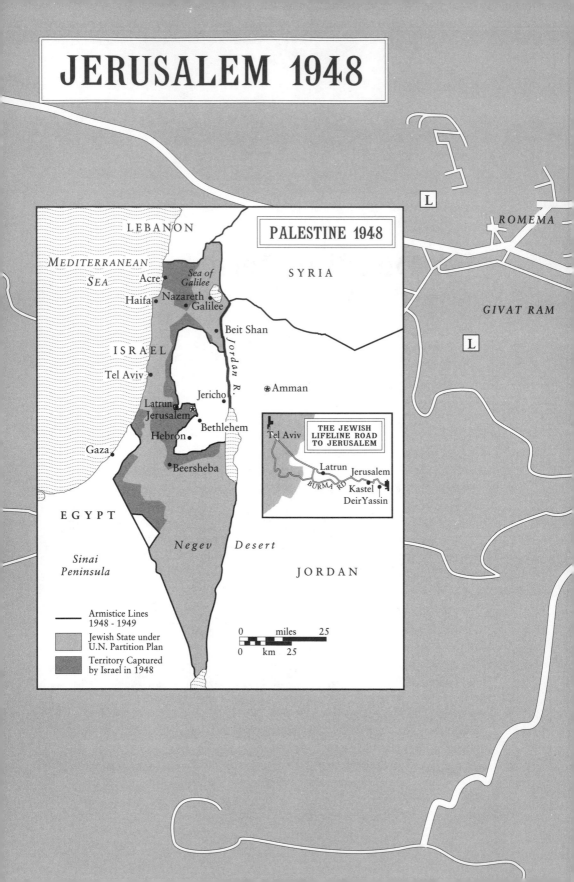

PALESTINE 1948

LEBANON

*MEDITERRANEAN
SEA*

SYRIA

Acre
*Sea of
Galilee*
Haifa
Nazareth
Galilee

Beit Shan

ISRAEL

Tel Aviv

Jordan R.

Jericho

⊛ Amman

Latrun
Jerusalem

Bethlehem

Hebron

Gaza

Beersheba

EGYPT

Negev Desert

*Sinai
Peninsula*

JORDAN

**THE JEWISH
LIFELINE ROAD
TO JERUSALEM**

Tel Aviv

Latrun
Jerusalem
BURMA RD
Kastel
Deir Yassin

L

ROMEMA

GIVAT RAM

L

	Armistice Lines 1948 - 1949
	Jewish State under U.N. Partition Plan
	Territory Captured by Israel in 1948

0   miles   25

0   km   25

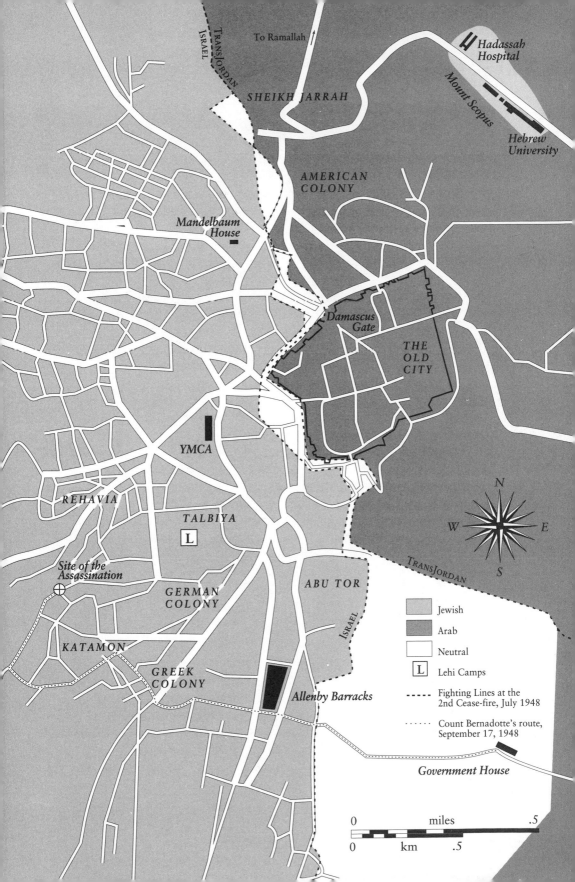

To Ramallah ↑

Hadassah
Hospital

SHEIKH JARRAH

Mount Scopus

ISRAEL

TransJordan

AMERICAN
COLONY

Hebrew
University

*Mandelbaum
House*

*Damascus
Gate*

THE
OLD
CITY

YMCA

N

REHAVIA

TALBIYA

W   E

L

TransJordan

S

*Site of the
Assassination*

GERMAN
COLONY

ABU TOR

	Jewish
	Arab
	Neutral
L	Lehi Camps

KATAMON

ISRAEL

GREEK
COLONY

- - - -   Fighting Lines at the
2nd Cease-fire, July 1948

Allenby Barracks

· · · · ·   Count Bernadotte's route,
September 17, 1948

Government House

0   miles   .5

0   km   .5

CHAPTER ONE

A DEATH
IN JERUSALEM

ON SEPTEMBER 17, 1948, AT TEN-FIFTEEN ON ONE OF THOSE PER-
fectly polished mornings the region offers up in early fall, Count
Folke Bernadotte's white DC-3 began its descent into the State of
Israel. The United Nations aircraft landed smoothly on the tiny
airstrip at Kalandia, north of Jerusalem. Folke Bernadotte, the
first United Nations mediator between Arabs and Jews, bounded
out of the plane.

Abdullah el-Tel, an Arab Legion colonel, strode forward to
escort the Swedish count to his armored car. Colonel el-Tel was
commander of the Transjordanian forces dispatched by King Abdullah to defend Jerusalem against Israeli incursions in the Arab-
Israeli conflict, now six months old.

Speed being the chief defense against snipers, the party raced
along the dusty road to Ramallah, where the Arab Legion's local
commander, Brigadier General Norman Lash, awaited them.
Deemed the most formidable fighting force in the Middle East,
the British-trained Arab Legion was charged with defending London's regional satellite, the Hashemite Kingdom of Transjordan.

Sandbags and barbed wire disfigured the facade of Ramallah's
Grand Hotel. Once the lure of Jerusalem's well-heeled residents,
it had been transformed into one more makeshift army headquarters during this summer of Israel's birth. Standing in the formal gardens, Bernadotte listened with a detached expression to
General Lash's lengthy litany of Jewish violations of the UN-
imposed truce.

Great Britain, awarded the Palestine Mandate by the League

of Nations in 1922, had been worn down by the Arabs' obsti-
nate opposition to London's promise of a Jewish home, and exhausted by terrorism from both sides. In March 1947, Prime
Minister Clement Atlee had turned to the United Nations to do
what London could not: restore a semblance of order to the region. The fledgling world body was thus presented with both the
greatest challenge of its three-year-old existence and the chance
to define its mission. For the UN was already proving impotent
to stop Great Power confrontations. Solving, or at least defusing,
smaller conflicts such as this one seemed to offer an opportunity
for the UN to succeed—somewhere. Following a May 27, 1948,
Security Council resolution ordering a truce between Israel and
the Arabs, Bernadotte had cajoled both sides into agreeing to lay
down their weapons. But the artillery fire that rumbled over the
Judean Hills mocked both the truce and the mediator.

General Lash, finished with his tirade, now urged Bernadotte
to take an armed Arab Legion escort to his next stop, Jerusalem.
But the count shook his head. "Eighty UN observers in Jerusalem
have no such protection," he said. "Why should I?" Nevertheless, as Bernadotte chatted with other members of the group,
General Aage Lundström, a tall, rangy fellow Swede who was
UN chief of staff in the region, took Lash aside and said, yes, we
would gratefully accept an armored car to escort Bernadotte's
convoy to the Mandelbaum Gate, which divided the Arab and
Jewish zones of Jerusalem. Hearing what Lundström had done,
Bernadotte shrugged and smiled resignedly.

The count's squared shoulders and frequent smiles belied his
fatigue. In his well-pressed khaki shirt and Bermuda shorts, his
Middle East uniform, the fifty-four-year-old Swede still looked
strikingly fit. As a young cavalry officer, he had learned the trick
of catching a five-minute nap between appointments, helpful
these days when he rose regularly in the predawn hours and
shuttled among half a dozen Middle Eastern capitals.

The optimism he had exuded in May, when he was appointed
to mediate the world's most rancorous dispute, had been eroded
by hours of empty negotiations with men who talked eloquently
of peace but put their faith in guns. Quitting had occurred to
Bernadotte only once, earlier that summer, when his frustration
reached a boiling point over UN delays in meeting his request for
a military unit to enforce the truce. His request had still not been
met, but Bernadotte had stayed on. In any case, abandoning his

post would have been next to impossible for a man described by Swedes close to him with the single word *rakryggad*— upright.

The convoy was finally on its way, bumping along the rutted dirt road just past the airstrip, when an Arab sniper's bullet hit the left rear fender of Bernadotte's Chrysler. Sitting in the front seat, Bernadotte's personal secretary, Barbro Wessel, a spirited twenty-eight-year-old the mediator called "Weasel," glanced at Lundström. Strange, she thought, for a general to look so anxious. But Folke Bernadotte, bred not to show fear, looked calm and his calm spread to Barbro. "Perhaps it would be safer to detour around Jerusalem through Latrun," General Lundström ventured.

"No, Aage," the count said, "I have to take the same risks as my observers. Besides, I must show them that no one has the right to prevent me from crossing the lines." Bernadotte deemed his presence in Jerusalem to be even more crucial since UN Secretary General Trygve Lie had declined to make the perilous journey himself.

Less than an hour later, his convoy reached the Holy City without further incident. "Good luck to you!" an American reporter called to Bernadotte as his car rolled across the line separating the Arab and the Jewish zones. "Thanks," the mediator waved back, flashing one of his wide smiles, "I shall need it."

When the convoy stopped on the Jewish side, a burly man saluted the mediator and introduced himself. "Captain Moshe Hillman, Israeli Army liaison." Noticing Hillman's service revolver tucked in its holster, Bernadotte said, "I'm afraid you'll have to leave that behind, Captain. None of our men are armed." Bernadotte pointed to the bullet hole in his car's fender. What was the use of one revolver against that? "The UN flag is our only protection."

At the dividing line, other UN officers waited to greet the count: Lt. Colonel William Cox, an American Marine in charge of UN peacekeeping operations in the city's Jewish sector; French Colonel André Sérot, the chief UN observer in Jerusalem; and Belgian Major Massart, head of observers in the Arab sector. Frank Begley, a former FBI officer now serving as UN security officer and Bernadotte's Jerusalem driver, joined the group, sliding in behind the Chrysler's wheel. Begley, a daredevil driver, knew his way around the mine field that the Holy City had become in the summer of 1948. He whisked the count, his newly expanded party in tow, to the YMCA on King David Street for lunch. There was no military escort, no offer of an armored car, nor anyone from whom General Lundström could request safe passage for the mediator's convoy.

A gaudy structure, the Y was America's contribution to Jerusalem's fantastic array of architectural landmarks. With its tall tower and its ornate, multicolored ceilings, it had more in common with a pharaoh's tomb than with Jerusalem's ramparts. As a result of a series of Byzantine negotiations involving the International Red Cross, the UN, and Arab and Israeli authorities, the Y and the equally fabled King David Hotel across the street were deemed to be a demilitarized "zone of sanctuary" under the unarmed "protection," first of the Red Cross, then later of the United Nations, and still later of the United States consulate. This little enclave was meant to be off-limits to the belligerents. Women and children were to be admitted at all times and temporary asylum was to be given to refugees while fighting was taking place. Those entering the "zone" had to surrender their arms. The count and his party planned to spend the night at the YMCA.

Also at the YMCA lunch table was a young Swede, Jan de Geer, who had recently joined Bernadotte's personal staff and traveled with the mediator from his headquarters on the Greek island of Rhodes. The count's presence was always a remarkable event in the besieged city, which had been abandoned by much of the world since it had become a war zone in May. With Bernadotte in their midst, the gathering took on the charged quality of a conversation between men in the field and their commanding officer.

They knew by now never to call him "count." Even Barbro called him "Folke." When someone in the group politely inquired after the health of "the countess," Bernadotte pointedly asked, "Are you speaking of my wife?" Not that he was an easygoing man. The military bearing, the arctic blue eyes, the impression he projected that wherever he was he was meant to be, precluded bonhomie. This self-assurance could perhaps be attributed to his heritage. Bernadotte was the king of Sweden's nephew. His godson was heir to the throne. His great-great-grandfather, the first Bernadotte to occupy the Swedish throne, had been a marshal in Napoleon's army.

But he was here now in this capital of fanaticism by choice. His personal courage could not be ignored. There had been other instances. He had faced Heinrich Himmler across a Berlin table while the Allied bombers unloaded their deadly cargo overhead. Folke Bernadotte had been among those who believed that bargaining for the lives of Hitler's hostages, even if only a handful at a time, was not a diversion from the war effort. Representing the Swedish Red Cross in 1945, he had started with a modest goal—to save Scandinavian captives of the Third Reich. In the end, he exceeded expectations, and managed, with the help of his Red Cross trucks and buses, to ferry thousands, Jews as well as Christians, to safety. His accomplishments skewed the observers' rapport with the mediator. Yet danger is also a great equalizer, and on this day in Jerusalem they were all courting danger.*

Neither side paid much attention any longer to the truce the mediator had pieced together. Twice he had succeeded—initially in June and then, when the first four-week truce expired and the combatants resumed their deadly business, again in mid-July. In the background, the random pop-pop of sniper fire and the dull thud of Arab mortars punctuated the group's conversation.

Bernadotte had seen the Jewish papers that morning. He was stung by the transcript of Israeli Foreign Minister Moshe Shertok's news conference. Shertok charged the count with turning a blind eye to Arab truce violations, while overreacting to Israel's minor infractions. This seemed an astonishingly undiplomatic message from a foreign minister whom Bernadotte had recently called his friend. The count was unaccustomed to such blunt treatment.

Bernadotte thought he had one more chance to bring the two sides together. He would present the United Nations General Assembly, convened in a special session in Paris, with his latest proposal for peace. He had learned a few things since the uproar caused by his first, rather ill-thought-out peace plan of late June. Surely, he thought, he could temper the Israeli rage at his sugges-

---

*Eighty UN observers were stationed in Jerusalem, which was sliced three ways by the 1947 UN partition of Palestine into a Jewish, an Arab, and an international sector, to safeguard the world's great religious shrines and their faithful in the Holy City.

tion that Jerusalem should go to the Arabs. After all, the Holy City lay well within the area allotted the Arabs by the UN's partition plan. It seemed more logical to the Swede that King Abdullah should have Jerusalem.

But Count Bernadotte had refused to recognize that logic had little to do with Jewish feelings on the subject of Jerusalem. He seemed equally oblivious of the fact that there was another struggle being waged for Israel's future. The six Arab armies that had breached the new state's borders the moment Israel declared her statehood were not alone in battling for control of the biblical land. Israelis themselves, Jews against Jews, were locked in a bitter struggle over the future of their own country. Zionist maximalists, impatient and fervent supernationalistic successors of Vladimir Jabotinsky, insisted on an Israel of biblical proportions on both sides of the Jordan River with Jerusalem its eternal capital, no matter the cost. Jabotinsky's offspring, members of the reviled Stern Gang, were Bernadotte's most dangerous foes. They perceived their more moderate, pragmatic brethren, Prime Minister David Ben-Gurion's Labor Zionists, as traitors to the Zionist dream. For Ben-Gurion was willing to bide his time to achieve his vision of a strong, safe Israel. Labor Zionists rejected the ideology of the so-called Revisionist Zionist movement, whose motto was "Conquer or die." The two camps were locked in a struggle of biblical intensity that at times skirted full-blown civil war. Folke Bernadotte was only dimly aware of this mostly subterranean strife, and the danger it posed for him.

Midway through lunch, an aide whispered to Bernadotte that Dr. Ralph Bunche, his chief advisor, had finished drafting the new plan and had just dispatched a copy to Paris. But Bunche, who almost never left Bernadotte's side, would be delayed reaching him, the aide explained. Bunche's secretary, a British subject, had aroused the suspicion of an anti-English Israeli officer in the port of Haifa, and, fuming and frustrated, Bunche had stayed in Haifa to help his secretary gain entry to Israel.

"Well, then, let's push on to Government House," the mediator announced. As an added security measure, Bernadotte's aides had taken the unprecedented step of not setting a formal schedule for his trip to Jerusalem. Not even Bernadotte, the implacable optimist, could now ignore the violent feelings he aroused wherever he went in Israel—especially in Jerusalem. Avoid the Holy City, seasoned diplomats had cautioned him. But Bernadotte was intrigued by the possibility of moving his residence from the Greek island of Rhodes to Jerusalem's Government House, the former home of the British high commissioner to Palestine. Rhodes was too far removed from the war zone. Now Bernadotte was eager to see Government House before dark.

Bernadotte asked de Geer to call Dr. Dov Joseph, Jewish Jerusalem's military governor, to schedule a meeting following the count's tour of Government House. As the group piled into their cars, Colonel Begley, for security reasons, ordered the convoy to take a roundabout route to Government House. Go through Talbiya and Katamon to escape the snipers, Begley told the drivers.

High on a bluff with the city spread beneath it, the former enclave of the highest British authority in Palestine held powerful symbolism for the citizens of the new State of Israel. In a supremely ironic move, which no doubt had eluded the architects, Government House had been constructed on the biblical Hill of Evil Counsel. Sir Winston Churchill had signed the documents creating the Kingdom of Transjordan in one of Government House's stately rooms in March 1921, thereby hoping to appease Arab nationalism east of the Jordan River. Some of the most passionately despised figures in the new Jewish state were the former occupants of this fortresslike building.

Folke Bernadotte was not a student of history. An eminently practical sort, he was looking for a place to live in Jerusalem. Government House, bequeathed by the departing British to the International Red Cross, seemed a good place from which he could keep an eye on both warring sides.

There was no denying the magic of the view. Bernadotte surveyed the landscape with a special eye. He still carried the Bible his uncle Prince Karl had given him during his negotiations with Himmler. For Bernadotte, a devout man, it was seductive simply to be able to contemplate the Old City of Jerusalem, with its spires, domes, and minarets backlit against the sky.

Like Rome, Jerusalem is a city of hilltops, clustered on a height of 750 meters, which plunges to the sea toward the west. The ancient, walled Old City contains many of the sacred places of three religions, enclosed by walls built in the sixteenth century. The mosque of Omar—on the site of Solomon's Temple—sits perilously close to the Wailing Wall, the Church of the Holy Sepulchre, and the Garden of Gethsemane. In 1948, most Jews lived in West Jerusalem, the so-called New City, built mainly since the late nineteenth century by Jewish immigrants, though a small, determined group of faithful had, until the recent siege by the Arabs, survived for millennia within the walled Old City. A few miles to the south and east of the city, the hills sloped down to the Dead Sea and the mountains where ancient Jewish and Christian zealots once sought refuge.

Bernadotte strolled through Government House's rose gardens, flanked by meticulously trimmed Aleppo pines. The last British high commissioner, Sir Alan Cunningham, had left four months before, on May 14, the day Britain's Palestine Mandate expired and David Ben-Gurion announced the birth of a new state.

On either side of this deceptively serene place, Arab and Jewish troops were dug in, poised to renew fighting. Egyptian units were encamped to the south, close enough so that with binoculars one could make out the type of English rifles they cradled. The Jordanians were to the north. Wherever you looked, Bernadotte's Israeli liaison, Captain Hillman, noted, you could see Jordanians—on the wall of the Old City, on Mount Zion. Jewish forces were to the west.

In the lookout tower, Bernadotte suddenly pointed to a group of dark figures in Arab kaffiyehs, deftly laying sticks of dynamite beneath the roadbed. As quickly as they had appeared, the Arab guerrillas melted into the shadows.

Before leaving Stockholm for the Middle East just two weeks earlier, Bernadotte had talked with his American-born wife Estelle about the danger. He had even left her precise instructions for his funeral. He refused, however, an offer from the Swedish police to fit him out with a flak jacket; he found it much too cumbersome, he said, for his high-energy style. Bernadotte was convinced his physical presence, as a man of peace, would dampen Jews' and Arabs' fervor to fight. He was willing to live at the very heart of the war zone while attempting to negotiate a peace he thought was within reach. But, then, hatred was not an emotion Folke Bernadotte could truly fathom.

Almost no one agreed with the Swede's choice of residence:

not Israeli officials, who had no wish to take responsibility for the mediator's safety in the next round of serious fighting; not his own advisors, who saw the place as impossible to keep supplied through hostile lines.

As he toured the Hill of Evil Counsel, Bernadotte finally realized that his aides were right, and he abandoned his dream of living there. But the Israeli newspapers had already carried stories about the mediator's interest in the residence, and in a place where history and symbols matter enormously, another message—it was not the first—had linked Folke Bernadotte with the despised British.

Before leaving the mausoleumlike residence, the mediator invited Dr. Pierre Façel, the Swiss doctor who had improvised a Red Cross hospital within its walls, to accompany him back to the YMCA. A man who had worked within the battered city for months, Dr. Façel struck Bernadotte as having a clearer, less partisan grasp of the situation than most. Always hungry for fresh facts, Bernadotte wanted to elicit the doctor's views.

The mediator's next stop was a yellow stucco building, a short drive from Government House, that was officially an Israeli agricultural school. Though the school was well inside the official demilitarized zone that encompassed Government House, Bernadotte had heard that the Israelis had transformed it into an armed fort in direct violation of the truce. Under the fierce leadership of Rachel Yamait, a middle-aged Israeli woman, twenty armed Israeli "students" were housed here.

"Over my dead body will you take their guns away," Mrs. Yamait said to the mediator as they all stood outside the agricultural school. Captain Hillman was startled and slightly embarrassed by her aggressive tone. The "schoolmistress" insisted that the armed youths were necessary in case the Arabs attacked the Red Cross zone, sought by both sides for its strategic location high above the city. Hillman bent down to pluck a few tomatoes from Mrs. Yamait's vines and noticed just in time that her tomato patch was mined.

Colonel André Sérot pulled Hillman aside. "When we get back in the cars, would you change places with me, Captain?" the French officer asked. "I need a few minutes privately with the mediator." Hillman had been sitting between Count Bernadotte and General Lundström in the convoy. Sérot explained to the puzzled Hillman that "My wife spent the war in Dachau.

She owes her survival to Bernadotte. I want to thank him." Hillman ceded his place to the colonel when they climbed back into their cars.

With the blue and white United Nations flags and the Red Cross banner snapping off the cars' front fenders, the three-car convoy accelerated for the final, most treacherous strip of road back to Jewish-held Jerusalem, and the relative security of the YMCA, where they would spend the night. They followed, in reverse, the route they had taken after lunch, to Government House, along one of only two roads leading to the New City that were not blocked by fortified positions of one side or the other. The convoy passed through the so-called Greek and German colonies, bruised remnants of a more peaceful era when the Holy City had been a magnet for the faithful of every nationality, and through the Katamon quarter, full of stately but now largely deserted Arab and British villas, two-story homes with large terraces and balconies whose elaborate grillwork spoke of another life. Their former residents were now part of the mass exodus. At the moment, in the late afternoon of Friday, September 17, the exhausted city was quiet. Even the distant snipers seemed temporarily to honor the Sabbath eve.

In the first car, Lundström's DeSoto, Major Massart sat behind the wheel, with Barbro Wessel squeezed between him and Captain Hillman. Jan de Geer and Lundström's aide-de-camp, Jan Flach, sat in the back. De Geer and Barbro had made a secret pact. Alarmed at the hostility Bernadotte aroused wherever he went in Israel, the two young Swedes agreed to form a human shield between the count and potential danger by occupying the first car of every convoy in which he traveled. The Swiss Dr. Façel followed the DeSoto in his own car. The mediator's car, a shiny new Chrysler, was last. Colonel Frank Begley drove, with U.S. Marine Commander Cox next to him. The count sat in the back, on the right-hand side, with Serot next to him. General Lundström folded his long frame into the left-hand corner.

As the convoy began to climb the steep, narrow road, Palmach Street, which leads to the affluent Talbiya section, the familiar sight of yet another Army roadblock forced them to slow down. An Israeli soldier dropped the barrier across the road as they approached. Captain Hillman shouted, *"Shalom Haverim!*

It's OK, it's the UN mediator," and the soldier lifted the barrier with a wave of his hand for them to pass. The convoy passed an Army truck full of Israeli soldiers and shifted down for the final climb toward the New City.

The road looked innocent. Open fields lay on either side, punctuated by a few scattered three- and four-story apartment houses of pale Jerusalem stone. Two children pushed bicycles up the steep hill. Slowly, the convoy's passengers began to lose some of their tension. A small store where thirsty children bought drinks after school came into view. And from behind it emerged a large Israeli Army jeep, resembling, except for the fact that it looked new, every other jeep in the city. Four soldiers, their caps pulled low over their faces, appeared to be drowsing inside.

As the convoy slowly rose over the hill, the jeep and its passengers stirred. It nosed into the narrow road, forcing Bernadotte's convoy to come to a full stop. Three men in the khaki shorts and visored military hats of the Israeli Army sprang, with military precision, from the jeep while the fourth man kept one hand on the steering wheel and the other on his revolver. Fingers on the triggers of their submachine guns, two men approached the left side of the convoy. Inside the DeSoto, the three young Swedes and the Belgian major groped for their papers. "It's OK, boys," Hillman's jaunty voice boomed out. "Let us pass. It's the UN mediator." Ignoring the Israeli officer, the gunmen sprayed the DeSoto's tires and radiator with gunfire. Then they moved rapidly on to the next car, which belonged to the Red Cross doctor. Meanwhile, the third man raced toward the Chrysler, and thrust the barrel of his Schmeisser into the open window of the back seat.

Folke Bernadotte saw the glint of metal. His companions heard him utter something "like an exclamation," as the blast blew him back against the seat. He toppled forward; blood spattered across his face and soaked his shirt. Six bullets tore into his left arm, his throat, and his chest. The assassin kept firing, pumping eighteen bullets into the French officer who had wanted to thank Bernadotte for saving his wife from Dachau.

"Folke?" Lundström, sitting next to the Frenchman, cried out. The mediator did not answer. The gunmen fled. Hillman sprang from his car and groaned at the sight of the carnage. "My God," he kept repeating. "Oh my God." The man whose job it was to assure the UN mediator safe passage through Jewish Jerusalem felt a knot of panic. Jumping in next to Begley and Cox, he barked, "Drive to Hadassah—go straight, just go!"

Hadassah Hospital was only a few minutes' drive, but the trip, with two silent, bleeding bodies in the back seat and the cars' tires oozing air from their bullet holes, was the longest of Hillman's life. At the hospital entrance, Barbro and Jan, the two young Swedes, rushed from their car to the Chrysler. With help from Hillman and Lundström, they carefully carried Bernadotte's bleeding body into the hospital. But for one of Europe's most privileged sons, it was already too late. Count Folke Bernadotte, the first United Nations mediator between Arabs and Jews, had died instantly on a narrow dirt road in Jerusalem.

CHAPTER TWO

THE SHOCK OF
THE NEWS

AT HADASSAH HOSPITAL, HILLMAN, LUNDSTRÖM, AND WESSEL, their clothes smeared with blood, waited silently outside the emergency room. Jan de Geer arrived from the nearby YMCA, where he had found Dr. Rudolf Ullmark, Bernadotte's personal physician. Because of the count's chronic case of bleeding ulcers, Ullmark always traveled with him, carrying a supply of Bernadotte's own blood for emergencies. Dr. Ullmark emerged minutes later from the operating room and silently shook his head.

There was nothing more for the stunned group to do but return to the YMCA and await the two bodies, which would lie in state there overnight. One of the first Israelis to reach the hospital was the dashing young military commander of Jewish Jerusalem, a thirty-three-year-old colonel named Moshe Dayan. "Extra Urgent," he cabled Prime Minister David Ben-Gurion in Tel Aviv before racing to the hospital. "Just now at 17:30 I have received word that Bernadotte and the UN chief of staff have been shot in Katamon." Dayan's cable sent waves of apprehension through the Israeli prime minister. He knew that Jews held Katamon. He realized that his darkest fear had come to pass: the UN mediator had been killed by Jews—extremist Jews, undoubtedly—the same group with whom Ben-Gurion had collided at every juncture of his rise to the pinnacle of the Zionist movement. Ben-Gurion, the white-haired lion of Israel, the Founding Father, had failed to curb these *terrorists*.

To the prime minister, the brazen ambush of a man sent by the world to make peace bore the unmistakable signature of the Irgun or the Stern Group. The disregard of world opinion, the blatant challenge to the frail new state's authority, the swift professionalism of the crime's execution—all these suggested the underground's work. The crime was a threat to the legitimacy of the four-month-old state. Acts of terror to protest the venal British Mandate were one thing, but Israel was a state at last, and this crime had been committed under Ben-Gurion's leadership. And Palestine was the first great test of the United Nations as international crisis manager. The UN's first attempt at mediation had climaxed in blood on a Jerusalem street. Would the world forgive Israel?

An hour and a half after Ben-Gurion first received word of the crime from Jerusalem, Dayan was on the phone and confirmed the prime minister's fears. He said he was certain the killers were either Irgun or Lehi.

In fact, the Irgun, under the leadership of a former Polish lawyer and editor named Menachem Begin, had denounced the crime as soon as he learned of it. Founded in 1937 as a breakaway faction of the Haganah (Palestine Jewry's self-defense organization) to repel British occupation by any means short of personal terror, the Irgun was less extreme in its philosophy than Lehi. At eight-thirty, Isser Harel, Ben-Gurion's Secret Service director, arrived and asserted "from the highest sources" that the Irgun was not behind the assassination of Bernadotte.

Lehi, founded in 1940 by Avraham Stern, a former member of the Irgun, believed in individual terror as a legitimate means toward the goal of a Zionist state of biblical proportions, as defined in Genesis 15:18, "from the brook of Egypt to the great river, the river Euphrates," a goal that went far beyond what Ben-Gurion thought realistic for the infant state.

Nor was Lehi willing to disband peacefully, as the Irgun had largely done, and join the new state. Lehi deemed Ben-Gurion a dangerous compromiser willing to settle for a diminished version of Eretz Israel (the Land of Israel). In Lehi's eyes, Ben-Gurion was too accommodating to outside pressures, particularly those coming from the United Nations—and from Count Folke Bernadotte.

Now Ben-Gurion ordered the Army to surround Lehi's three Jerusalem camps and arrest 260 of its members. The prime minister also ordered the Jerusalem–Tel Aviv road, the main thoroughfare out of the Holy City, blocked.

Dr. Ralph Bunche, Bernadotte's closest advisor, landed at the same airstrip where the Swede had arrived earlier the same day. An Israeli officer broke the news of the murder to Bunche. General Lundström, still wearing his bloodstained uniform, stood there, in silent shock. Bunche, an American with a stellar record of United Nations service (he was one of the authors of the United Nations Charter), had in four highly charged months formed an exceptionally close bond with Bernadotte. Bunche rushed to the YMCA, where his friend lay in the same room in which they had conducted talks with Arabs and Jews during that summer of fluctuating hopes. Two Israeli soldiers stood at attention over the UN-flag-draped coffins, Bernadotte's first armed guards since his arrival in Israel.

Bunche, a man of legendary self-discipline, found release from his distress in an uncharacteristic way, pouring his pain and his anger into a cable dispatched to the foreign minister of Israel.

"The murder in cold blood of Count Bernadotte, United Nations Mediator in Palestine, and of Colonel Sérot of the French Air Force and United Nations Observer, in the Katamon quarter of Jerusalem today by Jewish assailants is an outrage against the international community and an unspeakable violation of elementary morality. This tragic act occurred when Count Bernadotte, acting under the authority of the United Nations, was on an official tour of duty in Jerusalem and in the presence of a liaison officer assigned to him by the Jewish authorities.

"He was well within the lines of the armed forces of your government which has by official act assumed responsibility for that part of Jerusalem controlled by Jewish forces. His safety therefore and that of his lieutenants, under the ordinary rules of law and order was a responsibility of the Provisional Government of Israel whose armed forces and representatives control and administer the area.

"This act constitutes a breach of the truce of utmost gravity for which the Provisional Government of Israel must assume full responsibility."

The message filled Prime Minister Ben-Gurion with foreboding, all the more so as Bunche had just been appointed as the new UN mediator. The announcement, cabled to the UN's Haifa headquarters and relayed to Bunche in Jerusalem by telephone, came from the secretary-general's Soviet deputy, Arkady Sobolev, as Secretary-General Lie was on vacation in Norway and could not be reached.

After an hour's news blackout on the events in Jerusalem, the harsh trill of the alarm bell reserved for major breaking stories sounded on wires in newsrooms around the world. Working fast, the *New York Times*'s overnight editor rearranged the front page and composed a new banner headline: "Bernadotte Is Slain in Jerusalem; Killers Called 'Jewish Irregulars,' Security Council Will Act Today."

That evening in Jerusalem, the representatives of the world's major news organization found the following single-page message in their mailboxes.

On the 17th of September 1948 we have executed Count Bernadotte.

Count Bernadotte served as an open agent of the British enemy. His task was to implement the British plans for the surrender of our country to a foreign rule and the exposure of the Yishuv [i.e., the Jewish population of Palestine]. He did not hesitate to suggest the handing over of Jerusalem to Abdullah. Bernadotte acted without interruption towards the weakening of our military efforts and was responsible for the bloodshed.

This will be the end of all the enemies and their agents. This will be the end of all the enemies of Jewish freedom in the Homeland.

There will be no foreign rule in the Homeland. There shall be no longer foreign Commissioners in Jerusalem.

HAZIT HAMOLEDETH, SEPT. 17, 1948

Hazit Hamoledeth, or Fatherland Front, did not exist. It was a name, borrowed from the Bulgarian Communist Party, that Lehi's three-man leadership chose as cover for their crime.

Thousands of miles from the tumult of Jerusalem, in a stately home at the edge of a Stockholm park, a twelve-year-old boy was passing the time tinkering with his absent father's shortwave radio set. A tremulous voice, announcing itself as belonging to an amateur radio operator from the Swedish town of Helenelund, made the boy pause. "Count Folke Bernadotte has been shot and killed in Jerusalem," the radio operator announced. Stunned, Bertil Bernadotte rushed to his mother. "I can understand Count Bernadotte being shot," he cried. "But not Daddy."

CHAPTER THREE

THE ROAD TO KATAMON

THE BLOODY ENCOUNTER ON A JERUSALEM STREET BETWEEN A Swedish aristocrat determined to do good, and four men equally determined to bring about the redemption of the Jews through strength, began on May 14, 1948. On that day, the last British troops in Palestine boarded their ships at Haifa's harbor. Random gunfire in the distance punctated the eerie wail of the regimental bagpipes sounding retreat. It was a deliberately ragged, chaotic end to London's thirty-one-year sojourn in the Holy Land. "We had no instructions on what to do," Sir Alan Cunningham, the last high commissioner for Palestine, would later attest. The war that most clear-eyed observers of the region had predicted and Britain had done nothing to prevent was hours away.

When, on that Friday, May 14, at midnight Jerusalem time, David Ben-Gurion and his Council of Thirteen declared Israel the first Jewish state in nearly two thousand years, the armies of Egypt, Lebanon, Transjordan, Syria, and Saudi Arabia were arrayed on the new nation's borders. One of the world's most respected statesmen, US Secretary of State George C. Marshall, had warned that a truce between the two sides must precede this proclamation. But nothing could stop Ben-Gurion, who felt the moment was now or never.

Ben-Gurion's bold action set off shock waves from Washington to New York to Moscow. The decision as to whether or not to recognize the new Jewish state—its name still unknown minutes before it was declared—had split the Truman administration into two fiercely opposed camps. One, led by the president's closest domestic advisor, Clark Clifford, favored immediate recognition; the other, led by the revered secretary of state, George C. Marshall, opposed it as a "double cross" of the United Nations and a "pig in a poke."

Truman overruled Marshall. Thus, eleven minutes after Ben-Gurion spoke in Jerusalem, the United States became the first nation to recognize the new Jewish state. A few minutes later, the Soviet Union followed suit.

The news of American recognition hit the United Nations, meeting at its temporary headquarters in Flushing Meadow, New York, like a bombshell. It represented a turnaround for the United States, which had previously been committed to support of a United Nations trusteeship over Palestine until a solution between Arabs and Jews could be worked out.

Caught without instruction, the chief US delegate to the UN, Warren Austin, simply walked out of the hall and escaped to Manhattan, while the UN erupted in what more than forty years later Dean Rusk (then head of the State Department's UN Desk) still remembered as "pandemonium." "I'm not exaggerating. I was later told that one of our US mission delegates sat on the lap of the Cuban delegate to keep him from going to the podium to withdraw Cuba from the UN. Warren Austin (chief US delegate) just went home. He thought that would make it clear we hadn't deliberately hoodwinked the UN delegates by not preparing them for this. I thought that was a wise move."

The United Nations, with its fifty-seven members, including all of the Arab states, had come into existence three years earlier to prevent just this sort of conflict. "We have tried for years to solve the problem of Palestine," British envoy Sir Alexander Cadogan told the General Assembly delegates in March 1947. "Having failed so far, we now bring the Palestine question to the United Nations, in the hope that it can succeed where we have not." London, after running Palestine under a League of Nations mandate, was worn out. Imperial responsibilities no longer suited the war-weary British.

But though London was asking for help, it was unwilling to offer any to avert the bloodshed between Arabs and Jews that was widely expected to erupt after British forces left. There were solid reasons for Britain's noncooperation in the transition. Above all, it did not wish to provoke the oil-rich Arabs at a time when its foothold in the region was increasingly tenuous. Britain was also bitter toward the Israelis, for Jewish terrorists had killed 127 British servicemen between May 1945 and October 1947.

London's *après-moi-le-déluge* attitude, coming as it did from one of the five permanent members of the UN's ruling Security Council, which, under the UN Charter, has "primary responsibility for the maintenance of international peace and security," undermined the legitimacy of the world body and dismayed its secretary-general. "If the Great Powers accepted that this situation in the Middle East could best be settled by leaving the forces concerned to fight it out amongst themselves," wrote Secretary-General Trygve Lie, "it was quite clear that they would be tacitly admitting that the Security Council and the United Nations was a useless instrument in attempting to preserve peace."

Proposing another investigation of the problem was out of the question—there had been almost two dozen international commissions on the "Question of Palestine" over the years. Moreover, this war seemed tailored for a more forceful United Nations intervention. For once, the UN had a clear mandate for action. Whereas normally the world body lacks the power to impose a political settlement, in the case of Palestine, Britain had handed over the whole territory to the United Nations for disposition. The secretary-general thus felt that the organization had full constitutional power to both restore order within Palestine and to repel intervention from outside.

The war in the Middle East was the international organization's first real test, and came at a time when the world was still reeling from the aftershock of the deadliest of all wars. Unrealistic hopes were held that the UN could somehow solve an ancient conflict that had been further inflamed by the Holocaust and by the surge of Arab nationalism. It would soon become apparent that those wild hopes were supported by little of substance.

On May 15, the secretary-general wrote a "Secret and Personal" letter to Secretary of State Marshall, saying that the Egyptian government had informed him it was about to invade Palestine. "My primary concern," Lie wrote, "is for the future usefulness of the United Nations and its Security Council." The Council must act quickly and decisively, he continued, irrespective of whether its efforts succeed or fail. If the Egyptian government is allowed to get away with this aggression beyond its own frontiers, a precedent will have been created that will endanger the future usefulness of both the United Nations and the Security Council. "I must do everything to prevent this," Lie wrote; "otherwise, the Security Council will have . . . created a precedent for any nation to take aggressive action in direct contravention to the Charter of the United Nations."

While Trygve Lie seemed dedicated to building the authority of the United Nations during this testing episode, many doubted his ability to provide the crucial leadership. Though Lie was a former Norwegian foreign minister and labor-union leader, he was "totally out of his depth and unsuited to the job" of UN secretary-general, according to his personal assistant, Sir Brian Urquhart, who later became UN under secretary-general. Lie's legendary temper was not an occupational asset. "I remember being in his office one day when Lie started berating me," A. M. Rosenthal, then in the *New York Times* UN Bureau, recalled, years later. " 'Your country,' he fumed, 'they expect me to come and go as the secretary-general and still make me get a visa each time. Well, this is what I think of your visa,' and he proceeded to rip out from his passport the page with the US visa."

"He was a very tricky and jealous human being," Urquhart noted.

Complicating matters further was that two members of the Security Council who normally sided with each other, the United States and Great Britain, were at odds on Palestine. Britain was far from resigned to giving up her historic stake in the Middle East. Though the devastation of the Second World War had forced Britain to dismantle much of its empire, generations of Britons regarded the Mediterranean, the Red Sea, the Persian Gulf, and adjacent territories as English provinces. Cyprus, the Sudan, and Egypt all continued to have strong ties to London, while Iraq and Transjordan formed an integral part of her sphere of interest. World War II had vividly demonstrated that the Middle East, with its rich reserves of oil and its strategic location linking Europe, Asia, and Africa was of paramount importance to a state with global ambitions. With British Army bases scattered throughout the region, the Middle East was a vast military preserve for London. If her former Palestine Mandate went up in smoke after her departure, well, that would only demonstrate that she had not done such a poor job keeping the lid on the region after all.

Meanwhile, even after Truman's decision to recognize Israel, Washington remained divided between the pro-Israel faction of men like Clark Clifford and Israel's powerful domestic allies on one hand, and the pro-Arab leadership of the Departments of State and Defense on the other. For its part, Moscow hoped to exploit all these differences.

The day after Israel's declaration of statehood, France, Britain, China, the Soviet Union, and the United States, the so-called Great Powers who formed the permanent membership of the United Nations' Security Council, assembled on Long Island, in a place ironically named Lake Success. Their primary aim was to determine a response to the Arabs' violent challenge to the new state.

As the Great Powers met at Lake Success, Egyptian armored columns had advanced to within twenty-five miles of Tel Aviv. Fifty-eight miles to the south, additional Egyptian forces rained bombs on Beersheba, the largest town in the Negev Desert. Iraqi troops were joined by the Arab Legion in their drive for the sea. Few outsiders, including George C. Marshall, thought the one-day-old Jewish state would survive for long against the advancing Arab armies.

CHAPTER FOUR

JEWS AGAINST JEWS

BY MAY 28, 1948, THE PEOPLE IN THE JEWISH QUARTER, HUDDLED behind the Turkish wall of the Old City, could take no more of the Arab Legion's artillery barrage. The Haganah had failed to defend the 1,300 Orthodox Jews who lived amid the cramped warren of narrow streets, close by Judaism's sacred shrines. Kaffiyeh-clad Arab Legionnaires marched the rabbis and their young students, their hands above their heads, out of the Old City toward New Jerusalem. News that the revered site had fallen to Arab control rocked Jews everywhere.

Lehi blamed David Shaltiel, commander of Israeli forces in Jerusalem, and the man who entrusted him with that responsibility, David Ben-Gurion. Shaltiel seemed content to hold on to the predominantly Jewish New City in West Jerusalem rather than push to recapture the Old City, a few hundred yards behind the medieval ramparts. David Shaltiel fit perfectly the Stern Gang's image of a weak, eternally accommodating Jew from the Diaspora. And they felt contempt for Ben-Gurion; his foreign minister, Moshe Shertok; President Chaim Weizmann; and those Jews who were willing to negotiate away land that Lehi considered the unalienable birthright of all Jews. The fact that Ben-Gurion seemed to care more about an uninhabited sandy stretch of the Negev than the redemption of the Sacred City, the site of the future Third Temple, was to them a betrayal.

In November 1947, the UN had voted to partition Palestine into two states, one Arab and one Jewish. Ben-Gurion had accepted the decision as the wisest route to a Jewish state, even if smaller than he wanted. The rich coastal plains and the Negev Desert had been awarded to the Jews. Central Palestine, from Beersheba, the biblical town in the northern Negev, forty-six miles southwest of Jerusalem, to Jenin, south of Tiberias, as well as a northern triangle of the Galilee from Nazareth to the Lebanese border, was designated Arab territory. The UN partition plan gave the Arabs 4,500 square miles with a population of 804,000, while the 538,000 Jews were allotted 5,500 square miles. The two awkwardly configured "states" were to be linked in an economic union. Jerusalem, with its many holy places, would be under international rule. Ben-Gurion, Weizmann, and their comrades in the mainstream Zionist leadership saw the UN vote as offering a legitimacy they could convert—as they soon would—into statehood. But in the Stern Gang's eyes, agreeing to the partition of Palestine rather than fighting for all of Eretz Israel was yet another sellout by passive Jews.

The Arabs had been as outraged by the UN decision as Lehi. The eminent Arab scholar Albert Hourani attributed it to Western feelings of guilt for inaction during the Holocaust. "The [Westerners] were attracted by the gallant little people with a great and tormented past, by the pioneers taming the wilderness, the planners using science to increase production, the collective farmers turning away from the guilt and complexity of personal life, the terrorist making his gesture in the face of authority—all images of a new world . . . hopeful, violent and earnest."

Now, in the spring of 1948, after the loss of Jerusalem's Old City to the Arabs, Ben-Gurion had again "betrayed" Israel by bowing to the UN's truce resolution rather than waging a battle—no matter how futile it might have been—to wrest all of the Holy City from the Arabs. Lehi's single greatest grievance against the country's first prime minister was his seeming indifference to what mattered most to the underground, the fate of Jerusalem.

Lehi's view of Ben-Gurion would lead to tragedy, but it was not accurate. As his biographer Shabtai Teveth noted later, "There is no question that Ben-Gurion was attached to Jerusalem. But he was a pragmatic politician, willing to wait for the right moment to press his claim. Ben-Gurion once said, 'In history, great things do not get lost. If we give up Jerusalem now, we will not lose it in the future.' These Lehi people were obsessed with boldness, strength and virility. They thought Ben-

Gurion was not a proud Jew. To them, the weakling Jews were the ones who had tea with the High Commissioner. A proud Jew would have spilled tea on him. The weakling Jews were corrupt figures from the Diaspora, used to crawling before their lords and masters, and then having tea with them."

There was, in fact, a sharp difference between the Stern Gang's uncompromising, mystical attachment to Jerusalem, and the complex views of the Holy City held by Chaim Weizmann and even Theodor Herzl, modern Zionism's founder.

"I would say that in Zionist history there has always been a kind of ambivalence about Jerusalem," observed Abba Eban, a member of the Israeli UN delegation in 1948. "On the one hand attachment to it, on the other hand a certain recoiling from it. Herzl himself said the only place where the capital should *not* be is Jerusalem. He spoke of its squalor and its intense religiosity and he used very insulting words to describe it. He said it was full of 'Yids,' meaning the most unprogressive Jews. Weizmann understood intellectually the pull of Jerusalem, but he used to say that it will never be a place where Jews can take off their coats and relax. He said it was too full of rabbis and priests and incense. Zionism to all of them, Ben-Gurion included, is the green plains and orchards of Sharon and the great, sandy stretches of the Negev.

"I remember Weizmann once saying as we were driving away from Jerusalem, 'Well, now we can breathe again.' Weizmann built his own home in Rehovot, which became Israel's scientific center, not Jerusalem. And when he first arrived in Palestine from Russia, Ben-Gurion wrote voluble accounts of everything he saw in Palestine, but not a word about Jerusalem. I doubt he even went there." Eban noted, "The fact is that when the UN suggested internationalizing Jerusalem, that seemed like a pretty reasonable compromise, leaving open the prospect of it eventually becoming Jewish, once we were the majority."

In Lehi's eyes, this sort of pragmatism about the symbolic center of Judaism was blasphemy. Their fury toward Israel's leaders was intensified by their conviction that reclaiming the land that was rightfully the Jews' would have taken little effort. "The British left on May fourteenth. The Arab Legion arrived on the nineteenth," Lehi veteran Baruch Nadel explained. "In those few days the Jews could have taken all of Jerusalem, exploded the bridges. But nobody did anything. The Legion went into

Jerusalem and took the Old City. Five hundred well-trained men could have turned back the Arabs from Jerusalem in the very beginning, before the Arab Legion arrived. The Irgun began doing what they had in 1937, '38. They planted bombs in Arab centers, killing civilians. And everybody said the Haganah was standing by to protect the Jews. As for Lehi, we had no money, and arms immediately became very expensive. I don't remember Lehi doing anything in the first months [after statehood] in Jerusalem, which is unforgivable, given our ideology that Jerusalem should be the capital of the Great Jewish State, from El Arish to the Syrian desert, as God told Abraham a long time ago."

Among Lehi's band in Jerusalem was Yehoshua Zetler, one of Avraham Stern's old guard. Like many members of the underground, Zetler had served time as a British captive. He had escaped from the Jerusalem prison through the sewers and, by the spring of Israel's birth, was restlessly waiting to reclaim all of Jerusalem for the Jews. "Zetler was a fighter, no question about it," Baruch Nadel remembered. "A brave man who had spent seven of the last eight years in British prisons and concentration camps. He was quite bald, though still very young. He was a self-educated man they called *Fallah* in the Jerusalem prison, which means 'peasant' in Arabic, a simple guy born in Kibbutz Kfar Saba who managed to accomplish unbelievable things."

Because the Sternists were determined to fight for Jerusalem, they attracted many new recruits. One who left the Irgun to join Lehi was Meshulam Makover. Dubbed "Tall Yoav," he compensated for his well-over-six-foot height, which made him too conspicuous to be a good urban guerrilla, by becoming one of the underground's best drivers. Men like Tall Yoav and Nadel had little interest in the politics of the new state.

"People in Jerusalem were very different from people in Tel Aviv," asserted Sternist commando Baruch Nadel. "We didn't want to be 'internationalized.' And we were under fire all the time, which also changes you. The spring and summer of 1948 in Jerusalem, we used to say that a Jerusalem Mapainik [a member of Ben-Gurion's Labor Party] is better than a Tel Aviv Sternist. That's an unbelievable thing to say, since we hated Mapai. But that's how we in Lehi felt."

The Sternists were "under fire" not only from Arabs, but also from Israeli government forces. When Israel declared its statehood, the new government ordered the militant underground groups, the Irgun and Lehi, to disband. Some members obeyed. Those who didn't were now officially outlaws. According to Nadel, "the Irgun made some kind of a secret deal with the Haganah, which afterwards left them alone, while they hunted us. There were Arab gangs, hundreds and hundreds of them around Jerusalem. And we had thirty people." Ben-Gurion's determination to root out the underground forces had been strengthened by one of the most infamous terrorist operations in Palestine's history: the destruction of Deir Yassin. The operation had been planned as a joint Lehi-Irgun effort to "force Ben-Gurion's hand" to show that Jews could and should begin reclaiming Arab-occupied land by force.

"Lehi decided," Nadel recalled, "we should take an Arab village, clear it of Arabs, give it to the Haganah." The choice was Deir Yassin, a tiny Arab village at the entrance of Jerusalem. On April 9, 1948, only five weeks before Independence, 130 Lehi and Irgun fighters and a unit of the Haganah's crack Palmach commandos descended on the still-slumbering village in the predawn hours. The guerrillas had intended to give some warning to the villagers to evacuate, but their truck's loudspeaker accidentally tumbled into a ditch. The attackers, unhinged by the Arabs' surprisingly stubborn resistance, unleashed a random orgy of killing and looting. The mutilated bodies of old men, women, and children lay strewn in grotesque heaps in the terrorists' wake. Nadel, who arrived in Deir Yassin the day after the massacre, remembered: "There were people killed in the most brutal way. One Israeli took a piece of explosive with a fifteen-second fuse, stuck it on an old Arab's head, lit it, and told the man to walk. Ten steps later his head exploded. Why did they do this? I am not a psychiatrist, but they were frustrated. They wanted to fight for Jerusalem. A lot of people wanted to fight, but they were held back for too long. So they exploded at Deir Yassin. When we drove through the poor neighborhoods of Jerusalem with our trucks filled with Arab prisoners from Deir Yassin, people applauded us as we passed."

When a distressed Ben-Gurion sent a message of apology for the carnage to Transjordan's King Abdullah, the Sternists were furious. "Ben-Gurion made the Transjordan king the monarch of Arab Palestine," Nadel exclaimed. A measure of the Stern Gang's power to intimidate was demonstrated by Jerusalem

Commander David Shaltiel's unwillingness to attempt to disarm the terrorists even after Deir Yassin.

Terrorism provoked more terrorism. The week following Deir Yassin, an armored convoy of over seventy-five Jewish doctors, professors, and researchers were making the slow, perilous journey through Arab-held Sheikh Jarrah to the Hadassah Hospital on Jerusalem's Mount Scopus. Suddenly, brandishing rifles and hurling blazing gasoline-soaked rags, hundreds of Arab guerrillas swooped down on the convoy, turning its armor-plated cars into blazing, steel-trap prisons.

Holocaust survivors from Berlin, Vienna, and Budapest could not escape the fiery vengeance of the angry mobs crying revenge for Deir Yassin. The British infantry charged with maintaining order in the area did not arrive on the scene until the Jews trapped inside their bulletproof vehicles had been burned alive, twenty-four of them beyond recognition.

The Arab press had embellished the already horrifying details of Deir Yassin. One consequence was a flood of panic-driven refugees from towns across Palestine toward Jordan, Lebanon, and elsewhere, terrified that Deir Yassin was only the beginning of the systematic extermination of their people. Until the mid-May invasion of Israel by six Arab armies, entire Arab villages fled before Jewish forces. By that time, 250,000 Arabs composed the world's largest refugee population.

CHAPTER FIVE

ENTER THE
MEDIATOR

ON MAY 17, THE UNITED STATES RESPONDED TO SECRETARY-General Lie's plea for action to stop the Arab invasion of Israel by introducing a resolution declaring the situation a breach of peace within the meaning of Article 39 of the UN Charter. Thus implied, but not expressed, was the possibility of the use of force by the Great Powers to stop the aggression. Washington called for a cease-fire within thirty-six hours. London, however, was not yet ready for the guns to be silenced. The British envoy to the United Nations, Sir Alexander Cadogan, described as an "iceberg that never melted" by his colleagues at the UN, hastily substituted an amendment that rendered toothless the American attempt to stop the invasion. This amendment was passed, enabling Britain's Arab allies in the region to proceed with their invasion of Israel.

And thus, with armed intervention by the UN out of the question, the stage was set for the first of the Mideast peacekeepers, the first international mediator, someone who would take the problem off its hands at least temporarily. The General Assembly created for the still-unnamed mediator a mandate remarkably detached from the realities of a country under attack by its six neighbors. Empowered to "use his good offices with the local and community authorities in Palestine to promote a peaceful adjustment of the future situation . . . [and to] assure the protection of the Holy Places . . . the mediator was to arrange for the operation of services necessary to the safety and well being of the population of Palestine." In other words, restore order and harmony to a place that had only a dim memory of such things, and this without the benefit of an armed UN force to back him up. The mediator would be assisted by a staff of "observers."

Secretary-General Lie claimed credit for first suggesting Count Folke Bernadotte for the position, after a Belgian politician named Paul van Zeeland declined the offer. There was never any discussion in the Security Council regarding what sort of man (about the appointee's gender there was little doubt) they were seeking to serve as the first mediator between Arabs and Jews. Nor was there any discussion about the character, personality, or background required for the United Nations' most sensitive position. "The discussions took place behind closed doors," Sir Brian Urquhart, then assistant to the secretary-general, recalls, "and in a rush. There was simply no time for an in-depth discussion of the man's background or character. All five permanent members of the Secretariat agreed on Bernadotte." Nahum Goldmann of the Jewish Agency later told Bernadotte that the Zionist body favored the Swede over the Belgian, since van Zeeland was a devout Catholic and had been financial advisor to the Lebanese government.

The first American reference to the possibility of Bernadotte as Middle East mediator was in a telegram from Secretary of State George Marshall to the American embassy in Stockholm, dated May 12, 1948: "For your secret information, name of Count Folke Bernadotte has been mentioned in this connection [as mediator]. While this is strictly a UN appointment we are favorably impressed by Bernadotte's qualifications and would like your immediate indication whether you feel he would be available for such an important post and whether Swedish government would object to his accepting that appointment.

"You should not give any indication that this government is pressing for Bernadotte. Marshall."

In his hometown of Stockholm, the choice of Count Bernadotte was not greeted with universal jubilation. In his journal of May 19, 1948, the veteran Swedish diplomat Sven Grafström wrote, "[U.S. Ambassador H. Freeman] Mathews called today and informed me that the Big Five decided to appoint a mediator. Folke Bernadotte was one of the candidates, and Mathews wondered what attitude the Swedish government would take toward his candidacy. Keeping in mind this absolutely hopeless task, I said that I assumed the Swedish government would reject it out of hand, but that I of course would pass on their inquiry. In conversation with [Foreign Minister] Unden a bit later, he [Unden] said that this would be a matter the government didn't want to be involved in. That had to be decided by [Bernadotte]. When I got hold of Bernadotte by telephone, he said at once that it was a fascinating mission. My objections and purely personal warnings fell on deaf ears. I feel that this is just awful. We're not talking about a scouting mission here."

To ponder his startling new prospect, Folke Bernadotte retreated to the leafy serenity of the uninhabited island of Stora Karlsö, off Gotland, for the long Whitsun weekend. As always, he relied on his wife Estelle's counsel. "We knew that the task was one of enormous size and might possibly prove completely insoluble," Bernadotte admitted. "We argued this way, that if, in the event of my being definitely offered the post, I were to refuse it, I should probably reproach myself for the rest of my life because I had not even tried to make any contribution toward clearing up this difficult situation."

On May 20, Sven Grafström tried once again to temper some of Bernadotte's alarming enthusiasm with his own tough-minded cynicism. "Bernadotte came up [to the Swedish Foreign Ministry] and spoke to Beck-Friis [a ministry official] and me. We both warned him. He had received a telegram from Lie with an inquiry whether he would like to be a candidate [for mediator].

"Bernadotte had with him a draft when he arrived, in which he gave a positive answer, and it was sent, after the cabinet secretary and the political chief had made some changes and additions. When Bernadotte was leaving, he said with a sigh that it might not be him after all, but van Zeeland, who would be selected. 'Yes, I wish that were so, dear Folke,' I said, 'and if so, I think you should open a bottle of champagne.' "

On May 20, as Arab snipers positioned themselves along the Jerusalem–Tel Aviv road that was the Holy City's lifeline, a man whose knowledge of the region came almost exclusively from the Bible accepted the position of first United Nations mediator in Palestine. "He decided that he probably had one chance in a hundred to succeed, but accepted on the possibility of that one chance," his widow remembered.

Folke's friends in the Foreign Ministry were terrified at the prospect of this well-meaning but innocent man striding toward the world's most volatile intersection.

"Gunnar Hägglöf [a veteran Swedish diplomat], who sees the danger, has sent Bernadotte heart-wrenching warnings," Grafström wrote in his diary of May 21, "and at least tried to get him not to go right away to Palestine, but urged him to go to Lake Success and try to find out more about the utterly complex Palestine situation. But nothing has helped. Hägglöf's reasoning was most likely to get through to him, since going to America might convince Bernadotte that the wise move would be to resign. Bernadotte had a conversation with [Secretary-General] Lie and immediately thereafter called a press conference. He will travel to Palestine via Paris the 25th of May. His mission is not only to try to get a truce and then peace, but he will even outline the direction for the future order in the Holy Land."

Three days later, on May 25, 1948, Folke Bernadotte boarded a plane for Paris, the first leg of his journey to Palestine.

Earlier that same week, the first in the life of the new State of Israel, a terrorist who had spent the last two years as a British captive in a special prison camp in Asmara, Eritrea, also made his way to Tel Aviv—after a spectacular prison break, the second of his life. A short, compact, powerfully built man, he had tunneled his way out of the African camp, then spent a week nearly suffocating inside a petrol tanker that carried him to Abyssinia. From there, with the help of an underground railroad of sympathizers, he made his way to French Djibouti, then on to Toulon. The French government, fully aware they had a sworn enemy of the British in their grasp, nonetheless arranged for his safe passage back to Israel.

And thus Yitzhak Shamir, leader of Lehi, landed in the new state five days after its declaration of independence. Free at last of the British occupation, Israel began life with six Arab armies bent on her destruction. For Shamir, a prison-hardened man whose only profession was the underground, the Army was not an option. Shamir had much to learn of the new State of Israel, whose birth pangs he had missed because of his imprisonment. In common with Lehi, the underground organization he built,

Shamir rejected the notion that outside mediation should determine the size and shape of the Land of Israel. Shamir's story, and thus Lehi's, begins, however, not in 1948, not in Jerusalem, but in the shtetls, or small Jewish communities, of Poland, more than two decades earlier.

CHAPTER SIX

YITZHAK

It has been said that a European Jew survived the Holocaust only by dint of guile, luck, courage, corruption, or crime. A Jew could not survive Hitler's war simply by existing. Those who did survive did so as a result of some asserted act that represented either the best in a man or woman's character, or the darkest aspect. These acts of survival were born of the realization that no one would come to their rescue: in the end, they were alone. The miracle of their survival was forever tied to *not* trusting, to taking things into their own hands. Those who survived and reached Palestine took this lesson of survival with them. Israel, they felt, was not a gift bestowed on deserving Jews by the world. Israel had to be fought for and secured, using any and all means. Compliant behavior, accommodation of any sort, had led their parents, their brothers and sisters, to march toward open graves, to be shot in groups of several hundred or more, in silence. This was the bitter lesson of their youth. This was the essential spirit that animated the four men who were to kill Folke Bernadotte and that defined those who ordered the assassination; most particularly it shaped the steely determination of Yitzhak Shamir.

Yitzhak Shamir began his life as Yitzhak Yezernitsky, in the small shtetl of Rozhnoi, in what is now Belarus. Laws passed by the czars beginning in 1795 confined Yezernitsky's family, part of the 4 million Jews under Russian rule, to the largest of all ghettos, the Pale of Settlement.

Yitzhak Yezernitsky's childhood was spent in an almost exclusively Jewish world. Though the Judaism practiced by his family was of the secular variety, it embraced every facet of their lives:

their holidays, the music they played, the songs they sang, the newspapers they read—all were steeped in their ancient culture. Yitzhak's father, Shlomo Yezernitsky, married to his distant cousin Pearl Szawzien, practiced one of the professions allowed Polish Jews: he was a tanner. The family of five (two daughters, Miriam and Rivka, preceded Yitzhak) was relatively comfortable. The tanner was busy, since leather was a strategic material in a country where the cavalry was still a vital institution.

Jewish life went on after the Germans occupied Rozhnoi during World War I, the year before Yitzhak's birth; in fact, the Germans were less anti-Semitic than the Poles. The elder Yezernitsky helped to organize a hospital for the 2,000 Jewish residents of Rozhnoi. Though Polish was their official language, Yiddish was the language of the family table and of young Yitzhak's dreams. The uncertain national identity of their hometown did nothing to dilute the Jews' passionate attachment to their ancient faith. For Rozhnoi was one of those East European border towns whose flag seemed to change after each war. It became the front line between Polish and Russian forces following Germany's defeat in 1918. As so often when European armies were on the march, the Jews became the first victims. This was the future Israeli prime minister's first experience of the particular brutality for which there is only a Russian-Yiddish word: pogrom.

The Jews in Rozhnoi—as elswhere in Europe—were filled with a growing sense of foreboding about their future. They grappled with the question of how to confront the gathering darkness: to assimilate, to rise up in armed struggle, or to abandon the Old World altogether for the uncertain promise of Palestine.

Yitzhak was four years old when the Polish cavalry that had helped provide sustenance to the tanner's family unleashed a massacre on the Jews of the surrounding countryside. Thirty thousand Jews were dead in the wake of this rampage in Bialystok. His friends claim that Yitzhak could not forget the six lined up and shot in front of Rozhnoi's synagogue.

With Rozhnoi integrated into the new Polish Republic created after World War I, life again settled down to the dreary but predictable routine of a muddy shtetl. "Ytsel," as young Yezernitsky was nicknamed by his family, was no scholar. Only in the study of Hebrew, for which he had a genuine appetite, did he distinguish himself in school.

In 1927 his studies were interrupted when his father was forced to close his tannery and move the family from Rozhnoi to Volkovysk, a city of 20,000, in search of work. Shlomo was looking for work in a society in which Jews were increasingly marginalized, with an economic *numerus clausus* already in effect. The Yezernitskys' lives, like those of Poland's 3 million other Jews, had become a daily struggle.

The elder Yezernitskys tried their hand at running a small inn. Their son was more and more absent from the family circle, however, caught up in the rich political life of Volkovysk. Zionism was the hottest subject of the Jewish youth of Volkovysk, as it was in hundreds of other small towns in eastern Poland. In 1929, Yitzhak read in the local Hebrew-language newspaper of a terrible massacre of Jews by Arabs in Hebron. So even in Palestine, the land of redemption, Jews seemed defenseless.

The adolescent had heard talk of a Russian-Jewish writer, poet, linguist, a maverick Zionist, who was pressing for the formation of a Jewish Legion in Palestine, initially to help the British battle the Turks, and later for self-defense. His name was Vladimir Jabotinsky. His militant Zionism called for the immediate creation of a Jewish majority in Palestine on both sides of the Jordan River, as Zionism's first priority. "Treason," charged mainstream Zionists such as the venerated Chaim Weizmann, who saw that Jabotinsky threatened his more gradualist, diplomatic approach.

Yitzhak and his friends were increasingly impatient with the apparent failure of any power to stem Polish anti-Semitism and the great failure of Britain to deliver on the promise of the Balfour Declaration: a Jewish Homeland. For these Jewish youth, Jabotinsky's words had the clarity and wisdom of the Gospel. At last someone was suggesting action rather than more rhetoric. In an attempt to put his muscular Zionism to work, Jabotinsky launched the Revisionist movement in 1924. He chose the term "Revisionist" to emphasize his call for the revision of the Palestine Mandate to include both sides of the Jordan River.

A spellbinding speaker who is still one of Zionism's most hotly debated figures, Jabotinsky included in his program the immediate transportation of thousands of Jews to British Mandated Palestine, to be declared the Jewish Homeland. "The Jewish race," he had written in 1913, "will never be subjugated." Again and again, he echoed his theme: "The iron law of every colonizing movement, a law which knows of no exceptions, a law which existed in all times and under all circumstance [is]: if you wish to colonize a land in which people are already living, you must provide a garrison on your behalf. Or else—or else, give up your colonization, for without an armed force which will render physically impossible any attempts to destroy or prevent this colonization, colonization is impossible, not 'difficult,' not 'dangerous,' but IMPOSSIBLE!" he thundered.

Though Jabotinsky admired the British for their self-government and their culture, the Russian firebrand felt that Jewish statehood would have to be achieved by force of Jewish arms. Insisting he was not anti-Arab, in November 1923 Jabotinsky wrote: "My emotional relationship to the Arabs is the same as it is to all other peoples: polite indifference. My political relationship is characterized by two principles. First: the expulsion of the Arabs from Palestine is absolutely impossible in any form. There will always be two peoples in Palestine. Second: . . . I am prepared to swear, for us and for our descendants, that we will never destroy this equality [between Arabs and Jews] and we will never attempt to expel or oppress the Arabs. Our credo, as the reader can see, is peaceful. But it is absolutely another matter if it will be impossible to achieve our peaceful aims through peaceful means. This depends, not on our relationship with the Arabs, but exclusively on the Arabs' relationship to Zionism. . . . Any native people . . . it's all the same whether they are civilized or savage—views their country as their national home, of which they will always be the complete masters. They will not voluntarily allow, not only a new master, but even a new partner. And so it is with the Arabs."

For the youth of the old shtetls, this kind of blunt talk and assertiveness from their elders was like a square meal for a starving man. Yitzhak Yezernitsky joined Jabotinsky's militant youth group, Betar (Brith Trumpeldor, named after Joseph Trumpeldor, a Jewish soldier killed defending the settlement of Tel Chai in the Galilee in 1921). Devoted at the outset to the study of Hebrew language and culture, the Betaris also trained in self-defense. Their martial airs, the brown shirts they wore, the reverence they paid their leader, and their incessant drilling all made them an easy mark for charges of fascism from those Zionists repelled by this brand of flashy militarism. Wrapped in an almost mythical aura, Betar was alien to the predominantly

European, liberal-socialist-utopian strain of the Zionism of Weizmann and Ben-Gurion.

The fourteen-year-old Yitzhak Yezernitsky, a freshly minted
Betari and a student at the Hebrew Herzlyah High School in
Volkovysk, delivered his first political speech in 1929 and his
words echoed those of his new political mentor. "One more
cow, one more house, a goat or a farm?" he asked rhetorically
of his fellow students. "Is that how you wish to build a state?
He who wants a country has to fight for it. Buying one more
cow, one more goat, building one more farm in Palestine won't
lead you anywhere. That isn't for me. I couldn't build Eretz Israel
that way!"

In that same year, 1929, Chaim Weizmann was the undis-
puted leader of world Zionism, which saw the acquisition of one
more cow, one more goat, and one more farm as the road to a
carefully constructed Jewish Homeland. Weizmann, a Russian-
born British subject, was a distinguished scientist whose friendship with Lord Arthur Balfour had much to do with the 1917
Balfour Declaration promising Jews a homeland in Palestine. But
Weizmann and his British mentors sought to attain the homeland in a way that would somehow manage not to "violate the
legitimate rights" of its Arab occupants. Underestimating the
simmering fervor of Palestinian Arab nationalism, Weizmann
deemed good economic relations between the two communities
as paramount to achieving this goal. Centuries of Turkish rule
had depleted Palestine, ruled by a corrupt class of landowners,
the so-called *effendi*, whose lifestyle was propped up by a vast
sea of ignorant and poverty-stricken masses. Weizmann, like
many other moderate Zionists, nursed the illusion that the economic benefits of Jewish settlement would soon calm Arab fears
and lead to good relations between the two communities.

But young Yitzhak Yezernitsky had taken his first step along a
different path. The choice involved a break with his own father.
More and more of Ytsel's time was spent in Betar-related activities. The quiet, self-contained adolescent soon showed himself
an excellent organizer of Betari cells, one of which he started in
his hometown of Rozhnoi during a summer vacation there. As
government-sanctioned anti-Semitism became more and more
virulent in Poland in the early thirties, squeezing Jews out of
nearly all economic positions, the Zionist debate gained urgency.
Emigration to America, the traditional haven of Russian and

Polish Jews, was becoming more difficult. Emigration to Palestine, increasingly the last hope of Central European Jews, was still hotly debated among Zionists. Yezernitsky's own father opposed Jabotinsky's plan for the mass evacuation of Polish Jews to Palestine. This plan, which Jabotinsky hoped would transport 1.5 million Jews, (the bulk of them Polish), from Eastern Europe, had the implicit support of the Polish government as a means of getting rid of "their" Jews. In the spring of 1939, it set up a guerrilla training school for Jabotinsky's followers at Zakopane, in the Tatra Mountains. Polish Army officers taught them the tricks of sabotage and insurrection. The Poles provided them with weapons for 10,000 men, due to launch an invasion of Palestine in April 1940. Jabotinsky's lieutenants were engaged in negotiations with Turkey and Italy for passage to Palestine, but made little headway with either country.

Yezernitsky's father was appalled. "I have the right to live here if I want to. Besides," he asked his son, "how can you oppose Chaim Weizmann, who has the respect of the whole world?" Yet the determined young Yezernitsky graduated from Bialystok Hebrew Gymnasium wearing a brown Betari shirt under his school uniform. In 1933, the same year Adolf Hitler became chancellor of Germany, the future prime minister of Israel won a coveted place at Warsaw University Law School. But in his mind, law school was just an excuse for his deepening involvement with the Revisionists and with Betar.

At Warsaw University, Yitzhak noted signs of spreading alarm among his fellow Jewish students. "Many Jewish students walked around equipped with some means of defence against gangs of anti-Semitic hooligans whose attacks were becoming increasingly frequent. Later in life I got used to being armed . . . but in those first weeks in Warsaw, it was jarring for me to have to remember to slip a knife in my pocket—as more experienced Jewish students told me to do—before I set out to study."

The study of law struck him as absurdly irrelevant in a conspicuously lawless world. Yitzhak was among those who heard Joseph Goebbels, the Nazi master propagandist, lecture on the subject of National Socialism before a rapt audience of one thousand students and teachers at the law school.

A month after assuming power, Hitler suspended the constitutional rights of German Jews. Two months later, they were prohibited from holding civil-service jobs. Watching the drama unfolding next door in Germany, Yitzhak Yezernitsky began to plan the passage he had been contemplating for years—emigration to Palestine. Meanwhile, the rest of his family—his parents, sisters and brothers-in-law, as well as their young children—returned to Rozhnoi to try to eke out a living. In Rozhnoi, where the family was well known, they assumed they would be safe.

Aware that Hebrew University in Jerusalem preferred well-off students, Yitzhak said in his application that his father owned a large factory in Rozhnoi. The ploy worked and the determined twenty-year-old Pole, inspired by militant Zionism, was accepted by Hebrew University as a student of Hebrew literature and the social and economic history of Judaism. He also received a certificate of immigration to Palestine, becoming one of the thousands of European Jews to "make aliya"—Hebrew for "ascent"—to the Promised Land—that year.

Hardened well beyond his years, alienated from the world outside this tight circle of intimates, Yitzhak Yezernitsky now cut most of his ties to Poland. He carried virtually no baggage to Palestine save for a few hard lessons. This much he knew: Trust no one and keep your own counsel.

Jewish policemen on the streets of a Jewish city. A remarkable sight. Such was the twenty-year-old's first impression of Tel Aviv after his ship dropped anchor on November 11, 1935. Palestine in 1935 was in full economic and social bloom. Sixty-six thousand Jews arrived that year, pushing the Jewish population to nearly a half million. The Arab population had nearly doubled to almost a million by 1936. Yezernitsky had a name in his pocket, that of a friend of his father's from Rozhnoi who had moved to Tel Aviv. The man offered him lodgings and introduced him to other Polish immigrants. Still in his rough shtetl clothes, his head much too large for his small, squat body, his jutting jaw and eyes nearly buried beneath bushy brows, Yezernitsky was hardly an imposing figure. Yet there was an intensity about him, an absence of sentimentality that was surprising in one so young. He did not pretend to be interested in anything other than Jabotinsky's brand of militant Zionism. "I heard of him in the Youth Movement [Betar]," one of the future leaders of Lehi, Natan Yalin-Mor recalled, "when I first came to Warsaw in 1933. Everyone there spoke highly of him and recalled him with . . . nostalgia."

Yitzhak's days at Hebrew University were to be extremely brief. Arts, letters, and science held no interest for him. He was there long enough to make a few contacts, and to replace his immigrant's garb with the ubiquitous khaki shorts and open-neck shirt favored by Jews of the region.

When the Arab uprising against mass Jewish immigration erupted in Palestine in 1936, the Haganah preached and practiced *havlaga*, Hebrew for "self-restraint." Thus, while Arabs rampaged and looted, the British forces in Palestine, now numbering 15,000, were reluctant to antagonize the already enraged Arab majority, and stood by. When Jews were advised to lock their doors and wait for the terror to subside, the new arrival must surely have wondered if Palestine was any safer than Rozhnoi. Would the monotonous routine of cowering behind the bolted door waiting for the pogrom to pass never end? The principle of *havlaga* struck Yezernitsky as about as rational a response to violence as prayer would be to an atheist.

Havlaga, despised by some Jews, embraced by others, finally forced into the open the split inside Zionism's ranks. The Haganah was made up primarily of liberal, Labor members with a minority of Revisionists. Now Jabotinsky's Revisionist minority split from the Haganah and declared it would not accept the authority of the Jewish Agency in Palestine. Recognized by the League of Nations since 1922, the Jewish Agency was the organization responsible for the settlement of Jews in Palestine. Its leaders included Chaim Weizmann and David Ben-Gurion, the future president and future prime minister of Israel.

The breakaway faction, calling itself the Irgun Zvai Leumi, the National Military Organization, promised that henceforth it would return every Arab punch with a counterpunch. It was the message Yitzhak Yezernitsky wanted to hear, the starting gun in the young loner's life in the underground.

From contacts back home in Bialystok, Yitzhak had obtained the name of a Betari, David Orlovski, living in Tel Aviv. Orlovski had already joined the embryonic Irgun. The two young Polish immigrants, Yezernitsky and Orlovski, rented a small apartment at 34 Balfour Street, a grimy, indifferently furnished flat that they soon transformed into a meeting place for more Irgun recruits. Yezernitsky, trained by Betar in self-defense, now learned other useful terrorist tools. To these instructions, he brought a passion absent from his scholarly pursuits. He earned the name "Shooter" for the remarkable aptitude he showed in the handling of small arms. As part of his training, he had to learn to take apart and reassemble blindfolded every type of pistol, gun, and rifle.

At night, on the rooftops of "safe" Tel Aviv buildings, Yitzhak joined a growing army of adolescents and young men who marched and drilled. The recruits were fired by Jabotinsky's notion of *hadar,* dignity, as an antidote to centuries of what they deemed to be Jewish "slackness." For *havlaga* they felt only contempt.

In the darkness of abandoned Arab houses just outside Tel Aviv Yezernitsky and nearly eight hundred other young men and women pledged their lives to the underground in ritual-filled ceremonies, answering "Yes!" to disembodied voices that asked them a series of questions: "Are you here of your own free will? Can you bear pain? Suppose you are arrested—do you know how to keep silent?" And then, the voice in the dark instructed the new recruit: "Place your left hand on the gun that is on the Bible, raise your right hand, and repeat after me: I do solemnly swear full allegiance to the Irgun Zvai Leumi, and to its commander, to its goal, and its aims, and I am ready to make every sacrifice even of my life, giving first preference at all times to the Irgun, above my parents, my brothers, my sisters, my family . . . until we achieve a sovereign Israel. So help me, God."

CHAPTER SEVEN

STERN

THE TARGET OF YEZERNITSKY'S IRGUN IN THE LATE THIRTIES WAS the Arab population of Palestine, which was beginning to resist the growing Jewish presence. On July 4, 1938, Irgunists threw homemade bombs into the Arab suburb of Jaffa. Five people were killed and 20 injured. Two days later, Irgun bombs killed 23 Arabs and injured 79 others. The same month, the Irgun claimed 10 Arabs dead in Jerusalem, and on July 25, 29 more joined the Irgun's body count in Palestine. According to his friends from those early days in the underground, the new recruit from Rozhnoi was an active participant in these operations. One former Irgunist recalled the time he and Yitzhak hurled a hand grenade onto a train carrying Arabs.

In 1939, everything changed for the Jews. While Zionist leaders still debated how to construct their future state, a death sentence was passed on their people. Six months after he temporarily placated Hitler in Munich by abandoning Czechoslovakia to its fate, British Prime Minister Neville Chamberlain announced that the Balfour Declaration "could not have intended that Palestine should be converted into a Jewish state against the will of the Arab population of the country." After a final group of 75,000 Jews, to be admitted to Palestine between 1939 and 1944, the Arabs would have veto power over further Jewish immigration. The document, issued on May 17, 1939, commonly known as "the White Paper on Palestine," provided for the establishment of an Arab state within ten years' time, in which the Jews were not to exceed one-third of the population.

One of history's most despised documents, the White Paper would have condemned the Jews to remain a permanent minority in Palestine. It deprived their community of its lifeblood, immigration, and denied them the right to purchase land. Rising from his seat in Parliament, Winston Churchill pronounced the document "a base betrayal, a petition in moral bankruptcy." Chamberlain was barring the door to Jews at the same moment that Hitler was setting in motion the machinery of genocide. "That he could do this!" Chaim Weizmann, loyal British subject and chief dreamer of the Zionist dream, exclaimed upon leaving the office of Colonial Secretary Malcolm MacDonald. "He who made me believe he was a friend."

London's new policy had been felt in Palestine even before the publication of the White Paper. In April 1939, three refugee ships, packed with Jews who had managed to escape from Germany to Rumania, reached Palestine. The ships were refused permission to dock. Control of Jewish immigration (even within the 75,000 limit set by the White Paper) was strictly at the discretion of the colonial power.

In the House of Commons, when he was asked what would happen to the people on the ships, MacDonald coolly replied that they had been sent back to where they came from. "Does that mean to concentration camps?" MP Noel Baker asked. The colonial secretary answered, "The responsibility rests with those responsible for organizing illegal immigration."

In Jerusalem, Tel Aviv, and Haifa, stunned crowds poured into the streets in spontaneous demonstrations of anger and disbelief. That summer, at the Twenty-first Zionist Congress, convened in Geneva, even moderate Zionists boiled over in anger at the breach of British faith. David Ben-Gurion, head of Palestine's shadow government, urged a militant policy of resistance to the White Paper that had "created a vacuum which must be filled by the Jews themselves. The Jews should act as though they were the State in Palestine and should so continue to act until there will be a Jewish State there."

But, once again, Chaim Weizmann urged solidarity with the British war effort. "We have grievances," he told the congress, "but above our regret and bitterness are higher interests. What the democracies are fighting for is the minimum . . . necessary for Jewish life. Their anxiety is our anxiety; their war is our war."

Arthur Koestler, the noted author and sometime resident of Palestine, and like Weizmann a British subject, met often with the elder statesman of Zionism. "Weizmann believed in maximum pressure [on the British] for minimum demands. He believed that the British would partition Palestine [into an Arab and an Israeli state]. And if the frontiers imposed were impossible, there would be rectification later, either by force or by negotiations." This was the opposite of Jabotinsky's belief that Zionists should make maximum demands—an immediate Jewish state on both sides of the Jordan.

The delegates to the Geneva conference parted in what Weizmann called "a thick, black gloom." Their final hope of escape had been barred by their former patron, Great Britain. Few of them would survive the war.

In Palestine, Yezernitsky and his fellow members of the Irgun had a radically different response to the White Paper. "The Jewish Agency reacted to this step by proclaiming a half day general strike throughout the Jewish community of Palestine," wrote Natan Yalin-Mor, Yezernitsky's comrade in arms in the underground. "The strike was meticulously observed by one and all. The results were absolutely nil. The nature of the enemy was no longer in doubt. Britain's adoption of the White Paper was no mere tactical measure intended to mollify the Arab nationalist movement. Britain, it was clear, would activate the White Paper . . . as a tool to achieve an end: a permanent minority status for the Jewish community." Henceforth, the enemy was not only the Arab, but the British in the Homeland, Eretz Israel.

The underground launched full-scale warfare against both Arab and British targets. Irgunists mined the Rex Cinema in Jerusalem. Five Arabs were killed in the blast, eighteen more wounded. Forty-eight hours later, the Irgun attacked the village of Bir Adas, this time killing five Arabs. They bombed British installations, railroad tracks, mail and telephone boxes, and slashed telephone wires. The British Army in Palestine responded to this fresh wave of Irgun terror with much more vigor than when the Arabs had been the Irgun's target. Palestine thus began its transformation from just another nettlesome colonial outpost into a garrison state where the ratio of Jews to Englishmen in uniform would soon be five to one. In late May 1939, the British picked up Irgun commander David Raziel. One by one, they ambushed and jailed others among the leadership. The underground's wave of anti-British violence was temporarily checked.

On September 1, 1939, Hitler's soldiers crossed into Poland. Jabotinsky's dream of a Polish-sanctioned Jewish mass immigration to Palestine was dashed. Now, under the force of events, even Jabotinsky reluctantly fell in line with British war aims. In common with his great adversary, Chaim Weizmann, he conceded that London's ultimate objective was identical to that of the Jews. For the sake of the war effort, he was jettisoning his anti-British policy in Palestine. Defeating Hitler had to be the Revisionists' first priority.

One important member of the Irgun leadership had escaped the British net—Avraham Stern, who was in Poland during the roundup. He was there to arrange for the training by the Polish Army of 40,000 Irgun youth, Polish Jews, for an invasion of Palestine. The invasion, planned for October, was meant to wrest Palestine from the British. Poland's own occupation by the Third Reich in September 1939 shattered these plans. There is no hard historical evidence as to how seriously Polish officials took Stern's plan, but they did supply arms and training facilities to the Irgun.

Avraham Stern had other, equally fantastic schemes in mind. A remarkable character, the thirty-two-year-old Polish-born zealot with the melancholy features of a portrait by Modigliani was not one to trim his obsessions to political realities. Stern claimed he saw the enemy of the Jews—and it was not Adolf Hitler. Great Britain was the real oppressor, Stern asserted. It was a supreme act of heresy at the moment when Britain stood alone against the Nazis. Almost alone among Jews, Stern called for war not against Berlin but against London.

"We knew that our people's freedom could come about only after a struggle against Britain and the replacement of its regime in Palestine with Hebrew dominion," wrote Natan Yalin-Mor, one of Stern's disciples. "The bulk of the Jewish population, following the furrow plowed by its leaders, had been deceiving itself into believing that a sort of National Home could be nurtured and developed within the boundaries of British rule."

In common with other totalitarian thinkers, Stern was willing to take any measure to bring down the tyrant. In common with other powerless groups, he chose the weapon of terror. Stern clashed with the Irgun over the issue of the underground's self-imposed truce during the war. The British, according to Stern, were collaborating with Hitler by refusing to save Jewish refugees.

Whether seen as saint or demon in the Zionist pantheon,

Stern leaves few indifferent. His imprint on history stems from his powerful hold on those with whom he came in contact. "No fervor marked his statements, although in his voice I could sense a constant effort to keep the flame from exploding," Yalin-Mor recalled. "His voice was dry, metallic. His power lay in the logical analysis, the dialectic reasoning, leading his listeners to making a choice between contrasting possibilities, based on his own judgment, will and conscience."

To his followers in the underground, Stern was "the world's first truly free Jew," the messenger of a radical new brand of Zionism. "His Zionism was not just excess baggage to the aims of Churchill or Stalin," Yalin-Mor observed in his memoirs. "Stern was not prepared to serve either of the combatant sides. To him this was simply a war of Gog and Magog, inasmuch as neither side had declared support for the national aspirations of the Jews, and both had done harm to our people in one way or another."

Samuel Merlin, Stern's friend in the Irgun, remembered him in Poland in 1939. "He was an unusual man. He didn't look at all like a terrorist, or a man of violence. For one thing, he was immaculate, always dressed to the nines, while the rest of us didn't own a necktie. And a womanizer. Women found him handsome. And he thought himself so. I think he went to the barber every day. And he was a poet. A bona fide poet."

Stern was also a scholar, a protégé of Dr. Judah Magnes, the president of Hebrew University, who described him as "a pure, enlightened soul," and predicted a brilliant career for him. An avid student of the classics, equally fluent in Greek and Latin, Stern won a scholarship to Florence in the thirties, when fascism was on the march, and there was seduced by certain aspects of fascism. Stern admired Mussolini's leadership, the Duce's ability to bend the population to his powerful will. Stern wrote to Merlin, by then the Irgun's representative in New York, to ask him to raise money for his breakaway organization in America. "I got letters from Stern in code, asking me to represent him in New York and to try to create something here, but"—Merlin shook his head—"nothing came of it. American Jews found Stern too extreme, too threatening to everything cherished by mainstream Zionists. There was some minimal support," Merlin recalled, "but so secretive even I didn't know who it was." Within the underground, Stern was valued for qualities other than his mastery of the classics. He coauthored (with Irgun Commander David Raziel) a handbook on the revolver. He taught courses on the use of small arms and the manufacture of homemade explosives. But his long-term influence lay elsewhere.

When the German Army marched into Poland on September 1, 1939, Stern, like all 3 million Polish Jews, was a marked man. Unlike most of them, however, he managed to escape to Palestine. The young zealot burned to seize control of the underground and steer it toward a new, more violent path. He found a great many of his comrades chafing because of Jabotinsky's decision to cease terrorism against the British. To Stern, Jabotinsky's Revisionists had already sold out. Stern was more influenced by Abba Achimeir and his Brith Habiryonim, the most militant wing of the Revisionist Party in Palestine, than he was by Jabotinsky. The way Stern saw it, it was Britain that illegally occupied Eretz Israel, bestowed by God on the Hebrews. Britain was the alien presence in the land. Nazi Germany might be a foe of the Jews— one in a long line—but the British who refused to cede to Jews the land of their forefathers were the real enemy. The Bible, and not the Balfour Declaration, was Stern's point of reference.

"Stern's origins are in European fascism," asserts Professor Joseph Heller, the Israeli expert on the underground. "They're the most extreme group Zionism ever produced. They didn't just want a Jewish state, they wanted a Jewish kingdom. Nor did they fully grasp the portent of Hitler. They thought he was just another anti-Semite, and a vegetarian at that. Stern never read *Mein Kampf*. He and his followers simply didn't want to understand the Holocaust. For them the symbol of the Holocaust was not Auschwitz but the ships bearing Jews which the British turned away from Palestine. It was important for the Sternists to establish that the British were worse than the Nazis.

"They claimed the British were the nation which established anti-Semitism, with Houston Stewart Chamberlain. This is nonsense, but they needed to establish that the British were the greatest enemies of the Jewish people. The Nazis never occupied the Fatherland, the British did. The Nazis were troublemakers, but not the enemy. The chief enemy is he who occupies the Fatherland."

Ben-Gurion's words, "We shall fight the war as if there were no White Paper, and fight the White Paper as if there were no war," rang hollow for Stern and his followers. All the more so as they observed Britain's hard-hearted policy toward rescuing their trapped brethren.

They were called "the little death ships," steamers groaning under their burden of ten or twenty times their intended human cargo of Jews. Though the British had announced they would turn back refugees from Nazi-occupied Europe, still the Jews arrived. With help from the Haganah or the Irgun, they defied both the laws of their land and reason. As the ships of hope approached Palestine, their passengers half-delirious from thirst, hunger, and the prospect of what lay ahead, bayonet-bearing British soldiers forced the dazed passengers back. A kind of madness overtook those helplessly watching from the shore.

"Try to put yourself in the place of a Jew of your own age on the jetty of Haifa," Arthur Koestler wrote in "An Open Letter to a Parent of a British Soldier in Palestine," "shouting and waving to a relative—your son for instance—on the deck of one of those ships. He is not permitted to land; the ship lifts anchor to take its doomed hysterical load back to where it came from. The figure of your boy grows smaller; a few years later you hear that he has been gassed in Auschwitz. If instead of Smith, your name were Schmulewitz, it might have happened to you."

In September 1940, Stern stalked out of the Irgun to form his own underground. The British derisively dubbed it the Stern Gang. Stern's aim was to fight the British not only in Palestine, but on any terrain he could reach them. He rejected all other authority, even that of the Irgun's patron saint, Jabotinsky. A small but resolute group of supporters from the Irgun joined Stern's new movement, which would become known as Lehi—Lohmey Heruth Israel, Fighters for the Freedom of Israel.

Among Avraham Stern's most enthusiastic recruits were boys who had stood on the Palestinian coast and seen the "little death ships" collapse under the weight of their human cargo, leaving hundreds to drown, or watched them sail slowly away, back to the continent they had tried to flee.

Yitzhak Yezernistsky responded to Stern's magnetic zealotry. "I heard a lot about him before I met him," Yezernitsky/Shamir recalled decades later. "He was very highly thought of in the underground. He was a mixture of statesman, philosopher, poet, and also fighter. . . . At that time, I occupied a flat belonging to the underground, on Balfour Street. He would come there for meetings and we would talk a little." It took Yezernitsky several months to decide to leave the Irgun, his only family since his arrival in Palestine three years earlier. "It was a difficult experience for me. I knew everyone, and they were dear to me. . . . It was not easy to split up with friends with whom you had been for a long time, with whom you identified one hundred percent, and suddenly they became enemies. . . . This is a very hard experience. Very hard." Nevertheless, Yitzhak, who had assumed the underground name "Michael" after a famed Irish guerrilla named Michael Collins, followed Stern to the radical new underground. "The Irgun were only attacking buildings. And we were laughing at them," Natan Yalin-Mor explained. "We thought it more effective to aim at British lives."

Yezernitsky/Shamir later defended the strategy of the Stern Gang, saying it was more humane than that of the Irgun. Frontal attacks on army camps or a bomb hurled in a police station, Yezernitsky pointed out, kill men at random. The Sternists were selective in their targets, killing on an individual basis for a specific tactical reason. In his recently published memoirs, Yitzhak Shamir writes of the wide gulf separating Menachem Begin's Irgun from his own underground. "He [Begin] could not accept nor understand the modes of operation of the Lehi. Attacking one individual man seemed to him to be unethical. Going to war for lack of choice seemed to him to be completely kosher but execution of an enemy or an informant was wrong in his eyes. He wanted court houses, trials, legal legitimacy, precise legal procedures—things that were impossible in the underground."

In a matter of months, the stolid, reliable Yezernitsky had shown himself so adept at the terrorist's craft that Stern promoted him to membership in his high command. Yezernitsky's first task was one of his hardest: recruiting others to Stern's movement. "Our position demanded a special motivation," he recalled. "This we did not often succeed in arousing. There wasn't a basis of manpower. . . . The Irgun had Betar and the nationalist youth and all those who followed Jabotinsky. We didn't have an alternative source of manpower. Apart from that, the British immediately started fierce pursuit. Eighty percent of our people were sitting in jail. Until I was arrested in 1941, I built up part of this force, in Tel Aviv, where I was living. It was hard."

"We were of diverse mentality united by one thing," another former Sternist, Y. S. Brenner, observes today. "There must be a Jewish state. This was the only thing which we had in common. The need for a National Home. We rejected the Diaspora. We thought of ourselves as a superclass, and all those Jews in the rest of the world were either knaves or fools. We felt this kind of superiority. I felt it, though we had no reason to. The damage we did for the future was tremendous. We cut ourselves loose from the Jewish liberal tradition and, instead of picking out what was worthwhile in that tradition, we rejected everything."

Not all Sternists share Brenner's rethinking of the messianic impulse. "For a moment," Baruch Nadel asserts with pride, "we became the Sons of God. That is what our Revolution meant. We have never forgotten this feeling."

Speaking a half century later from the prime minister's office, Yezernitsky—by then known as Yitzhak Shamir—recalled, "That period in the underground was the best part of my life."

Yezernitsky's recruiting job was not made easier by Stern's most brazen innovation: to deal with Hitler. In 1941, Stern decided to approach the people who were responsible for the existence of the little death ships, those who had passed the death sentence on millions of his fellow Jews. Though Stern managed to keep his audacious policy secret from British authorities, it gradually seeped into the consciousness of those who made up the almost hermetically sealed universe of the Jewish underground. Stern dispatched one of his men, Naftali Lubentchik, to Vichy-controlled Beirut. In early January 1941, Lubentchik met two Germans, Alfred Röser, a Military Intelligence agent, and Werner Otto von Hentig, a Foreign Ministry official. On January 11, 1941, von Hentig and Röser sent Stern's memorandum to the German ambassador in neutral Turkey. It proposed collaboration between the Nazis and the Jewish underground. The document's receipt was acknowledged by the signature of the German ambassador to Turkey, [Franz] "von Papen," and it was found in Ankara after the war. Dated November 1, 1940, and marked "Secret," it read:

> . . . I am happy to pass on to you the proposal of the [Stern faction of the Irgun] regarding the solution of the Jewish question

in Europe. . . . It is frequently expressed in announcements and speeches by central policy-makers in Nazi Germany that a secret solution of the Jewish question via evacuation ("Europe free of Jews") is one of the foundations of the new order in Europe.

The evacuation of the Jewish masses from Europe is a prior condition for the solution of the Jewish question. But the only possible final solution can be enacted by bringing these masses to the homeland of the Jewish people, to the Land of Israel, and by establishing a Jewish state within its historic boundaries. . . .

The Irgun knows well *the Reich's enthusiastic attitude towards Zionist activities within Germany* to encourage the Zionist emigration and therefore it believes that:

1. There are mutual interests between the designers of the new order in Europe according to the German outlook and the nationalistic aspirations of the Jewish people and its representation by the Irgun.
2. *Cooperation is possible between the new Germany and the renewed National Popular Hebrew Movement.* [Emphasis added.]
3. The establishment of the historical Jewish state on a national and totalitarian foundation, *linked by alliance with the German Reich, will safeguard and strengthen the powerful position of Germany in the future of the Near East.* [Emphasis added.]

From these factors, Irgun turns to the government of the German Reich with the suggestion to cooperate in the war on Germany's side, on the condition that the above-mentioned aspirations of the Israeli liberation movement will be recognized.

. . . The participation of the Israeli Liberation Movement also matches the line taken by one of the Reich chancellor's recent speeches, in which Herr Hitler emphasized that he would take advantage of any combination and coalition in order to isolate England. . . .

According to its world view and structure, Irgun is extremely close to the totalitarian movements of Europe. Irgun's military talents have not been silenced or seriously injured at any time, not by the policy of the English authorities nor by the Arabs nor by the Jewish socialists. [Emphasis added.]

In neither the German nor the Israeli archives is there a record of an answer to the letter from Hitler, though Stern's document is on file in the Bonn Public Record Office. As for Stern's hapless messenger, Lubentchik, he was picked up by British agents in Syria, imprisoned in Palestine's Mazra Detention Camp, and transferred from there to Eritrea, where he died on April 20, 1946.

Stern's astonishing and now-forgotten proposal of a Jewish-German alliance against Britain came as the eastbound trains transporting Jews had begun to pull out of European stations. It preceded by less than six weeks the Berlin Wannsee Conference, at which the Nazis planned the implementation of the Final Solution. The Reich chancellor and his colleagues had worked out their own solution to the "Jewish problem."

Unwilling to jettison his *idée fixe* of a Nazi-Jewish collaboration, later in 1941 Stern dispatched Natan Yalin-Mor to Turkey (the Vichy regimes in Syria and Lebanon having been defeated in July 1941) to make contact with German agents there. Yalin-Mor was arrested by British agents in Aleppo, Syria, en route to Turkey in December 1941.

"I can tell you why Stern contacted Hitler," former Sternist Baruch Nadel explains. "Hitler was the guy with power. Our famous nationalist poet Uri Zvi Greenberg advised one of Stern's lieutenants, 'Contact Hitler, he's the landlord.'"

In truth, there is some historic precedent for this. Theodor Herzl traveled to Russia in 1903 to make contact with the man who orchestrated the pogroms, the despised Vyacheslav von Plehve, thinking he might be interested in expediting the transfer of Jews out of Russia. But Stern was proposing more than a way for Hitler to solve his "Jewish problem." He was offering an alliance based on shared goals and convictions. As to the reaction of Stern's loyal disciple, Yezernitsky/Shamir—a man who normally shrinks from discussions of the past—on the subject of his underground's overture to Hitler, he has declared, "What was, was justified. We believed in what we did. We believed in what we said, spoke, and wrote. Therefore, it was right."

Years later, speaking as prime minister of Israel, Shamir attempted to explain his position regarding Stern's overtures to the Nazis. "I did not trust it. I knew very well what the Nazi movement was. I read a lot and I came from there. In the year before I emigrated to Palestine, I was a student in Warsaw. I encountered students who were mostly anti-Semitic, as well as the Nazi atmosphere in the streets. Persecution of the Jews was very deeply rooted ideologically, philosophically. I did not believe that they would suddenly perceive any kind of shared interests with Jews, with any Jews."

But Shamir has never actually disavowed a policy which, as a member of Stern's command, he clearly supported at the time. Dealing with Hitler, like murder for a cause, was not a moral issue for Shamir. It was, rather, a pragmatic decision, one for which he has never expressed remorse. "No shame," he told Israeli commentator Dan Margalit in 1992. "It was not a question of shame. It was just not the right policy. Because nothing came of it."

In a prophetic move, Stern had assumed the underground name "Yair," after Eliezer ben Yair, the hero of Masada, the Jewish symbol for all-out resistance. After the fall of Jerusalem to the Romans in A.D. 70, Yair led 1,000 of his followers to the nearby mountain fortress of Masada, and made them take an oath never to let themselves become servants of the foreign ruler. When, after a three-year siege, defeat was inevitable, Yair led his men in a mass suicide, rather than face capture.

Stern put the indelible stamp of his personality on the new underground. His disciple Yitzhak Shamir recalled in 1994, "Yair believed that people should think for themselves. 'Study, train and think,' he told us. He schooled us in the rudiments of covert life, including the art of camouflage: be inconspicuous, quiet, walk in the shade, be a little stooped, a little shabby, never preen or show off. Although he was a master of practical conspiracy, his craving for secrecy came out in unexpected ways sometimes. For instance, he wrote by hand, in capital letters, extremely quickly so that his handwriting would reveal as little as possible about him, be as anonymous, as impersonal as possible."

Guerrilla warfare against the well-defended British garrison involved increasingly higher risks. Stern/Yair's mind turned to another outlet for his agitated spirit. He churned out poetry that was soaked in blood and sacrifice. A loner who kept even his closest comrades at arm's length, Stern revealed himself most clearly in his poetry. "Yes, we shall pray for freedom—we shall pray with the revolver, the machine gun and the mine," he wrote.

Elsewhere he warned, "We are struck with the madness for kingdom." The dark visionary also sketched his image of the new nation of the Jews. Entitled "The Eighteen Principles of the Renaissance," the document contains Stern's legacy to his followers: "The Jewish people are unlike any other people. . . . Their country is the Land of Israel, with its frontiers as promised Abraham in the Bible—stretching from the Nile to the Euphrates. . . . The problem of aliens in the Land of Israel will be decided by an exchange of populations. . . . Alliances should be formed with anyone who has an interest in the organization's war and who is ready to give it direct help. . . ."

On crudely stenciled pieces of paper that his two hundred or so followers distributed under cover of night, the Jewish community in Palestine read Stern's poetry and his manifesto, Ikarei ha Tehiyyah (The Principles of Revival). One of those who distributed Stern's leaflets was Geulah Cohen, today a vocal right-wing member of the Knesset, in the forties a teenage fighter for Lehi. "I went about with a young man so we looked like a boy and his girlfriend," she recalls. "Our job was to stick up posters and hand out leaflets."

"Our headquarters were always on the move," Shamir recalled. Like medieval outlaws, Shamir and his gang often hid in caves and sand dunes near Tel Aviv. (In those days, when Palestine was still under the British Mandate, Tel Aviv—with its overwhelmingly Jewish population, easy access to sea and land transport—rather than Jerusalem, was the location of choice for the underground.)

After a series of violent attacks on British soldiers and policemen by his underground, Stern became a hunted man, unable any longer to leave his Tel Aviv hideout. All over Palestine, his unmistakable aquiline features on wanted signs offering a $5,000 reward for his capture were pasted on trees and telephone poles. Still, he refused to flee Tel Aviv. On the morning of February 12, 1942, Captain Geoffrey Morton of the Criminal Investigation Division banged on the door of No. 8 Mizrahi Street, in a working-class neighborhood of Tel Aviv. Stern had been hiding in the top-floor apartment belonging to one of his men, who was in British custody after being wounded in a shootout with police. Six khaki-uniformed, helmeted British officers and policemen flanked Captain Morton. Avraham Stern/ Yair slipped into a large wardrobe, while Tova Svorai, the wife of the wounded Sternist, slowly opened the front door.

It did not take the English soldiers long to find Stern. One of the officers pushed Mrs. Svorai out the front door while another fastened handcuffs on Stern. Three shots rang out. "Jews!" Tova Svorai screamed into the street. "They are killing Yair! Help him!" Seconds later, two policemen kicked Yair, dying and wrapped in a bloody blanket, down the stairwell.

"Our loss was abysmal, irreparable, when Yair fell," Yalin-Mor wrote. "Most of humanity was not with us; even our own people, almost all of them, were against us. But the few who remained swore, each unto himself, to persevere in Yair's footsteps, until the battle for freedom was won. . . . We would win freedom, even if life itself would be the price."

In the end, Avraham Stern had proved a disappointing underground leader. From his astounding and ultimately fruitless attempt to strike a deal with Hitler, to his fantastic plan for the redemption of the Land of Israel, to his blood-drenched poetry, his was a troubling legacy, the product of a tormented mind. Even the way he met death struck some as unworthy. "It was not a very good way for a leader of a guerrilla group to die, being dragged out of a cupboard," noted Efraim Dekel, the head of Haganah intelligence. "He could at least have shot his way out, taken one of the policemen with him, died like a hero. He was more of a poet than a fighter."

The British record states that Stern was "shot dead while attempting to escape." The man who shot Stern, Captain Geoffrey Morton, objects to that explanation. "I dislike the term 'Shot trying to escape' both because of its inaccuracy in relation to the death of Stern and because of its emotive, Nazi-like connotations. . . . When Stern dived for the window, I shot him. Full stop." "Captain Morton helped us in a way," Yalin-Mor told British historian Nicholas Bethell. "He destroyed our illusions . . . brought us to the Rubicon."

Avraham Stern's greatest single contribution to the underground was his death at the hands of Captain Morton and his six policemen. Yair left his followers the priceless gift of his martyrdom.

Yitzhak Shamir, known to Stern as "Michael," was in British custody at the Mazra Detention Camp near the Crusader fortress town of Acre when word of Yair's murder reached him. "I thought that my world was falling apart."

CHAPTER EIGHT

A PRIVILEGED
YOUTH

IT IS A LONG JOURNEY FROM A BARE, BLOOD-SPATTERED STAIR-well on Mizrahi Street in Tel Aviv's working-class quarter to a graceful, yellow stucco villa called Dragongården, tucked away in a serene Stockholm park. The leap is even greater if the resident of the villa is the nephew of the king of Sweden and the husband of an American asbestos heiress.

Count Folke Bernadotte, coddled as the youngest of five children within the privileged shelter of the Swedish royal family, had not attracted much attention until middle age. "I am one of those who have spent their youths in a peaceful and affectionate environment," Bernadotte recalled, in an attempt to explain why he would volunteer for dangerous assignments. "I have enjoyed so much good fortune that I deserved to be included among criminals and misfits if I did not try in some fashion to share part of my own good fortune and happiness."

Despite his high birth, Bernadotte's was the very opposite of a life of luxurious self-indulgence. His father, Prince Oscar, brother of King Gustav, was a stern, ascetic figure who imposed a strict regimen of daily prayers and relentless good works upon his family.

"I remember that my father often said a child should learn to obey before he reached two years of age," Bernadotte noted. "My parents very much insisted on honesty, obedience and punctuality. Already when we were small our thoughts were directed towards trying to help others. My father and his brothers had themselves been brought up in the same atmosphere."

Folke's was a secure and comfortable childhood punctuated by those timeless Nordic rituals that interrupt the seemingly endless winters and uncertain summers. The Festival of St. Lucia, when every Swedish town and village crowns a fair-haired girl with candles to salute the lengthening of the days; Christmas Eve, when the entire Bernadotte tribe gathered in Stockholm's baroque Royal Palace, and Midsummer Night, when the families of the four princes, Oscar, Karl, Eugene, and their eldest brother, King Gustav, and their children celebrated the longest day of the year by lighting bonfires. Young Folke seemed no different from his leggy, tow-headed, not overly intellectual cousins, with whom he danced, skated, played bridge, skied, and rode. He was a man most comfortable outdoors, in motion, preferably on horseback. Dyslexia, though undiagnosed in the early part of the century, was a common condition in the Bernadotte family and made reading a struggle for the count. This disability, plus a nature not much given to introspection or analytical thinking, produced a weak appetite for literature, which never really evolved past the Bible and a lifelong affection for comics. His world was closed and seemingly complete within itself. There was no need for a Bernadotte to change anything, to struggle against injustice, or even to be curious about the rest of the world.

Young Folke had no higher ambition than to be a cavalry officer in the Royal Horse Guards. Because he was excluded from the line to the throne as a result of his mother's commoner status, "the service, horses and pleasure captured my entire interest," he wrote years later. "I do not believe that I was aware of any emptiness in my life. My motto was to live life with a smile." And so he did, until 1916, when, at the age of twenty-one, while on a grueling nighttime cavalry patrol, the young count suddenly slumped off his horse, unconscious. Examining him by lantern light, one of his comrades touched Folke's tunic and found it soaked, not with perspiration, but with blood. Bernadotte was sped to the nearest hospital and the flow was stanched. This episode was the beginning of a lifelong, and at times incapacitating, condition of bleeding stomach ulcers. Throughout the rest of his life, Bernadotte required massive injections of vitamin C and periodic hospitalization.

Though he almost never referred to his condition, he had, at twenty-one, come face-to-face with his own mortality. "He had a feeling that his hemorrhages eventually might lead to his death, because his maternal grandfather succumbed to a series of them," his widow Estelle recalled.

Only a few of Folke's intimates were even aware of this recurrent internal bleeding, which occasionally forced him to spend weeks confined to a hospital bed. A relentless optimist by nature, Bernadotte turned his condition into something like a blessing. "Life in a hospital is certainly somewhat depressing," he wrote. "But I would nevertheless not have that experience undone. When one doesn't know how the future will turn out, and when one realizes that the distance between life and death is short, at that moment the importance of all difficulties disappears, although they normally bulk so large. . . . I am glad that I had that experience in the hospital. It was of great use to me."

In 1918, by now a lieutenant in the cavalry, Bernadotte survived another close call. That winter, while he was riding on the frozen Deer Park Bridge Creek in the outskirts of Stockholm, his horse suddenly broke through the ice and quickly sank below the surface. Instead of crawling to shore, the twenty-three-year-old cavalry officer plunged after the animal into the icy black hole, but despite Folke's efforts, the animal soon slipped out of his grip and disappeared under the ice. Bernadotte barely managed to save himself, and his exertions provoked another serious bout of internal bleeding.

By the early 1920s, Folke's life as a cavalry officer was becoming a picturesque anachronism. The Dragoons were gradually absorbed by the Swedish Army, and this brave and gifted horseman found himself without an occupation.

"This was one of the most painful things for him to deal with," his son Bertil recalled, "losing a career. He was a military man and he was forced to give it up. And he didn't have anything to go to."

One of Folke's uncles, Prince Eugene, known as the artistic and worldly one among the otherwise dour princes, suggested a trip as a way to divert his nephew, as well as a chance to expose the sheltered young man to the world. The two tall, spare Swedish noblemen, uncle and nephew, thus set off for Paris, a city that was everything Stockholm was not: avant-garde, bohemian, and vaguely dangerous. "With his usual methodical precision he conducted me round the Louvre and other museums in Paris," Folke recalled of his Uncle Eugene. "He took unbelievable pride in pointing out the most beautiful pictures and the finest sculptures. . . . We wandered around the streets of Paris, to teach me the layout and architecture. He loved to move about freely and unrecognized among the people and delighted to chat with people he didn't know." Passing the Arc de Triomphe, Folke, trying to reassure his uncle that his attentions were paying off, asked if the same architect had designed that monument as had designed the Cathedral of Notre Dame, which they had visited earlier in the day. "How does it feel to live in such darkness?" the dismayed uncle asked his nephew, thereafter abandoning his cultural enlightenment. This anecdote became one of Folke Bernadotte's favorites, which he would tell on himself often and with great relish.

In 1928, another bout of ill health sent Folke to southern France. His companion, traveling incognito as "Mr. G.," was King Gustav. It was at a banquet in honor of Mr. G. that Bernadotte met Estelle Romaine Manville, the twenty-three-year-old daughter of New York asbestos millionaire Edward Manville. The tall, slender, self-possessed brunette later painted a telling portrait of her future husband. "I wondered to myself whether he wasn't actually quite an ordinary and somewhat self-preoccupied gentleman," she recalled of their first meeting. "One day, however, I found him laughing, in the special and completely irresistible way of his, and in that instant I understood for the first time something of his inner essence . . . his face exploded in a bright and lusty laugh and I suddenly realized that he had extraordinarily blue eyes. . . . I thought for a moment I could see the spirit in his soul and in the same instant I realized that he was a good man."

Folke, though too reserved a man to declare himself on first meeting Estelle, was, by all accounts, totally captivated by the striking, outgoing American girl, in such contrast to the wellborn but diffident young women of the royal circle. The king's nephew and the American millionaire's daughter were married later that same year, on December 1, 1928, amid great pomp, at her parents' estate in Pleasantville, New York. On the bridge of the luxury liner that carried the newlyweds to Sweden, Estelle had another glimpse into her thirty-eight-year-old husband's still-unfulfilled longing for public service. "I hope," the earnest young Swede told her, "that I may do something great and honorable for my country someday."

In 1933, Folke Bernadotte discovered the Boy Scouts as his

vocation. King Gustav, traditional patron of scouting—worried that this decent and amiable nephew, in his late thirties, not spurred by a quest for either money or position, would forever founder in the small royal pond—urged the merger of two needs. For Bernadotte, a man who thrived in the outdoors with little appetite for books, scouting was an ideal occupation. His direct, down-to-earth style, combined with a natural authority which was the result of meticulous breeding, made him the ideal scoutmaster to the nation. Scouting would also be a transition to bigger things.

As the husband of a very wealthy woman, Bernadotte gradually freed himself from the spartan restrictions of his parents' lifestyle. He and Estelle converted his former regimental mess, called Dragongården, into a princely residence. "The idea of making Dragongården our home came to us after a few years of living in an apartment [in Stockholm], as we sat on some steps looking over the wonderful oak trees which had grown there in Djurgården for hundreds of years and where Folke could point out spots where his fellow officers had buried their favorite horses."

But there was tragedy. Just over a year after their marriage, the first of their four sons was born, followed in fairly rapid succession by the other three. In 1934, their infant son Frederick died of a coughing fit while his parents were out for the evening. Two years later, six-year-old Gustav died of an ear infection. The boys' father retreated to his childhood faith for solace. "He was a very deeply convinced Christian," Bertil Bernadotte said of his father. "Those who were like him in those days were either priests or did missionary work. But he never made the rest of us go to church. He considered his religion his own business."

"We didn't come to this world to be happy," Folke told his wife during their grief, "but to make others happy." Bereft, Estelle Bernadotte withdrew to a sanitarium for several months. "I almost never saw her cry," Bertil, her youngest son, recalled. "She was very self-disciplined."

Bertil remembers his father as an authority figure, whose single steely glance could wither the children. "Father was a person with what I would call serious charm. He was very humorous, liked to laugh, but he could make you feel as if you'd done something terribly wrong if you said something off-color or slightly dishonest. Once, he came into my room to see if I was doing my homework, and I hid the book I was reading (which of course had nothing to do with school) under the desk, by propping it up with my knee. 'Are you doing your homework?' he asked. Yes, I answered. Then he asked me to stand up, which of course made the book fall down, and I got a spanking from him.

"Another time, I had put my clothes over my pajamas. I was going to surprise him by tearing them off like Clark Kent and turn into Superman. But my mother gave the surprise away, which upset me. 'You're so stupid!' I shouted at her, and got spanked by Father for it."

Bertil Bernadotte claims he did not feel "royal" growing up in their spacious house in Djurgården, Stockholm's Hyde Park. "Father didn't let us feel important. He himself rode his bicycle to his office at the Red Cross. But we did spend a lot of time with the royal family, because the heir apparent was Father's closest friend. In fact, Father was asked to take charge of Prince Gustav Adolf's public life, to teach him how to be more at ease with all sorts of people."

The Bernadotte family would spend summers at the Manville estate in Pleasantville. "We liked it much better there than at my Swedish grandparents' summerhouse in Malmsjo," recalled Bertil Bernadotte. "In Malmsjo we had to start each day with prayers, which even the servants had to attend. We prayed before meals and for forty-five minutes each evening. It was all very spartan, with no running water or indoor plumbing."

By the 1940s, not even the Bernadottes could escape Hitler's long reach. Sweden's cherished neutrality, dating back to 1815, the last time the nation had engaged in a European conflict, was directly threatened by Hitler's attack on her sister Scandinavian states, Norway and Denmark. Stay out of the northern war, Hitler threatened the Swedes, or risk the Third Reich's occupation of Sweden. Stockholm's foreign policy during the early years of the war was mostly one of placating the Germans. Between 1940 and 1943, Stockholm permitted over 650,000 soldiers of the Reich to cross Swedish territory to reach Germany's occupied Nordic neighbors. The Swedes, perched on Germany's northern flank, granted no such transit or other privileges to the Allies. To soften its image as a selfish neutral ever so slightly, Sweden initiated humanitarian actions for thousands of victims of Nazi aggression.

It thus happened that the forty-seven-year-old Folke

Bernadotte would finally be able to satisfy his growing appetite for humanitarian service. Bernadotte's coming of age had been a slow process. At an age when most men and women begin to trim back their expectations, Folke was somehow unfulfilled. "He was one of those who develop late," his wife noted. "But this type of person often goes further than those who have reached adulthood early. Besides the tremendous advantage of understanding children all their lives, they grasp humanity as a whole. He did ripen markedly at forty, and continued to do so, which enabled him to attempt things others didn't dare."

In 1942, the Swedish Red Cross asked him to be its vice chairman. Folke's eighty-three-year-old uncle, Prince Karl, was chairman of the Red Cross, and would not retire until a successor was found. Sven Grafström, Swedish diplomat and diarist, noted in his journal of May 1, 1943, "The Swedish-American Society, along with many other organizations, held a big dinner at the Grand Hotel [in Stockholm]. Folke Bernadotte presided and gave a very good welcoming speech. He gives a much more energetic and intelligent impression than his royal cousins. . . . The hothouse atmosphere at the court is definitely not a good one, either for the development of character or the gift of reason."

Bernadotte's chance to test his leadership skills came the same year, when the Swiss Red Cross enlisted the help of its Swedish colleagues in the exchange between Germany and Great Britain of 10,000 wounded prisoners of war. The Swedish port of Göteborg was chosen as the location for the exchange. From registering and feeding thousands of exhausted and disoriented soldiers, to engaging a brass band to play "It's a Long Way to Tipperary" for the British troops and "Lili Marlene" for the German POWs, Bernadotte skillfully stage-managed every detail of the venture.

On a damp October morning in 1943, Bernadotte stood on the quay in his neatly pressed Red Cross uniform and savored the unaccustomed sense of accomplishment. It was his first taste of the reward for having organized a successful, large-scale humanitarian effort. For this child of parents for whom serving others was the highest Christian calling, parents who reserved their praise mostly for its fulfillment, it was a proud moment. It was also the first time most Americans heard both Folke Bernadotte's name and his voice on their airwaves. On October 20, 1943, a special NBC News broadcast from aboard the hospital ship *Atlantis,* in port at Göteborg, carried this report by correspondent David Anderson:

"As I came on this ship less than a half hour ago, wounded German soldiers were being disembarked on stretchers. . . . Before she leaves port she will have on board somewhere around 8,000 British wounded or protected personnel who will be repatriated. Her Red Cross flag is as good an assurance as any ship can have in these days of total war that she'll arrive safely back in port. . . . The man responsible for the arrangements in Sweden is Count Folke Bernadotte, the vice president of the Swedish Red Cross. I've asked him to say a few words. Count Bernadotte:

"May I first express the gratitude of the Swedish Government and Swedish Red Cross for the privilege of taking part in this humanitarian work. Our facilities have always been at the disposal of this type of international work. At this very moment the exchange of 4,159 British soldiers is taking place in this Swedish port. 831 German repatriables are being sent back to Germany by train and boat. It is our sincere hope that this type of exchange may be repeated in the future and then, as now, we will be most willing to lend our cooperation. . . ."

The next day, CBS News carried a similar report from correspondent Bernhard Valery: "We, the allied correspondents who came to Göteborg to follow the exchange, were afraid of meeting all these boys. We feared that physical and moral suffering has made them bitter and resentful. We discovered, however, that it takes more than a lost leg or arm to make an invalid out of a brave man. . . . The man whose authority and untiring energy was largely responsible for the success of the exchange operation, the vice president of the Swedish Red Cross, Count Folke Bernadotte, the nephew of the King of Sweden, is by my side now. . . . Count Bernadotte."

"These rather strenuous days have been some of the most happy days of my life," Bernadotte responded. "From all sides, both American, British and German, I have received many times word of appreciation and thanks, and that of course makes me very happy. But when I will think back on the result of these days I know that I am the one who ought to be thankful. Thankful for having had the privilege to lead this operation and see how lights of happiness have come in the eyes of all these American, British and German repatriables when they came to Sweden and knew that in a couple of days they were going to come back to their beloved mother country. To have seen their happiness has been the best reward for my work."

At last, the middle-aged man had found an outlet for a well of unfocused energy and idealism. The "baby" of the family had earned the respect of his stern, devout parents. Folke Bernadotte's own spirituality would always be of a more generous variety than their slightly pinched, conventional Christianity. "Folke was not a churchgoer," said Estelle Bernadotte. "God to him was the 'Chief.' I'm sure Folke never felt that he had been 'chosen' by God for any of his missions."

The international press had also discovered this accessible almost-prince, and doted on him. With his sleek dark hair brushed back to reveal the strong features of a face tanned and lined by a life spent outdoors, and his strong military bearing, he was good copy and photogenic besides. "At his first of many large international press conferences, Folke Bernadotte was, I remember, remarkably at ease," his uncritical biographer, British journalist Ralph Hewins wrote of the Göteborg expedition. "He leaned up against the bar with his hand in his pocket and smoked a cigarette as if he had been holding such meetings all his life. He was in uniform and spoke in clear staccato tones, which sounded like orders but somehow raised no hackles in his audience composed of men habitually disinclined to be ordered about."

Throughout 1943 and 1944, Bernadotte traveled widely on Red Cross missions across the battered continent. He wore his innate optimism like armor against the abundant horror around him. "Beneath the hatred," he insisted, "there is a deep core of humanity in all people." It was this humanity, seemingly ruptured by the war, which Bernadotte, above the fray, tried to reach. In mid-November 1943, he flew to Switzerland, where he tried to persuade the leadership of the prestigious Swiss Red Cross to accept Swedish help in a German-Russian POW exchange. As a personal friend of Moscow's ambassador to Sweden, the heroine of the Russian Revolution, Alexandra Kollontai, Bernadotte felt he might be able to slash through the morass of red tape in which the Swiss effort was mired. But not even Bernadotte's high connections could get Germany and Russia to cooperate in the prisoner-of-war exchange. Each side had treated the other's prisoners so savagely that they feared the world's reaction to the release of thousands of brutalized enemy soldiers.

As he moved from one battle zone to the next, Bernadotte seemed remarkably impervious to danger. On November 22, 1944, he was in Berlin negotiating with the German Red Cross on distributing postwar relief for the German population during a night when the skies glowed from the Allies' bombs and sections of the city were pulverized into smoke and ash. He emerged from the burnt shell of the Swedish legation unshaken and hungry for a still more intense role in reaching "that core of humanity in all people."

"Even though the night of 22nd November was one of the most terrible I have experienced, I would not have missed it. I felt how insignificant the individual becomes in the overall picture. None has the right to boast about what he or she may have accomplished. That fiery night in Berlin thoroughly impressed upon me the appalling realities of total war." But Bernadotte had yet to glimpse the still-camouflaged features of the war's most barbaric face.

Late that autumn of 1944, with the end of history's deadliest war in sight, Bernadotte took part in talks in London for the allocation of areas for Red Cross relief work. The Swedish count sat across the conference table from the supreme Allied commander, General Dwight D. Eisenhower. While these talks were under way, the Wehrmacht launched a final offensive in Belgium, forcing General Eisenhower to abandon Bernadotte's postwar relief plans.

By late 1944, as the outcome of the war became clear, Folke Bernadotte's name was mentioned more and more frequently in the Swedish Foreign Office, as it searched for a wider role for itself, and a better image for the country. The conditions were now ripe for a large-scale rescue of the thousands of people of all races, religions, and nationalities still held captive by the retreating Nazis. Apart from Sweden's genuine humanitarian impulse, Stockholm was eager to establish a good record with which to face an Anglo-American–dominated future.

Sweden's first concern was for her Scandinavian neighbors, Denmark and Norway, in their fifth year of German occupation. The November 1942 deportation of 700 Norwegian Jews to Poland caught Swedes by surprise and shocked Sweden into action. Stockholm hastily made an offer to the German Foreign Ministry to take the remainder, approximately 750 of Norway's Jewish population. Germany vetoed the offer, but Sweden was nevertheless able to quietly save most of these Norwegians, who fled across the long border separating the two Scandinavian countries. Sweden had discovered that the Final Solution could be circumvented.

On October 3, 1943, Sweden announced that all Danish Jews were welcome in Sweden. Overnight, nearly 7,500 of the 8,000 Danish Jews virtually "disappeared." Protected by their fellow Danes, they slipped underground before the anticipated German roundup of Jews. Most of them made the short but hazardous North Sea crossing to Sweden in fishing vessels. Thousands of other Danish and Norwegian "undesirables," however, Jews and non-Jews alike, were still captives of the Reich. Neutral Sweden was virtually the only power with the mobility to attempt their rescue. The Red Army, lumbering westward, had captured the main extermination camps in Poland. Scandinavian prisoners were held primarily in camps on German soil, still firmly in the Nazis' grip.

In late 1944, the Norwegian government-in-exile in Stockholm urged the Swedes to mount a rescue of Nazi-held Norwegians, both Jews and non-Jews. Niels Christian Ditleff, Norway's representative in Stockholm, persuaded the Swedish Foreign Office sometime during the fall of 1944 that the moment was ripe for a bold move. The Danish government also submitted a list of Danish prisoners, including 500 Danish Jews held in Theresienstadt, in Nazi-occupied Czechoslovakia. The Swedes had reason to hope for success. In January 1944, President Roosevelt had established the War Refugee Board, with a mandate to help those Jews still alive. Raoul Wallenberg, Folke Bernadotte's fellow Swede, was hastily dispatched that summer of 1944 to do what he could for the Jews of Hungary, the last intact Jewish community in Nazi-occupied Europe. Wallenberg surpassed all expectations for his mission, and entered into legendary status.

By late 1944, Hitler's authority seemed, even to many inside his own camp, to be less than absolute. Some of the Führer's closest aides were not as eager for self-immolation as the Führer himself seemed to be. Heinrich Himmler, head of the Gestapo and the Waffen-SS and minister of the interior, and the second-most-feared and -despised man in Europe, was among those beginning to worry about Hitler's future.

Enter one of the war's more baffling characters, Felix Kersten, masseur to the Gestapo chief. Kersten, who did not share his patient's political beliefs, presented himself as a potential tool in the hands of Swedish officials, a go-between who would continue to care for Himmler while serving the Swedish rescue effort.

A corpulent, Latvian-born Finn, Kersten practiced the oriental art of pain relief though massage. Though not a real physician, he had prospered from this healing gift, which he practiced on members of Europe's pedigreed and wealthy sufferers of back and abdominal pains, including Duke Friedrich of Mecklenburg and his brother Prince Hendrick, the husband of Queen Wilhelmina of the Netherlands. Kersten had settled in Sweden in 1942, and thereafter divided his time between Stockholm and his country estate, Gute Harzwalde, forty miles from Berlin. Since March 1939, when a German potassium magnate named Dr. Aügust Diehn introduced him to Reichsführer Heinrich Himmler, his "magic fingers" had kept the high-strung Nazi hypochrondriac in functioning order. So dependent was Himmler, who suffered from crippling intestinal pains, on Kersten's ministrations, that he called him "the magic Buddha who cures everything by massage."

Kersten's revulsion toward the Nazi hierarchy that supported his lavish lifestyle grew with his exposure to its members. Himmler's dependency enabled Kersten to command an unheard-of price for his services. The masseur asked to be paid in human lives. "Kersten massages a life out of me," Himmler once complained "with every rub."

A mysterious amalgam of the generous and the opportunistic, Kersten was eager for Swedish citizenship as protection against being repatriated to his native Latvia, now under Soviet occupation. Thus, like Bernadotte at roughly the same time, he came to the attention of Swedish officials in October 1944. Newly established in the Swedish capital and eager to make a place for himself in Stockholm society, Kersten persuaded Himmler to free seven Swedish businessmen on the eve of their execution as Allied spies in Warsaw. In December 1944, Himmler allowed the masseur personally to take the Swedes back to their homeland as a "Christmas present" from his grateful patient. The Swedish foreign minister, Christian Günther, quickly saw a chance to make further use of Himmler's therapist in the rescue operations that were simultaneously under discussion.

In early 1945, the World Jewish Congress also appealed to the Swedish government to pursue the rescue of those Jews who had

survived the Nazi extermination campaign. Other events reinforced the impulse for some audacious Swedish rescue effort. In
the fall of 1944, word reached the Swedes that a former Swiss
president, Jean-Marie Musy, representing a Swiss-Jewish rescue
committee, had begun negotiations with Himmler to buy train-
loads of Jews from Theresienstadt in exchange for deposits in
Swiss banks. The facilitator behind this money-for-blood deal
had been Himmler's right-hand man, chief of the German Strategic Intelligence, Walter Schellenberg. On February 9, 1945, a
trainload of 1,210 Jews from Theresienstadt arrived in Switzerland. More were expected to follow. This eleventh-hour surge of
activity encouraged the Swedish Foreign Ministry, the Swedish
Red Cross, the World Jewish Congress in Stockholm, and Folke
Bernadotte to expand their embryonic mission to include not
only the Scandinavian prisoners, but non-Scandinavian Jews as
well.

By February 10, 1945, the Swedish government was finally
ready to make its move. Count Folke Bernadotte was instructed
to open negotiations with the Germans regarding "civilian prisoners in Germany . . . their internment and their possible re-
moval." There was no mention of either the religion or the
nationality of those to be saved. Bernadotte's instructions were
no more specific than that. He understood, however, that his
first priority was the Reich's approximately 13,000 Scandinavian prisoners.

Embarked on the most hazardous mission of his career,
Bernadotte was armed with a plan of his own. "It would be futile to ask the Germans to open their concentration camps," he
told his friend and comrade in the rescue operation, Major Sven
Frykman, "and allow us to take their inmates away immediately.
We must proceed by stages. . . . In the process we must lay our
hands on anybody else we can and anyway, by showing our
faces, shame the Gestapo into mitigating some of the horrors of
the camps. . . .

"This will not be achieved by table thumping—only by firmness, tact and perseverance. If necessary we must talk and
behave like *Herrenvolk,* which the German officials will understand. We must use bribery—cigarettes, drink, chocolate or any
other means we can think of—in order to achieve our purpose.
We must not talk politics or get into any quarrels with the Germans. We must even, if necessary, flatter, or cajole them—how-

ever much it may stick in our throats. The object is to save human life and to mitigate human suffering and any means to this end is legitimate."

Aware that the success or failure of the mission depended largely on Himmler, Swedish Foreign Minister Christian Günther called on Kersten to smooth Bernadotte's way. Simultaneously, Arvid Richert, Swedish ambassador in Berlin, also requested Himmler's adjutant, Walter Schellenberg, to arrange for Bernadotte's meeting with his chief. The Swedes informed the Allies of these otherwise top-secret talks, without winning either Washington or London's support for the enterprise. The Allies held to their previously stated policy: no retreat from the principle of "unconditional surrender," announced by President Roosevelt in January 1944. Thus, no direct negotiations were to be undertaken with the Nazi government, not even on the subject of prisoner rescue, for fear of stirring Stalin's easily aroused paranoia regarding his Western partners.

"Discussions were held in the Foreign Ministry," noted Sven Grafström in his journal of February 11, 1945, "about what could be done in case the Germans start massacres in Norway prior to their evacuation. Do we threaten with Swedish intervention? . . . One such threat is intended to be delivered by Folke Bernadotte to Himmler. He shall request the return of Norwegian students and demand the end of violence in Norway, all this as a Red Cross representative and as a person in the wings of the Royal Family. He shall, at least according to the opinion of Erik Boheman [the secretary-general of the Foreign Office], mutter something about the public sentiment in Sweden and that it is impossible to determine what might happen if the Germans continue in the present path. We will see if [Foreign Minister] Günther likes these instructions. The devil knows. One message in any case went to Swedish envoy in Berlin Richert last Saturday. Arrange a meeting between Folke Bernadotte and Hitler's premier executioner."

The war's most unsung, most controversial, and yet most successful rescue effort inside Germany was under way. The fifty-year-old Count Bernadotte was about to be tested in ways he had not imagined.

CHAPTER NINE

RESCUE

THE FÜHRER MUST NOT KNOW. THE SWEDE'S PRESENCE IN BERLIN
would have to be kept under the tightest security wraps. If Hitler
found out that the Swede was there—to rescue Scandinavians
and, more provocatively, Jews—he would undoubtedly blow the
whole mission out of the water.*

It was clear that only one man had the power to negotiate for
Jews and other prisoners behind Hitler's back: Reichsführer
Heinrich Himmler. At Swedish Foreign Minister Günther's request, the cunning Kersten smoothed the way for Bernadotte's
meeting with the man the Führer called "the faithful Heinrich."

Himmler's mental and physical state, like that of the Third
Reich itself, teetered on the brink. In mid-February, General
Zhukov's advance units of the Red Army had crossed the River
Oder and reached a point a scant thirty-three miles from Berlin.
Roosevelt, Churchill, and Stalin were meeting at Yalta, mapping
their final assault as well as the future of Europe. On all fronts,
the Wehrmacht was collapsing in disarray. But the Führer had
proclaimed that if he could not realize the dream of a Thousand-
Year Reich, he would create a Wagnerian twilight of the gods.

Maneuvering behind the scenes throughout all these clandestine dealings was one of the Nazi high command's smoothest operators, Walter Schellenberg, Himmler's right-hand man and

---

*In fact, Hitler personally thwarted a similar effort by the former Swiss
president Jean-Marie Musy that same month, for the release of 30,000 Jews in
exchange for 5 million Swiss francs, to be paid to Heinrich Himmler and the
Gestapo.

head of espionage services. He did not resemble his colleagues. In his late thirties, Schellenberg cut the slightly studied figure of an English squire in speech, manner, and appearance. Schellenberg knew the war was lost, and long before Himmler, he began an effort to save his and his chief's skins. Schellenberg hoped that opening channels to the Allies through the Swedish rescue mission would be his passage to safety as the Third Reich collapsed.

Bernadotte found Schellenberg ready to arrange a meeting with Himmler, and able to untangle bureaucratic knots that blocked the Swedish Red Cross's way. Prior to his meetings with Himmler, Schellenberg briefed Bernadotte on how best to approach the Reichsführer. "From the start," Bernadotte later wrote, "I conceived a certain trust in [Schellenberg], and in any case, I shall always be grateful to him for the positive assistance he rendered me in connection with Red Cross work in Germany."

Bernadotte slipped into Berlin on February 16, 1945, in great secrecy, and the meeting took place three days later in a hospital seventy miles north of Berlin. To the tall, athletic Swedish aristocrat in his immaculately tailored Red Cross uniform, the short, stoop-shouldered, agitated Gestapo chief, Heinrich Himmler, seemed ordinary—in a sense, he personified what Hannah Arendt would later call the banality of evil.

> When I suddenly saw him before me in the green Waffenschützstaffel uniform [Bernadotte wrote later], without any decorations and wearing horn-rimmed spectacles, he looked like a typical unimportant official, and one would certainly have passed him in the street without noticing him. He had small, well-shaped and delicate hands, and they were carefully manicured. . . . It was a most extraordinary experience to hear this man, who has sent millions of human beings to their death by the most monstrous methods, speak with enthusiasm of the chivalrous manner in which the English and the Germans had waged war in France in the summer of 1944, on occasion interrupting actions in order that each might gather up their wounded.

Following Stockholm's guidelines, Bernadotte hinted at postwar Swedish retribution if the Nazis carried out their rumored plan to massacre people as they withdrew.

He said there could be no question but that I was misinformed. At a subsequent meeting, he himself brought up an example I had cited and admitted that an inquiry he had instituted showed my facts to be correct. If this was a premeditated piece of acting, it was certainly well done. Then came the usual question: Had I any concrete proposals? . . . It was at this point that I made the proposal about the release of Norwegians and Danes for internment in Sweden, to which Himmler reacted . . . violently. He said that, whether or not, Sweden and the Allies would have to give some compensation for such a concession, e.g., an assurance that sabotage would cease in Norway. The shadow of Hitler fell across the room at that moment. . . . It was so evident that Himmler's hands were tied; that he was not so powerful as many believed. The Führer was alive and for one reason or another, he could not be ignored. I told Himmler that the concession he had mentioned was quite unthinkable.

Quickly, so as not to lose ground, the Swede asked for permission to gather 13,000 interned Scandinavians into two camps and allow Swedish Red Cross workers to operate in those camps. Himmler agreed. Bernadotte had pushed the door slightly ajar.

Eager to change the subject, Himmler turned sentimental, talked of how at "the beginning of this century a boy was growing up in South Germany whose name was to become known throughout the world. He came of a simple middle class family, and his father had been a tutor to one of the princes of the Bavarian royal house. During the Great War the boy enlisted in the Bavarian Guards and attained the rank of sergeant major at the age of sixteen. When the war ended he returned home and joined the Nazi movement at its very inception. 'Those were the glorious days,' Himmler said, talking of his own life. 'Then I could fight for what I regarded as Germany's rebirth.'

"He failed to make any mention of the millions of Jews who had been murdered while the 'movement' was in power," wrote Bernadotte later. In keeping with his original strategy to avoid "table thumping," he calmly asked the Nazi "if he would not admit that there were decent people among the Jews just as there were among all races. I told him that I had many Jewish friends. To my surprise he admitted that I was right, but added that we in Sweden had no Jewish problem and could therefore not understand the German point of view. . . . Later on Himmler, at my suggestion, agreed that if the necessity should arise, he would allow interned Jews to be handed over to the Allied military authorities instead of having them removed from the concentration camps where they were held."

Starting with a modest mandate from his government to collect Danish and Norwegian internees, Bernadotte had achieved a great deal. Yet even in his own country, particularly among professionals offended by his improvised diplomacy, his efforts were treated with pious disdain.

"Regarding the Bernadotte Mission," Sven Grafström wrote dismissively in his diary on March 13, 1945, "when the government didn't consider itself able to intervene militarily against the German's brutal ravages in Norway and Denmark, some bright boy thought of . . . sending Folke Bernadotte to see Himmler to procure the release of those Norwegians and Danes imprisoned in Germany, to be sent home. During discussions inside the political department [of the Swedish Foreign Office] I advised strongly against any such action that would not lead to any results. . . . Such Swedish contact with one of the biggest war criminals in this stage of the war could become exceedingly compromising for us. Well, my line of reasoning found no echo . . . and Folke went on his way. He met with both Ribbentrop and Himmler and according to the very odd report he turned in, he had conducted himself with very sharp tongue and vague threats as to the worst. In addition, he gave a rather amusing account of Ribbentrop and Himmler. . . . The result of Bernadotte's efforts were that the Germans consented to the Norwegian and Danish prisoners (in Germany) being brought together in two big camps . . . to which Swedish Red Cross personnel would have access for medical and spiritual care. [Swedish envoy to Paris Arvid] Richert has written a panegyrical report regarding the splendid result of Folke's mission and the German cooperation. . . . Not only do I myself consider the result to be utterly meager, but it also contains many dangerous and doubtful elements."

Upon his return to Stockholm, on February 23, Bernadotte assured a leader of the capital's Jewish community, Hillel Storch, that "Swedish authorities have made very serious attempts, and given permission for some Jews to come to Sweden . . . even in this Swedish action [i.e., Bernadotte's mission] some positive results [for Jews] should be achievable." At the same time, Storch was also using Felix Kersten as an intermediary to persuade Himmler to release Jews to Sweden. On March 12, 1945, he extracted from his patient a remarkable document. Drafted in Himmler's own hand, it is called "A Contract for Humanity" and it promises:

1. That concentration camps will not be blown up.
2. A white flag would be raised over them at the Allies' approach.
3. Not a single Jew would be executed from that day forward, and Jews would be treated like other prisoners.
4. Sweden could send Jewish prisoners packages.

The "contract" bears the signatures of both Kersten and Himmler and two witnesses.

Bernadotte returned to Germany on March 5, this time accompanied by twelve white buses bearing the Red Cross insignia and twelve trucks filled with medical and other supplies. The convoy collected 2,200 Danes and Norwegians from Sachsenhausen, 600 from Dachau, and 1,600 Scandinavian policemen from various German concentration camps, and transported them to the Neuengamme camp on the Elbe River, close to the Baltic ports of Hamburg and Lübeck, where the inmates would be under Red Cross care.

Back once more in Stockholm, on March 26 Bernadotte met with two members of the Foreign Office and agreed to a broader scope for the rescue effort, which was exceeding everyone's expectations. Though the thrust of his rescue would still be Scandinavian inmates, the new policy empowered Bernadotte to "request that a number of Jews be sent to Sweden."

The stately Bismarck family estate of Schönhausen in Friedrichsruhe was the operational headquarters for a grueling mission that involved seven relays between March 15 and March 30 to the nearby Oranienburg and Sachsenhausen camps, and farther south to Dachau, Mauthausen, and Schomberg. By March 27 the Swedes had collected nearly 5,000 inmates, transporting them to the collection camp of Neuengamme.

The rescue work proceeded in feverish haste and under "friendly" (that is, Allied) fire from the air. It was a high-risk operation. In fact, the British tried to warn the Swedes off the whole enterprise.

Bernadotte often trailed the procession in his private car, painted white and bearing the Red Cross insignia on its roof. The man who had almost drowned trying to save his horse took meager precautions for his own safety. He placed an extra chauffeur on the back trunk of his car, with instructions to bang on the top of the car as soon as he saw Allied planes approaching, "thus warning us to stop, jump out, and take whatever cover we could find." On April 24, near Padborg on the Danish-German border, Allied bombers strafed the count and his party. All told, Allied bombs hit the convoy three times during the weeks of frenetic activity, killing sixteen of the newly freed inmates.

On March 30, Bernadotte entered Neuengamme Concentration Camp, the first representative of a neutral, humanitarian organization to set foot in one of the Reich's death camps. "It was with feelings of great emotion that I prepared to see these, the most revolting creations of the Third Reich. . . . The commandant, Obersturmbannführer Pauli, received us in his green SS uniform, looking very smart and military and efficient. . . . He had the reputation of being one of the very worst representatives of his profession, if it can be called that. . . . The guns were roaring near Bremen, the front was approaching nearer and nearer to Berlin, and the Obersturmbannführer probably realized that his professional days were numbered. . . ."

Once Bernadotte was inside the factory of death, his movements were limited to the area where the Scandinavian prisoners (who, as a result of Himmler's reluctance to give the green light until the very last moment, did not yet include Jews) had been gathered. "When I took my departure of the Danes and Norwegians gathered along the enclosure of electric wire that surrounded the camp, I called to them, 'Paa gjensyn' (Au revoir), and saw the joy in their eyes. . . . But I thought, too, of the prisoners of whom I had caught a glimpse in a part of the camp where we had no power. There were thousands of unhappy human beings there or rather human wrecks, wandering aimlessly about the camp, apathetic, vacant, incapable of ever returning to a normal existence."

The British continued to take a dim view of this mission. In a

memo to Prime Minister Winston Churchill the British Foreign
Office opposed "Jewish societies" who insist on the rescue of
Jews "at any price." Both Foreign Minister Anthony Eden and
the prime minister, fearing Stalin's ire concerning any Allied-
German contacts, agreed with this advice. Churchill scribbled on
the document, "I agree. No truck with Himmler."

On April 21, over a sumptuous breakfast served up at the SS
hospital at Hohenluchen, Himmler informed Bernadotte that the
Swedes could take *all* surviving Jewish inmates. Taken aback,
Bernadotte was unaware of two events that preceded and partly
explained this unexpected offer. The previous day, Himmler had
visited the Führer in the bunker in Berlin. Not even "faithful
Heinrich" could delude himself any longer as to Hitler's manic,
glassy-eyed state. From this moment, Heinrich Himmler thought
of himself as the Third Reich's true leader, though no one had offered him such a position. For Himmler still hoped to somehow
salvage something of his country, and if not, then at least to
somehow cut a good deal for himself. And the surviving Jewish
inmates were among his last remaining bargaining chips.

Also on April 20, during an extraordinary confrontation
arranged by the peripatetic masseur Felix Kersten, Norbert
Mazur, a prominent Swedish Jew, had flown to Berlin to meet
with Himmler, with lists of Jews he wished to have freed.
Himmler allowed Mazur to take only 1,000 Jews back to Sweden, but he told Bernadotte—obviously a more important player
to Himmler—he could take them all. The last-minute game
was under way. Walter Schellenberg now made an all-out effort to persuade Himmler to offer the Anglo-Americans a
separate peace through Bernadotte. While convincing the end-
lessly vacillating Himmler to abandon the Führer was very difficult, winning over Bernadotte proved relatively simple. During
Himmler's final meeting with Bernadotte on the night of
April 23, 1945, an increasingly distraught Reichsführer told
Bernadotte, "Take anyone you wish." The next day, 4,000 dazed
Jewish women from the Ravensbrück camp were on a train
bound for Sweden. By the end, Bernadotte's mission had rescued nearly 21,000 inmates, citizens of more than twenty
different countries. An estimate of the number of Jews saved was
about 6,500.

With the Red Army's guns pounding just outside Berlin,
Himmler, too, was eager now to make a hasty bid for a separate

peace with the West. On the night of April 23, in the dank, pitch-black air raid shelter of the Swedish consulate in the ancient Baltic port of Lübeck, the little man who had failed as a poultry farmer but proved brilliant in his chosen vocation, offered, via Bernadotte, to surrender to the British and Americans. Bernadotte, acting on his government's instructions, declined to take Himmler's offer to the supreme Allied commander, Dwight D. Eisenhower. The Swede did agree, however, to transmit Himmler's proposal to his own government, adding as a condition the immediate surrender of German troops in Denmark and Norway.

Bernadotte's message from Himmler provoked a flurry of telegrams among Churchill, Truman, and Stalin. "You will no doubt have received some hours ago the report from Stockholm . . . on the Bernadotte-Himmler talks," the British prime minister cabled the American president on April 25, 1945. "As Himmler is evidently speaking for the German State, as much as anybody can, the reply that should be sent him through the Swedish Government is in principle a matter for the Triple Powers, since no one of us can enter into separate negotiations. This fact, however, in no way abrogates Gen. Eisenhower's or Field Marshal Alexander's authority to accept local surrenders as they occur."

Churchill added in his war memoirs: "In view of the importance of this German peace offer, and of our experience of Russian suspicions . . . I think it well to record our attitude [toward Bernadotte's message] in detail. . . . I spoke to President Truman at 8:10 PM . . . also told him that we were convinced the surrender should be unconditional and simultaneous to the three major Powers. Truman expressed strong agreement with this."

They did not have long to wait. The German high command surrendered to the Allied armies on May 7, 1945. The surrender ending the five-year war, the deadliest in history, was unconditional.

On April 27, Churchill wrote in his memoirs: "Count Bernadotte conveyed our demand to Himmler. No more was heard of the Nazi leader till May 21, when he was arrested by a British control post at Bremervörde. He was disguised and was not recognized, but his papers made the sentries suspicious and he was taken to a camp near Second Army Headquarters. He then told the commandant who he was. He was put under armed guard, stripped, and searched for poison by a doctor. During the final stage of the examination he bit open a phial of cyanide, which he had apparently hidden in his mouth for some hours. He died almost instantly just after eleven o'clock at night on Wednesday, May 23, 1945."

Bernadotte's own role in this chapter did not end with the war's long-awaited finale. Rumors and, later, when secrecy was no longer an issue, news reports of the count's astonishing meetings with Himmler under the rain of Allied bombs, raced around the globe. The fifty-year-old aristocrat's name, along with those of Churchill, Eisenhower, Hitler, and Himmler, was now woven into conversations touching on the last days of the war. It was not the stories of the white buses and their cargo of 20,000 inmates that made the count an instant world figure. The fact that Bernadotte was the first non-Nazi to sit across a conference table from one of history's great monsters would be forever intertwined with his name. Later, as Israeli resistance to Bernadotte's peace plan hardened, rumors that he had once appeased the Nazis circulated in Israel.

Along with the sudden fame came a flurry of honors, awards, and decorations from Scandinavian monarchs; the Grand Cross of the Legion of Honor, the highest civilian decoration from France; as well as a citation from the World Jewish Congress and an offer from a publisher eager for his memoirs. In a matter of weeks, with considerable help from a ghostwriter, Bernadotte published a runaway bestseller. *The Curtain Falls,* or *Slutet,* in the Swedish version, was translated into more than a dozen languages for a world hungry for every scrap of information describing the war's final days as seen from inside the Nazis' twilight world. Bernadotte was not a literary man. *The Curtain Falls* is written in the stilted, simplistic style of a book the publisher rushes into print. This enterprise would also embroil its author in a storm of controversy.

Estelle Bernadotte claimed her husband only wanted to give his own story, and leave others to write theirs. Whatever the motive, his account mentioned neither Felix Kersten nor Norbert Mazur nor the extensive groundwork laid by members of the Swedish Foreign Office prior to Bernadotte's arrival on the scene. In *The Curtain Falls,* Bernadotte claimed another source of inspiration for his role. The Swedish consul general in Paris,

Raoul Nordling, whom Bernadotte visited in late 1944, inspired him to act. Nordling had smuggled to safety scores of French men and women threatened with arrest by the Nazis. "I asked myself," Bernadotte wrote, "whether it wouldn't be possible for me to do something comparable for those who lingered in German concentration camps."

Bernadotte was even more expansive on the contributions of Himmler's right-hand man, Walter Schellenberg. Bernadotte had offered the Nazi shelter in his own home in May 1945, during the final weeks of the war. While there, Schellenberg drafted his own version of events before he faced Allied justice. Part of the motive for the count's hospitality was that Schellenberg continued to play an intermediary role in the German surrender in Norway and Denmark. Whatever the reason, granting a high-ranking Nazi asylum in May 1945 was an extraordinary lapse of judgment on Bernadotte's part. Estelle Bernadotte thought so even at the time. "Schellenberg was an excellent actor. . . . [I] was not fooled by his attitude, but Folke felt he owed Schellenberg a good deal for the success he achieved with Himmler. . . . It was a delicate situation. Being American-born, Folke realized I would be against accepting Schellenberg under our roof! But he pointed out the importance of hiding Schellenberg's presence in Sweden just then in order to protect the outcome of the return of the concentration-camp prisoners. But of course the military attachés of the U.S. and Britain were notified [by the Swedish Foreign Ministry] and actually met him at our home."

Bertil Bernadotte remembers the excitement of having "a real Nazi" staying with the family. "I was very impressed by his dueling scars. I remember him as very soft-spoken, very well educated and intelligent. In my father's mind he was one hundred percent pure. Father was a very positive person. Mother always said one of his virtues was also a weakness. When he met somebody he liked, he ignored the negatives. He just didn't see the things that could go wrong. He was very single-minded about his mission, and without Schellenberg it wouldn't have happened."

Estelle Bernadotte kept another memory of those extraordinary weeks in May 1945. "Schellenberg and Folke and I sat and listened to the Deutsche Rundfunk's report on Hitler's death . . . following some funeral music. When Schellenberg heard that Admiral von Dönitz would take over [instead of Himmler], his shock was enormous. Both he and Himmler had counted on it being Himmler who would have that job."

Schellenberg was eventually tried by the American military tribunal at Nuremberg and acquitted of genocide charges. The judges accepted his claim that he had no direct involvement in the Final Solution. Despite Bernadotte's witness to his good character, however, Schellenberg served a six-year prison term. Released in 1952, he died two years later, aged forty-two. Of much longer duration would be the damage Bernadotte's somewhat heedless friendship for this man caused the count's good name.

Heinrich Himmler's "magic Buddha," Felix Kersten, was not among those who greeted the Nazi Götterdämmerung with unalloyed joy. The prosperous masseur now faced the possibility of becoming one of the thousands of displaced persons who swarmed a continent bled dry by war. He had no intention of repatriating to Latvia, the country of his birth, now a Soviet province. His reputation in the Swedish capital, where both his family and a stately home awaited him, was mixed at best. "Kersten is known to me as a Nazi," Victor Mallet, the British minister in Sweden, had cabled London a few months earlier, "and a thoroughly bad man. He has a home in Stockholm to which he has brought a big collection of pictures. They are reported to be Dutch but I have little information on this point."

Kersten had accumulated considerable wealth by keeping Himmler and several lesser lights in the Reichsführer's entourage fit for service. What he needed now was a state to call his own. Swedish Foreign Minister Christian Günther, to whom he had rendered the same sort of service Schellenberg had rendered Bernadotte, was willing to support Kersten's bid for Swedish citizenship.

Folke Bernadotte was less enthusiastic. "Folke met him only once," Estelle Bernadotte recalled. "He put a slip of paper in Kersten's pocket with three names on it and asked Kersten, 'Can you massage these out of Himmler? It would be a good turn. . . . Kersten wanted to speed up his application [for Swedish citizenship] . . . which was and still is, seven years. . . . Folke was too honest to get involved with something illegal as far as Swedish law went."

By late 1945, Kersten was desperate. Despite the foreign minister's support, his application for Swedish citizenship had been turned down. Folke Bernadotte's widely acclaimed account of the rescue of German inmates gave Kersten no credit for the role that might have shored up his dubious reputation in Stockholm. In December, he twice wrote Bernadotte asking for his help in locating and rescuing members of his family caught in the Russian zone. Bernadotte, who by then had been elected chairman of the Swedish Red Cross, received hundreds of such letters, but promised to do what he could for Kersten. He stopped short of supporting the masseur's bid for Swedish citizenship.

If the Swedes felt no obligation to grant him permanent asylum, Holland, where dozens of people owed their lives to Kersten's having "massaged them out of Himmler," surely would. That was Kersten's premise, and before he was finished, he had succeeded in convincing the Dutch people he had single-handedly rescued them from mass genocide. He provided Holland's Institute for War Documentation "proof" of a Nazi plan to exile 3 million "unreliable" Dutch people to Eastern Europe, to the region around Lublin. Only Kersten's bold intervention through his patient Heinrich Himmler foiled the plan. Kersten produced a diary he claimed he had been keeping since 1941, the year this alleged mass deportation of the Dutch was to occur. He followed this with "copies" of letters, though he produced no originals, to confirm the Nazi plan. He even provided the institute with supporting testimony from former SS officers facing the war-crimes tribunal.

N. W. Posthumus, a respected historian at the Institute for War Documentation, gave Kersten's "evidence" his seal of approval. Dutch citizenship, as well as the country's highest honors and a nomination for a Nobel Peace Prize, followed in rapid succession. The rotund masseur responsible for Reichsführer Heinrich Himmler's good health throughout the Final Solution had reinvented himself as Holland's postwar hero. In 1991, David Barnow, a historian at the same institute that certified Kersten, explained, "Kersten was trying to save his neck and it suited the Dutch to think they were such a menace to Hitler that he would want to deport three million of them. The Dutch people were all too willing to believe Kersten. Three historians certified his 'evidence.' "

Kersten became the subject of flattering biographies, including *The Man with the Miraculous Hands* by Joseph Kessel, and a self-congratulatory autobiography the masseur published in 1956, *The Kersten Memoirs,* with an introduction by the eminent Oxford historian of the Nazi period, H. R. Trevor-Roper. In these accounts, Bernadotte's role in the Swedish rescue is reduced to that of a "mere transport officer, nothing more." Moreover, Bernadotte is described as an anti-Semite and a grasping self-promoter who, without Kersten, would not have been able to rescue any Jews at all.

Kersten's maneuverings ultimately cast a shadow over what should have been a proud achievement for Folke Bernadotte. Nevertheless, the episode illuminates much about Bernadotte's character. He thrived in the limelight and he liked to take charge of situations where another, perhaps slightly less arrogant man might have tread more gingerly. For a man of his years, Bernadotte was also strangely innocent in the ways of the world. Befriending Schellenberg because he was "his sort of man," and alienating the desperate Kersten, who was not, proved to be a dangerous miscalculation. A half century as a privileged member of a European royal house was not the best school for the rough-and-tumble world of international politics to which he aspired.

Sven Grafström, a cynical but shrewd observer of Swedish affairs, noted in his diary entry of November 29, 1945, "The very renowned General Patton has been invited by Bernadotte without consulting the authorities [to the Swedish American Club's dinner] . . . the Foreign office had tried to prevent [Patton's] arrival. . . . I saw Bernadotte self-importantly engaged with the press. . . ."

In another revealing entry in Grafström's diary, on January 26, 1947, on the occasion of the sudden death in a plane crash of Prince Gustav Adolf, the heir to the throne, "Folke Bernadotte among others delivered an oration in memory of the prince on the radio, which, with its bombast and exaggerations, if one didn't already know it, clearly showed that Folke has more heart than brain."

"He liked to think well of people," Bertil Bernadotte noted of his father. A letter Bernadotte wrote to the wife of Walter Schellenberg, then in Allied custody as a potential war criminal, throws light on this well-meaning but naive side of the Swede: "Because of his position in the SS, his situation is obviously precarious. Indeed, one cannot argue against the fact that his *personnel* committed things which were not in accordance with international principles of legality, whether they were known or unknown to your husband—*I personally like to think the latter*—accordingly, he must be made responsible for them. . . . As your husband was extremely helpful to me in the course of my latest activities, I am personally interested in helping you and your children—as far as possible—while you are separated from your husband."

By 1945, Folke Bernadotte was no longer just another presentable member of the extended Swedish royal family, searching for a purpose in life. Folke, and not the aging King Gustav, was the Bernadotte known to Truman, Churchill, and Eisenhower. A *New York Times* story headlined "Swede Sees Flaw in War Guilt Trial" under C. L. Sulzberger's byline, dated November 29, 1945, read: "Count Folke Bernadotte, president of the Swedish Red Cross and the man who served as envoy in the final negotiations between the Allies and Heinrich Himmler, said today in an interview that while he agreed in principle with the theory of designating war criminals, he did not believe that high-ranking officers such as Field Marshal Gen. Wilhelm Keitel and Field Marshal Gen. Albert Kesselring should be tried if they were merely doing their duty and following military commands."

Bernadotte had achieved his dream: he was now indisputably a player on the world stage.

CHAPTER TEN

THE
UNDERGROUND
REBORN

IN PALESTINE, WHILE THE WHEELS OF HITLER'S WAR MACHINE still rolled smoothly over the Continent, while the trains meant for cattle still ground daily into the factories of death, a captive in the Crusader fortress of Mazra prison, Yitzhak Shamir, had taken a few steps toward the day his path would intersect with that of the faraway Swedish aristocrat. "Michael," as Shamir was known to his fellows, was a British prisoner in 1942. A significant number of prisoners in Palestine were disciples of Avraham Stern. "Michael" received Stern's last letter days before the British policemen gunned down Stern in his hideout. Shamir was determined now to revive and reorganize the underground. But first he had to break out of jail. Jail was death for the movement whose motto was "Kill, be killed, but do not surrender."

Even among the inmates of Mazra, near the ancient coastal town of Acre, Michael and his fellow Sternists, including Eliahu Giladi, Mattiyahu Shmulovitz, and Natan Yalin-Mor, were treated as lepers. Prisoners who were members of the Haganah— or even the Irgun—shunned them, refusing even to partake of the prison-prepared Pesach feast in their company. Matti Meged, Shamir's fellow inmate, who was an officer in the Palmach, the crack Haganah unit, and had been picked up for arms smuggling, recalled Shamir and the other Sternists as people who "never got any food packages, no cigarettes, nothing from the outside, which the rest of us did. Our commanders didn't want us to get friendly with them. Yes, they were fanatics, but there was something sympathetic about them. Shamir never said much, he was a real tough guy, the type who probably read one book in his life and that was about bombs and sabotage."

While "Michael" and Natan Yalin-Mor began quietly to plan their escape, outside, hidden among the orange groves of Bat Yam near Tel Aviv, one member of their group carried on the struggle—Yehoshua Cohen, a blade-thin seventeen-year-old Sabra who lived on oranges and Yair's memory. He had taken enough shots at passing British trains to provoke the ire of the Mandatory authority. In 1942, Cohen and his girlfriend and courier, Nehama, were about all that remained of Stern's "movement" outside prison. Cohen had a $3,000 reward on his head. In the Bat Yam orange groves, Cohen quietly amassed a small arsenal, practiced his already legendary marksmanship, and waited, certain others would soon join him.

On September 1, 1942, just after midnight, Shamir and his comrade Eliahu Giladi crawled out from under three layers of barbed wire that encircled Mazra. The next day, still wearing Polish Army uniforms Cohen had smuggled to them, they met Yehoshua and Nehama, and two other recruits of Cohen's, in the shelter of the orange grove. Shamir stayed in the grove long enough for his hair and beard to grow out. Weeks later, his transformation complete, he emerged from hiding and made his way to a small rented room in Tel Aviv. The fierce fighter with the barrel chest and bulldog face now became Rabbi Shamir, with long hair, beard, and black robe camouflaging eyes, hands, and arms skilled in things other than the study of the Talmud.

Armed with Yair's posthumous blessing, Shamir, the quiet man recognized as the group's best organizer, had no trouble imposing control over the new underground. "We start anew," he announced in his flat voice to the small group assembled in the orange grove. He reorganized Lehi, as it would henceforth be known. It would become a nearly airtight conspiracy. No one was to know anyone else's real name, only his or her code name. Operations, all of them planned by Shamir, were to be carried out by cells of three or four. The dead Yair was still the inspiration, the guiding spirit, but the hard-nosed new leader jettisoned Yair's more extravagant schemes. For one thing, "Michael" abandoned dreams of links to the Axis, a notion even more bizarre in 1943 than it had been two years earlier.

Shamir was a hunted man after his prison break. His bushy-eyebrowed, jut-jawed portrait, on wanted posters that described him as having "large ears, unkempt appearance and sallow complexion," was nailed to trees and telephone poles throughout Palestine. A reward was offered for help leading to his arrest. British intelligence officials, enraged at the humiliating evidence that their penal system was insecure, called Shamir "among the most fanatical terrorist leaders . . . imprisonment is the only satisfactory means of preventing [him] from carrying out further outrages."

Shamir resumed his nocturnal life, moving often from one safe room to another in Tel Aviv's rabbit warren of working-class neighborhoods. By day, he stayed indoors. But with so many of his comrades still in jail, Shamir needed to recruit new members to his decimated underground.

Before he could start recruiting, however, Shamir had an extraordinarily difficult problem to solve. The behavior of the man with whom he had broken out of Mazra, Eliahu Giladi—"Shaul" in the underground—was threatening the safety of the entire movement. "His behavior towards other people," recalled Yehoshua Cohen, "was very brutal. He used crude language. With him the end justified any means." Giladi, Yalin-Mor wrote in his diary, was "free from loyalty to any idea or person. He was a professional revolutionary, without a national . . . ideal." To raise money for the underground, Giladi robbed private homes, something the others eschewed, preferring instead to hold up banks and other businesses.

"Giladi," Shamir would recall many years later, "was perhaps the only one of us who was, by nature, an extremist, a fanatic, a man free of the fetters of personal loyalties or ordinary sentiments, who found it difficult to function within any framework or discipline but was fast moving, imaginative, daring and fearless. . . . Then he developed a new *idée fixe*: Lehi should 'do away' as he put it, with the Zionist leadership, kill Ben-Gurion and clear the stage. He was not a traitor or an informer but he was irrational. I waited for him to change, for the dreadful fantasies to leave him, but he went on, talking icily about the need to kill. I knew then that I'd have to make a fateful decision and I did. I decided that we couldn't go on like that; Giladi was far too dangerous to the movement."

But Giladi was also Shamir's friend. Both men were born in 1915, both were products of Betar, and both had arrived in Palestine (Giladi from Rumania) at roughly the same time. They had simultaneously broken from the Irgun and followed Stern. But Giladi seemed too eager to lead Lehi, a post Shamir did not wish to relinquish. Yehoshua Cohen recalled Giladi/Shaul as "a man who had great influence on me. He was brave and strong. But Shaul could have gotten to the point where he would have killed Shamir. And then the underground would have fallen apart."

The details surrounding the murder of Giladi/Shaul are only those Yitzhak Shamir has seen fit to disclose. What is known is that Yitzhak Shamir and Eliahu Giladi took a walk alone together on a deserted strip of Tel Aviv beach in early 1943. Only Shamir returned. The future prime minister never evaded responsibility for the crime. "The execution of Shaul was essential. . . . The decision about the execution was my personal decision," he told Tsvi Tsameret in a November 1973 taped interview, kept at Hebrew University's Institute of Contemporary Jewry.

"Of course he shot him," asserted Dr. Amitsur Ilan, author and Israeli Defense Forces historian, in October 1992. Dr. Joseph Heller, a preeminent Israeli scholar of the underground, concurred. Shamir still refuses to disclose the location of Giladi's grave, through the murdered man's family continues to this day to plead with him to do so. In the Lehi Museum in Tel Aviv, Giladi is listed as among the movement's fallen heroes.

Only after Giladi's elimination did Shamir summon the other twenty-six members of the reborn movement. Not surprisingly, none of the terrorists disagreed with the decision Shamir had already taken. "After the execution," Shamir said in 1973, "I invited some [Lehi members] who were on [Giladi's] side to personal conversations . . . Schmulovitz . . . Nehama and Yehoshua Cohen . . . I spoke to each of them personally." None dissented from the decision, though Yehoshua Cohen remained silent for a long time. But then Shamir, whose favorite expression is *kacha*—Hebrew for "because it is so"—was not a man to encourage discussion.

"In large measure," Yalin-Mor noted, " 'Michael' reinforced our movement with his willpower and his cruelty. I don't want to say that he has no feeling. He has more than others, but he knows how to be cruel toward others as he does toward himself, for the cause." Shamir has never expressed doubt or remorse for the execution of his close friend and comrade. "With Giladi, it was really a tragedy," Shamir said in a 1992 interview. "He was a friend but suddenly we reached a situation where we had to make a terrible decision and there was no choice. I didn't accept this decision quickly. I thought perhaps . . . perhaps. . . . I consulted with Yalin-Mor, who was still in the Latrun jail, by letter. He really encouraged me in this direction, and amongst all the comrades who were in my circle and who knew about the matter, there was never a word against the killing."

"The decision was difficult and cruel," Shamir observed in 1991 in another interview. "But this is one of the decisions which the commander of an underground movement has to face when his movement is in danger. He cannot give in to weakness." Murder for Shamir was, at least in this case, a pragmatic decision: kill or be killed. The only sign that could be interpreted as remorse came with the birth of Shamir's daughter in 1949. He named her Gilada.

With Giladi out of the way, Shamir and the newly free Natan Yalin-Mor (who escaped from the Latrun prison, to which he had recently been transferred from Mazra, on November 1, 1942) began organizing a guerrilla movement based on personal terror. Joining the two as the head of the revived underground was a thirty-two-year-old Polish-born Bible teacher named Israel Eldad. They formed a triumvirate they called the Center. Yalin-Mor, a civil engineer and mathematician who once edited the Revisionist newspaper in Warsaw, was in charge of political activities, and represented Lehi in negotiations with the Irgun and the Haganah. With his thin wisp of a voice and tall, shapeless body, he looked more like a café poet than a ruthless guerrilla.

Eldad, known as the Doctor, was a brilliant, electric personality enthralled by the fiery power of his own voice and its biblical message. He handled ideological indoctrination and "wrote propaganda the way Mozart composed music," in the words of his former colleague Baruch Nadel. "If you take Eldad and put him on the pedestal, he will talk for ten hours without trouble. He is what we in Israel call an 'astronaut.' He knows nothing about what is happening on earth."

There was no competition among the three for control of Lehi operations. Yalin-Mor and Eldad, genuine intellectuals and thinkers, knew and cared little about the nuts and bolts of terrorism, while Shamir, the supreme pragmatist, had little patience for ideas. Operations were his domain. With his image as the tough, uncompromising leader solidified by Giladi's execution, he pondered the group's next action. He wanted something that would make the world sit up and take notice.

All the while, the organization's ranks were swelling. Because Lehi had abandoned the elaborate military trappings and rhetoric of the Irgun, it drew a different breed of terrorists to its ranks—men like Y. S. Brenner, today the head of the Department of Economics at the University of Utrecht. Growing up in an Arab-Jewish village where Bedouin camels once grazed and which was later absorbed by the Tel Aviv garden town of Ramat Gan, the teenage Brenner signed on with Lehi and took the code name "Benjamin." "Lehi was logical," the former guerrilla explained. "We saw that a Jewish-British alliance didn't really fit London's needs, not when they had an empire with so many Arabs in it. The Irgun people under Menachem Begin wanted to show the British how strong the Jews were. That we Jews are better allies than the Arabs, and will defend the interests of the British empire, so that in exchange they'll give us Palestine. This made no sense to me. At that time, there were 200 million Arabs under British rule and we were maybe 300,000. There was no communion of interests between Jews in Palestine and the British. Lehi saw this and said we have no choice but to get rid of the British. Besides, there was something in the Irgun's style, a kind of militarism, with ranks and subordinates and the sort of climate which was very fashionable in the thirties in Franco's Spain and of course in Germany, which didn't fit with my liberal upbringing. As a young person, you go with your friends. My friends were joining Lehi." So secretive was this new underground that Brenner's parents never knew he had joined.

Learning to use a gun was as natural a part of growing up as kicking a ball would have been in a different era. The tools of killing were the childhood toys of this generation coming of age in Palestine. "I don't remember how I learned," Brenner said fifty years later. "It was probably during the Arab uprising in 1936. You had to learn. I grew up with arms. So when I turned nineteen, and Lehi needed an arms instructor, I was ready. I remember there was a famous Hebrew poet who came to my father's house (my father was a playwright from Berlin) and tried to convince my parents not to let us play with toy soldiers. But this was the wrong moment for this particular view. I was relieved when Lehi chose violence as policy. It was the right thing at the time."

On a steamy day in August 1944, Shamir, Eldad, and Yalin-Mor met at Shamir's sparsely furnished Tel Aviv apartment and decided on a dramatic strike at the heart of the British Empire. The three men passed a sentence of death on Walter Edward Guinness, Lord Moyne, His Majesty's minister of state for the Middle East, a close friend of Winston Churchill's, and the ranking British official in the entire region.

For several weeks, Shamir focused on how to carry out this sentence. He was determined to compensate for his inglorious first year as chief of operations, when Lehi had tried and failed to penetrate the curtain of security that protected the high commissioner in Palestine, Sir Harold MacMichael. Shamir still smarted from several unsuccessful assassination attempts on MacMichael, whose administration was responsible for Yair's humiliating massacre, for the jailing of hundreds of Jews (including, of course, Shamir, Yalin-Mor, and scores of other Lehi men), for the exile of still others to Mauritius and Eritrea, for imposed curfews, house arrests, and other draconian measures intended to bend Palestine to His Majesty's rule.

In the best-known and most embarrassing incident, Lehi had ambushed MacMichael's car on the way from Jerusalem to Jaffa. The high commissioner's car managed to escape the hail of machine-gun fire and hand grenades. The most hated man in Palestine suffered only minor wounds.

Lehi *had* to show the world its mettle. It *had* to set itself apart from the Irgun with a spectacular "deed," as Shamir called it. "He would take something into his thought process, concentrate with body and soul with the full weight of his will and then carry it out," Eldad recalled.

Benjamin/Brenner, like most of the Lehi rank and file, approved the decision to assassinate Lord Moyne. "By that time we knew what was happening to Jews in Europe," Brenner remembered. "We knew, in spite of denials, that Moyne had frustrated efforts to give Hungarian Jews safe passage, knew he was opposed to Jews coming to Palestine. So it was no longer the problem of creating a state, just saving people. Days of prayer, hunger strikes, and all sorts of powerless demonstrations were going on all over Palestine. Finally, we were cutting ourselves off from these useless gestures."

Lord Moyne was picked as Lehi's target because he was the most conspicuous symbol of the despised British presence in the region. Never mind that Moyne did not bring the same steely indifference to Jewish dreams for a homeland that MacMichael did. Never mind that Moyne's good friend Winston Churchill regarded him as a friend of the Jews. Everything about the spare, six-foot-two, sixty-four-year-old Lord Moyne, from his sleek black Humber with the Union Jack snapping off the front fender, to the Savile Row perfection of the white linen suits he affected in the sweltering Cairo summer, to his family name, Guinness, synonym for the best Irish stout, spoke of the hated Empire.

A story, true or not, about Moyne had roared like a forest fire across the parched Palestinian landscape. It provided Lehi's three-man leadership the final piece of "evidence" to seal the Englishman's fate. The previous summer, British security in Syria had picked up a Hungarian Jew named Joel Brand. Purporting to be an agent sent by Adolf Eichmann, the chief of the Gestapo's Jewish section, Brand claimed to be empowered by the Nazi to negotiate with London for the lives of Hungarian Jews in exchange for 10,000 trucks and other supplies. British security agents conducted Brand to Cairo and presented him to His Majesty's minister of state for the Middle East. Moyne, in keeping with the same British policy of no negotiation with the enemy that months later would condemn Folke Bernadotte's exchanges with Himmler, reportedly dismissed Brand with, "My dear fellow, whatever would I do with a million Jews?" True or not, in Palestine, the oft-told tale had catapulted Moyne to the status of chief demon.

For Lehi, Moyne had another distinct advantage as a target. In contrast to High Commissioner MacMichael, Moyne was vulnerable. With only a driver and an unarmed aide-de-camp composing his regular entourage, on cool evenings the minister of state had the habit of strolling unaccompanied along the Nile. Cairo was not the vigilant fortress Jerusalem had become.

Outside the three-man Center, only the two men chosen by Shamir to assassinate Moyne, and the man he picked to train them for the job, Yehoshua Cohen, were privy to the death sentence. Recruited to Lehi by Shamir, and now picked by him for this operation, were Eliahu Hakim, a seventeen-year-old

Sephardic Jew from Haifa, and Eliahu Bet-Zouri, five years older and from Tel Aviv. Both were former members of the Irgun. Shamir's faith in the youths was absolute. "What influenced [Bet-Zouri]," Shamir recounted, "were our careful and definite statements that we wanted to free our country from foreign rule. Not because that rule was British, but because it was foreign. Not because of the Jewish problem, or because Zionism was the answer to that problem—but simply and basically because this is our country, our homeland, the land of our ancestors, and in it we—not strangers—must rule."

The blue-eyed, blond Bet-Zouri impressed Yehoshua Cohen, with "his rough face, as if hewn out of rock, not round and smooth." The dark-eyed Eliahu Hakim had caught Shamir's eye the moment he joined the underground. Hakim compensated for his inexperience with a barely contained anger and a need to do something to salve a childhood memory. The sinking of a Jewish refugee ship, the *Struma,* off the Turkish coast on February 24, 1942, was a tragedy in which 740 Jews fleeing Hitler drowned because the British authorities in Palestine refused to allow it to dock. The disaster "dumbfounded" the adolescent Hakim. "The 740 Jews who escaped the Nazis' sword," Eliahu Hakim wrote, "thought they had escaped from the frying pan. Little could they know they would fall into the fire. How can I ignore them? They are our brothers! How is it even possible for people to think about parties and good times? If we do not mourn them, who will?"

Yehoshua Cohen, Lehi's most valued fighter, traveled from Tel Aviv to Jerusalem to prepare the two Eliahus for their mission. Cohen was ideally suited for the task. Since the age of sixteen, the wiry zealot with the marksman's steady gaze had been preparing for combat against the enemies of Zion. After weeks of rigorous training in Jerusalem's back streets and deserted lots, the two Eliahus faced their commander for the final time. In solemn tones, Shamir exhorted them. "A man who goes forth to take the life of another," Shamir repeated the mantra he would intone to others he sent to kill, "whom he does not know, must believe one thing only—that by this act he will change the course of history."

"Our attack on Moyne will clarify exactly who the enemy is," he told the youths. "We smash the dragon's head, not the tail. . . . We believe Great Britain simply cannot carry out her promises to both Jews and Arabs. . . . The deed against Moyne will bring the whole issue into the world forum where it will merit the attention of world opinion and world diplomacy."

Having passed Shamir's final inspection, the two assassins, barely out of their adolescence but burning to prove themselves, set off by train for Cairo. Of the 30,000 Palestinian Jews enlisted in the British forces, 15,000 were stationed in Egypt. Twelve of that group had secretly signed on with Lehi. Their services would now be called upon to help the two Eliahus melt into the teeming Egyptian metropolis.

With the help of the underground, the assassins stalked Lord Moyne for several weeks, familiarizing themselves with his habits. They observed his penchant for a midday trip home for a quick meal and a siesta. They scrutinized old copies of the *Illustrated London News* with close-up photographs of the Right Honorable Walter Edward Guinness's chiseled features and his patrician air. Ambushing him as he arrived or left his stately residence by the Nile seemed like the best strategy.

Very early on the morning of November 6, 1944, the two men pedaled their bicycles to the redbrick home on the Rue Gabalya of a man who was not a man to them, but only the Enemy: His Majesty's minister of state for the Middle East.

In the shimmering midday heat of Cairo, the two Eliahus crouched in the shrubbery and listened for the crunch of gravel under the minister's tires. Alert to the faintest tremor in the air, the Eliahus waited for over an hour for Lord Moyne to arrive for his customary lunch. Just after 1 P.M., the black Humber finally rolled up the long sweep of the driveway, coming to a smooth stop in front of the residence's double doors. The driver, Corporal A. T. Fuller, leapt out to open his chief's door. Captain Andrew Hughes-Onslow, Moyne's aide-de-camp, strode straight toward the front door. In a split second, the assassins pounced from behind their hiding place and bounded toward the car's back door. It was the dark-haired Eliahu who got there first, took careful aim, and, before the Englishman had a chance to react, pumped three shots into Lord Moyne. In a trance, Fuller sprang toward the blond Eliahu, who fired three shots into the chauffeur's chest. Leaving Moyne slumped in the blood-soaked back seat of the Humber, the killers jumped on the bicycles they had left propped up against the wrought-iron fence and raced down the gravel road. Suddenly, an Egyptian motorcycle policeman appeared and, sensing trouble, blocked their way. This was not something Cohen had prepared them for. Bet-Zouri fired at the officer's motorcycle, and missed. The policeman took aim and hit his target, hitting the older Eliahu in the chest. The two offered no further resistance as they were taken in.

They were tried by an Egyptian court. Despite their forceful and headline-making courtroom testimony, explaining with an almost serene conviction their motive for the murder, the two Eliahus were sentenced to death. On March 22, 1945, an Egyptian hangman tightened the noose first around Hakim's neck, then around Bet-Zouri's. The Fighters for the Freedom of Israel had two more martyrs. "The Deed," as Shamir called it, had put Lehi on the map.

The Yishuv was stunned by the murder. "Since Zionism began," *Ha'aretz*, the respected daily, said, "no more grievous blow has been struck to our cause." In London, Winston Churchill, Lord Moyne's lifelong friend, was too upset to speak at a special session of Parliament. In a voice drenched in cold fury, Anthony Eden gave the details of the assassination. Dr. Chaim Weizmann claimed the news had been a greater shock to him than "the death of my own son," a Royal Air Force flight lieutenant shot down over Germany.

Five decades later, Shamir was still concerned with accusations that his underground had been wantonly brutal. In 1994 he insisted that "we were exceedingly sensitive to the charge, expended much time and effort on explaining that there was no other way, examined our motives and aims over and over again and undertook no action blindly or automatically or for brutality's sake. Our goal . . . was not so much to punish as to deter, to warn and to raise the price of each Jewish life taken or damaged. Reprisals were not acts that called for . . . celebration; they had to be, and were, part of the payment demanded from us for national survival, and I recall them as such, without apology or regret."

Eleven days after the murder of his friend, Winston Churchill delivered Moyne's eulogy in the House of Commons. "This shameful crime has shocked the world, none more sharply than those like myself who in the past have been consistent friends of the Jews and constant architects of their future. . . . If our dreams for Zionism are to end in the smoke of assassins' guns and our labors for its future to produce only a new set of gangsters worthy of Nazi Germany"—the prime minister paused—then, many, like himself, he asserted, "would have to reconsider the position we have maintained so consistently and so long in the past."

The hard men of the Lehi leadership were elated by the storm the deed had provoked. "We didn't have to wait for the British Royal Institute for International Affairs," wrote Yalin-Mor in his memoirs, "to tell us that the assassination of Lord Moyne had drawn worldwide attention to Palestine. This was our prime purpose and we achieved it fully. . . . We knew that we had reached the summit. A British Minister to the Middle East was probably the highest-ranking target we could have set."

"The Government of Palestine will award the following prizes in return for information leading to the arrest of members of the Stern Gang," ran the full-page ads, complete with physical descriptions and photographs, carried by the Hebrew press, "who call themselves Fighters for the Freedom of Israel . . . Natan Yalin-Mor, 500 pounds, Yitzhak Yezernitsky, 200 pounds, Yehoshua Cohen, 200 pounds." The large reward for Yalin-Mor was presumably a reflection of his higher profile as the underground's political chief, higher than that of the man who never left the shadows but had orchestrated this and other Lehi operations, Yitzhak Shamir.

" 'Michael' and I," wrote Yalin-Mor, describing the squalid life of constant fear of capture of this period, "didn't meet with many outsiders, but we wished to keep our identities from those few we did. Many of the men in our ranks didn't know who we were until then. . . . Such was Lehi discipline."

"At the end of 1944 the Stern Group had maybe ninety members," recalled Baruch Nadel, who quit the Haganah to join Lehi sometime later. "It was nothing. The Irgun had about fifteen hundred or two thousand, and after Moyne's murder, which the Stern Group carried out, Ben-Gurion decided to go after the Irgun. He was a shrewd politician and he saw the Irgun as a bigger threat than we were. I also think Yalin-Mor made some kind of a secret deal with the Haganah. So they left us more or less in peace."

In exchange for being left alone by Ben-Gurion, Lehi more or less retired from the field during this period. Not so the Irgun, which, with its core of 800 members and thousands of sympathizers, presented Ben-Gurion with the prospect of a Jewish civil war, and thus bore the brunt of Ben-Gurion's ire. Called "the Season," it was a time of Jew hunting Jew, of Haganah men rounding up suspected members of the Irgun and turning them over to the British authorities for interrogation, which was often a code word for torture. For since January 1944, the Irgun, under the leadership of a thirty-year-old Warsaw lawyer and editor named Menachem Begin, had called on all Jews to revolt against British rule.

Like Shamir's, Begin's roots were in Jabotinsky's militant right-wing youth movement Betar, which Begin had once headed in Poland. But whereas Shamir's background was small-town working-class, Begin had been shaped by the culture of an urban professional class. Begin never approved of Lehi's policy of personal terror and did not believe it would speed the creation of a strong independent Israel.

"Four years have passed since the war began," Begin exhorted his fellow Jews in a pamphlet that burned with frustration and rage, "and all the hopes that beat in our heart then have evaporated without a trace. We have not been accorded international status, no Jewish Army has been set up; the gates of the country have not been opened. The British regime has sealed its shameful betrayal of the Jewish people. . . . There is no longer any armistice between the Jewish people and the British administration which hands our brothers over to Hitler. Our people are at war with this regime—a war to the end."

While continuing to condemn sharply Lehi's policy of individual terrorism, on March 23, 1944, the Irgun attacked British police stations in Haifa, Tel Aviv, and Jerusalem. Two Irgun men and six Britons were killed in the fighting. Two months later, Begin's troops captured a British radio station near the Arab town of Ramallah. Like Shamir and Yalin-Mor, Begin, too, thought Ben-Gurion a dangerous compromiser, too intimidated by the British ever to win the Jews their long-promised state.

Teddy Kollek, chief of intelligence for the Jewish Agency—and subsequently Jerusalem's longtime mayor—admits to having turned over to the British the names of 1,000 Jews connected to the underground. Kollek never repented of this, for he felt it was the only way to stop Jewish terrorists. Thus, one by one, Begin's comrades in the Irgun fell into the British net. Still, their commander counseled restraint, and the Irgun held its fire. Begin abhorred the prospect of Jews fighting Jews.

Still under deep cover in the wake of Moyne's murder, Shamir consolidated his grip on his small underground. "In his determination to avoid failure," wrote Yalin-Mor in his memoirs, "Shamir felt obliged to supervise every detail, to check on every individual and examine every particular. . . . 'Michael's' vigilance never relaxed. His system bore fruit."

"We respected Shamir," Y. S. Brenner recalled. "He was a hell of an organizer. Before we would set off on an operation . . . he would inspect everybody to make sure each man had everything he needed, to see if your shoes were all right and you had enough ammunition. But I would say he was more respected than liked."

To avoid capture, Shamir was constantly on the move, spending time in the small village of Bnei-Brak, with a largely Orthodox Jewish population. To keep up the terrorists' spirits, Eldad, the chief propagandist, preached fiery sermons to his idle disciples in safe houses late at night. Skimming from the Old Testament and drawing on the example of Yair's blood-soaked martyrdom, "Eldad lectured on the ideology of the movement at courses we gave along with the military instruction. We knew from past experience that for the underground fighter, awareness of the justice of his cause was no less vital than his ability to draw and hit his targets," Yalin-Mor recalled. ". . . Infused with the righteousness of our cause, Eldad at times became hopelessly aggressive. His listeners would seek to escape the scalding torrent. . . ."

For at least one of Eldad's faithful, his torrent of hate was never too scalding. Operating from a clandestine radio station, a Moroccan-born Sephardic Jew named Geulah Cohen soon became the voice of Lehi in the Yishuv. "Geulah's voice," Yalin-Mor noted, "was tinged with hoarseness, a matter not of her vocal cords, but of the excitement which gripped her as she read the emotion-laden material. . . . Her fluency in Hebrew, acquired in school and at home, was superlative. . . . Geulah's was the sensuous voice which stimulated the fighter as he went forth to give battle. It was the heartbeat of life and death, beyond logic and calculation. . . . When Geulah's voice came on the air, they felt a surge of emotion."*

Preparing for sustained battle, the Center set a new policy: Lehi fighters must marry and have children, or they risked losing heart for the long haul. At the end of the summer of 1944, Shamir decided to set a good example. His courier, Sara Levi, code name Shulamit, was earning an unfair reputation as a prostitute for her late-night visits to "Rabbi" Shamir; in fact, they were in love, Sara, a short, tenacious Bulgarian refugee, became Mrs. Yitzhak Shamir. "I married clandestinely," Shamir recalled many years later. "The wedding was underground. . . . The rabbi who performed the ceremonies was Rabbi Aryeh Levine. It was organized secretly in Jerusalem, at Machaneh Yehudah [a neighborhood], without fanfare or formality. The *chuppah* was in a courtyard, we drank a toast and returned to work. That same evening my wife returned to Tel Aviv with 'messages.' Poor thing!"

The couple, reborn in the underground, would continue to call each other "Michael" and "Shulamit." A year later, a son was born to the Shamirs, the first of many Lehi male progeny to bear the name Yair.

At around the same time, friends from Poland arrived with the news Shamir had been fearing. Although his parents and sisters had escaped the November 1942 deportations from Rozhnoi, they had not survived the war. His father, Shlomo, was shot by childhood friends in Derecyn, in eastern Poland, where he had gone in search of a hiding place. From that day, Yitzhak Yezernitsky never again used his family name. Henceforth he used only his underground name. It was an appropriate choice. *Shamir* in Hebrew means either a particularly hard rock or, according to legend, a tiny worm that broke up rocks for the construction of the Temple.

Shamir only once referred publicly to the fate of the family he left behind in Poland. In 1989, at a public gathering commemorating the victims of the Holocaust, the normally expressionless prime minister trembled slightly as he told the story of his father's murder. "While seeking shelter among friends in the

---

*Geulah Cohen's voice would continue to be heard for decades to come, as she became the most vocal and articulate right-winger in the Knesset.

village where he grew up, his friends from childhood killed him." The prime minister then listed, for the first and last time, each member of the family whom he had not seen since he began his journey to Palestine in 1935: Shlomo Yezernitsky, his father; Pearl, his mother; his sisters, Miriam and Rivka; their husbands, Mordechai and Yaakov; and their children. Shamir's icy unsentimentality is the strength of a man who never forgot, never forgave.

Lehi, still derisively called the Stern Gang by the British, continued to expand. Some members estimated the membership to have reached 200 by 1946, but precise figures on the clandestine group are impossible to ascertain. Apart from their individual three-or-four-man cells, the terrorists did not know the real identities of fellow members. "That way if you got caught, they couldn't get much information from you," Y. S. Brenner recalled. "Even within your cell you didn't know each other's real names or addresses. This was all Shamir's idea, of course. But in such a small country as Israel, sometimes you recognized someone you knew, and if there was an operation in Haifa where we blew up some British refineries . . . you might recognize somebody's brother. But the idea was that it shouldn't happen, and mostly it didn't happen. We really were anonymous soldiers."

The majority of the Jewish population of Palestine, however, "hated us like poison," according to Baruch Nadel. The group survived as a result of its genius for evading the authorities. "Your order would come on a piece of paper," Brenner recalled. "Meet so and so—his code name; we never knew anybody's real name—on such a block. You were supposed to walk the block east while the other guy walked in the opposite direction and you would recognize each other. If he didn't stop, it meant one of you was being watched, and we would try again in an hour."

On July 26, 1945, Lehi received support from an unexpected source: London. With the election of a British Labour government, many mainstream Zionists expected the end of the reviled White Paper, and the opening, at long last, of Palestine's doors to the European Jews who survived the war. Almost immediately, President Truman sent a message to the new British prime minister, Clement Atlee, expressing "the hope that the British Government may find it possible without delay to take steps to lift the restrictions of the White Paper on Jewish immigration to Palestine." Truman's was not a wild hope, as the Labour Party had been staunchly opposed to the White Paper policy from its birth. Still, when the new prime minister failed to respond, the Truman Administration fired off a second letter. "To anyone who has visited the concentration camps and who has talked with the despairing survivors," wrote the president's representative, Earl G. Harrison, "it is nothing short of calamitous to contemplate that the gates of Palestine should be soon closed." In a reply dated September 16, making Atlee's policy on Jewish immigration official, the Labour prime minister answered with a line worthy of his Conservative predecessor. Allowing more Jews into Palestine would "set the Middle East ablaze." To avert that dire scenario, the Labour government would permit a trickle of 1,500 Jews a month to enter Palestine.

From Lehi's trained assassins to the most idealistic kibbutznik in Palestine, from Yitzhak Shamir to David Ben-Gurion, this latest British betrayal was a call to arms. By October 1945, the Haganah, which only months before had been hunting down suspected members of Lehi and the Irgun, had joined forces with them against the hated British presence. Suddenly, Shamir and his men were no longer automatically dismissed by mainstream Jews as a dangerous band of criminals. Lehi had grasped London's treachery before anyone else, and had used it successfully for recruiting. In the fall of 1945 and in early 1946, scores of new recruits signed on with Lehi. British soldiers in Palestine became prisoners in a garrison state of their own making.

Shamir did not trust the new relationship among Lehi, the Haganah, and the Irgun. Still in the shadows, he ran Lehi without showing his face. Natan Yalin-Mor represented Lehi in meetings with Haganah chief Moshe Sneh and Irgun commander Menachem Begin. For a ten-month period beginning in October 1945, the three men coordinated a joint effort to rid the country of the hated army of occupation. Working together, they blew up bridges and refineries, exploded railroad lines, and robbed banks to finance their activities.

The wave of terror crested with the famous bombing of the King David Hotel. A powerful symbol of British presence in the Holy Land, the King David was not only the military headquarters of the British, but the center of their social life as well. Until July 22, 1946, it was considered both sacrosanct and safe. Despite a telephone warning from the Irgun to the King David Hotel operator, eighty people—Britons, Arabs, and Jews—were killed in the bombing. Roughly the same number were seriously wounded.

With the blast, the frayed nerves of the war-weary British people finally snapped. General Sir Evelyn Barker, commanding officer in Palestine, issued an order to his troops that confirmed Lehi's darkest vision of British anti-Semitism:

> No British soldier is to have any social intercourse with any Jew, and any intercourse in the way of duty should be as brief as possible and kept strictly to business in hand. I appreciate that these measures will inflict some hardship on the troops but I am certain that if my reasons are fully explained to them they will understand their propriety and will be punishing the Jews in a way that race dislikes as much as any, by striking at their pockets and showing our contempt for them.

The Yishuv, too, was shaken by the audacity of the King David bombing. Perhaps, people reflected, the wave of terror had gone too far. Confirming Shamir's innate wariness, Ben-Gurion pulled out of the united effort, leaving the Irgun and Lehi to go it alone once more. And once more came the British roundup of suspected terrorists, the arrests without charge or bail. In one such house-to-house search in the late summer of 1946, the authorities finally caught up with the quiet, cautious man they had been stalking since his escape from Mazra four years earlier.

"I was sure nothing would happen to me," Shamir recalled more than two decades later. "I had passed all sorts of ID checks and searches. I said to myself, I'll get past this one, too. I therefore put off leaving town. The British concentrated the men in our area in a school in Ben Yehuda, and there I was recognized by a British detective who had a special gift for identifying people from photographs. His name was Martin. He identified me immediately by my bushy eyebrows. He said to me straight away, 'You are Yitzhak Yezernitsky!' "

Yalin-Mor recalled how he heard the news.

> Shulamit, Michael's wife, arrived. I read the bad news in her face. Michael had been arrested. We got the details about the arrest from the London papers. They had high praise for Officer Martin of the Criminal Investigation Division. He had identified

Michael by his thick eyebrows. This was verified a few days later
in a letter that Michael smuggled out from the Central prison in
Jerusalem . . . before he was flown to the detention camp in
Eritrea. Of the two items in Michael's note, one called for immediate action: Martin was the one directly responsible for his arrest . . . the Operations Department was instructed [by Michael]
to work out plans to execute Martin and to wait for word when
to strike. The decision came not only as a matter of concern for
the prestige of the underground, important though it was, but
also to remove a threat to the underground and its men.

Shamir, his wrists and ankles manacled, was in a Halifax
bomber on the way to Eritrea when, on September 9, 1946,
Sergeant T. G. Martin approached the tennis court near his
home on Mount Carmel in Haifa, for his weekly game. Something about the two players on the next court struck Martin as
not quite right. The sergeant's hand reached for his service revolver, but he was not fast enough. A burst of automatic-
weapons fire ripped into him. The men on the next court
vanished without a trace, leaving the English detective dying on
the red clay of the Haifa Tennis Club.

CHAPTER ELEVEN

PARTITION WITHOUT PEACE

IN 1946, AS FOLKE BERNADOTTE'S REPUTATION AS A HUMANITAR-
ian grew, the Holy Land, which had largely escaped the war, was
transformed into an armed camp. The British, ostensibly there to
maintain law and order, stayed behind nests of barbed wire, or
ventured out inside their armored personnel carriers. Around
them the population boiled with anger. The streets of Jerusalem
rumbled with the sounds of jeeps unloading more sandbags.
"One hundred thousand Englishmen," Winston Churchill, no
longer prime minister, announced in the House of Commons,
"are being kept away from their homes and work for a senseless
squalid war with the Jews. We are getting ourselves hated and
mocked by the world at a cost of eighty millions."

Despite Lehi's and the Irgun's relentless raids on British
soldiers and installations, London kept Jewish immigration
to Palestine to a dribble. Nor did Britain envision giving up
its Mandate. After all, with the imminent loss of Egypt as a
colony, the Empire needed Palestine more than ever. Under pressure to do something about this increasingly embarrassing situation, London and Washington appointed an Anglo-American
Commission of Inquiry, the eighteenth such commission since
London was awarded the Mandate for Palestine. Foreign Minister Ernest Bevin pledged that if the commission, convened between January 1 and April 30, 1946, and composed of six
British and six American members, presented him with a unani-
mous recommendation, he would heed it, whatever its recommendations.

The commission proceeded to meet Bevin's challenge. It unanimously recommended that 100,000 Jews from European DP (displaced-person) camps be admitted immediately to Palestine, an end to Britain's White Paper policy, and the abolition of restrictions on Jewish land purchases. The commission did not make the disarming of the underground a precondition for the admission of the 100,000. In its final report, released on April 30, the Anglo-American Commission stopped short of endorsing a Jewish state.

President Truman immediately endorsed the commission's conclusions. But despite Bevin's pledge, Bevin declared that "it would not be possible for the Government of Palestine to admit so large a body of immigrants" without American help. In addition, the British made the admission of DPs dependent on a condition: the "illegal armies in Palestine" (including the Haganah) must be "disbanded and their arms surrendered."

This condition sounded more reasonable than it really was. The British had demanded the disarming of the Jews without simultaneously asking the same of the armies of the Arab League—Egypt, Syria, Iraq, and Transjordan—all protégés of London. The Jews were not about to accept this precondition. Thus, the British were provided with a handy pretext for not implementing the Anglo-American Commission's proposals.

The British public, however, was sickened by the image of Jewish survivors, recently gazing hollow-faced from behind Hitler's barbed wire, now held in camps in Cyprus and Mauritius, His Majesty's captives. This was not the way most Britons wished to close the imperial day.

In 1946, Samuel Merlin, friend to Lehi and a fund-raiser for the Irgun, called on the British ambassador to France, Alfred Duff Cooper, who presented Merlin with a Bible inscribed, "I am with you." Merlin recalled, "Cooper spoke of Bevin with such contempt. 'The Foreign Office commits blunder after blunder,' he told me. 'Bevin believes everything his civil servants tell him. And they believe in a bluff: the power of the Arabs.'"

By early 1947, the obdurate foreign secretary's frustration over Britain's inability to find a way out of the Palestine quagmire boiled over. Ernest Bevin felt that granting the Jews a homeland would shatter London's plans for a regional Pax Britannica, buttressed by her Arab alliances. He also realized that postwar

Britain needed Washington's financial and economic support to stay in the high-stakes game of Great Power politics. The appalling images telegraphed from Tel Aviv and Jerusalem depicted a cycle of terror and counterterror in the Holy Land that risked contaminating London's special relationship with Washington. British Tommies, pictured using rubber truncheons to round up Jewish suspects, were seen by some as not much better than Hitler's storm troopers.

Some American Zionist extremists openly applauded acts of Jewish violence aimed at the coldhearted imperial power. In a "Letter to the Terrorists in Palestine" published in the *New York Herald Tribune,* Ben Hecht, the famed Hollywood screenwriter, asserted, "The Jews of America are for you. You are their champion. You are the grin they wear. You are the feather in their hats. In the past fifteen hundred years every nation in Europe has taken a crack at the Jews. This time the British are at bat. You are the first answer that makes sense to the New World. Every time you blow up a British arsenal, or wreck a British jail or send a British railroad train sky high or rob a British bank, or let go with your guns and bombs at the British betrayers and invaders of your homeland, the Jews in America make a little holiday in their hearts. . . . "

Responding to his countrymen's growing wish to be done with the whole degrading business, Bevin finally took the Palestine question to the United Nations in February 1947. The result was the appointment of yet another commission—the nineteenth—to once more till this well-turned ground. The United Nations Special Commission on Palestine (UNSCOP), composed of members from eleven nations (Australia, Canada, Czechoslovakia, Guatemala, India, Iran, the Netherlands, Peru, Sweden, Uruguay, and Yugoslavia), spent from mid-June to mid-July in Palestine.

Arriving in Jerusalem on June 14, Secretary-General Trygve Lie's representative on UNSCOP, Ralph Bunche, noted: "the British are everywhere and they all carry guns. As you go thr [sic] the streets you're constantly stopped by sentries and control centers and required to show your pass. Buildings are surrounded by barbed wire, pillboxes and road blocks are abundant. Armed guards patrol the building in which we live." On UNSCOP's first working day, June 16, the British passed the death sentence on five members of the Irgun for terrorism. The five men were hanged on July 30, and the underground retaliated by kidnapping and hanging two British sergeants.

"The longer we stay," Bunche wrote at the end of the month, "the more confused all of us get. The only thing that seems clear to me after five weeks in Palestine is that the British have made a terrible mess of things here. About the only subject on which both Arabs and Jews seem to be in agreement is that the British must go." In its report on August 31, UNSCOP pronounced the Mandate unworkable. The majority of the committee recommended the partition of Palestine into two states, one Arab, the other Jewish, but called for the economic unity of "Palestine." The UN General Assembly, it further maintained, should take "measures" to solve the problem of a quarter-million Jewish refugees in Europe.

On the critical issue of borders, UNSCOP's partition proposal resembled, in its critics' eyes, "two fighting serpents." The majority of UNSCOP members recommended an Arab area comprising western Galilee, the hill country of central Palestine (except for the Jerusalem enclave), and the coastal plain from south of Isdud (Ashdod) to the Egyptian border. The Jewish territory would embrace the rest, except for the Jerusalem area, which would be internationalized. During a two-year interim period starting in September 1947, Britain would administer Palestine under United Nations supervision. The United States would play an as-yet-undefined role in this transition period. Jewish immigration would continue at the rate of 6,250 monthly during the first two years, totaling 150,000 immigrants. After this period, 60,000 Jews a year would be permitted to enter Palestine.

Once more, the British, given the solution they had solicited, rejected it. On September 26, the British colonial secretary, Arthur Creech-Jones, told the United Nations that he had been "instructed by His Majesty's Government to announce with all solemnity, that they have . . . decided that in the absence of a settlement they must plan for an early withdrawal of British forces and of the British administration from Palestine." The colonial secretary did not specify the date this withdrawal from Palestine would take place, but less than a month later, Creech-Jones said that London "would not accept responsibility for the enforcement, either alone or in cooperation with other nations, of any settlement antagonistic to either the Jews or the Arabs or both, which was likely to necessitate the use of force."

To Arthur Koestler, watching with contempt, British policy was ridiculous: "To appeal for the judgment of an international body in order to stop two parties from quarreling, and then to reject the judgment because it meant enforcing peace between them, was no longer diplomacy but sheer Harpo Marx logic."

This was the beginning of a period that baffled London's closest ally and wreaked havoc in Palestine. For though the British barred any other authority, including the United Nations, from maintaining order in Palestine, they declined to do the job themselves. Sir Alexander Cadogan, Britain's first permanent representative at the UN, announced, "So long as my Government will continue to hold the Mandate for Palestine, *they must insist upon their undivided control of that country.*" [Italics added.]

Thus, London precluded any orderly transition from colonial to independent rule in a place that was among the most bitterly contested places on earth. The British had decided simply to withdraw and let the Arabs and Jews fight it out. *"Après moi le déluge"* is how some observers described London's new policy of imperialist nihilism.

The disaster that ensued was preordained. One of the architects of Bevin's policy, Harold Beeley, many years later tried to explain the rationale for Britain's refusal to accept a collective settlement. "Maybe we were wrong. Maybe we should have put troops along the partition frontiers and made sure that partition was carried through. I agree that this would have been a more dignified posture. But in the Foreign Office's view, it would have involved a serious injustice to the Arabs. And it would not have been in Britain's national interests. All through 1947, Bevin was negotiating with the prime ministers . . . of Egypt and Iraq for the protection of the Suez Canal and our oil concessions, and to integrate the two countries into the Western alliance. All this would have been ruined if we had played a part in creating the state of Israel."

It seemed a little late in the day for Britain, author of the Balfour Declaration, not to "play a part in creating the state of Israel." But once again London repudiated, as it had in 1939 with the White Paper policy, its own historic role in the region. It was perhaps not by chance that only weeks earlier the "Jewel in the

Crown"—India—had been given independence and been engulfed by bloodshed.

On November 29, 1947, delegates representing all fifty-seven member states of the United Nations gathered in the cavernous skating rink of the former World's Fair grounds in Flushing Meadow, Long Island. The dreary setting did not diminish the mystical aura of the moment. There was a palpable sense of history in the making—Jewish dreams, born out of genocide and guilt, collided with Arab anger. Wild hopes confronted a bedraggled and disintegrating Empire. All this was played out in the drafty hall.

"The United Nations really mattered in those days," recalls A. M. Rosenthal, then a twenty-six-year-old *New York Times* correspondent, one of a dozen reporters assigned by the paper to this beat. "There were such high hopes attached to the place. It was a huge story. . . . People were fascinated by all this. Palestine was the biggest, most emotional story of the day." Rosenthal still recalls Abba Eban's simple eloquence following the Lebanese delegate's impassioned speech calling Jerusalem the center of his universe, which could never be surrendered to the Jews. "Eban stood up and said, 'This was a very fine speech but let me point out that the distinguished speaker who lives in a Lebanese village 100 miles from Jerusalem has never visited Jerusalem.'"

Just two years after the end of the Second World War, during which more Jews had been killed than in any other period in their two-thousand-year exile, the majority of the General Assembly voted in favor (33 to 13, with 10 abstentions) of the partition of Palestine into an Arab and a Jewish state. A coalition of Arab-Muslim states voted against the motion. Britain abstained. Still, the vote represented a victory for the US and Israeli delegations, which had engaged in vigorous lobbying. In Palestine, the Arabs declared a three-day general strike. In the streets of Jerusalem, Jews danced to the music of the "Hatikva." "Nobody who lived that moment will ever lose its memory from his heart," recalled Abba Eban, who accompanied Chaim Weizmann to a tumultuous Zionist rally in Madison Square Garden that evening. A Jewish state, although smaller than hoped for by Zionists, had been legitimized by the world body.

Eban's celebratory mood was tempered, however, by the

memory of a late-summer afternoon four months before, when he and Azzam Pasha, the secretary-general of the Arab League, had been lured to a rendezvous arranged by a resourceful Reuters correspondent at London's Savoy Hotel. Over cups of tea, Azzam "kept muttering something about war," Eban recalled. "If there is a war," Eban argued, "there will have to be negotiations after it. Why not negotiate before—and instead of—war?"

"Azzam's reply was indignant but shatteringly candid," Eban recalled forty-five years later. " 'If you win the war, you will get your state. If you do not win the war, then you will not get it. We Arabs once ruled Iran and once ruled Spain. We no longer have Iran or Spain. If you establish your state the Arabs might one day have to accept it, although even that is not certain. But do you really think that we have the option of not trying to prevent you from achieving something that violates our emotion and our interest? It is a question of historic pride. There is no shame in being compelled by force to accept an unjust and unwanted situation. What would be shameful would be to accept this without attempting to prevent it. No, there will have to be a decision and the decision will have to be by force.' "

In his bunkerlike headquarters in Tel Aviv, David Ben-Gurion did not celebrate either. The Old Man, as he was familiarly known, dropped his grizzled head into his hands. He saw too clearly what Jerusalem's celebrants chose not to see: that the biggest battle was still to come.

Nor did Yitzhak Shamir, Natan Yalin-Mor, or the volatile Dr. Eldad toast partition that evening. Their fiercest struggle was also about to begin. They did not want *part* of Palestine; they wanted all of it—both sides of the Jordan River, as ordained by the Bible and prescribed by Avraham Stern.

The Arabs reacted to the UN decision with fury. As early as September 16, upon learning of UNCSOP's pro-partition line, Prime Minister Salih Jabr of Iraq hastily called fellow members of the Arab League's Political Committee to Sofar, Lebanon. The two-and-a-half-year-old League, composed of all Arab states, voted to impose economic reprisals against Great Britain and the United States and to supply weapons and men to the Palestinian Arabs. Three weeks later, the group met again in the Lebanese town of Alay to plan military reprisal against the emerging Jewish state. Iraq's prime minister thundered loudest for an armed invasion of Palestine, while Transjordan and Egypt still hesitated. An Arab Liberation Army was eventually organized under the command of Iraqi General Sir Ismail Safwat Pasha. The League decided to arrange for the passage of 3,000 Arab volunteers through Syria into Palestine and to supply approximately $2 million toward the cost of the "defense of Palestine."

By the end of that winter, few would still celebrate the partition of Palestine. Soon, enraged Arabs attacked Jewish quarters in Jerusalem, Haifa, and Jaffa. These hit-and-run assaults on isolated Jewish settlements were the opening shots in the war still to come. On February 28, 1948, the Central Intelligence Agency summarized the situation for President Truman in cold terms:

> . . . the partition of Palestine into separate Arab and Jewish states . . . cannot be implemented. The Arab reaction to the recommendation has been violent and the Arab refusal to cooperate in any way with the five-nation United Nations Commission will prevent the formation of an Arab state and the organization of economic union. . . . The British have also declared that when the mandate terminates on 15 May they will not transfer authority to the UN Commission but will merely relinquish that authority. . . . Thus without Arab and British cooperation the [UN] Commission will be unable to carry out the task assigned to it.
>
> Even among the Jews there is dissatisfaction over the partition plan. The Irgun Zvai Leumi and the Stern Gang, the two extremist groups, have refused to accept the plan and continue to claim all of Palestine and even Transjordan for the Jewish state.

It was Harry Truman's most intractable problem: what to do about Palestine. "Truman was schizophrenic about Palestine," recalled Dean Rusk, then serving as the State Department's director of the Office of Special Political Affairs. "On the one hand, he believed in the Jewish home after the Holocaust; on the other hand, he wanted to avoid a succession of wars in the Middle East. The result was that he gave very contradictory signals. So we just went ahead and took our lumps." Rusk and most other State Department officials, including Secretary of State George C. Marshall and his deputy, Robert A. Lovett, favored a United Nations Trusteeship over Palestine. Many, like George

Kennan, considered the Palestine situation beyond solution for the immediate future. Secretary of Defense James Forrestal also weighed in with a strong antipartition vote. He voiced concern over the risks to America's access to Saudi Arabian oil.

Perhaps no one in the State Department fought harder against both the partition of Palestine and American recognition of Israel than Loy Henderson, director since 1945 of the department's Near Eastern Affairs bureau. A cool, consummate professional known as "Mr. Foreign Service," Henderson was also a fervent practitioner of *Realpolitik.* With the end of the war against the Nazis, he quickly perceived the danger posed to American global interests by Soviet expansion. The Arabs, in Henderson's eyes, had oil, were strategically located, and possessed a huge population. What did the Jews have, other than a sentimental choke hold on America? In Henderson's eyes, if Washington backed the frail new state of Israel, it would mean nothing but decades of trouble and "the rise of fanatic Mohammedanism."

Though his views were largely supported by Secretary of State Marshall, others viewed Henderson's cold logic as plain anti-Semitism. "Perhaps Palestine is a new subject for Mr. Marshall," Emanuel Celler, congressman from a largely Jewish section of New York City intoned. "Perhaps he is being briefed by Mr. Loy Henderson, the Arabophile [and] striped-trousered underling saboteur." *

Jewish organizations, sensing danger, redoubled their efforts to regain the president's support. Truman received 100,000 letters and telegrams concerning Palestine during the winter of 1947. The sometimes heavy-handed lobbying rubbed the president the wrong way. "Individuals and groups asked me, usually in rather quarrelsome and emotional ways, to stop the Arabs, to keep the British from supporting the Arabs, to furnish American soldiers, to do this, that, and the other. I think I can say that I kept the faith in the rightness of my policy in spite of some of the Jews." During an overheated session with a group of Zionists, the president blurted out in frustration, "All these people are pleading a special interest. I am an American."

On March 19, 1948, the situation exploded with a speech,

---

*Today, the main auditorium of the Department of State is named the Loy Henderson Auditorium.

still controversial to this day, given by the United States ambassador to the United Nations, Warren Austin. Speaking before the Security Council, Austin stunned the world—and, as it turned out, President Truman—by asking for the suspension of the partition plan in favor of a temporary trusteeship for Palestine under the United Nations Trusteeship Council. Austin had not cleared his speech with the White House.

In addition, Austin had no way of knowing that only the day before his speech, Chaim Weizmann, the venerable wise man of the Zionist movement, had slipped into the Oval Office without the usual fanfare, through the back door efforts of the president's friend and former business partner, Eddie Jacobson, who persuaded Truman to see Weizmann. Though it was only their second meeting, an unusual current of sympathy passed between the sixty-one-year-old Missouri farmer's son and the seventy-one-year-old shtetl-bred chemist. Truman was deeply moved by the aging, half-blind scientist who had led the Zionist movement over so many rough years. He told Weizmann that he would continue to support the partition of Palestine. Now Truman felt as though the rug had been pulled out from under him by Austin and the State Department. He was now caught between Marshall, whom he regarded as "the greatest living American," and his pledge to Weizmann. "It was one of the worst messes of my father's career," Margaret Truman Daniel later said, "and he could do nothing but suffer."

Little wonder, then, that Harry Truman breathed a sigh of relief when Folke Bernadotte assumed his position as the first United Nations Mediator between Arabs and Jews. "It was my hope," Truman wrote in his memoirs, "that out of the efforts of the United Nations mediator there might come a solution that would give the Jews a homeland in which they might safely build their future."

Such were the hopes pinned on one man, a stranger to the region, as he embarked on his journey to the Holy Land.

CHAPTER TWELVE

TO JERUSALEM

On May 26, 1948, two brief items appeared on page 5 of the London *Times*. "Count Folke Bernadotte, the recently appointed United Nations Mediator in Palestine, arrived in Paris by air this afternoon from Stockholm. He expects to leave on Thursday." The second item, bearing a Vienna dateline, read, "The Austrian office of the Jewish Agency has called to the colors today all Palestinian citizens between the ages of 17 and 35 and invited all able-bodied Jewish men and women in the displaced persons camps of the United States zone of Austria to volunteer for the armed forces of Israel. The response is understood to have been very strong, and it is estimated that more than a third of the 60,000 Jewish displaced persons now in this country will succeed in reaching Israel before autumn."

That same week, a young officer of the Haganah, Matti Meged, accompanying 1,500 men from Europe's displaced-persons camps, was aboard a rickety hulk, the SS *Kalanit*, crawling toward the port of Haifa. The tall, wiry Israeli officer had been with the men, all of them survivors of the Holocaust, since February. His job was to mold the pale, skinny refugees into a fighting force that could hold off the Arab advance on Israel's most endangered city. "We had been training with sticks while still in the DP camps," Meged recalled. "Our biggest problem was language: the boys spoke Polish, Hungarian, Russian, Rumanian, and smatterings of Yiddish. But not a word of Hebrew and no common language among them. The word 'Jerusalem' they understood, and what they wanted more than anything was to help save the city. When we sighted Haifa harbor, they all shouted, each in his own tongue. They could hardly wait to get off that ship and fight for their new land."

But the refugees were far from battle-ready. Meged was summoned to the Red House, Ben-Gurion's headquarters on the Tel Aviv seafront, by the prime minister. "How many are there?" he asked. "Who are they? Where did they come from? How much training have they had?" the prime minister demanded gruffly. Meged told him the sad truth.

"You know why they are here?" Ben-Gurion asked. "Because we need them." "But surely not right away," Meged interrupted. "That is not your business," the prime minister snapped. "You don't know how bad it is in Jerusalem."

There was nothing more Meged could do for the 450 immigrants. They were whisked by yellow buses from Haifa harbor to the dusty village of Tel Hashomer, on the road to Jerusalem. A Russian-born officer named Zvi Hurewitz, after receiving blank stares from most of the new recruits as he barked Hebrew commands at them, quickly taught them a few basic Hebrew words and issued them the first real weapons (British Lee-Enfield rifles) most of them had ever handled. The men were designated as the 72nd Battalion; it seemed a joke.

Most of the men had never heard of Latrun, the promontory that stands like a gateway at the mouth of the Jerusalem road. On May 24, the new battalion, equipped with neither helmets nor packs nor canteens—a "battalion of beggars," in the words of Chaim Herzog, Israel's future president—launched an assault on the village of Latrun, then in the firm grip of the Arab Legion. Stunned by Arab artillery, their flank unprotected, the *hamsin* and the unforgiving desert sun beating down on them, the refugee army could not understand the few words of Hebrew their officers screamed at them.

The officer who had trained them and brought them to Palestine now arrived to lead them to safety. "They didn't even know how to crawl under fire," Meged recalled. In the frantic rush to prepare them to fight, nobody had even compiled an accurate list of the new recruits' names. Thus, there was never an official record of how many men lost their lives that day in the fight for Latrun. "I found a seventeen-year-old Polish boy named Malamed, whom I knew from the *Kalanit*, dying in a ditch," Meged recalled. " 'Oh, we must have disappointed you,' the boy whispered to me. I will never forget his face. For me it was the worst trauma of my life,"

The Haganah admitted to 75 dead in the battle of Latrun. The Arab Legion claimed 800 Jews killed, undoubtedly an inflated figure. At the end of the day, the Arabs were richer by 220 rifles and the Israeli Army had suffered the war's bloodiest defeat.

As the battle of Latrun ebbed, Ralph Bunche waited for Folke and Estelle Bernadotte in the lobby of the Crillon Hotel in Paris. The city was still gray and shabby that spring, three years after the war's end. After flying all night, Bunche was not thrilled to be heading back to Palestine, where he had already undertaken several troubleshooting missions for the UN. He did not like leaving his wife Ruth and their three children, and UN Secretary General Lie had given him only four days of warning. "A great shock to both Ruth and me," he noted in his diary on May 20.

Upstairs in the famous old hotel, where a double room with bath cost six dollars a night, the Bernadottes prepared to meet the man Lie was sending with the mediator to Palestine to guide him through the Middle Eastern maze.

The short man in the lobby, smoking a cigarette and wearing a rumpled suit, was an unlikely companion for the aristocratic Swede. But Ralph Bunche was an unusual man. Then forty-four, he had made his way out of the black ghetto of Detroit, earned a Phi Beta Kappa key at UCLA, a Ph.D. from Harvard, and the respect of all with whom he worked. An educator, an OSS officer in the war, a scholar, and a civil-rights leader, Bunche now headed the UN Trusteeship Department. He was known for his remarkable intellect and his prodigious energy.

Bunche was startled by his first glimpse of the man who would be his new chief. The Swedish count, impressive in his crisp Red Cross uniform with its many service ribbons, his silver hair carefully brushed back, was accompanied by his exquisitely turned-out wife, his secretary, and his valet. Bunche and Bernadotte—the black from the ghetto, the count from Stockholm—shook hands, sized each other up, and instantly became friends.

"The Count is affable"—Bunche recorded his first impression in his diary—"speaks good English, is fairly tall, slender, with a deep-lined face, but nice looking. . . . He is eager to get to work. He emphasized frankness and punctuality. He says that if he advances an idea he relishes criticism provided it is accompanied by an alternative plan." To his wife Ruth, Bunche wrote, "I think we will get on well, for he seems to be a man who will listen seriously to advice."

"They became fast friends during that tense period," Estelle Bernadotte recalled. Meeting Ralph Bunche made her feel somewhat better about her husband's daunting new assignment. "He was an invaluable copartner [as a result of] his previous knowledge of the many attempts made by the UN in this problem, of which Folke had no knowledge. Besides, Ralph's command of the English language was brilliant, which was definitely not the case with Folke."

For the next three months, these two men, separated by culture, geography, and social position, formed an inseparable union. "Ralph was a Negro, burdened with much which that stood for in America during that time. The fact that Folke had no acquired opinions on this subject, nor was discriminating in any way, made Ralph feel that Folke took him at the level of human dignity and admired many of Ralph's fine qualities. It was thoroughly mutual," Estelle Bernadotte asserted.

"My treasured friend," Bunche called Bernadotte a few months later, "an utterly honest and fearless man, completely independent in his thinking, and thoroughly devoted to the effort to bring peace to Palestine." Bunche, too, saw through the older man's cool surface and "took him at the level of human dignity."

The following morning, the two men were joined by one of the most influential members of the World Zionist movement. Nahum Goldmann, chairman since 1936 of the World Jewish Congress and the World Zionist Organization,* was a dapper and worldly figure. He had traveled from London to have this

---

*Founded by Theodor Herzl in 1897, the World Zionist Organization was the most prominent institution of the Zionist movement. Its leadership was elected by the biannual World Jewish Congress. Between 1920 and 1946 (excepting the years 1931–35), Chaim Weizmann was the WZO's president. With the gradual ascendancy of the Jewish Agency, set up in Palestine to function as a shadow government, the World Zionist Organization became an international lobbying group for the cause of Zionism.

conversation with the new mediator. As it was the Swede's first real window into the conundrum of Palestine, the conversation left a deep mark on Bernadotte. "He is a moderate," Bunche told Bernadotte, regarding their visitor. A man of dazzling linguistic and diplomatic skills, the German-born and -educated Goldmann was a smooth and persuasive negotiator, on first-name terms with statesmen around the world. He had, at Dean Rusk's urging, advised the Zionists against a "premature" proclamation of sovereignty.

Speaking "personally and confidentially," Goldmann advised Bernadotte that "the Jews would probably join a Middle East confederation of states if such a confederation were on a geographical rather than a racial basis." He explained that "the Jews were quite willing to do this as a means of offsetting Arab fears of the Jews in the Middle East as a foreign wedge. . . . It is clear that the Jews must have peace with the Arabs," Goldmann continued, for they cannot hope to live permanently in the midst of millions of hostile Arabs. But, he stressed, the Arabs must recognize Israel's right to exist. Then, as if he himself still had trouble accepting the new state's legitimacy, Goldmann pointed out that one of the count's initial difficulties would be that the Jewish negotiating party consisted of representatives of the Provisional Government of Israel. The Zionist leader, indulging more in wishful thinking than relying on hard facts, reassured Bernadotte that the "Jewish State is now in a position to assure its complete responsibility for the acts of Sternists and the Irgunists. It has recently been revealed," he noted, "that there are less than 500 Sternists, 2,000 Irgunists."

Dr. Goldmann advised the mediator that British Foreign Secretary Bevin wished King Abdullah of Transjordan to hold on to Jerusalem. "This explains the present concentration of the [Transjordanian] Arab Legion in Jerusalem. The British," Goldmann said, "think that if Abdullah sits in Jerusalem he will become the titular head of the Arab world, and that their deadly enemy, the Grand Mufti of Jerusalem, would be permanently eliminated." On the key points of unfettered Jewish immigration to Israel and the vital role of the Negev, as yet a sparsely settled, undeveloped region that Ben-Gurion fervently hoped to cultivate, Goldmann implied that the count had room to negotiate.

All in all, Goldmann's briefing misled the new mediator and reinforced his innate optimism. Taken as a whole, the picture

Goldmann painted for the inexperienced and impressionable mediator was very poor preparation for what lay ahead. Only Israel's existence was nonnegotiable, the Zionist leader implied. Israel might agree to Transjordan's claim to Arab Palestine and might be amenable to a confederate status with Transjordan.

Bernadotte also met with the French foreign minister, Georges Bidault, and a group of British diplomats before retiring for the night. While he slept, at his request, the DC-3 aircraft chartered by Bunche from KLM Royal Dutch Airlines was painted white, with UN and Red Cross markings on its wings and fuselage. "I wanted to emphasize that my mission had a strongly humanitarian background and that I would try to be completely objective and neutral when I met the various representatives of the conflicting forces."

At day's end, Bunche sent the secretary-general this message: "Count considers it inadvisable for political, psychological reasons to proceed directly to Tel Aviv. I agree. Present intention is to go to Cairo . . . for consultation . . . after Cairo, Count's tentative itinerary is Amman and Tel Aviv. Realize consultations in capitals of Arab states not strictly within paragraph 1A Assembly Resolution, but Bernadotte correctly points out inability to 'uncover local Arab authorities' [i.e., Palestinian leaders]."

"It was the Arabs after all who were adopting the offensive," Bernadotte explained. "It was consequently with them we ought to seek contact first in any question of truce or cease-fire." Bernadotte's first task was to stop the fighting, which spluttered on throughout the country. However, since the Israelis had captured Haifa and Jaffa, on April 22 and May 12, respectively, the energy had dribbled out of the Arab offensive. Except for the Jerusalem area, which was still threatened by King Abdullah's Arab Legion, the military balance had unexpectedly tipped in Israel's favor. The Haganah had defeated the Arab Liberation Army in the north. Since early May, the Israelis had controlled the whole of western Galilee. The Egyptians, responsible for the southern half of Palestine, were hampered by poor communications across the 250-mile desert terrain. The Arab invasion's single greatest shortcoming, however, was the absence of a unified command of the six armies. Coordination among the various Arab armies was pathetically weak.

In the eyes of many Jewish officials, Folke Bernadotte had committed his first blunder before he even touched Israeli soil.

By stopping first in Cairo, he had already given offense. "Instead of coming straight to Palestine," Dov Joseph, the Israeli civilian commander of Jerusalem, wrote many years after the fact, "the Mediator's first step was to visit the Arab states which had openly and arrogantly defied the UN, to consult with the Arab leaders." In a region where symbols often outweigh reality, the wrong signal sent by his first stop eluded Bernadotte.

Before taking off from Le Bourget Airport outside Paris, Bernadotte met with Secretary-General Lie's chief of staff, Commander Robert Jackson, or "Jacko," as the flamboyant Australian naval officer was universally known. Jackson, recognized as the guiding spirit of UNRRA, the United Nations Relief and Rehabilitation Administration, remembered his first meeting with the new man on the UN team. "As I stepped from my aircraft a tall slim man with a distinctive military bearing emerged from the mist, and I immediately assumed that it was Folke Bernadotte. . . . We sat together in a quiet room in the airport and he asked many questions—about the Palestine conflict itself, and the United Nations, about its staff. I think I was able to give him some useful background about the respective viewpoints of the Jewish and Arab authorities and their supporters. . . . Towards the end of our talk, Bernadotte turned to me and asked, 'How important do you consider my mission to be?' My answer came easily. 'I know of no more important mission that anyone could be asked to undertake. I believe that the future of the United Nations depends on the manner in which this crisis is handled. The League of Nations failed because it failed to deal effectively with aggression in Manchuria and Abyssinia. The United Nations cannot afford to fail in the Middle East. . . .' Bernadotte was silent for a few moments and then he said very quietly, 'I fully understand and I fully agree.' "

The mediator then boarded his sparkling white aircraft, bound for Cairo. It was not an auspicious arrival. The Egyptian control tower refused to give the UN mission permission to land, since "this would give the enemy the direction of the wind and Egypt is at war." Having dramatized their point, however, the Egyptians relented and allowed the mediator's party to land. Bunche recorded the incident in his diary as "comic opera stuff."

The group checked into the once-sumptuous, now-tattered Shepheard's Hotel, the legendary meeting place of journalists, diplomats, and the region's wide collection of traveling ne'er-dowells. There was almost no time for Bunche to brief his new chief before their first meeting, with the Egyptian foreign minister, Ahmed Mohammed Khachaba Pasha, a session that Bunche referred to later as "absolutely meaningless." (The foreign minister told them, for example, there were three conditions for the Arabs entering into a cease-fire but he could remember only two of them.)

The same afternoon, Bernadotte, Bunche, and Paul Mohn, a Swedish aide, were ushered into the reception rooms of the Egyptian prime minister, Nokrashy Pasha. The count addressed the first man he spotted wearing a fez as "Prime Minister." It turned out to be a doorman, who in embarrassment pointed Bernadotte toward a mustachioed, roly-poly figure shambling through the reception room's French doors.

An hour and a half in the presence of the Egyptian leader gave Bernadotte his first taste of the fabled Arab elusiveness and intransigence. The Arab position was that there must be a *single* Palestinian state in which the Jewish minority population would be granted full protection and even local autonomy in such places as Tel Aviv. There could be no sovereign Jewish state in Palestine, the prime minister asserted. Bernadotte still found cause for "not being too depressed," however, as Nokrashy Pasha was in favor of a British-sponsored resolution calling for a cease-fire before the Security Council.

That evening, Bernadotte and Bunche changed into black tie for dinner at the British embassy, an imposing place set among wide lawns on the edge of the Nile, facing the pyramids. Crisply saluting sentries and the Union Jack snapping against an orange sky greeted the two visitors and conveyed a false image of the Empire in its prime.

Bernadotte understood that he must keep the British at arm's length during his delicate passage through the region's shoals. "I won't let them spy on me," he told his secretary, Barbro Wessel. In fact, one of Bevin's complaints about Bernadotte was that he never knew where to find him. "A hard man to catch," the scrappy Bevin muttered on the subject of the mediator.

The pleasant atmosphere of Ambassador Sir Ronald Campbell's dinner was interrupted when an aide handed the mediator the latest Reuters wire-service copy regarding the poisonous exchanges between British UN delegate Sir Alexander Cadogan and Israel's Abba Eban on the subject of the British truce proposal. (The British proposal called upon "both parties to order a cessation of all acts of armed force for a period of four weeks . . . that they will not introduce fighting personnel . . . into Palestine during the cease-fire. . . . Instructs the Mediator to make contact with both parties . . . with a view to making recommendations to the Security Council about an eventual settlement for Palestine. . . . Invites the . . . members of the Arab League and the Jewish and Arab authorities in Palestine to communicate their acceptance of this resolution not later than 6 P.M. NY Standard Time on 1st June, 1948." The resolution also warned that a party that did not obey the truce would be subject to UN sanctions.)

Bernadotte had no way of knowing that, during the same night, David Ben-Gurion had called Eban and, over the crackle of the transatlantic line, told him Israel was desperate for a break from the fighting. Despite Israeli successes elsewhere, Jerusalem was virtually cut off from the rest of the country by the Arab Legion and various bands of armed Arab "irregulars."

Bernadotte awoke the next morning to find an overnight telegram from Secretary-General Lie bearing unexpected good news. Despite the heated rhetoric of the previous day's session, the Security Council had adopted the British resolution that called on all parties to lay down their weapons for four weeks. The resolution also banned shipments of arms and military personnel from the outside world. The British, who had resisted a cease-fire resolution as long as the Arabs had been on the offensive, now saw that the combined forces of five Arab armies had not "pushed the Jews into the sea," and they fell into line with the American policy of calling for an immediate halt to the fighting to let mediation, rather than the battlefield, determine the future of Palestine.

Anglo-American policy henceforth would entail close cooperation with Bernadotte to achieve that end. The mediator was instructed (in concert with the UN-appointed Truce Commission, made up of the Jerusalem consuls of France, Belgium, and the United States) to supervise the observance of the truce and to organize military observers (drawn primarily from the military ranks of the Truce Commission member nations) for the task.

Bernadotte was elated by the Security Council's unexpected consensus, and anxious now to begin the business of cajoling the warring parties into accepting the cease-fire. He had one final appointment in Cairo, with Azzam Pasha, the secretary of the Arab League, a three-year-old British creation originally meant to bring the Arabs under British control. Azzam, a reedy and austere-looking man with an iron devotion to the Arab cause, made a strong impression on the Swede. "I felt an instinctive liking for him," Bernadotte wrote of the learned and courtly Azzam. Like Nokrashy Pasha, Azzam, too, asked the question "Why . . . must it be necessary for the approximate number of 700,000 Jews who are at present in Palestine to have a State of their own, when there are far larger numbers of Jews in other parts of the world without any question of establishing separate states?" As a solution, Azzam offered "a sort of Vatican state" status to Jews in Palestine.

Bernadotte wasted no time in exerting pressure on the wan Azzam to agree to the cease-fire. "Whichever side rejects it"— the mediator's threat was thinly veiled—"would assume a terrible responsibility for the future. Personally," Bernadotte pushed on, "I am not bound by the UN resolution on partition. I have a free hand as far as putting forward new proposals for the future of Palestine." Indeed, so relieved was Secretary-General Lie to have this problem out of his hands, he had not disabused Bernadotte of his idea that he had a "free hand" in Palestine.

Having been briefed on the actual battlefield strength of the two sides, Bernadotte knew Azzam was deluding himself if he truly believed, as he claimed, that the Arabs were about to overwhelm the Jewish defense. But in Azzam Pasha, Bernadotte thought he had found a man who feared God as much as he himself did. "We are all members of the same religion," Azzam Pasha told the Swede, "with the same origins and the same high ideals."

"I left this interesting man," Bernadotte recounted, "firstly hoping that I should soon see him again, secondly with a feeling that I had in him a friend who would help me in every way in my difficult task." But Azzam's silken manners were camouflage. While reasonable and courtly with foreign dignitaries such as Folke Bernadotte, in public Azzam and his fellow Arab leaders turned into fiery hawkers of hate.

Bernadotte, as guileless as Azzam Pasha was cunning, did not have a sharp nose for deception in others. Knowing next to nothing about the culture and mentality that spawned this "interesting man," he could not calibrate the depth of the Arab pol-

icy of "nonknowledge" of Israel. For in 1948 the Arabs had determined that by building a psychological wall around the new
state, by prohibiting the word "Israel" itself from being spoken,
Israel would simply be isolated and fade away.

It would have been useful for the mediator to have been ap-
prised of Azzam Pasha's stern warning to Abba Eban, delivered
over cups of tea at the Savoy Hotel, regarding the inevitability of
war. Shame comes not in war, or even in losing a war, Azzam
had told Eban, shame is in accepting an "unwanted situation"
without war.

Four Royal Air Force Tempest fighters escorted the mediator's
plane from Egyptian airspace to the ancient Mediterranean port
of Haifa, Folke Bernadotte's first stop in Israel. The count spent
the several-hours-long drive to Tel Aviv under heavy Haganah
military escort, transfixed by the unfolding landscape. "No incidents occurred during the car journey," he wrote, "but it was interesting all the same in that it provided us with a clear picture of
the amazing work the Jews had done in cultivating this desert-
like countryside. From the car we were able to follow the work
of the population out on the land, and observe the very sharp
lines of demarcation between the desert on the one hand and the
fertile gardens and orange-groves on the other."

CHAPTER THIRTEEN

"STATESMANSHIP
AT ITS BEST"

RECALLING THE FIRST TIME BERNADOTTE ARRIVED IN ISRAEL, Walter Eytan, director general of the embryonic Israeli Foreign Ministry, said: "I remember standing on the roof of the Jewish Agency Building. The first sight we caught was of this small, very white plane, against a deep blue sky. I felt something akin to salvation at the sight of this white streak descending towards us. Here was the United Nations coming to help settle the crisis. We had been besieged for so many weeks. There was no food, barely any water, but finally the world had taken notice of us. Something was finally happening."

Young men and women in improvised uniforms of khaki shorts and unisex shirts manned the roadblock surrounding Ben-Gurion's Tel Aviv headquarters. The Red House, an unadorned, faded pink stucco house on the Tel Aviv seafront at 44 Hayarkon Street, was a world away from the musty Royal Palace, weighed down by centuries of dust and tradition, which Bernadotte had left behind in Cairo that morning, May 31. Here everything was rough and new and improvised, a defiant challenge to an inhospitable land and climate. Sunburned youngsters flanked sandbags, their Sten guns slung casually on their shoulders. A short, stocky man with wide Slavic features framed by twin tufts of flaring white hair, David Ben-Gurion had no patience with ceremony. The prime minister greeted the mediator with a few plain words before getting down to business.

Despite the fact that the UN truce resolution was, in the words of one Israeli, "manna from heaven," three days after the May 28 surrender of Jews in the Old City of Jerusalem to the Arab Legion, Ben-Gurion struck a tough, combative tone with Bernadotte during their first meeting. The Jews know, Ben-Gurion asserted, that the British want King Abdullah, their puppet monarch, to reign over Jerusalem and the whole Arab world. His foreign minister, Moshe Shertok, a wan-looking man with a deeply furrowed brow and a small mustache, interrupted with a rumor he had heard that a white horse was standing by, waiting for Abdullah to mount and ride it victoriously into Jerusalem! The count, when he finally had a chance to speak, tried in vain to assure the agitated prime minister that UN observers would be dispatched to Jerusalem to report any sign of Arab Legion movement to the Security Council. Yes, but could the count guarantee the flow of supplies to Jerusalem during the truce? the Jewish leaders demanded. He would, Bernadotte assured them, at the same time threatening UN sanctions against Israel if the conditions of the truce banning arms and military men were broken. You are treating both sides the same way, Ben-Gurion scolded the mediator, when it is the Arabs who are the aggressors here.

Bernadotte, whose first task was to stop the fighting and get the combatants to agree to the Security Council's cease-fire resolution, found it a hard-edged first meeting. The count had never been spoken to in this brusque, unceremonious fashion. "I tried to reason with the Prime Minister [Ben Gurion]," Bernadotte notes plaintively in his memoirs. "[He] showed a very bitter spirit. . . ." Bunche called the meeting "unpleasant" and claimed there was too much tension in the air for anything constructive to happen. It is clear from Ben Gurion's own noncommittal diary entry—"I was visited at 6 P.M. by Count Folke Bernadotte accompanied by Dr. Ralph Bunche. If an armistice is arranged, peace talks will be possible. . . ."—that no particular current of good feeling was produced between the two men.

Lacking an emotional or historic connection to the region, the mediator could not appreciate that keeping Israel's doors open to Jews from anywhere on earth, whether they were of military age (as proscribed by the UN Security Council cease-fire resolution on the table, but not yet agreed to by the parties) or not, was at the very heart of the new state's reason for existence.

Meeting Ben-Gurion had given Bernadotte his first taste of the deep well of suspicion toward the outside world that unified Israelis during those precarious early days. But why he, who considered himself a humanitarian first of all, would arouse such feelings, this the count could not understand.

The travel-weary Bernadotte's spirits picked up somewhat later that evening upon entering Ohel Shem Auditorium to hear the Tel Aviv Philharmonic, conducted by Solomon Eissler. "The Jewish audience seemed gratified by my presence," he noted, referring to the spontaneous standing ovation he was accorded.

The next day, again confirming Israeli mistrust of UN mediation, Prime Minister Ben-Gurion wrote in his diary, "There was a cabinet meeting at my office at 11 o'clock. At that very moment it was hit by bombs and machine-gun fire from Arab planes. Apparently, a spy in Bernadotte's party had informed the Arabs of the location of my office." The Israeli press, mirroring this innate suspicion, incorrectly reported that "again the truce has failed," even before the time for the truce to begin had been set.

Bernadotte (though he was called Folke by his own team, Ben-Gurion's circle referred to him as "Ha Rozen," or "the count") was up at five-thirty the next morning strolling the seafront of his hotel, the Gat Rimon. He was joined by John Reedman, a young economist, who, though English-born (Bernadotte did not want any British subjects on his staff, given the Israelis' strong feelings on the subject), held a South African passport and had been dispatched by Trygve Lie to assist in the eventual truce supervision. Reedman was astonished at how little sleep the Swede seemed to need, and how vigorously he attacked his mission.

"Though he had no great knowledge of the area," Reedman recalled, "this was an advantage. He had no preconceptions. His interest was humane, but he also had a good mind. My impression of him was that he was his own man in many ways, but he kept very firmly to the notion that he wasn't there to tell the parties to the dispute what to do, but to point out how they could improve on the situation and get together. He never tried to impose a solution on them. . . . He did not have a domineering personality, but, after all, he was the king's nephew, everyone knew his background. He was absolutely at home in meeting anyone in government. He was unselfconscious with heads of state. Bernadotte met everyone on equal terms. He had perfect manners and could deal as well with King Abdullah as with Moshe Shertok."

Bernadotte already had his bags packed to go to Amman, though Reedman stayed on in Tel Aviv, a city he describes as "a growing, pulsing place, in full construction and in very sharp contrast to Arab Jaffa, just next door, which was destroyed. Tel Aviv was quite a pleasant place to be in those days."

A message from King Abdullah caught up to Bernadotte in flight to Amman. The Transjordanians asked him to delay his visit to Amman, as the Arab League delegates had gathered there to discuss the Security Council truce proposal. "I could not accept this," Bernadotte noted. "I wished particularly to get in touch with the Arab leaders before they had definitely decided their attitude on the truce question." So he and Bunche proceeded, unbidden, to Amman, confirming Reedman's point that Bernadotte was unintimidated by royalty or anyone else.

"We flew over well-known tracts, over some of the most famous places in Bible history," Bernadotte noted, transported for the first time by the region's biblical, rather than political, associations, "over the town of Nazareth and the Lake of Gennesareth and the place where Jesus preached the Sermon on the Mount—scenes which I saw now for the first time, from a height of 4,000 feet."

Upon landing, Bernadotte's party was immediately reminded of the obvious fact that Transjordan was very much London's creature, a linchpin of the Empire's regional policy. "The strategic importance of Transjordan lies in its central position in relation to the Middle East area as a whole"—a Foreign Office memo bluntly stated the role the little kingdom played for the British Empire in the Middle East—"and in the fact that communications between the oil-producing areas of Iraq and Persia and our main base and supply areas in Palestine and Egypt traverse the country."

Brigadier General Norman Lash, deputy commander of Transjordan's celebrated Arab Legion, was first to greet the mediator with a crisp salute. "I'm sorry to see, sir," Lash remarked to Bernadotte, pointing to the mediator's blue and white United Nations armband, "that you are wearing an arm band in the Israeli colors." "Ah," the mediator replied, growing aware of the region's acute sensibilities, "but I do not wear my heart on my sleeve. My heart is of a strictly neutral tint."

Amman was a modest little capital in those days, snuggled in the hills of Moab. The palace of King Abdullah ibn Hussein stood on a ridge outside the town, guarded by Arab Legionnaires in well-pressed khakis wearing the traditional red and white Arab kaffiyeh. The seventy-year-old king, son of the grand sherif of Mecca, direct descendant of the Prophet, immaculate in his black robes and snow-white turban, greeted the mediator whose visit he had tried to discourage. "I tried to express myself in the elaborate and somewhat ceremonial style that is so characteristic of the East," Bernadotte noted in his memoirs. Abdullah was lavish in his courtesy and flattery of the Swedish count. "Like myself you are of royal blood and you must know what it means to govern a kingdom." The king assured him, "I am always at your disposal as your counsellor, if you wish to talk things over with me. . . . I will call you brother."

Sir Alec Kirkbride, London's minister in Amman, doubling as Abdullah's chief British advisor, entertained Bernadotte and Bunche at lunch. A beefy, affable Scot, Kirkbride spun tales of his time in the desert with the Bedouins under Lawrence of Arabia's command. Bernadotte was presented to yet another legendary British Arabist, Sir John Bagot Glubb, one of the generation of Englishmen who so relished the adventure provided by imperial service in the Middle East, he had made his life there. After many years of service in the region, Glubb grew to genuinely admire the Bedouin Arabs he tried to discipline into the British-style soldiers of the Arab Legion, London's surrogate fighting force in Transjordan. Glubb Pasha, as he was affectionately known, had been commander of the Arab Legion since 1939. With his weak chin, unimposing physique, and shy smile, Glubb was every inch the antihero. He had by now assumed many of the airs and mannerisms of the desert tribesmen he had forged into the Arab world's most feared army. "If God wills it!" peppered Glubb's speech and sounded an odd note coming from a man who was the image of an English county clerk.

The afternoon, spent in the company of these breezy, expansive Englishmen with their tales of swashbuckling in the colonial service, enthralled Bernadotte, who seemed to savor their tweedy charm. It would only gradually become clear to the mediator that, though a full-fledged member of the Arab League that had declared war on Israel, Transjordan was motivated by a quite separate agenda of its own. The king had for some months been conducting secret negotiations with Israeli officials on the subject of his own ambitions to control Arab Palestine. Then, as now, however, the tiny, meagerly endowed nation lived at the sufferance of vastly more powerful and better-endowed neighbors and a distant mentor, Britain. Abdullah performed a precarious high-wire act trying to maintain the goodwill of his "fraternal" Arab nations, all the while searching for some sort of modus operandi with Israel. The king's entourage of moderate (certainly by Arab standards) Englishmen—Glubb, Lash, and Kirkbride—considered the fledgling State of Israel a potentially formidable foe, almost from the day of her birth, and thus cautioned Abdullah to exercise restraint in the conflict.

On May 27, a new agreement between Washington and London further dampened whatever appetite King Abdullah's British advisors had for war against Israel. This accord cut off British shipments of arms and military aid to Transjordan and all other Arab countries, and ordered the withdrawal of British personnel from the Arab Legion. Glubb Pasha and Brigadier General Lash escaped this new government regulation, however, as they had officially resigned from the colonial service and signed on as mercenaries of the Hashemite Kingdom.

On the subject of the Arabs' (in this case meaning Abdullah's) historic claim over Jerusalem, Islam's third-holiest city, however, the king, as Bernadotte would soon discover, was as unrelenting as the most zealous of Lehi's rank and file.

Shortly after lunch, Bernadotte received word that the Arab League had decided to accept the truce, but had mistakenly sent its reply to Lake Success rather than to the mediator. Bernadotte immediately scribbled a cable to Secretary-General Lie, asking for authorization to set the actual date and time the truce would start, as well as its specific terms. He eventually received a positive reply, but global communications were at a primitive stage in 1948. During the several days that Ben-Gurion did not hear from the mediator regarding the truce deadline, the Israelis' deep-seated suspicion of both the Security Council and the Swede was fueled by rumors of the latter's pro-Arab tendencies. Then, as now, rumor, the staff of Middle Eastern life, took no time at all to fly from capital to capital.

"Bernadotte represented everything the Israelis were not," recalled Bunche's Haifa-based assistant, William Mashler. "He was regal, he had wealth, and he had security. And he was a Swede, which means he was not particularly warm. He was slightly detached, not like an American who tries to fit into every situation. The Israelis clearly liked Bunche, in part, I suppose, because he was a black American who didn't have any airs about him. Bunche liked to talk about baseball; wherever we went, he always got the score. Bunche was an egalitarian. Bernadotte was an aristocrat. How many aristocrats are there in Israel?"

During the following week, with Cairo, the region's chief urban center, as his base, the mediator embarked on a frenzied prototype of the Middle East shuttle, trying to nail down the terms of the truce. This frenetic pace was maintained without the benefit of modern technology to smooth the way, with at times near-fatal results. "We would send a message by commercial cable," Bunche noted, "stating for example that we would arrive at Mafrak, Amman, the Transjordanian airfield, at a certain hour. We would come down and . . . would be immediately surrounded by officers, and they would assure us that we were very lucky indeed, for they had their anti-aircraft guns trained on us and were just about to pull the string when they caught sight of the United Nations' letters painted on the white plane, and that if it had been a little cloudy and they had not seen it, we would have been dead ducks. We told them, 'But we informed you that we were coming.' They replied, 'We never received the cable.' Some hours later our cable would arrive."

Between June 3 and 7, Bernadotte zigzagged relentlessly from Cairo, to Amman, Haifa, and Beirut. Bunche noted in his journal on a typical day, "8 AM cable from headquarters, swing into action, rouse Doreen [Daughton, his secretary] . . . sent copies around, had conference with Count and we decided to confer with Nokrashy Pasha. From Cairo to Amman . . . tea with Glubb Pasha . . . saw the Foreign Minister . . . to Haifa saw Shertok in the Zion Hotel, then Beirut." On the evening of June 6 in Haifa, Bernadotte's physician, Dr. Ulf Nordwall, found him so exhausted he feared Bernadotte might have to be hospitalized.

The *hamsin*, the hot, dry desert wind, was blowing, and both Bernadotte's and Bunche's nerves were frayed. "Both sides love to haggle and bargain," Glubb told Bunche during one of their meetings in Amman; "they should be told to take it or leave it." Bunche noted, however, that the Arabs were cordial to

Bernadotte, so he preferred conferring with them rather than with the blunt-spoken Jews. About the Arab tendency to hype nonexistent battlefield successes against the Jews, Bunche commented, "These guys seem to believe their phony generals, or are bluffing." For while one Egyptian armored column had bogged down in the Negev, another reached the southern gateway to Jerusalem at Ramat Rachel without receiving desperately needed support from Abdullah's Arab Legion, which was almost within touching range of the Egyptians. Other Egyptian troops were within artillery range of Tel Aviv, encamped near the suburbs of Jerusalem by June 11.

Food and water, which the Israeli government was unable to provide for 100,000 Jews held hostage by Arab forces in Jerusalem, as well as Jewish insistence on the free flow of Jewish immigration to the new country, were Bernadotte's two big hurdles on the road to nailing down the truce. On the question of food and water, the king of Transjordan revealed that under his ceremonial robes beat a steely heart. Not one drop of water or a single pound of provisions would he permit to be brought into Jerusalem for Arab or Jew during the truce. "The Arabs living in Jerusalem and in Jaffa," the king thundered at the mediator, "are not worthy of remaining alive, as they have not fulfilled the expectations that the Arab peoples rightfully are holding with regard to them."

Israel, established to provide unhampered safe haven to Jews around the world, refused to relinquish this right even during the truce. The immigration issue made Folke Bernadotte realize how little support or even compassion he could expect from the organization he represented in the region. During the first two weeks in June, Bunche kept working the precarious Cairo phones, trying to get the Secretariat to give the mediator some guidance on just what the Great Powers had in mind on the subject of Jewish immigration to Israel during the truce. Bernadotte, as Bunche remembered, wanted assurances that he would not be accused of preempting the Security Council's functions if he made his own interpretations of the Council resolution. But the mediator soon discovered how reluctant the Secretariat was to take a strong position on anything.

"They had explained there," Bernadotte noted, "that it might lead to unfortunate consequences if the Security Council sat down and gave a definite reply to my questions. It might even mean that the whole question of a truce might be torn up afresh. It would be better, they maintained, that I should be left free to make up my own mind on the question and try to find a formula which, according to what my own conscience told me, was in accordance with the spirit of the resolution." On this, possibly the most sensitive of all issues for the new State of Israel, the message delivered to Bernadotte by a phone call from the secretary-general's office was: You are on your own.

This was Bernadotte's first real test, one that would strain the remainder of his mediation. The Arab leaders were pressing hard to ban all immigration during the truce. The president of the Security Council, who happened to be a Syrian, Faris el-Khouri, wired Bernadotte on June 5, saying that the intent of the UN resolution was that "no military advantage shall accrue to either side as a result of the . . . truce."

When Bernadotte read this to Israeli Foreign Minister Shertok at their meeting on June 9 in Haifa, "His reaction was immediate and violent," Bernadotte noted. "Barely had I finished my reading before he interjected in a very irritated tone that as the president of the Security Council for the month of June was a Syrian, and the telegram was consequently signed by a national of a country which was at war with the State of Israel, it was impossible for him to accept his ruling."

"In the end," Bernadotte admitted for the first time, "I lost patience." The mediator threatened to make Shertok's objections public, which he said clearly showed Israel's lack of faith in the UN and in Bernadotte as mediator. Shertok seemed to realize he had taken the wrong approach with the mediator. The normally soft-spoken, cerebral foreign minister had been advised by a member of the Stockholm Jewish Council that Bernadotte responded well to a severe, almost patronizing tone.

Now Shertok backed off and promised to present Bernadotte's proposals for "controlled" immigration during the truce, and for the holding of immigrant men of military age in special UN-controlled camps for its duration, to his government. Shertok knew that Israel needed the truce "like air for breathing" and that the mediator's terms were "not disastrous." Starvation threatened the Jews of Jerusalem, and the Israeli Defense Forces were on the verge of exhaustion. Though Bernadotte noted, "We parted the best of friends," the game of high-stakes bluff marked both men. "The Israeli view of Bernadotte," Reedman asserted, "began to change during these discussions with Shertok. They were very bitter because they didn't seem to be getting what they wanted. Shertok was an interesting man, with the kind of mind which makes a good foreign secretary: very subtle. But he would talk very bitterly, in language that went way beyond the language of diplomacy, with Bernadotte."

Bernadotte was slowly learning one of the hard truths of his mission. The hothouse of United Nations politics and the distance separating him from New York meant his would be a lonely effort. "In Lake Success they evidently could not, or would not, understand that the difference between the views of the two parties was in fact enormous," he noted with typical understatement.

June 9 began, in Bunche's words, "in watchful waiting" to hear if all parties would accept Bernadotte's proposals for the truce, which included a ban on the entry of men bearing arms or belonging to a military organization, and precluded any change in the military status quo existing before the truce. Waiting was one of the things the count enjoyed least of all.

To kill time, Bernadotte had arranged for a private audience with Egyptian King Farouk. A pudgy, prematurely balding figure, the sybaritic king told the Swede that his uncle, King Gustav, was regarded in Egypt as strongly pro-Zionist. Bernadotte agreed that King Gustav had saved Jews from Hitler, adding, "I myself had been in charge of this work," which resulted in the rescue of 20,000 people. Was it not true, Farouk pressed, that the Bernadotte family was part Jewish? In one report of this conversation, Bernadotte is quoted as having answered, "I regret that is not the case"; however, no full transcript survives this interview. Farouk tried to draw Bernadotte out on King Abdullah's attitude toward the truce, and cautioned the mediator against relying on his fellow Arab monarch's word on anything. It was an instructive session for Bernadotte. The rotund young Farouk had lifted the filmy veil of the "United Arab Front" to reveal a sham.

At noon on June 9, another sweltering day in Cairo, Count Bernadotte received the word he had been impatiently awaiting. The governments of Egypt, Lebanon, Syria, and Saudi Arabia accepted without conditions the four-week truce in Palestine, starting at 6 A.M. on June 11. Two hours later, Transjordan acquiesced. At two-forty the Israelis sent their reply. They, too, accepted the count's terms for a truce, which included not only a ban on "all acts of armed force in Palestine for a period of four weeks," but a promise of "relief to populations of both sides in municipal areas which have suffered severely from the conflicts, as in Jerusalem and Jaffa . . . administered by the International Red Cross . . . to ensure that reserve stocks of essential supplies shall not be substantially greater or less at the end of the truce than they are at the beginning." For Israelis, the most sensitive clause of the truce proposal was that "during the first week following the truce, in consideration of the time required for setting up the controls essential to effective application of the resolution, *the Mediator shall exercise his discretion as regards the entry of any immigrant irrespective of age or sex.* (Italics added.) It was the same issue that not long before had torpedoed British rule over Palestine: a check, however limited, on the free flow of immigrants, the lifeblood of the new state.

"The Count hugged me," Bunche noted in his diary, adding, "He was the only one who could have done it." Later, when he was already a Nobel Peace Prize–winning negotiator, Bunche would call this truce the result of "the most intensive diplomatic negotiation that has ever been undertaken in the history of diplomacy." Bernadotte gave all credit for the truce to God. It was, he noted, a moment of "intense joy and deep gratitude to God."

In two weeks, he had achieved what both the British and, until now, the United Nations had failed to do. By dint of relentless persuasion and the implicit intimidation of his title and position, he had won a truce between the two belligerents. He still had no mechanism for enforcing the truce, however. The Security Council had promised him sixty-eight observers; so far, however, only five Swedish colonels had arrived in Palestine.

In Washington, Secretary of State Marshall dispatched a message to Cairo: "Tell Bernadotte," the American embassy was instructed, "his work is statesmanship at its best." At Lake Success, the French delegate, Alexandre Parodi, told reporters not to bother the Security Council with questions regarding Palestine. "The matter is entirely in the hands of Bernadotte."

Both sides needed the truce "like air for breathing," in Shertok's words. Neither side was sufficiently humbled, however, to accept a negotiated, rather than a battlefield, solution to the future as anything more than a temporary, tactical device. John Reedman, who had served in the League of Nations and knew something about the difference between a truce and peace, was left uneasy. "This job was beyond anybody's capacity at that particular time. From the point of view of a real settlement, the truce came too soon. Neither side was ready to think beyond their battlefield goals. It would have been better to let the fighting go on a bit longer."

Not all concerned parties were jubilant on that early summer day in Palestine. One of Lehi's three-man leadership, Dr. Israel Eldad, issued the following statement on June 9: "The Fighters for Freedom of Israel [Lehi] will not regard itself as bound by any cease-fire order anywhere, anyplace, anytime. . . . Any military delegation of outsiders . . . who come to Palestine to implement cease-fire orders will be regarded [by Lehi] as enemy invaders and treated as such."

CHAPTER FOURTEEN

A PHONY TRUCE

THE NOTION OF PUTTING JEWISH IMMIGRANTS OF MILITARY AGE into special camps under the mediator's supervision, referred to even by Ben-Gurion as "Bernadotte's Camps," was the part of the truce agreement that most rankled the Sternists. They were equally infuriated that their own leaders, Ben-Gurion and Shertok, would agree to such a condition. "These were British-built camps, and they put Jewish immigrants in these concentration camps," Baruch Nadel insists. "Bernadotte told them to do it and they did it. And one of the immigrants shouted (I read this in the Labor Party newspaper), 'I've been freed from a Nazi concentration camp, now in my own country you put me in a camp!'"

Nadel and others in the underground, demonized and isolated by their own countrymen, were ignorant of Ben-Gurion's own revulsion toward Bernadotte's proposals curbing arms and immigration. Though he badly wanted a break in the fighting, Israel's first prime minister was not about to bend on what he regarded as the most fundamental tenet of the new country's sovereignty: the right to build an army. Chronically and universally suspicious, the Sternists had no way of gauging Ben-Gurion's own defiance of the mediator. "The Arabs have nothing to lose by not receiving arms for four weeks," Ben-Gurion told his cabinet on June 4, striking a tone similar to Lehi's, ". . . they have been receiving them for years. For us the four weeks can be decisive. . . . We cannot be treated in the same way as the Arab states. They already have weapons of all kinds. We do not. There is another, very basic question involved: national sovereignty. . . . The Arabs don't need people from the outside, though no one will prevent a thirty-year-old Englishman from entering Lebanon even if he happens to be a military officer who has come to teach the local people how to make dynamite. . . . I am not concerned with the political consequences of our refusal to accept the Bernadotte proposals. The Security Council is not a homogeneous body; every member has his own policies. The military consequences may be more serious. . . . I suggest that we reject the Bernadotte proposals. There are two elements basic to our existence, immigration and independence. We must determine what happens in our own country."

The prime minister's closing comments to his cabinet would have astonished Shamir, Eldad, and Yalin-Mor. "Why does Bernadotte think we have to trust him?" Ben-Gurion demanded to know. "Did we choose him? And why is he preparing his final draft [of the truce proposal] in Egypt?" However, with its troops exhausted, their arms and ammunition depleted by the first wave of fighting, and to appease world opinion, the cabinet accepted Bernadotte's conditions. But Prime Minister David Ben-Gurion did not for a moment intend to adhere to those restrictions that proclaimed "no military advantage [was to] accrue to either side" while the truce was in effect.

Oblivious to these complex undercurrents, Bernadotte savored the apparent success of the truce. With only a handful of observers in UN jeeps bumping along Palestine's rutted roads to enforce the cease-fire, both sides seemed relieved to have this imposed break from the exhausting business of trying to wipe each other out. In reality, the entire grandiose-sounding United Nations Truce Supervision Organization (UNTSO) was a jerry-built business with an ungainly task. The truce applied not only to Palestine, but to seven Arab states as well. Shipment of war matériel as well as the influx of immigrants had to be checked and controlled. Airfields, ports, military lines were all part of the mediator's responsibility. A tiny staff of Secretariat employees was improvised to fulfill these far-flung tasks. Bunche remembered Paul Cremona, a thin wisp of a man from the Secretariat, forced to sit on top of the British supply dump at Suez, with only his UN armband as defense against Egyptians eager to grab abandoned British weaponry.

More observers from New York, Stockholm, Paris, and Brussels began to trickle into their headquarters in Haifa on June 11, wearing their khakis and light blue UN berets for the first time.

They improvised every step of the way. "Things that worked, we institutionalized," Mashler remembered. "We had nothing to draw on, and faced a lot of sticky incidents. We lived in miserable conditions, just about any place, any village the Israelis would billet us. We commuted from villages to the front." With a per diem of fifteen dollars, the observers had neither much money nor any arms. The New York Police Department had donated a crate of fifty pistols to the observers, but Bernadotte had decreed, "No arms." "I told the guys to get rid of the guns," Mashler says, "or you're dead. Before the truce, both sides had been shooting as if it were the Wild West. You give a guy a pistol with six slugs and you get him in a prone position very fast against a man with a submachine gun. Besides, we were there to carry the UN banner. We were observers, not a peacekeeping force."

John Reedman, an economist with no military experience, recalled the first truce violation. "Foreign Minister Shertok called me and told me in a very agitated way, 'The Arabs are shooting.' I decided I'd better go myself and have a look. He gave me a car and a driver, a Jew who spoke Arabic and had lived in the area in question since childhood. We tore off with a white flag flying. When we got near this village, I jumped out of the car and started walking. From behind a tree an Arab captain spotted me. He spoke a few words of English. They stopped shooting when I got there. It was an Arab Legion stronghold. I asked to see the man in charge, a colonel. I pointed out to him that he was jeopardizing the truce which his government had accepted. Do you really think it's worthwhile, I asked him, to fight over these few yards between you? In a very excited voice, the colonel said, 'Every inch matters!' And that's how both sides felt—they were talking about inches."

Thus, the truce in no way tempered either side's ardent wish to gain ground, even in inches. "The Security Council had laid down the fatuous provision that no military advantage should be gained by either side," Abba Eban noted. "Why two belligerents should accept a truce unless each hopes to improve its position seems incomprehensible to ordinary minds."

On June 13, Bernadotte had abandoned the heat and frenzy of Shepheard's Hotel in Cairo for the serenity of the Greek island of Rhodes in the Aegean Sea (a three-and-a-half-hour flight from Palestine), which he chose as his headquarters during the mediation. Rhodes was removed from the tumult of the war zone and the nervous truce that held by a thread. Amid the tatty grandeur of the beachfront Hôtel des Roses, with Bunche beside him, Bernadotte began drafting what he hoped would be a "just solution" to the long-term problem of Palestine.

Bunche himself was overwhelmed with the administrative burden of running this multinational effort from his hotel room. Not an early riser by nature, particularly as he regularly worked into the early-morning hours, Bunche often appeared in a pink nightshirt for his daily morning meeting with the count on Barbro Wessel's balcony. They had to scrounge for the most basic supplies and pleaded with New York to send everything from secretarial help to bookkeepers and maintenance men. "Don't send me any social butterflies," Bunche warned Andrew Cordier of the Secretariat over the phone. "I want hardworking secretaries of the good old-fashioned type."

Even the shipment of UN flags and armbands sent by New York posed a problem. The UN flag looked too much like Israel's blue and white banner, and thus offered little protection for the observers in Arab areas. Cordier suggested that they paint huge black UN initials on the cars they used in Arab territory. And this they proceeded to do, setting another precedent. UN observers' vehicles have been emblazoned with these outsized initials ever since. By late June, the mediator realized his Red Cross uniform was inappropriate for his present job. "I considered the humanitarian part of my task finished now, for the time being at any rate. The negotiations had reached a more pronouncedly political stage." He switched to the plain khaki shorts and open-neck shirt that became his Middle East field uniform.

Not until July 22 were the first forty-four observers in place, though by late August their number had more than doubled. The US, Belgium, and France each supplied thirty-one officers from their armed forces. Five Swedish colonels acted as Bernadotte's personal representatives. Bernadotte appointed one of them, Colonel Torde Bond, as his chief of staff for the truce supervision. On a call to New York, William Stoneman, a journalist sent to Palestine by Secretary-General Lie to act as the UN's press liaison, commented to Andrew Cordier, "The Swedes strike me as being first class, tell that to your friend Mr. Lie. Bernadotte is punctual, treats everybody with great consideration and earns the respect of the local yokels by conducting himself like a gentleman. It's a pleasure to work with him."

Secretary Lie recruited and dispatched to Palestine fifty-one extra guards from his Secretariat. The UN had no transportation and communications equipment of its own and had to borrow it from American and British stores. It all took time. The truce supervision was also hampered by the fact that none of the UN observers spoke Hebrew. Arthur Koestler, in Palestine at the time, recounts the tragicomic scene of one such inexperienced American truce observer assembling six Jewish and six Arab officers on a bridge in the Galilee and asking them in pidgin English, "Who shoot after truce?—who break truce?—who shoot, say—eh?" Of course, both groups started yelling at the top of their lungs, each in his own language, and charging the other side with the violation. As Koestler noted, if they had not been covered by machine guns from the other side, the shouting would have been accompanied by shooting.

As time passed, the violations of the shaky truce only increased in frequency and audacity. The Israelis claimed that Jews couldn't get to the holy places in the Old City of Jerusalem and, more seriously, that the Arabs were blocking Jerusalem's water supply. Bernadotte protested to the Arabs, but this, too, took time to rectify. The Israelis refused Bernadotte permission to control the influx of men of military age and war matériel landing on Israeli airfields. The Egyptians would not permit the UN to control their airports. On June 21, in the most serious truce violation, an Irgun ship named the *Altalena,* Jabotinsky's nom de plume, laden with arms and men, landed close to Tel Aviv. Bernadotte's observers had advance warning of the ship's departure from the French harbor of Port le Bouc, near Marseille.

Ben-Gurion, though himself quietly defying the provisions of the truce regarding a ban on arms and men of military age, refused to let the underground challenge his authority by bringing in its own arms and men. Haganah troops were arrayed for battle when the *Altalena* docked. From his Palmach unit headquarters close by at Tel Aviv's Ritz Hotel, commando Chaim Hefer watched the *Altalena* drop anchor. "Somebody fired a shot. I don't know which side it came from, but suddenly bullets were whizzing everywhere. I picked up a grenade, threw it in the direction of the *Altalena* and ducked. The whole vessel erupted in flames. I knew a lot of Jews were on board and it was an awful feeling." Seventy Irgun recruits and twelve crew members burned to death on board the *Altalena*. But Ben-Gurion had asserted his authority over the underground and dealt a near-fatal blow to its commander, Menachem Begin. But the incident made plain the dangerous fault line separating the left and the right of the Israeli political landscape.

The mediator's widow recalled that Bernadotte's moods rose and fell with these unfolding events. Both he and Bunche missed their families painfully, though Bernadotte never saw his position as one with a deadline. "There was never a question of Folke tiring of the Palestine problem," Estelle Bernadotte insisted. "There was a job to be done, and when the first cease-fire was achieved, finding a satisfactory solution was imperative. . . . Folke's sole preconception was that the job had to get done." During one of his calls to New York, Bunche reminded Cordier that he had been promised only a short stay in the field, perhaps ten days or two weeks, and then back to Lake Success. Cordier told Bunche that the high quality of his work made replacing him difficult. "I'll soon fix that," Bunche promised. On another call to the home office during the truce, Secretary-General Lie grabbed the phone from Cordier to tell Bunche how much he appreciated the work he and Bernadotte were doing. "Tell Bernadotte I am very pleased with his work and would have followed the same course had I been in his shoes."

After a few days at the Hôtel des Roses, both men felt restored. The waves lapped gently a few yards from the hotel, and the fish at dinner was fresh. On the night of June 13, both men had their first solid night's sleep since arriving in Rhodes. Bernadotte even insisted on some sightseeing during the day, traipsing around the Crusader Palace of the Knights of St. John. Despite the island's oppressive humidity, however, they worked all afternoon, not even taking time out for a swim. Time was short; the following week they were to resume their airborne mediation. "Rhodes is a beautiful island," Ralph Bunche wrote his wife on June 13, "but the weather is extremely humid—everything is damp, even the paper I'm writing on. The sea breezes keep the temperature down, however. The hotel is very close to the sea and I can look out my window and see the Turkish coast not far away."

While Bernadotte and Bunche had been exploring the ramparts of Rhodes, the Secretariat of Israel's ruling Labor Party met in Tel Aviv and heard Foreign Minister Moshe Shertok announce: "The Count (Ha Rozen) is devoting himself entirely to broad-based policy and is not dealing with the details of the truce, for which he has a Swedish goy who is his Chief of Staff. Under this Swedish goy there are four more Swedish goys, and under these, five American, French and Belgian officers. . . ."

The day before, on June 12, Chaim Weizmann wrote to Shertok and Ben-Gurion from Paris: "I do not know what you foresee at the end of this truce. . . . I understand that the Mediator may press for a revision of frontiers, and for our relinquishment of the Southern Negev, including Akaba. I would not agree to this, certainly not so far as Akaba is concerned. It will be a dagger in our backs if it falls into the others' hands. You remember how we fought for it at Lake Success."

On June 13, the *Sunday Times* of London trumpeted: ". . . that remarkable, energetic and optimistic Swede, Count Folke Bernadotte, will take upon his broad shoulders the Herculean task which has defeated countless negotiators and brought dozens of conferences to abject failure during the past twenty years. What are his chances? The view of British officials in the Middle East is that Count Bernadotte is a tremendous 'go-getter,' who will face the Arab and Jewish representatives with the single advantage that he is the supreme arbiter, that he will have to consult no one, refer nothing back to a Government or even to the United Nations. If he can achieve the modern miracle of obtaining both parties' consent to any plan, then that plan becomes the solution to the Palestine problem. If anyone can achieve that result, it is Bernadotte."

Calling Folke Bernadotte the "supreme arbiter" may have been flattering, but it also fueled both official and underground Israeli paranoia regarding "Ha Rozen's" daunting global influence.

Back in Tel Aviv once more toward the end of June, the mediator found a changed foreign minister. Shertok "was graciousness itself," Bernadotte noted. But as to the war, the Israelis' attitude had hardened since the truce began. "What he said only confirmed the fact that the Jewish attitude was diametrically opposed on practically every point to that of the Arabs. It certainly gave me little hope of ever finding a middle course that would be acceptable to both parties." Despite all external evidence, Bernadotte's natural optimism seemed to nourish itself. "I com-

Theodor Herzl, the revered Hungarian-born founder of modern Zionism, was exposed to virulent anti-Semitism while covering the Dreyfus Affair as a Paris-based newspaper correspondent. Thereafter he abandoned assimilation in favor of Zionist activism. Herzl went on to organize the first Zionist World Congress (1897) and was its president until his death at age 44 in 1904.

Vladimir Jabotinsky (in 1940), the fiery Russian-born writer and political leader, is still among Zionism's most controversial figures. Denounced by some as the prophet of violence, hailed by others as a statesman, he rejected mainstream Zionist gradualism and demanded an independent Jewish state with the historical boundaries of Palestine on both sides of the Jordan River. Jabotinsky was the spiritual guide of Avraham Stern, Yitzhak Shamir, and Menachem Begin.

Theodor Herzl *(center, with beard)* and Chaim Weizmann *(second row, first on left)*, with other delegates to the Fifth Zionist Congress in Basle, 1902. This photograph is the only one known to show the two most revered figures of Zionist history together.

Dr. Chaim Weizmann, the revered and nearly blind first president of Israel, speaks to members of the ruling State Council in Tel Aviv on October 2, 1948. A portrait of Theodore Herzl, the founder of the State, is behind him while David Ben-Gurion, the prime minister, with whom Weizmann did not always agree, is seated in front of him.

The Zionist Congress met in Geneva from August 16-24, 1939, on the eve of the German invasion of Poland and the outbreak of World War II. The Zionist leaders Moshe Shertok, David Ben-Gurion, and Chaim Weizmann *(front row, left to right)* make no attempt to mask the despair they felt at the approaching nightmare. Most of the other delegates to this congress did not survive the war.

In May 1939, in cities all across Palestine, outraged Jewish residents demonstrated against London's new policy, the so-called White Paper, which repudiated partition and the Balfour Declaration's promise of a Jewish National Home.

Walter Edward Guiness, Lord Moyne, a close friend of Winston Churchill, British resident minister in the Middle East, was the highest-ranking Englishman in the region. Moyne was gunned down by two members of the Stern Gang at his home in Cairo on November 11, 1944. The incident gained the underground the notoriety it sought and speeded British withdrawal from Palestine.

Sir Harold MacMichael, high commissioner for Palestine and Transjordan in the early forties, presided over some of Britain's most draconian measures for maintaining law and order in Palestine. MacMichael was demonized by the the Stern Gang, which tried and failed on several occasions to assassinate this dour but well-protected Englishman.

At eighteen months, in 1896 Count Bernadotte was already holding the riding crop that would play an important role in his future. *Below:* Two-year-old Folke Bernadotte *(the first on the left)* is shown with his four older siblings—Elsa, Sophia, Carl, and Maria. Despite being the offspring of a prince (though their mother was a commoner), they were raised in a spartan environment by strict and religious parents.

As a young cavalry officer, Bernadotte *(second row, center)* discovered his great love of both horses and the outdoors. When his unit, deemed an anachronism, was disbanded in the 1920s, the young aristocrat was left without a vocation.

The wedding portrait of Count Folke Bernadotte and Estelle Manville of Pleasantville, New York, on December 1, 1928. The American-born bride, ten years the groom's junior, was heiress to the Manville asbestos fortune.

Folke Bernadotte with his twelve-year-old son Bertil at their home in Stockholm. The Bernadottes lost two of their four children to childhood ailments.

Folke Bernadotte, wearing his Red Cross uniform, oversees his first major humanitarian mission, a German-British prisoner of war exchange at Goteborg, Sweden, in October 1943. The success of this enterprise led to his selection as intermediary between the Swedish Foreign Ministry and Reichsführer Heinrich Himmler in a large-scale rescue of concentration camp inmates in the spring of 1945.

Count Folke Bernadotte *(center, in hat)* speaks to women prisoners at the German concentration camp of Ravensbruck. During March and April 1945, Bernadotte negotiated with Reichsführer Heinrich Himmler for the release of some 14,000 camp inmates. The women with an "X" on their backs have been chosen for release. These negotitations behind Nazi lines, which earned Bernadotte a global reputation as an effective humanitarian, led to his selection as the UN's Middle East mediator.

Folke Bernadotte's rescue of thousands of German-held inmates was achieved with the use of these so-called White Busses, which collected prisoners at German concentration camps and ferried them to freedom in Sweden.

During the siege of Jerusalem in May 1948, Arab artillery pounds the Old City, whose residents, hungry and outnumbered by King Abdullah's Arab Legion, surrendered on May 28.

Above: During a visit to Jerusalem on August 3, 1948, Bernadotte is flanked by Dr. Dov Joseph, the Israeli military governor of Jerusalem *(left)* and Swedish General Aage Lundstrum. *Left:* King Abdullah of Transjordan, the grandfather of the present King Hussein who, in common with Abdullah, walked a tightrope between seeking better relations with Israel while at the same time looking to enlarge his own kingdom without alienating his fellow Arab leaders.

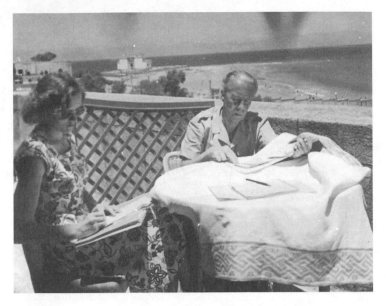

Folke Bernadotte working with his secretary, Barbro Wessel, on the balcony of the Hôtel des Roses in Rhodes in July 1948.

Bernadotte toured the Old City of Jerusalem with the legendary English-born commander of the Arab Legion, Glubb Pasha *(center)*, and General Lundstrum.

Bernadotte addresses the United Nations Security Council on July 13, 1948. The mediator remained composed under a barrage of hostile Russian questioning of his inability to silence the guns of Jerusalem.

The mediator faces Israeli delegate (and future foreign minister) Abba Eban in the delegates' lounge at Lake Success, New York, before the Security Council meeting on the Middle East war on July 13, 1948.

Bernadotte greets Soviet delegate to the UN, Andrei Gromyko, as the mediator prepares to report to the Security Council on his effort to extend the Middle East truce on July 13, 1948. Secretary General Trygve Lie is in the center. Gromyko refused to meet alone with the mediator and showed intense hostility toward him during the Security Council session.

Folke Bernadotte during his shuttle diplomacy of July-August 1948, shown here in Beirut, Lebanon, in front of his white United Nations' plane with *(from left)* Paul Mohne (of the Swedish Red Cross), Ralph Bunche, and *(wearing a fez)* the Lebanese chief of protocol.

As the summer of Bernadotte's mediation progressed, relations with Israeli officials, such as Foreign Minister Moshe Shertok, shown here *(left)* talking with the mediator and Ralph Bunche at his office in the Foreign Ministry in Tel Aviv, became more strained.

Armed and vigilant members of Lehi are shown inside one of their three Jerusalem camps during the summer of 1948. *Left:* Estelle Bernadotte is greeted by her husband as she arrives in Rhodes to spend part of the summer with him at his UN mediation headquarters at the Hôtel des Roses.

Lehi members stand at attention during an inspection of their ranks inside one of their Jerusalem compounds.

Count Folke Bernadotte and Colonel André Sérot lie in state in the YMCA in Jerusalem on September 18, 1948. Bernadotte's Boy Scout hat is atop his UN flag-draped body. His longtime secretary, Barbro Wessel, stands in the back. This is the same room where Bernadotte and Bunche engaged in talks with Israeli authorities during the summer.

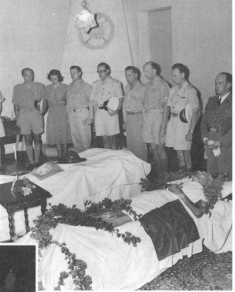

Members of the Security Council, meeting in a special session in Paris on September 18, 1948, rise to mark the assassination of Count Folke Bernadotte with a moment of silence.

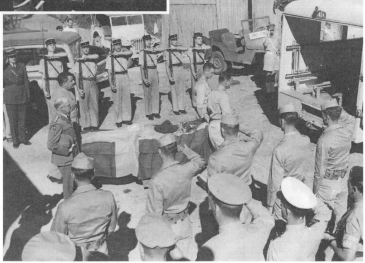

Bernadotte's coffin, watched over by an Israeli honor guard, begins its long journey, with stops in Haifa and Paris, home to Stockholm.

Natan Yalin-Mor, one of the Stern Gang's three commanders, enters a Jewish military court in Acre on December 6, 1948, to face charges relating to the murder of Count Bernadotte. Mattiyahu Shmulovitz, another member of the Stern Gang also arrested in connection with the assassination, follows. The court sentenced them to light prison terms. They were pardoned after two weeks in jail.

Dr. Ralph Bunche, who succeeded Bernadotte as Middle East mediator, addresses the Security Council at the Palais de Chaillot in Paris on October 19, 1948. *From left to right:* Faris El Khouri of Syria, Vasili Tarasenko of the Ukraine, Jakov Malik of the Soviet Union, Sir Alexander Cadogan of Great Britain, Dr. Bunche, Secretary General Trygve Lie, U.S. Ambassador Warren Austin, and A.A. Sobolev of the Soviet Union, serving as assistant secretary general.

This plaque hangs in the lobby of the UN General Assembly building. The only other plaque there commemorates the death of Count Bernadotte's fellow Swede, Secretary General Dag Hammarskjold, killed in a plane crash in 1961 in the Congo (now Zaire) on the same day as Bernadotte's assassination thirteen years earlier.

An official portrait of former Lehi commander-turned-prime minister
Yitzhak Shamir. A portrait of Avraham Stern, the founder of the Stern
Group—or Lehi—is shown behind his faithful disciple Shamir.

David Ben-Gurion strolling with Yehushua Cohen, his friend and bodyguard—and Bernadotte's assassin—in Ein Avdat, Israel.

forted myself, however, with the thought that the representatives of both parties would naturally feel bound to adopt a very firm attitude in these preliminary discussions on the future of Palestine. They would obviously argue that if they showed any sort of willingness to compromise at this stage of the negotiations, it would weaken their positions."

Typically for Bernadotte, his was a rosy interpretation of reality. Walter Eytan, who, as secretary-general of the Israeli Foreign Ministry, participated in these sessions with the mediator, retained a different memory of them. "I remember the scene of our talks, an old German Templar villa. It was summer, so we sat out of doors—Mr. Shertok, myself and this tall, impressive man, Bernadotte. He seemed out of touch in some way. Bernadotte showed absolutely no understanding or familiarity with the existential problem, you know, the real psychological problem that existed and unfortunately still exists between the Arabs and ourselves. He came to this problem the way you might approach any legal or territorial dispute. He was more like a conciliator or a lawyer, somebody who is looking at the situation very factually. Whereas it was such a complicated situation, emotionally and psychologically. We had the feeling that he didn't grasp that aspect of the problem at all."

"Jerusalem," Eytan insists, "was one of the problems then and still is today. The various bodies which had been examining and making recommendations about Palestine realized that Jerusalem occupied a really special place for us. For example, the British Royal Commission, which first recommended the partition of Palestine, had left Jerusalem out of its plans and said that Jerusalem should not be part of the partition because of its special history, but should remain part of the British Mandate. It was an elegant way of perpetuating British rule, but they showed they understood that Jerusalem could not be disposed of by putting it in either the Arab or the Jewish state. The United Nations had reached exactly the same conclusion in 1947."

Bunche noted a visit from Dov Joseph, whom he refers to as the "Jewish mayor of Jerusalem" in his diary. The black American was stung by the Israeli's insensitive comment regarding his trip on the newly built so-called Burma Road from Jerusalem to Tel Aviv. "We had to work like niggers to get through," Joseph commented to Bunche.

"On the flight from Tel Aviv to Rhodes," Bernadotte noted,

"I read an article in an evidently very fanatical Jewish newspaper. The article contained a number of sharp attacks both on the measures I had taken and on me personally. The writer tried to make out that I had forced the truce on the Jews and that I was a lackey of the British and Americans. He took it for granted that I had been in direct contact with both the London and Washington Governments, which shows better than anything else how irresponsible the article was. . . . He accused me of having prohibited the use of a road into Jerusalem built by the Jews during the war, an accusation which once again was completely untrue."

As if to confirm the Swede's disclaimer of Anglo-American influence, on June 18 the American ambassador to London cabled Secretary Marshall: "Bevin said he felt that Foreign Office knows too little of how the mind of Bernadotte is working and suggested that since the Mediator is a hard man to catch, it would be advisable for United States Government and His Majesty's Government to pool their information in this regard." A week later, Secretary Marshall cabled the American ambassador to the UN, Philip Jessup, that "it would be extremely helpful for the Department [of State] to have more explicit knowledge of the details of Bernadotte's plan."

After less than a month spent breathing the rarefied air of Palestine, Bernadotte was beginning, however dimly, to perceive something he had previously banished from his consciousness. "I began to realize what an exposed position I was in. I also began to understand that all my attempts to think and act objectively would inevitably be misunderstood and misinterpreted by irresponsible and fanatical writers." What he did not yet realize was that it was not only "irresponsible and fanatical writers" who would cast his efforts in such a light.

Others with more sensitive antennae registered the danger ahead. The American vice-consul in Jerusalem sent a secret cable to the secretary of state on June 24, 1948: "Reliable Jewish sources indicate that two groups (Irgun and Stern) are augmenting their forces here to serve as threat and reminder to Israeli Government that Irgun and Stern will not tolerate any concession on immigration or the status of Jerusalem. Regarding latter it is possible that Irgun (IZL) and Stern will reject international status for the city believing that Jerusalem should be the capital of Jewish State which they regard as ultimately including all of

Palestine. Dr. Bernard (Dov) Joseph, Chairman of Jewish Jerusalem Emergency Committee has stated . . . his inability to be responsible for the acts of Irgun and Stern. Moreover, as proven in recent failure by Haganah to dislodge Stern members from their enclave in Talbieh quarter of Jerusalem, Haganah is unable to cope with the situation. It is also known that Haganah commander, David Shaltiel, is under severe censure by Stern for what they consider his conciliatory attitude in the present truce negotiations."

There is no record of a copy of this secret telegram's being sent to Folke Bernadotte. However, on May 26, during his very first briefing on Israel, the optimistic Dr. Nahum Goldmann had assured the mediator that "the State of Israel was now in a position to take full and complete responsibility for the acts committed by the Stern Gang and the members of the Irgun."

CHAPTER FIFTEEN

THE END OF AN ILLUSION

As the truce deadline of July 9 neared, Bernadotte, with Bunche's drafting assistance, poured all his energy into his long-term proposal for peace in Palestine. "Two important developments have taken place in Palestine since the adoption by the United Nations General Assembly of the resolution of 29th November 1947," he noted; "the first was the political and military intervention of the Arab States, and the second the complete collapse of the Palestine Arabs. . . . The Palestine Arabs have at present no will of their own. Neither have they ever developed any specifically Palestinian nationalism. The demand for a separate Arab State in Palestine is consequently relatively weak. It would seem as though in existing circumstances most of the Palestinian Arabs would be quite content to be incorporated in Transjordan." Bernadotte's conclusion, astonishing in light of subsequent events, was nonetheless borne out by the fact that no cohesive Palestinian leadership had emerged to fill a void King Abdullah was only too eager to fill himself.

Some of the mediator's early bravado had begun to fade, as he started to grasp just how monumental his task was: ". . . in putting forward any proposal for the solution of the Palestine problem one must bear in mind the aspirations of the Jews, the political difficulties and differences of opinion of the Arab leaders, the strategic interests of Great Britain, the financial commitments of the United States and the Soviet Union [i.e., to the United Nations], the outcome of the war, and finally the authority and prestige of the United Nations."

As the two men worked side by side on Barbro Wessel's sun-drenched balcony, Bunche drafted a message on Bernadotte's behalf which, though in the terse language of international cables, spoke volumes of their sense of isolation from the organization they served: "To the Secretary-General, June 20: It may prove useful," Bunche wrote, "if I elaborate my reasons for suggesting . . . to you that you might make a short visit to this theater. One: this has become a huge elaborate and complex operation growing every day and in view of UN investment and stake, it would be useful for you to see it first hand. Two: in view of the possibility of the extensive use of UN guards it has broad implications for the permanent establishment of UN Guards or a Security Force. Three: the evidence of the fullest UN support of the Mediator's efforts regarding the application of the truce controls and the settlement would be of psychological advantage to the Mediator. Four: first-hand knowledge of the operations here would provide you clearer basis than our cables can give for you to interpret the Mediator's efforts for Security Council.

"The full picture of the operation can be obtained by visits to Rhodes, Mediator's Headquarters, and Haifa, seat of the [truce] Controls.

"If you should decide to come, I would advise publication of intent along these lines in order to avoid any political implications: Purpose of your visit is to meet and consult with the Mediator and observe the Truce controls, operations and role. Signed, Bunche."

The answer to this plea for a show of support came the following day, when the secretary-general cabled Bernadotte: "I have very carefully weighed the suggestions set forth in your cable. . . . I am in full agreement with your strategy in keeping negotiations fluid and in extending the truce. I am sure that there would be certain advantages in exchanging views and in familiarizing myself with your growing operations, but the disadvantages might outweigh the advantages at this time. My visit there might, for example, create the impression that negotiations have come to a head and that a serious crisis was developing. Furthermore, I feel that it is important to remain here for the purpose of keeping all of our lines at headquarters thoroughly coordinated with your plans. Therefore, I feel that it would be better for me not to come at the present time. . . . Signed, Trygve Lie, Secretary-General."

On June 18, Press Liaison Stoneman added his urgent voice
to the same request, bluntly telling Lie that a personal visit
from the secretary-general "might make the difference between
success and failure" of the mission. "Lie was afraid to go,"
recalls Sir Brian Urquhart. "It was a source of great irritation for
Bernadotte and Bunche that he refused to make the trip."

Remote from the world body, the two men labored on a solution to one of the world's most urgent and intractable problems.
It was not only a question of war or peace in Palestine that
weighed heavily upon them. They were also burdened by the full
knowledge that the prestige of the United Nations and its future
as a credible peacekeeper rested on their shoulders.

"The job couldn't have been more important," Brian Urquhart
insisted decades later. Urquhart, then a young British officer,
went on to lead UN peacekeeping operations for the next four
decades. "Bernadotte's was the first bona fide effort of the UN,
just before it got really smashed by the Cold War, to actually
mediate a terribly important problem which nobody, not the
British, not the Americans, could tackle on their own. Bernadotte was the symbol of that effort, and I think he was absolutely
unique in that way." The support Bernadotte received fell tragically short of the mission's importance.

On June 27, Bernadotte's plan was ready. Since he was physically unable to present his proposals to both sides simultaneously, John Reedman handed Foreign Minister Shertok one
copy, while his aides Paul Mohn and Constantine Stavropoulos
presented another to the Egyptian prime minister, who was
also chairman of the Arab League. In cover letters, Bernadotte
explained that his proposal was "only intended as a basis
for further discussion," and pleaded with both sides not to
dismiss it out of hand before they had a chance to discuss their
objections with the mediator. His suggestions, later dubbed "the
First Bernadotte Plan," were as follows:

1. Palestine, as defined in the original Mandate entrusted to
   the United Kingdom in 1922, might form a Union, comprising two members, one Arab and one Jewish. The
   Arab area would be the Kingdom of Transjordan; the
   Jewish would be Israel.
2. The boundaries of the two members should be determined in the first instance by negotiations with the assis-

tance of the Mediator, and on the basis of suggestions to
be made by him.

3. The purpose and function of this Union should be to
   promote common economic interests, to operate and
   maintain common services, including customs and ex-
   cise, to undertake development projects and to coordi-
   nate foreign policy and measures for common defense.

4. Each member of the Union is to exercise full control over
   its own affairs, including foreign relations.

5. Immigration within its own borders should be within the
   control of each member of the Union, provided that, following a period of two years from the establishment of
   the Union, either member would be entitled to request
   the Council of the Union to review the immigration policy of the other member.

6. Holy Places, religious buildings and sites should be pre-
   served, and existing rights to their use fully guaranteed.

7. Refugees from the Palestine conflict should have the
   right to return to their homes and regain possession of
   their property.

In an annex to the suggestions, entitled "Territorial Matters,"
Bernadotte further proposed:

1. The inclusion of the whole or part of the Negev in Arab
   territory.

2. The inclusion of the whole or part of Western Galilee in
   Jewish territory.

3. The inclusion of the City of Jerusalem in Arab territory,
   with municipal autonomy for the Jewish community.

There were other provisions regarding Jaffa and free ports
at Haifa and Lydda. But the main implications of the modestly
entitled "Suggestions" were unmistakable. King Abdullah would
have not only Arab Palestine but also the city of Jerusalem and
the whole or part of the Negev incorporated into his Kingdom of Transjordan. Thus, the other Arab states would see Palestine divided between the Enemy and their main Arab rival, King
Abdullah. The Palestinian Arabs would lose the UN-promised
state of their own. Israel would have to give up chunks of both its
sovereignty and its land.

In his diary note for June 27, Bunche claims, "Drafting of introductory statement, most of the ideas and suggestions and territorial annex were mine" and were meant to be "deliberately vague and designed to gain time." Somehow, neither of these two critical points (the thinking behind which will later be apparent), that Bunche was the originator of the territorial suggestions and that they were meant to be preliminary and by no means final, was taken into account by those already possessed of a visceral distrust of Bernadotte.

Once these bold proposals, identified entirely with Folke Bernadotte and only secondarily with Ralph Bunche, had been sent off to both parties, Bunche noted, "Count Bernadotte can't stand waiting. . . . Difficult period waiting for reactions to our suggestions." The waiting fortunately coincided with the arrival on Rhodes of Estelle and the two children. Suddenly, the all-but-deserted Hôtel des Roses resounded with the boisterous laughter of two preadolescent boys, often joined by Barbro Wessel in their games of hide-and-seek. During one of these games, Barbro and the boys vanished from the hotel for such a long time that Greek security police began to comb the island for them. "We were all like a family," Barbro Wessel recalled. Bernadotte even dressed his elder son Oke in a Red Cross uniform and "smuggled" him into Jerusalem during one of his trips there in July.

For the first time since his arrival in Rhodes, Bernadotte took time out to swim, stroll on the beach with his wife, and throw a ball to his sons. In the evening, the four of them had supper in the dusty hotel garden, festooned in bougainvillea and oleander, while a tired violin scraped in the background. "I was glad to have my family gathered about me in my second home," Bernadotte noted, "for that was how I had come to regard Rhodes, that wonderful island. . . ."

The first reactions to his plan were encouraging. Secretary-General Lie and Secretary of State Marshall both unofficially let Bernadotte know they strongly endorsed his proposal, which cannot have displeased the British, given Abdullah's handsome treatment. Foreign Secretary Bevin, still smarting from the ragged British retreat from Palestine, and concerned primarily with maintaining good relations with Washington, had a "pox on both your houses" attitude regarding the Arab-Israeli war. He was sufficiently pragmatic, however, to have resigned himself to the inescapable fact of Israel's existence and, unlike Bunche and

Bernadotte, did not think handing Jerusalem to the Arabs was a sound idea.

The first portents from Israel were favorable. "On 1st of July a coded telegram arrived from John Reedman in Tel Aviv," Bernadotte wrote. "It was decoded in tense excitement. It is perhaps not difficult to imagine my joy when I read Reedman's communications: Shertok was prepared to come to Rhodes to continue negotiations on condition that the Arabs also accepted my invitation. This was a wonderful piece of news. It meant that the Jews accepted my proposals in principle as a basis for future discussions, even though they doubtless would not agree to all the details."

It turned out to be one more Middle Eastern mirage, this early moderate reaction, a stalling tactic on the part of the Israeli government. Reality soon broke like a wave. "Count's suggestions utterly negative," Foreign Minister Shertok cabled Chaim Weizmann in late June in Switzerland; ". . . we are not interested to be the first to reject . . . therefore we are playing for time." On June 29, David Ben-Gurion jotted in his diary, "Today, the Count's suggestions were received. Whoever suspected that he was Bevin's agent did not do so entirely without reason."

On July 6, the full thunderclap of Israeli reaction to his plan finally hit Bernadotte. His welcome in Tel Aviv, where he had flown to throw his full weight behind the proposals, was not one degree warmer than the minimum required of the envoy of a nonbelligerent state. At the suburban former German colony of Sarona, which housed the Foreign Ministry, a pale and frosty Shertok handed the mediator the formal reply to his "Suggestions." Scanning it quickly, Bernadotte, though revealing no emotion, was finally and utterly drained of all his optimism. The Israeli government's rejection of his effort was total.

The reply expressed "surprise" that Bernadotte had "ignored" the UN partition resolution, "the only internationally valid adjudication on the Palestine question." Equally surprising, the reply continued, was the count's inclusion of Arab Palestine "in the territory of one of the neighboring Arab States." Nor would Israel agree to any limitation on her sovereignty, and claimed the right to "complete and unqualified freedom to determine the size and composition of Jewish immigration." The final paragraphs fairly boiled over with outrage and bitterness at the count's "Suggestions."

"The Provisional Government was deeply wounded by [the count's] suggestions concerning the future of the City of Jerusalem which it regards as disastrous. The idea that the relegation of Jerusalem to Arab rule might form part of a peaceful settlement could be conceived only in utter disregard of history and of the fundamental facts of the problem: the historic associations of Judaism with the Holy City; the unique place occupied by Jerusalem in Jewish history and present-day life; the Jewish inhabitants—two-thirds majority in the city before the commencement of Arab aggression. . . . The Jews of Jerusalem will never acquiesce in the imposition of Arab domination over Jerusalem, no matter what formal municipal autonomy and right of access to the Holy Places the Jews of Jerusalem might be allowed to enjoy. They will resist any such imposition with all the force at their command. . . . The Government did not find it necessary to comment upon the other points . . . hoping that Count Bernadotte might reconsider the whole approach to the problem."

With the barest trace of a bow, a grim-faced Bernadotte silently withdrew to his hotel room to draft, with Bunche's help, a reply to the Israeli objections. Within an hour and a half, he had a carefully worded, reasonable-sounding reply, elaborating on how he reached his proposal for peace in Palestine. "I have studied carefully the observations on my Suggestions set forth on your letter to me of 5th July 1948 . . ." Bernadotte's reply stated. "You will appreciate, I hope, the spirit in which my Suggestions have been advanced and the objectives which were sought. . . . these ideas were put forth with no intimation of finality; they were exploratory only and designed specifically to invite further discussion and counter-suggestions from the interested parties. The success of my Mediatory effort, you will agree, must inevitably depend upon the possibility of finding some common ground on which further discussions with the two parties may profitably proceed. There was . . . no question of formal acceptance or rejection of the specific ideas advanced, but only a determination as to whether there might be in those ideas some framework of reference within which progress towards ultimate agreement on details might reasonably be hoped for . . . it is true that I have not considered myself bound by the provisions of the [UN's] 29th November resolution [on partition of Palestine], since had I done so there would have been no meaning to my mediation. . . . As regards any territorial adjustments to which either party might lay claim as a result of successes on the field of battle, it must be said that, quite aside from the question of fundamental principle involved, the conflict was only in its very early stages when the truce began and the military outlook for either side is by no means clearly predictable. . . . *Jerusalem stands in the heart of what must be Arab territory in any partition of Palestine. To attempt to isolate this area politically and otherwise from surrounding territory presents enormous difficulties.* [Italics added.] The special condition of Jerusalem—its large Jewish population and its religious associations—needs special consideration, and the way for discussion of these questions was left open. Arab domination of legitimate Jewish and other non-Arab interests in Jerusalem was never intended or implied in the Suggestions. . . . I wish you to know that I have but one interest in the future of Palestine, and that is to do everything within my power to bring peace to this troubled land. I am willing at all times to carry on such discussions and seriously to consider all suggestions which may hold any promise for a peaceful settlement of the problem."

The injury inflicted by his first set of "Suggestions" was such, however, that no amount of explaining or backpedaling would lessen the sting. By suggesting that Israel might be amenable to giving up some of its bitterly won self-determination and equally amenable to forsaking Jerusalem, Bernadotte not only had lost the support of even the most moderate Jews, but had incurred their deepest rancor. "Nobody who has the slightest understanding of history," Walter Eytan noted, "of three thousand years of Jewish history, would make such a proposal. Yet such a proposal seemed rational to him because it was clean-cut. OK, let's give it to Abdullah. It showed he had none of the historical knowledge or the sensitivity to gauge the extreme delicacy of the whole situation. Nobody before or after has proposed any such thing."

Ralph Bunche, the originator of many of the "Suggestions," had the example of Berlin, the dominant international crisis of the summer of 1948, in mind when contemplating Jerusalem as a divided city held captive inside hostile territory. He and Bernadotte also felt that an international regime wouldn't work in Jerusalem, which lacked the manpower to enforce such an arrangement. Ironically, they were motivated in part by fear for the security of the city's Jewish population, which occupied a small, precarious corner of Jerusalem.

Moreover, Bernadotte and Bunche's "Suggestions" were genuinely meant to be just that, suggestions to provide an informal basis for further discussions. Leaks to the press in Tel Aviv and in Cairo, however, forced the mediator to publish the "Suggestions" as a document of the Security Council, thereby giving them a weight and a permanence Bernadotte and Bunche had not intended.

The Arabs were no more enthusiastic than the Israelis about Bernadotte's peace plan. The Arab League claimed that Bernadotte had failed to understand that the Arabs were the original owners of Palestine and that Bernadotte was advancing the Zionists' cause. The difference in the Arabs' reactions, both official and behind the scenes, was that it was free of the Israelis' personal animosity toward the mediator. "Unfortunately," ran the Arab reply of uncompromising bombast, "the suggestions have proved to be most disappointing to the Arabs, because they aim at the realization of all Zionist ambitions and tend to grant the Zionists more than was provided for by the partition plan, which was doomed to failure. Furthermore, the suggestions do not guarantee for the Arabs any of their demands, thus demonstrating that they did not weigh the causes of the present dispute. . . ." And so on.

Unmentioned in the official Arab reply was the deep resentment the Arab states felt toward the plan's conspicuous aggrandizement of Transjordan. The Egyptians' and Syrians' irritation at Bernadotte's unexpected generosity toward King Abdullah is made plain in a secret cable from the American chargé in Cairo to Secretary of State Marshall dated June 30, 1948. "[Syrian Prime Minister] Mardam declared suggestions worse than partition since, if accepted, they would make Transjordan a Jewish colony through joint economic functions and constitute even greater menace to Arab world. Both [Syria and Egypt] clearly indicated opposition to aggrandizement of Abdullah."

Such was the depth of Israeli resentment of Bernadotte that even his proud history of negotiating for Jewish lives during the Holocaust was now viewed with suspicion by Jewish leaders. Rumors of the Swede's "friendship" with Himmler were suddenly given credence in many quarters. Chaim Weizmann wrote to Abba Eban later that month: "Although I've never met the man [Bernadotte], I'm deeply prejudiced against him. The reason is his great friendship with Himmler. He's naturally in the tow of Mr. Bevin and his friends and only yesterday there was a curious statement in the Swiss press that Bevin considers Germany as the most favored nation from now on, so Bevin and his friends and Bernadotte and his friends make a nice kettle of fish which we should try to avoid like poison. . . . I have no doubt that attempts will be made at the next session of the UN in September to reopen our question and the more recognition we can get from the Western powers the more difficult we can make it for our enemies. . . . I would like to utter a warning against the Galilee-Negev exchange."

Walter Eytan, who only a few weeks before had seen the mediator's white plane as a symbol of hope, now also revised his opinion of Bernadotte. "We soon discovered that he had been actively engaged in conversations with Himmler, also on some sort of diplomatic mission. Somehow this gave us an awkward feeling about him. After all, he was a man who'd been dealing with the Nazi murderers in some sort of conciliatory way. He had spoken in a normal way to people like Himmler and others like him. That created some kind of feeling of discomfort. Looking at it objectively and with hindsight, our feelings were unjustified. But everybody's feelings about the Nazis were very raw still; after all, this was 1948. I had the feeling all the time that here I am talking to a man who not long ago was using the same pleasant tone with Heinrich Himmler."

Judah Magnes, the president of Hebrew University and a respected moderate Zionist with whom Bernadotte occasionally corresponded (and who, ironically, once referred to Avraham Stern as among his most gifted students), wrote in a rueful tone to the count on July 14, 1948. "I should have liked the opportunity of discussing the Jerusalem issue with you. In many ways Jerusalem seems to me to be the crux of the Palestine problem. . . ." Bernadotte replied briefly to Dr. Magnes on July 29. "I know that many people should not understand why I suggested Jerusalem as an Arab city. There are many reasons for this suggestion. First of all, I think that we have many experiences of having an international area in another state which are not very encouraging. Look at the present situation in Berlin, Vienna, Trieste and Tangiers. . . . From a financial point of view there will also be economic difficulties in the future if Jerusalem should be an international city, as the economic burden for the international organization has to be paid by the population of Jerusalem."

Letter writing did not come easily to Bernadotte; thus, the significance of his letter of July 23, 1948, to his brother Karl, devoted almost entirely to explaining the rationale for the plan that seemed to have offended all parties to the dispute. "I understand quite well," Bernadotte wrote his elder brother, "that you and many others were wondering about my opinions regarding the future of Palestine . . . and in which I made allusions that Jerusalem should be an Arab city. Following long discussions with my colleagues, who, in the main, reinforced this idea, I understood that this would arouse much criticism. So you might like to know the reasoning behind my proposal. You see, I feel that we have a lot of evidence showing that an international territory entirely surrounded by another state has proven to be quite unfortunate. You can point to examples like Berlin, Vienna, Trieste, and Tangiers. . . . I do not believe that such an arrangement would be lasting, but would only result in endless complications.

"The other reason behind my decision was that the UN had not, according to its November 27 resolution, been willing to finance the costs to internationalize Jerusalem . . . sooner or later Jerusalem's residents would start to complain about their money being used, through taxes, to finance this international machine, which they, at least, had no interest in.

"A third reason is that my proposal calls for an international committee to supervise all so-called 'holy' places, making sure that all different religions are guaranteed free access. From a religious standpoint, I could not come up with a single 'correct' suggestion.

"Finally, however, it is easy to refute another point the Jews emphasize: that there are 100,000 Jews and only 65,000 Arabs and therefore it is unreasonable for Jerusalem to be an Arab city. If we agree with that principle, then the basic premise of Israel itself is undermined. There is only one place in that state, namely the capital, Tel Aviv, where the majority of the population is Jewish.

"However," Bernadotte concluded, evidently chastened by bitter experience, "my understanding is that Jerusalem will not likely become an Arab city. I would say that it is more likely to become an international territory, and I suppose only the future will later prove my reflections right or wrong. You see"—he stressed yet again the point that the overwrought parties to the dispute missed—"my suggestions were only a basis for further discussions. . . . Yes, this is the way I now view this matter, but during these past few months I have learned that plans change constantly and rarely do events turn out the way one expected."

While all this sounded reasonable to the mediator, a deeper knowledge of the region and a more refined sensibility regarding its traumatized inhabitants might have averted this pitfall. Bernadotte might then have realized that for a people too long accustomed to a struggle for survival, his brand of cool, lawyer-like objectivity was not a virtue. But to Bernadotte, who boasted that his "heart is of a strictly neutral tint," an Arab Jerusalem was a reasonable topic for "future discussion." For a great many Jews, moderates to extremists, by even raising this as a possibility, he had already betrayed them.

By far the most puzzling aspect of all this is Ralph Bunche's role. How is it that Bunche, a vastly more seasoned negotiator and regional specialist than Bernadotte, failed to caution Bernadotte against disregarding eighteen months of painstaking UN investigation into the problem, and allowed the mediator to, in a stroke, enrage the Jews and outrage all the Arab states, save Transjordan.

Certainly, Bernadotte could not have been fully aware of Israel's growing self-confidence regarding its present and future battlefield strength. Both sides had violated Bernadotte's truce at every opportunity, but Israel had much more to show for her violations than the Arabs. The CIA had picked up on the region's rapidly shifting military balance. "The truce resulted in so great an improvement in the Jewish capabilities that the Jews may now be strong enough to launch a full-scale offensive and drive the Arab forces out of Palestine. Events during the truce, and the enormous increase in Jewish strength resulting from them, considerably change the previously held estimate of the probable course of the war in Palestine."

The arrival of daily arms shipments had fortified Israel's defense forces, which were now vastly better prepared, and less intimidated by the enemy, than during the first round of fighting in May. Israeli agents bought and smuggled a steady stream of arms, primarily from Czechoslovakia, Russia, and even Mexico.

Matériel from the United States included two boatloads of war-surplus jeeps, trucks and half-tracks, bombsights, chemicals for explosives production, radar, and bazookas. Thirty Sherman tanks arrived from Italy. The Israeli Air Force, which six months before featured a bunch of pleasure planes, now boasted fifteen C-46s, three B-17 Flying Fortresses, three Constellations, twenty Messerschmitts, and on and on. Volunteers, both Zionists and soldiers of fortune, signed on from all over the world to fly them.

By late summer, Israel had the most powerful air force in the region, as well as a fully functioning arms-production industry. Equally important, Israel had trained 60,000 new recruits for combat. Though still inferior in arms to her enemies, Israel had nonetheless significantly narrowed the margin. The new state no longer felt bound by the November 27, 1947, resolution on the partition of Palestine (though Shertok chided the mediator for ignoring it in his proposal), since the Arabs themselves had violated it by invading Israel in the first place. To both Ben-Gurion and Shertok, Israel's boundaries were now an open question, to be settled not at the negotiating table but by the next round of fighting.

An equally dramatic development for Israel was the flight since April of 300,000 Arabs from Palestine. "The most spectacular event in the contemporary history of Palestine," Shertok called it in mid-June, "more spectacular than the creation of the Jewish state . . . is the wholesale evacuation of its Arab population . . . after which revision of the status quo ante is unthinkable. It opens up a lasting radical solution of the most vexing problem of the Jewish state."

This "spectacular event," whereby hundreds of thousands of Palestinians became wards of established Arab states, was sometimes actively encouraged by Israel. Prime Minister Yitzhak Rabin, commander of the Har El Brigade during the 1948 war, described how this policy evolved:

"While the fighting was still in progress we had to grapple with a troublesome problem for whose solution we could not draw upon any previous experience: the fate of the civilian population of Lod [Lydda] and Ramle, numbering some 50,000. Not even Ben Gurion could offer any solution, and during the discussion at operation headquarters, he remained silent, as was his habit in such situations. Clearly, we could not leave Lod's hostile and armed populace in our rear, where it could endanger the supply route to Yiftach (another brigade) that was advancing eastward.

"We walked outside, Ben-Gurion accompanying us. (Yigal) Allon repeated his question: 'What is to be done with the population?' B.G. waved his hand in a gesture which said: 'Drive them out!' Allon and I held a consultation. I agreed that it was essential to drive the inhabitants out. We took them on foot toward the Ben Horon road, assuming that the [Arab] Legion would be obliged to look after them, thereby shouldering logistic difficulties which would burden its fighting capacity, making things easier for us.

" 'Driving out' is a term with a harsh ring," Rabin continued. "Psychologically, this was one of the most difficult actions we undertook. The population of Lod did not leave willingly. There was no way of avoiding the use of force and warning shots in order to make the inhabitants march the ten to fifteen miles to the point where they met up with the Legion. . . .

"Great suffering was inflicted upon the men taking part in the eviction action. Soldiers . . . included youth movement graduates, who had been inculcated with values such as international fraternity and humaneness. The eviction action went beyond the concepts they were used to. There were some fellows who refused to take part in the expulsion action. Prolonged propaganda activities were required after the action to remove the bitterness of these youth movement groups, and explain why we were obliged to undertake such a harsh and cruel action."

As temperate early summer turned into parched midsummer, in the cafés of Tel Aviv's Dizengoff Street and along Ben-Yehuda in Jerusalem, Bernadotte was increasingly referred to in the same bitter vein as the archvillain Ernest Bevin. The Swede had come to curb the dream of reclaiming the land, they said. This aloof man was not a friend, but a friend of the enemy. By late June, it was not only for the habitués of the sidewalk cafés, avid for gossip, that Bernadotte had lost his luster as a man of peace. Dr. Chaim Weizmann wrote a friend in New York on June 20: "Neither do I think that Bernadotte is a particular friend of ours. He constantly speaks of effecting a permanent settlement between us and the Arabs, and I am certain that he is thinking of appeasing the Arabs by giving them chunks of our territory, either in the Negev or in the North or both. The intention of the British is to keep the country in a ferment and to fish in troubled waters. You will no doubt warn our good friends in Washington of this state of affairs. . . . There is real danger ahead."

Reuters Jerusalem correspondent Jon Kimche remembered those weeks: "They had just got rid of the British who had strutted about telling them what they should do; and here, already, was another lot of superior persons to dictate to them what they might or might not do. The Jewish coffee house grapevine was also busy retailing gossip of Bernadotte's alleged Nazi sympathies, and many Israelis, who ought to have known better, confided to me that Bunche was in fact only a State Department agent, and they were certain that Bernadotte was a British agent and that he had discussed his mission with the British before coming to the Middle East. The fact that all this information was unfounded did not lessen the strong current of suspicions and hostility which pervaded Israeli relations with the UN observers and with the Mediator and his assistants. The Israeli press was full of it. Government officials right up to the top believed it. The army suspected the observers of spying for the Arabs. The observers themselves contributed to this mood by their own attitude to the local population; the Americans and Belgians (with a few outstanding exceptions) considered them as Bolshevik suspects or colonials who might have to be humored but could not be trusted or treated as equals."

A short distance from the rumor mills of Ben-Yehuda Street, among the 120 action-starved commandos of Lehi's three Jerusalem camps, the first nub of a plan began to gather shape. Land and power were their twin obsessions. They had gone without both for too long to be reasonable about how those things should be acquired now. Bernadotte, seen through their distorting lens, was all-powerful. Bernadotte's advice would be heeded by the Great Powers. Worst of all, they feared Bernadotte would prevail over their own leaders—servile figures, cowed by Ha Rozen from the north.

Among Lehi's three leaders, the fiery Eldad claims he was the first to articulate what he saw as inevitable: Bernadotte's assassination. "In history, individuals make events"—he repeated his familiar theme to Shamir and Yalin-Mor at their Camp Dror headquarters in midsummer. "Bernadotte is a British agent and he wants to give Jerusalem and the Negev to Abdullah because the British need a land bridge from the Suez to Jordan. The

British will come back through their puppet, Abdullah. Bernadotte has the power, he has the United Nations behind him. We
are a small, weak country."

The man called Michael, slow to make a move, slower still to
speak, only listened. Shamir knew that ultimately he and not the
combustible Eldad would have to turn the rhetoric into action.

CHAPTER SIXTEEN

"IN THE HANDS
OF THE
SECURITY COUNCIL"

WITH HIS DREAM OF INITIATING A LONG-TERM POLITICAL SETTLE-
ment tumbling like a house of cards, Bernadotte scrambled to
salvage what he could of the truce. Shertok privately assured him Israel would be willing to extend the cease-fire
for one month past its imminent July 9 deadline. Reuven
Shiloah, later an armistice negotiator for Israel, pulled Bunche
aside to tell him that the Jews were convinced Bernadotte was
under Anglo-American influence and that his suggestions were
British-inspired. "I denied this vehemently," Bunche wrote in
his diary.

Bunche called Secretary-General Lie's aide, Andrew Cordier,
to inquire if the Security Council might adopt strong measures to
back up the mediator's effort to reinstate the truce. Noting the
Security Council's habit of letting the mediator carry the ball,
Cordier was not optimistic.

From Cairo to Baghdad, the Arab press continued to beat
the drums of war. "The Arab people," a CIA memorandum of
July 27, 1948, alleged, "were confident of victory and were assured by their leaders that the truce would not be extended.
Their bitterness may well erupt into violence against their governments. . . . Arab leaders, however, will first make every effort
to turn the anger of their people against the UN, the US, and
the UK."

No one wanted peace more than King Abdullah, whose Arab
Legion, cut off from its British arms supply by London and

Washington's embargo on arms to the region (as well as by terms of the cease-fire), was in no condition to resume fighting. No one stood to gain more from the mediator's peace plan than the diminutive king of Transjordan. Abdullah's would-be allies in the Arab League, however, were clamoring for war. "Arabs must be either mad," noted Bunche, "or assured of British supplies." The answer turned out to be the former.

"The decision [to resume fighting] seemed to me fatal from a military and diplomatic point of view," noted the Legion's commander, Glubb Pasha. "The Jews had agreed to prolong the truce, the Arabs had refused; the United Nations and the Great Powers would all be alienated by such an action. I also reminded [Transjordan's prime minister] Taufiq Pasha that we had not much ammunition left. . . . 'All the others [in the League] wanted to renew the fighting,' Taufiq said. The King was as distressed as myself at this fatal decision."

Abdullah cabled Bernadotte on Rhodes and "asked for a talk of the utmost importance." But the clock had already run out on the cease-fire. On July 9, the rumble of artillery fire shattered the stillness of Jerusalem's dawn. The same morning, Count Bernadotte landed in Amman, rushing straight to the Royal Palace. An agitated monarch in flowing robes greeted him. "Abdullah was very nervous. . . . He urgently requested me to act quickly to change the situation. He had himself ordered the Arab Legion not to start hostilities or an offensive, but only to answer Jewish fire and to repulse Jewish attacks. . . . It was, the King closed, necessary for the Security Council to take serious measures to prevent a renewal of the war. . . . It was my turn to speak," Bernadotte recounted. "I had appealed to the Arab Committee . . . to come to their senses and not resist a prolongation of the truce. I had explained to them what effect a negative attitude would make on the United Nations . . . and on the Security Council. But all in vain. Therefore, I wanted to ask him if we had not better concentrate on the question of the demilitarization of Jerusalem. . . . 'Your Majesty is by now the most powerful factor in the Arab world,' I added. 'The Arab Legion is the greatest Arab military asset. Without the Legion, military successes would be out of the question for them.' "

Abdullah answered, "Yes, I, too, am interested in the demilitarization of Jerusalem, but first we must stop the war in Palestine. The Security Council must intervene with force."

Bunche scribbled during these talks: "King shaky, chagrined at Cairo decision [to resume war] . . . asked how to get Egyptians [with their foothold in the Negev] out of Palestine. Count said he couldn't—how about piece of Negev for Egypt—Abdullah says OK."

"The situation was strange indeed," Bernadotte noted. "Here I was sitting conferring with one of the leaders of the Arab world. And he demanded that I should try to induce the Security Council to intervene against the Arabs, his own kinsmen and allies, if they insisted in their refusal to prolong the truce—induce it first to use violent language against them and then, if nothing else helped, to apply sanctions.

"I asked him . . . if my proposals [for peace in Palestine] could be used as a basis for further discussions. He assented to this and added that the best would be if Arabs and Jews could be brought together to negotiate directly. To this, I could only reply that this was exactly what I had been working for; the Arabs, however, had declared that they certainly would not accept a round table conference with the Jews.

"I was rather puzzled when I left Abdullah. Something must have happened that made him go as far he had done in his request for help from my side. Later in the day I had the explanation."

Glubb Pasha provided the answer. "I saw Count Bernadotte for a few minutes," he recalled. "It was obvious to me that the longer the fighting went on the more the Arabs would lose. 'The only thing now,' I said to the Count, 'is for the Security Council to take really strong action. They must insist on an immediate cessation of the fighting.' 'I'll do my best,' he replied. . . . I never saw any report of the secret proceedings of the Arab League Political Committee," Glubb noted. "From what I could gather, Nokrashy Pasha [Prime Minister of Egypt] had pressed for a renewal of hostilities. . . . During the first period of fighting, the Egyptian Press had daily announced the dazzling victories of the Egyptian army. The public were expecting an early end to the war, the occupation of Tel Aviv by the Egyptian Army, and the surrender of Israel. Instead of that, they were told that a month's truce had been agreed to. The Egyptian people were incensed—they had been given to understand that complete victory was in their grasp.

"During the . . . truce, criticism of the government increased in Egypt. To silence this criticism, the Egyptian Prime Minister decided to start hostilities once more. The future of the Arabs of Palestine," Glubb Pasha ruefully concluded, "was sacrificed to Egyptian politics."

Barbro Wessel recalled feeling sorry for Glubb Pasha, as he stood beside the mediator, who "looked even taller and more imperial than normally, in his crisp white uniform, his jacket buttoned, next to this small, weak-chinned, unimpressive, and very worried man."

Never one to quail before a decision, and relishing action, Bernadotte flew back to Rhodes, stopping only long enough to inform New York he was on his way. Accompanied by Bunche and Estelle, he left the Hôtel des Roses at seven thirty-five the next morning. In an act of rebellion, Bunche packed all his luggage, saying he didn't want to see the place again unless his wife Ruth and his children were with him. They took off at 8 A.M., immediately plunging into work on the first draft of the mediator's report to the Security Council.

A rotund and perspiring Secretary-General Lie, his chief lieutenants, and a clutch of reporters awaited the mediator on the La Guardia Airport tarmac in the paralyzing humidity of New York in July. Bernadotte, exuding confidence, his face lined but tan, wearing a pale-colored, double-breasted summer suit, strode up to a bank of microphones. Estelle, cool and composed in a navy blue suit, white gloves, and a straw hat, stood smiling beside her husband. "The present situation can only improve," the count reassured the press. "I feel sorry for both Arabs and Jews who have resumed fighting again. Personally, I feel fine, had a good sleep on the plane . . . anxious to address the Security Council."

The Cold War's chill winds gusted through the dark corridors of the Lake Success hall where the members of the Security Council assembled to hear for the first time from their Middle East troubleshooter. Andrei Gromyko, the Soviet delegate (who viewed this and all other disputes through the prism of Cold War politics, which dictated that whatever position Washington supported, Moscow opposed), had already made a point of declining Bernadotte's invitation for a private meeting. As Bernadotte delivered his urgent appeal for Security Council intervention,

Gromyko shifted his gaze from the papers in front of him to the ceiling, never once acknowledging the Swede's presence. The president of the Council, Dimitri Manuilsky of Ukraine, kept his mustached upper lip tightly pursed.

"The question is now in the hands of the Security Council," Bernadotte told the body, barely looking down at his carefully studied notes. "I have done my utmost, and for the moment I cannot do more. It is necessary that quick decisions—I should like to say immediate decisions—be taken, because for every hour we discuss, hundreds and perhaps thousands of lives are lost in Palestine, lives of both Jews and Arabs. . . . Nothing could be more helpful to a solution of the Palestine question than a clear understanding by both parties that the use of force, in achieving one solution or another, is not to be tolerated. . . . A firm and unequivocal order—I repeat *order*—for an immediate cease-fire in Palestine . . . would be an indispensable first step . . . a second and very important step, particularly in view of the prospect of the virtual destruction of this historic city which belongs to the world, would be an order for the demilitarization of the city of Jerusalem as a whole. . . . One might hope," he concluded, "that the cease-fire in Palestine and the demilitarization of Jerusalem would eventually lead to an armistice, thus ensuring an extended period of peace during which mediation could be most effectively employed; and, if found feasible, a plebiscite of the two peoples might be held."

Hardly had he finished his plea for Security Council action than the two Soviets, Gromyko and Manuilsky, opened fire. "I assume the Mediator realizes"—Gromyko's tone was bone-dry—"that his proposal for a plebiscite for the whole of Palestine conflicts with the General Assembly decision on Palestine."

Bernadotte, transformed under fire into the ice-cold aristocrat, answered, "If I should have been one hundred per cent bound by the General Assembly decision . . . I think that the Security Council should not have had a Mediator because then no mediation would have been necessary."

Manuilsky and Gromyko took turns grilling him. "My sporting instincts had begun to assert themselves," the unflappable Swede noted. ". . . [T]he thing was to hit the balls back by finding suitable answers as quickly as possible and giving the facts clearly."

"The Mediator shares the responsibility for the resumption of hostilities," Manuilsky charged. Bernadotte was a stalking horse for Western oil companies, the Ukrainian asserted, claiming the mediator was not concerned about either Jews or Arabs, but merely Great Power interests in the region. Bernadotte maintained his composure and would not be provoked, however.

"I did not expect," Bernadotte finally replied, "in this very distinguished assembly, words would be said to me which indicated that I was more or less responsible for the fighting which has now started in Palestine. I think it would be rather easy for me to answer the representative of the Ukraine that his critical remarks, if I may use a rather mild expression, are somewhat unjustified. I am not, however, going to defend myself at all. . . . I believe it is of greater, very much greater, importance that this Council should get results from this meeting and reach a decision. . . . To save lives . . . is much more important . . . than for me to defend myself."

In remarks certain to arouse the hostility of the Arab delegates, the mediator gave his strongest endorsement of Israel and expressed his personal admiration for the new state, praising it "for exercising all the attributes of full sovereignty. . . . It is a situation the Arab states are fighting to eliminate, but the plain fact remains that it is there. It is a small state, precariously perched on the coastal shelf with its back to the sea, defiantly facing a hostile Arab world. If it survives," the mediator closed with powerfully prophetic words, "its security will be a problem for a good long time to come."

"We all admired him." Brian Urquhart recalled that taut session. "He was very feisty with the Russians; he wasn't putting up with any of their baloney. And he looked and sounded terrific. In the corridors, the Russians kept parroting that he was a British agent. And of course the Israeli press picked that up. Nobody could have pushed harder than Bernadotte to get a settlement. But the dominant event that summer was the Berlin blockade, so of course he was affected by the prospect of a city held hostage, when thinking about Jerusalem's future. But it's utter nonsense to say that he and Bunche were pushed around by the British or anybody else. He wanted to be absolutely sure that when he presented his next report to the Security Council it would not get shot down. So of course he sought their views."

"We thought Bernadotte was the best possible man to represent the UN," Urquhart noted. "Lie was the only one in the Secretariat who didn't like him. In part because he was a Swede and an aristocrat, and Lie was this great, fat, temperamental Norwegian trade-union lawyer. Lie would say things about Bernadotte when people came around, especially the Israelis. 'Of course I don't agree with Bernadotte,' he would say to them. Lie undermined him behind his back. But we never thought Bernadotte was in any real danger. After all, the UN was such a grand institution in those days, and he was its representative. Surely he was safe."

The unflappable Swede, rather than the indignant Soviets, prevailed that day in the Security Council. An American-sponsored resolution ordering the parties in Palestine to desist from military action and enter a truce at a time specified by the mediator was passed on July 15, with the Soviet and Ukrainian delegates abstaining and the Syrian voting no. Failure to comply would be "a breach of the peace within the meaning of Article 39," calling for unspecified action under Chapter VII of the UN; it was the heaviest weaponry ever aimed by the world body at any trouble spot.

The Security Council had no intention of backing up the strong words with forceful acts, however. For the mediator, who had mistaken rhetoric for reality, the Security Council's endorsement seemed a transfusion of new life for his mission. Suddenly, the pieces seemed to fall neatly into place for Bernadotte. The Israeli government agreed to lay down arms, as of July 18. The Arab League, after agonizing consultations in Lebanon, also accepted a cease-fire on July 17. Bernadotte did not want to leave New York without a commitment of UN troops from the Western powers to help maintain and control the truce. In a meeting with Philip Jessup, an American envoy to the UN, Bernadotte "emphasized that the type of service contemplated in no way involved combat, but would be confined to duty as drivers, guards, communications operators, etc. I assured Bernadotte that while we were in no position at present to commit our military establishment along these lines, prompt and serious consideration would be given to his proposal. He stated that time was valuable and that a prompt decision could make all the difference. . . . He concluded with the remark that having just received word of Arab assurance of the cease-fire for Jerusalem, he was taking off for the Middle East with high hopes and his 'flag at the top.' "

Promised "an adequate number" of American, Belgian, and French observers to enforce the truce, Folke Bernadotte had reason to feel exhilarated when on July 17 at La Guardia Airport he and Estelle boarded a KLM aircraft bound for Amsterdam and thence to Rhodes. With the optimism he wore like a second skin, he brushed aside the things he did not achieve. Nowhere in the resolution was there mention of a UN force to give teeth to the threatened sanctions. Nor was a call for the withdrawal of Israeli and Arab forces to their pre-June lines adopted. There was not a word regarding Bernadotte's growing unease regarding an issue both Israel and the Arabs preferred to ignore: the question of hundreds of thousands of Palestinian refugees.

By July 14, Israel had recaptured Lydda, Ramle, and Nazareth, three key Arab towns, establishing Israeli bridgeheads in the heart of Arab territory. The Israeli forces also smashed the Egyptian assault in the Negev.

A satisfied Israeli foreign minister noted, "We have had the best of both worlds. We behaved like good boys vis-à-vis the UN, and proved that we are good soldiers in battle. The results of the [Arab] gamble [to resume hostilities] were catastrophic." The mediator's efforts to bring peace to the region, but not necessarily on Israel's terms, now took on a different aspect. Israel, having profited from the June truce to build up her fighting forces, was becoming adept at circumventing Bernadotte's efforts, which the new state viewed as an impediment to her hopes. The young country's growing brashness on the battlefield was now matched on the diplomatic front. "What we resented," Abba Eban recalled, "was Bernadotte's suggestion that Israeli sovereignty was still optional. If the UN had expressed greater interest in our fate prior to Bernadotte's appointment, perhaps we would have had more faith in the body. But we had won our freedom unaided."

The Soviets' harsh treatment of Bernadotte also served to embolden Abba Eban to take a tougher line on the mediator's efforts to reign in Israel's territorial ambitions. On July 10, Eban sent a secret telegram to Foreign Minister Shertok. "Consider our interest requires early termination Bernadotte mission in order he not report to [General] Assembly, raising question of the future Government of Palestine, advocating his proposals. His existence is constantly exploited [by] the [Security] Council to avoid action against aggression. If Bernadotte is removed, no organ of potential revision remains, question becomes narrowed to peace preservation. If you concur, we can work discreetly, fruitfully here in circumstances, [with] President of the Council [Manuilsky], Secretary General [Lie], favorable Washington atmosphere. Please cable views, Eban."

CHAPTER SEVENTEEN

"THE SERVICE OF PEACE . . . IS . . . DANGEROUS"

AROUND THE END OF JUNE, BARUCH NADEL, A SINEWY, RED-bearded urban guerrilla was told by Lehi's Jerusalem commander, Yehoshua Zetler, to start collecting intelligence on the mediator's movements. Lehi's three-man command—particularly Yalin-Mor, flirting with socialism that summer—drew encouragement from Soviet propaganda on the mediator. Viscerally suspicious of this son of a European royal house with strong Anglo-American ties, Moscow's press seized every opportunity to vilify Bernadotte. "Bernadotte has arrogated to himself functions which were not entrusted to him and has taken the path of revising the UN decision," wrote *Pravda* on July 11. "Clearly to be seen in the plan proposed by Bernadotte for settling the Palestine problem is the label 'Made in England.' " The same day, the *Soviet Literary Gazette* accused Bernadotte of being "one of the most Americanized representatives of the Swedish aristocracy," whose motives in dealing with Nazi Germany were "anti-Soviet."

"We did not hate Bernadotte," Lehi fighter Nadel later insisted. "We hated the way Ben-Gurion and Shertok let him have his way. They would not stand up to him, so we had to. Because the one thing everybody in the Stern Group agreed on was that we would never again be under foreign rule. Never. One of our bullets could do much more to determine Israel's fate than a hundred of Shertok's speeches." Bernadotte's "Plan of Shame," as the mediator's "Suggestions" were dubbed by Lehi, could be stopped only by a single violent act.

Seen through Lehi's eyes, Bernadotte's attitude toward Ben-Gurion and Shertok was a reprise of the British high commissioner's treatment of the Jews. "He represented the new imperialism that wanted to rule our country. You might call it UN imperialism, you might say American imperialism, because the UN was then the vehicle of the United States," Nadel asserted. He and his fellow commandos saw Rhodes, the mediator's headquarters, as the new Munich, the place where Jews would be sold down the river yet again by the cynical Great Powers.

"Zetler asked me to find out whether the UN convoys were armed," Nadel recounted, "and whether the observers themselves carried personal weapons. I asked Zetler if he had any contacts inside the UN. He said, 'No, but we need the information within a week.' I was twenty-two; I didn't know what it meant to build contacts. So I said OK. I didn't know better. I asked Zetler for some cigarettes, which were very rare in Jerusalem, some money, and a car with a driver, who, if I tell him to wait for me in the middle of the Sahara Desert, will wait until he dies of thirst. We had enough cars, we had 'confiscated' them all over the city. We had even confiscated Golda Meir's armored car, which we used in Deir Yassin. We also confiscated gasoline, another luxury. We kept all this in the three camps which we made out of abandoned Arab houses, circled with barbed wire. The main camp was called Dror, in Katamon; another was in upper Lifta, called Yoav, which featured kosher food only, for our Orthodox members; and a third called El Daud, in southwest Jerusalem.

"Zetler supplied what I asked for, so I got to work right away. The driver was a young Sephardic boy. They were the most loyal in Lehi. I told him to drive me to the UN headquarters at the YMCA and the King David Hotel. The whole place had barbed wire around it and there was a military checkpoint with a barrier. I told the boy to drive at medium speed and don't stop at the barrier. 'Stop, stop!' the UN guard shouted. I shouted back in a very angry voice, 'Up! Raise it up!' And the guard was so taken aback that he did. I had on khakis; I looked like any military man in Israel. I was not armed, I had no documents. He didn't know who I was, but maybe I was a general of one of the many countries in the UN? How did he know? You have to remember, this was Jerusalem, the summer of 1948, anything was possible! The driver deposited me at the entrance of the King David, and then I told him to go.

"I went inside the hotel and there in the lobby I saw UN men sitting around, drinking at the bar. I sat down, turned to my neighbor and asked, 'May I?' They looked happy to have a new guy around. We began to talk. They were Americans, a captain and a lieutenant. What do you do, they asked me after a while. I'm a journalist, I told them, which was true. I was writing for *Mivrak,* our paper. Before long, we were talking about girls. I already had in mind two girls for these two guys—two girls who didn't have food, who didn't have cigarettes, with whom I stayed in touch. You have to understand we were starving in Jerusalem, and cigarettes were like gold, they were the currency which bought anything. So this helped my work. One of the girls I had in mind was an American volunteer in the Haganah. Women liked UN guys; they had a little money, food, cars.

"So I went in my big car to see the American girl, Marsha, who came back after the war to live in Israel, and her roommate, whose name was Ahuva and whose father was a truck driver who smuggled things into Jerusalem for us. I had known her from the Upper Galilee, since 1944. They didn't know I worked for Lehi. It didn't really matter anyway. Everything was turned upside down in those days. I told them I have these two friends from the UN, waiting in my car, let's go to a café and have a good time. So they came, and we all went to one of the three cafés that were still open on King George Street.

"And afterward I took the men back to the King David in my Studebaker and the guards there saw me with the UN guys and thought I was OK. We met again at the hotel the next afternoon and we were drinking when the captain said, 'Hey, we hear there is a dangerous gang here in Jerusalem and they want to kill us because we came to enforce the truce.' And I said, 'Don't worry, the Haganah can deal with those guys.' But they didn't even know what the Haganah was, so I told them and one of them said, 'We have arms, but Count Bernadotte won't let us use them. They are all in a safe in the cellar of the King David Hotel. Bernadotte has one key and General Lundström in Haifa has another.' He gave me the details of what they had in that cellar— Bren guns, handguns, and rifles. I thought it was a trap, it was so unbelievable that thirty hours after Zetler asked me to find these things, I had all the information. Was it a trap? Anyway, I told the guys we'd go out again that evening with the girls.

"I went back to the Lehi camp like a conqueror. I threw nineteen of the twenty pounds and two of the three packs of cigarettes in front of Zetler and said, 'There, you can have it back. It cost one pound and two shillings and twenty-five cigarettes to find out that all the UN arms are in the cellar of the King David, one key with Bernadotte, one key with Lundström.' It was thirty-two hours after he sent me to find out. 'That's impossible,' he said. 'How do you know this?' 'A couple of UN guys told me,' I said. 'And you believe them?' Zetler asked. I nodded. And I stayed in touch with those guys. Thanks to me, they got to know the two girls a lot better. But they repaid me for it."

Nadel's reckless audacity was Lehi's stock-in-trade. Dov Joseph, no admirer of Lehi, nonetheless acknowledged that "their dedication to their own programs was formidable, and their deception and subterfuge fantastic: the Stern Gang succeeded at different times in planting a man inside the Jewish Agency and another in the [British] High Commissioner's office." Joseph had no way of knowing Lehi had also effortlessly infiltrated the UN operation.

While Baruch Nadel was making contacts with UN observers, the Lehi Center was wavering on what to do about Bernadotte. Yalin-Mor had shifted his sights east, hoping for an eventual alliance with the Soviet Union, with a future in Israeli politics for himself. He was thus the most hesitant of the three leaders to plan a new hit. Shamir, the least ideological of the three, tended to follow Yalin-Mor's political cues. Shamir was an innately cautious operator, and the assassination of the mediator had not yet ripened in his thinking. Eldad, all fire and zeal, could barely contain his need for a renewed demonstration of Lehi's muscle.

While Lehi wavered, it floated menacing messages to warn off the mediator. On July 24, the *New York Times* foreign correspondent C. S. Sulzberger was jolted from his typing by a knock on the door of his Tel Aviv hotel room. A bellboy handed him a message urgently summoning him to the lobby. "Downstairs were two handsome, tall young fellows in khaki shorts and light-colored shirts. They shook hands and suggested we go out for a coffee because they had something to say. It turned out they were both South African Jews who had come here since the war and were not only ardent Zionists but members of the Stern Gang. They told me not to bother remembering their names because the names were phony.

"They discussed the aims of the Sternists and among other things horrified me by warning that the organization intended to assassinate Count Bernadotte and other advisors on the UN mission, just the way the Sternists had murdered Lord Moyne, because it was necessary to frustrate the UN effort to confine Israel within artificially constricted borders."

The *New York Times* correspondent wasn't sure how seriously to take this threat, though he did make a note to pass on the warning to Ben-Gurion's "high muckamuck in secret service and dirty tricks," Reuven Shiloah. Sulzberger did not report this incident until September 18, when he referred to it in a *New York Times* account of the assassination of the mediator.

In mid-July, the Stern Gang's underground newspaper, *Mivrak,* featured a scathing attack on the mediator by Eldad entitled "Please Meet the New Occupant." Beyond trusting their own government to defend them, and marooned in their impenetrable paranoia, Lehi saw the United Nations mediator as a life-threatening presence. The man's arrogance stirred primal fears in Lehi.

"A man comes to you without any military experience," Lehi Jerusalem commander Yehoshua Zetler recalled. "He arrives with nothing and suddenly becomes an institution. And this fictitious institution frightens everyone, makes everyone shake and be servile. You really should have seen how he would stand with his baton under his arm like the British with their hats. Everyone related to Bernadotte the way they used to relate to the British. The same fears. We needed to uproot this. If we had not uprooted this, then Jerusalem would have been in danger. He wanted to hand over Jerusalem to the Arabs."

"In Jerusalem, in the summer of 1948, human life was not only devalued," noted Lehi recruit Y. S. Brenner; "it didn't count. I have difficulty in conveying how different values were then. There was a war going on with the Arabs. Bullets were whistling by. You could have been shot any minute from behind any wall.

"One day in August, we went and robbed a jewelry shop. The jeweler was a German Jew. We had done this before and the shop owners just went to the insurance company and got their money. But this old man suddenly said, 'In the name of Dr. Weizmann, I arrest you!' He was crazy, but of course he was the only sane person in the place. We just pushed him aside and said, 'Yes, good, you do that.' But he was the only decent person there. It was a different world."

By now not even Bernadotte, his optimism as thick as armor, could ignore the hate swirling around him. Of a news conference he held in Tel Aviv, he noted: "The room was packed with people. From the expressions on the faces of many of those who sat nearest to me, I realized they strongly disapproved both of my proposals and myself." He tried to stay calm under the mounting pressure. As the attacks gained in venom and took on a personal edge, however, his armor of indifference began to fray. He was both pained and puzzled. ". . . [T]he Jewish Press had made very violent attacks on me. The extremist newspapers in particular . . . had torn my good name almost to shreds. . . . I had read a number of articles . . . which insinuated among other things that my activities during the final phase of the war and my conferences with Himmler had been of a dubious character. I said that I asked no sort of thanks for this work, but that I could not help thinking it was unjust that in particular this Red Cross work I had been in charge of should have been picked upon to cast aspersions on me, the more especially as it had been the means of saving the lives of about 10,000 Jews."

The dynamic quality which earlier served Bernadotte so well, when he overwhelmed all parties to the dispute with his high-octane negotiating style and persuaded them to agree to the truce, now aroused suspicion. "I got the impression of a man wholly preoccupied with the idea of speed and activity," Pablo de Azcárate, a member of the UN's Committee on Palestine, wrote, "anxious to appear as someone who came to the point at once and knew his own mind. . . . But whatever the characteristics of his personality and methods, no one could refuse to pay a tribute of admiration and respect to the wholehearted devotion with which he flung himself into his task, or to his impartiality and his fervent desire to accomplish a work of peace and justice in Palestine."

When an exploding land mine killed a French member of his team of observers, Bernadotte was again reminded of the nature and the territory of his mission. If his judgment was at times questionable, his courage was not. "Major Labarrière's death only confirmed what I had already established in Germany during the final phase of the war, namely that work in the service of peace and humanity is often extremely dangerous and unfortunately demands the sacrifice of human lives."

CHAPTER EIGHTEEN

THE CONSPIRACY
HARDENS

*"We warned him that we will kill him and he should
have taken it seriously."*

BARUCH NADEL

"IN JUNE, JULY, AND AUGUST, SHAMIR BECAME SOMETHING THAT
we in the Lehi never had before: a general. He sat in his headquarters in the Dror Camp in Katamon, wearing his khakis, and
he began to behave like a general," Baruch Nadel recalled. "He
told me to keep trailing the UN people, pick up information on
Bernadotte's movements. Later, he told me it took five weeks for
the Center to make their final plans. Shamir was a careful plan-
ner. Eldad only liked to send others to kill. He didn't know how
to fire a gun himself. We used to say that Eldad was built like
Lehi, he had a small body and a very big head; Lehi was a small
organization with very big ideas.

"I was within earshot of a meeting in July between Bernadotte, Shertok, and Dov Joseph at the King David Hotel in
Jerusalem. I had seen the big black government car at a military
roadblock and the MP on duty told me, 'It's Shertok.' I knew
what that meant: Bernadotte was in Jerusalem. What else would
bring the foreign minister? So I rounded up my car and driver
and had him drop me off at the King David. Thank God one of
my new friends was in the lobby, drinking. I hadn't seen him in a
few days, but he looked happy, he had his girl, he knew I was a

reporter, so of course I was interested in a meeting between the mediator, who had come from Amman, I think, and the foreign minister. But I couldn't stay in that hall while this meeting was going on in one of the conference rooms off the lobby, not without a blue UN armband. My friend had no problem with that. Within minutes, he provided me with one. I already wore khakis pretty much like theirs. So there we sat, thirty yards away from their conference room. It was difficult for me to hear what they were talking about, except when they raised their voices. From time to time I heard 'demilitarization.' I heard Bernadotte speak to the foreign minister like a lord to his butler. Shertok and Dov Joseph were like ghetto people talking with the *poritz* [gentile lord]. They gave Bernadotte the wrong impression about Jews. It made me furious.

"I left before it was over, worried maybe somebody would spot me. But I saw that Bernadotte had no bodyguards. He was a brave man. I give him that. But he was not brilliant enough to be that brave. We warned him that we will kill him and he should have taken it seriously.

"The next day when all the newspapers wrote that Bernadotte came to Jerusalem and spoke to Dov Joseph about bringing water and food, I wrote in our newspaper, 'Bernadotte came to Jerusalem to talk with Shertok about demilitarization,' which was supposed to be secret. Demilitarization of Jerusalem meant the Jews withdraw and the Arab Legion takes over."

Shertok and Dov Joseph did not, however, strike Bernadotte and Bunche as "ghetto people talking with the *poritz*," during their meeting with Israeli leaders on July 26. "On the question of demilitarization," Bernadotte wrote, "Shertok [who later Hebraicized his name to Sharett] refused to give me a definite answer, though I pressed him hard." Bunche scribbled in his diary, "Shertok was quite pompous and was opposed to the demilitarization of Jerusalem . . . the Jews now have a land bridge to Jerusalem and are thinking in terms of the possibility of Jewish Jerusalem being included in the Jewish state. There could be no question of the return of Arab refugees while the war is on. Shertok admitted that the Palestinian Arabs were the main victims of the war which is between Israel and the Arab states rather than with the Palestinian Arabs."

Two days later, the foreign minister dispatched the following sharply worded reply to the mediator:

1. The Provisional Government reaffirms its rejection of the Mediator's plan of demilitarization. The Provisional Government assumes that this particular scheme no longer stands.
2. The attitude of the Provisional Government to any plan of demilitarization emanating from the Mediator cannot but be influenced by the fact that the Mediator has proposed to place Jerusalem ultimately under Arab rule and that he has not withdrawn that proposal.

Gone was the exhilaration the Swede had felt when he left New York only weeks before. The three hundred observers he had been promised had not arrived. With a meager team to enforce the new cease-fire (for, with the end of the cease-fire and the resumption of war in early July, he could not risk leaving unarmed observers in place), a frustrated Bernadotte cabled New York from Rhodes on July 29: "Am still without reply to our cables 147, 167, 179. I must once more urgently request immediate action from Secretariat. As mentioned in cable . . . impossible to maintain present situation in Jerusalem if UN unable to meet as moderate a request as 40 armed guards. UN prestige and my position in Palestine impossible to maintain, if this lack of quick action from UN continues. I blame this fact entirely, repeat entirely, on UN organization not on me or members of my staff. You notice without doubt that I am mad, and I believe I have the right to be."

After a hurried trip to Beirut to confer with Arab leaders, Bunche jotted in his diary: "Arab position now is pitiful. They cannot continue to fight and know it. Yet their public opinions are so hot, the government officials are frightened stiff. Heads will fall . . . Syria and Iraq are especially dangerous. These were the countries which had insisted on fighting on . . . but in the end their military advisors had prevailed, because they had no ammunition and very little chance of getting any."

Not surprisingly, Bunche noted in his diary that both he and Bernadotte were "restless and despondent," and wondered, "How can we get an agreement on the demilitarization of Jerusalem if we can't provide 40 armed guards for the water pumping station at Latrun, now in UN control by agreement between the Arabs and Jews?"

"We knew that the United Nations prestige was sinking day

by day among both parties in Palestine," Bernadotte observed.
"They seemed to imagine . . . that once the [UN] resolution had
been adopted, all would be well. Both belligerent parties would
then keep quiet of their own accord, and there was no need for
anyone to see that the provisions of the resolution were in fact
observed. I cabled to the United Nations that if it proved impossible to maintain the second truce, I should lay the blame solely
and entirely at the door of the United Nations. Without effective
support I and my staff could get nowhere."

Secretary of State Marshall's attempt on July 28 to smooth
the mediator's ruffled feathers provoked the opposite effect. In a
secret cable, Marshall instructed the US Jerusalem consul
general to tell the mediator: "We have given most careful consideration to [his] . . . request for the temporary assignment of a
battalion of the US Marine Corps as a guard force for the policing of the Mt. Scopus area of Jerusalem. We regret that we are
unable to accept a military commitment of this nature in
Jerusalem. . . . We suggest for your earnest consideration the
possibility of a plan for policing Jerusalem which would enlist the
active cooperation and participation of Arab and Jewish authorities and armed forces. Responsibility for carrying out the Security Council resolution of July 15 rests primarily upon the Arabs
and Jews who should be able to undertake the policing of the city
without employing the services of UN personnel in other than an
observing capacity."

Secretary Marshall's suggestion regarding a joint Jewish-Arab
police force did provide the despairing Swede with a rare moment of levity. "Yes, we certainly had a good laugh at that
telegram. But at the same time we felt . . . bitterness at the
thought that it should rest in the hands of people so remote from
reality as to decide what was to be done in Palestine, while, in
the event of failure, they could automatically transfer the blame
to the shoulders of me and my staff."

Bernadotte told the American consul general, John J. Mac-
Donald, to warn the secretary of state that he would resign if no
help was forthcoming. Bernadotte, however, was unfamiliar with
the conventional wisdom of American politics, which deems
sending US troops to a foreign war zone during a presidential
election year tantamount to political suicide. Still another reason
for Marshall's reticence was contained in a CIA memorandum. If
Bernadotte belittled the presence of the Irgun and the Stern

Gang, the State Department, drawing on CIA intelligence, exaggerated the underground's potential. "At the present time," a CIA memo, drafted for the secretary of state in July, alleged, "[Israel] can control extremist elements within the partition boundaries, but it may not be able to control them in other parts of Palestine, especially in Jerusalem." The CIA estimated Lehi's strength at 400 to 800, roughly twice its actual size.

Remarkably, despite this intelligence, Secretary Marshall cabled UN Ambassador Jessup on July 21 that moving Bernadotte's headquarters from Rhodes to Jerusalem "would be desirable." Marshall's motive was a practical one: "Department has in mind that requirements for equipment and personnel might thereby be lessened. Jerusalem seems clearly preferable to Haifa for headquarters and mediation matters, since Haifa is within Jewish-controlled area." Yet the secretary of state was not oblivious to the danger such a move entailed for Bernadotte. Indeed, his reason for refusing the mediator's request for a battalion of US Marines to serve as temporary UN guards in Jerusalem was precisely this fear: "There is no assurance, that such units would not be subjected to attack by well armed groups such as the Irgun or the Stern gang." Jessup and British Foreign Secretary Bevin concurred that the mediator ought to set up shop in Jerusalem. "Our own opinion is that [the Jerusalem move] would be very desirable. He would thus not only be far closer to all parties in negotiation, both truce and mediation . . . we feel [his presence] would be important stabilizing factor for carrying out demilitarization and eventual establishment of the internationalization of that city." Bevin differed with Marshall on one key point: the British foreign secretary endorsed Bernadotte's call for a UN security force in Jerusalem.

On August 1, Bernadotte's legendary self-control snapped. While in Jerusalem, he announced to the American consul general, "It is impossible for me to supervise the observance of the truce without sufficient staff and equipment. I regret therefore to request you to inform Secretary Marshall that I am not prepared to continue under such conditions and unless the required personnel and equipment are forthcoming at once, I shall feel forced to resign as Mediator."

American Consul to Jerusalem John J. MacDonald added his own comment to bolster Bernadotte's plea for support. "Two weeks have elapsed since the truce went into effect, during which time the Mediator has been powerless to carry out properly its supervision, which has resulted in the UN rapidly losing prestige on both sides. Consequently, the situation has deteriorated steadily, making it more difficult and probably impossible to demilitarize Jerusalem. To date Mediator's staff consists of 30 American observers, 50 French, 47 Belgians and 10 Swedes, most of whom have arrived during the past five days."

But Secretary Marshall was too preoccupied during this period with the Soviet blockade of Berlin and by Moscow's generally confrontational attitude to devote much time to Bernadotte's travails. Besides, the secretary of state had little background knowledge or even much interest in Palestine, a field he left to his subordinates Dean Rusk and Robert Lovett, and the American delegates to the UN, under the leadership of former Vermont Senator Warren Austin.

Thus, it was Lovett as acting secretary of state in Marshall's absence who scribbled on the margin of a telegram drafted by the State Department to Bernadotte, "To suggest that the settlement might have to be enforced by troops? NO!" The last word was underlined three times.

Bernadotte was slowly learning the ways of the world organization, ruefully (and prophetically) noting in his journal, "The United Nations showed itself from its worst side. It was depressing to have to recognize the fact that even the most trivial decisions with regard to any measures designed to lend force to its words were dependent on the political calculations of the Great Powers. According to what I was told by a very reliable source, the American attitude was influenced by two considerations. If American troops were used in connection with the truce control, they were afraid in the first place that that might seriously complicate relations with Moscow. And in the second place they were afraid that if anything were to happen to American soldiers, if for example they were fired on by Arab or Jewish snipers, that would cause a storm of resentment in the USA which in its turn might influence the Presidential elections in November. If this information is correct, and I have no reason to doubt it, it throws a not very encouraging light on the ability of the United Nations to intervene effectively for the prevention of any future wars."

Behind the closed doors of Ben-Gurion's cabinet meeting, Israeli ministers voiced their growing resentment of the mediator and of the presence of even a small handful of UN observers in Jerusalem. The prime minister was now openly critical of the Swede. Using an ironic tone in referring to Bernadotte, who had let it be known he would return to Stockholm to chair the upcoming International Red Cross conference, Ben-Gurion noted, "We heard that Bernadotte will leave on August 15 for a month's rest at home, It is very hot here now; the climate in Sweden is certainly much more pleasant during this time of the year. . . ." He told his colleagues, "As for Jerusalem: the Old City is now in Arab hands, as is Sheikh Jarrah. Bernadotte has suggested demilitarization of the city. Because he represents the United Nations his proposals carry weight. This has created a political situation that serves the needs of our enemies and all those who are not our friends. . . . Meanwhile, a new status quo is created and the world learns to accept it. We are not a nation like all other nations. We are under supervision. There are supervisors here who do not even require our visas. The world is getting used to the idea that Israel is a dubious, problematical country."

It was as the most visible symbol of a scorned and unpopular organization that Folke Bernadotte arrived in Jerusalem on August 3. "The knowledge that there might be snipers about gives one a(n) . . . uncomfortable feeling," Bernadotte noted as he set off on foot from the craggy hill of Mount Scopus, where his headquarters were located, to the Augusta Victoria Hospital. Only seven of the original fifty UN guards were left to "enforce" a cease-fire that the chatter of automatic-weapons fire in the background turned into farce. "Originally there had been 50 guards on duty in Palestine. But some had declared they wanted to go home to the USA. They went—though they can hardly be described as returning heroes. In newspaper interviews some complained loudly firstly of the dangers they had been exposed to, secondly of the bad food they had had. Neither had the regulations about an eight-hour working day been adhered to. In their own eyes they were poor little boys deserving of all the pity the American public could give them. It is true," the mediator admitted, "that these guards had been hastily and haphazardly recruited in response to our urgent request."

One of the seven remaining guards, the Norwegian Ole Bakke, was fatally wounded by an Arab sniper's bullet while traveling in his jeep. Wearing his air of determined calm like a shield, Bernadotte shook hands with all his observers, telling them, "You are heroes to stay at your post."

The mediator, who earlier that summer had been treated as Jerusalem's salvation, was now received with all the warmth of a persistent gate crasher. An aloof Dov Joseph "took pride in never agreeing to any proposal" that Bernadotte suggested. The Jews, Joseph told him, have no confidence in the UN. "It's become a laughingstock," he told him. As for the mediator's plan for the demilitarization of Jerusalem, Joseph shrugged it off, saying, "I cannot commit my government on this."

With the Israeli foreign minister, it was the count who now played the role of supplicant, pleading with Shertok to do what he could to soften the shrill tone of the Israeli press treatment of Bernadotte and the UN. The *Palestine Post*'s headlines regarding the mediator during August and early September of 1948 all had the same arch tone: August 15, "Israel Rejects Mediator's Charges of Truce Breaches"; August 17, "Mediator Threatens to Report Jews as Violators"; August 23, "Mediator's Lack of Realism"; September 10, "Mediator's Fruitless Meeting."

"He [Shertok] admitted," Bernadotte noted, "that his Government's attitude had hardened after the military successes of the ten days' war. He admitted, too, that I and the United Nations Observers in a way were regarded as 'enemies.' The Jews looked at the matter in this way: they had at last got free from the British mandate. But they felt that they were not yet completely free. They had only come under a fresh control, the control exercised by the United Nations."

"Israelis now swashbuckling," Bunche wrote in his diary. "Shertok pompous. Jewish imperialism rampant."

"Nothing that I could propose," the frustrated mediator wrote, "aroused any response; I got nowhere. It was significant to read later in the Jewish newspaper *Palestine Post*: 'Count Bernadotte has had a fruitless meeting with the Foreign Minister of Israel.' "

British Foreign Secretary Bevin alluded to the similarity in tone between Israeli officials and the underground in a top-secret memo to Secretary Marshall. "[Bevin] thought that in larger picture, there is very little reality in disavowals by the Provisional Government of Israel of IZL (Irgun) and Stern activities. From the point of view of Arabs and Middle East peace they were Jews with the same objectives, only difference being that one group is more activist than the other."

Dispassion and detachment—the qualities Bernadotte felt were essential for his mediation—were the ones for which he was faulted by Israelis. These same qualities enabled him to carry on in an increasingly hostile atmosphere. Somehow he managed not to take personally the hate swirling around him. "Shertok"—the Swede recalled his chilly meeting—"was fighting for what was to him a holy cause; my impression was that in so doing he often used expressions and methods that he would have preferred not to have to adopt. His life had only one purpose and object, namely to fight for the State and people of Israel. . . ."

On one subject, Bernadotte lost his dispassion: the plight of thousands of Palestinian refugees. "Before we left Jerusalem," he recalled, "I visited Ramallah, where thousands of refugees from Lydda and Ramleh were assembled. I have made the acquaintance of a great many refugee camps; but never have I seen a more ghastly sight than that which met my eyes here at Ramallah. The car was literally stormed by excited masses shouting with Oriental fervor that they wanted food and wanted to return to their homes. There were plenty of frightening faces in that sea of suffering humanity. I remember . . . a group of scabby and helpless old men with tangled beards who thrust their emaciated faces into the car and held out scraps of bread that would certainly have been considered quite uneatable by ordinary people, but was their only food. Perhaps there was no immediate danger of this camp becoming a breeding ground of epidemic diseases that would spread all over Palestine. But what would happen at the beginning of October, when the rainy season began and the cold weather set in?"

The Swede proved prescient. In the decades to come, the refugee camps would become "breeding-grounds" not only of "epidemic diseases" but for a disease less known to Bernadotte, terrorism.

Let the old and women and children return to their homes, Bernadotte pleaded with Shertok, as an interim measure. Let the Arabs first recognize our right to exist, Shertok replied, not before.

Desperate for a sign of continued UN commitment to his cause, Bernadotte returned to Rhodes to confer with Commander Jackson, sent by the UN Secretariat to appease the Swede's mounting distress. As they sat together on the roof garden of the Hôtel des Roses, Bernadotte repeated his urgent plea for both men and arms for several critical locations in Jerusalem. Above all, he needed to safeguard the pumping station at Latrun, the source of the city's water supply, now under token UN "protection." Commander Jackson promised to do his best to get him the 250 UN guards armed with machine guns that the mediator considered the barest minimum to carry out his mission.

Bernadotte then shocked the Australian officer by announcing he planned to return to Jerusalem as soon as possible. "I pleaded with him not to do so," Jackson recalled, "pointing out that by doing so he would immediately become an obvious target for those who did not want the United Nations intervention to succeed. As I spoke," Jackson recalled, "my mind was fixed on the assassination of Lord Moyne, and other friends who had been killed recently for political reasons. Bernadotte was clearly reluctant to accept my reasoning and my reiterated pleas to bring the representatives to talk with him in Rhodes singly if that was necessary and then jointly if progress was made. We must have argued . . . for the best part of two hours until finally he said: 'Do you remember our first conversation at Le Bourget?' 'Very clearly.' 'And you said that nothing was more important than that the United Nations as an institution should not fail in this matter?' 'I did.' 'Then you cannot disagree with my view that any individual is insignificant compared to the cause to which we are all committed?' I had no answer to that question."

The next day, Bernadotte flew to Jerusalem, where he summoned the resident press corps to a news conference at the graceful villa of Belgian Consul General Jan Nieuwenhuys in the city's prosperous Talbiya district. Ringed by barbed wire and crammed full of weapons was Lehi's camp, under the command of its "general," Yitzhak Shamir, three hundred meters away. Bernadotte approached the Belgian residence flanked by the newly arrived Swedish General Aage Lundström and his driver, the boisterous former FBI officer Colonel Frank Begley. Right away, the three men spotted two jeeps parked outside the consular residence. Young men and women holding placards reading "You Work in Vain—We Are Here, Fighters for the Freedom of Israel" and "Stockholm Is Yours—Jerusalem is Ours" blocked the mediator's way.

Newsreel footage of the count's arrival shows Bernadotte brushing past a scruffy, bearded young man standing nonchalantly with a group of correspondents: Baruch Nadel. The terrorist took his first hard look at the man in Lehi's gunsights. "He looked very good, very fit, especially for his age. Tall and straight and slim in his shorts. But I felt nothing. Not hate or any other emotion. We knew we were going to kill him, so we did not fear him. The other Jews were all afraid of Bernadotte, but not us."

Nadel and "Benjamin" Brenner were ostensibly there to cover the event for *Mivrak*. "One of the foreign reporters asked Bernadotte to stand near the jeeps, so they could take his picture. He pushed them aside and entered the house. You could see how steamed up he was," Nadel recalled. "I remember that the room in which the press conference was held had a little pool in the middle, filled with goldfish. In Jerusalem we barely had enough water to drink and there was this pool full of water. Bernadotte sat near the Belgian consul and the journalists sat on the floor on the other side of the pool. It was all done to show us that he didn't care about us, you know," Nadel asserted.

"Everybody spoke English, all the Israeli reporters, too. But since I didn't know English very well, or at least I was in the city which was the capital of my country, I didn't want to talk in the language of those who enslaved us; I spoke the language of my country. I asked in Hebrew, but very politely, 'Respected Count, you say that Jerusalem should be internationalized because it has international institutions; why shouldn't Stockholm be internationalized, since it is the home of the Nobel Prize, an international institution?'

"He had a dark look on his face because he understood our message, 'Stockholm is yours, Jerusalem is ours.' And he turned to the Belgian consul at his side and asked, 'Who is this man?' And he was told, 'Lehi.' But nobody translated my question for him. So I said in a loud voice, in Hebrew, 'I am sorry but my question has not been answered yet. And I would like it to be answered.' And an Israeli journalist said to the count, 'No, don't answer it.' But Meltzer of the *New York Times* [Julian Louis Meltzer] translated the question for him. Bernadotte turned pale and then he said, 'No comment.' "

Brenner recalled asking the mediator, "Why not divide Stockholm, instead of Jerusalem?" "And Bernadotte turned to the Belgian Consul and whispered into the open microphone, 'Why do these Jews always ask such insolent questions?'

"Now, there was a war going on between us and the Arabs, you could hear shooting in the Old City while we were at the press conference. In that sort of an atmosphere you just don't make provocative comments like Bernadotte's," Brenner said.

Nadel was appalled at the meekness of the Israeli journalists. "Bernadotte spoke of himself in the third person, and he told them, 'Count Bernadotte said he would be tougher and tougher! Now write this down,' he told them. And they all began to write! And he reached for a cigarette and one of them jumped to give him a light. And the next day in the paper it said, 'Our reporter gave the mediator a light.' They were all ghetto Jews"— Nadel fairly spits out the term. "All of them."

The news conference was still in progress when two hastily summoned armored cars bearing the Israeli Defense Forces insignia screeched to a stop in front of the Belgian consul's residence. An agitated colonel wearing the eyepatch that would be his signature on the battlefield sprang out. "Get moving!" Moshe Dayan, newly named commander of the Israeli Defense Forces in Jerusalem, ordered the Lehi demonstrators. "Get out of here!" The terrorists saw the gun mounted on his car, and withdrew.

Following the mediator's press conference, Nadel "walked back to the Lehi camp. Nobody said a word about a decision having been taken by the Center to kill Bernadotte. But I noticed that there was a third jeep, in perfect condition, brought from Tel Aviv, which had not been sent out with the other two to the Belgian consulate. And this jeep would sit there for the rest of the month; nobody was allowed to use it. There were maybe a hundred fifty people there, thirty of them women, and Shamir and Eldad. I told them how the demonstration went. In his broadcast that night, Eldad announced, 'This time Lehi came unarmed and did not take the count's miserable life. But if he tries to dig his nails into Jerusalem again, we will deal with him the right way.' So, as far as we were concerned, we had warned him."

But the warning missed its mark. In his diary, Bernadotte wrote of the hostile press conference. "I soon became aware that I was being subjected, particularly from Irgun quarters, to a series of often fatuous questions, which it was hoped would trip me into giving replies that could be turned against me later. By this time, however, I was becoming quite practiced in warding off attacks of this nature." It was not in the Swede's nature to contemplate the possibility that "Irgun quarters" had weapons deadlier than "fatuous questions" in their armory.

"When we demonstrated in front of him and told him, 'Go away from our Jerusalem, go back to Stockholm!' he did not respond," asserted Lehi's Jerusalem commander, Yehoshua Zetler. "We should not have had to do what we did—all the people should have stood up, the state should have risen up. Ben-Gurion should have risen up! Go away, why are you here? But nobody stood up. So we had no choice."

If the meaning of the audacious demonstration was lost on Bernadotte, it was clear to Ben-Gurion. At his August 11 cabinet meeting, the prime minister announced, "Something very grave could have happened yesterday. Bernadotte was in Jerusalem and Lehi sent out some jeeps, nobody knows why. There are those who say that they wanted to kidnap him. I am not among Bernadotte's admirers," the jut-jawed leader with the flaring white hair noted, "but he is a representative of the United Nations."*

Nevertheless, the same week, Israeli Interior Minister Yitzhak Gruenbaum, charged with bringing the underground—which in Jerusalem openly flouted the state's authority—to heel, told the cabinet a "policy of continued tolerance" was better than using force. The prime minister agreed to let him try. We are now responsible for Jerusalem, Ben-Gurion reminded Gruenbaum. We have declared that Israeli law applies there as well. The situation is particularly grave there, the prime minister asserted, as the city is in the international spotlight. We will be judged by what we do there.

An unaccustomed heaviness in his step had replaced Bernadotte's buoyant stride as he alighted from his plane upon landing at Rhodes on August 11. "He had aged quite suddenly that sum-

---

*Though Jerusalem was not officially part of Israel proper, on July 26, Ben-Gurion had appointed a military governor, Dov Joseph, to govern New Jerusalem as Israeli-occupied territory.

mer, no question about it. Something of the quickness in him was gone," Barbro Wessel recalled. The forced smile and a sub- dued manner unusual in the man spoke of the discouragement he did not articulate. Nor was Estelle there to lift his spirits. She and the boys had returned to Stockholm. Absent, too, was the loyal, irreverent Bunche. Bernadotte had dispatched him to America to plead once more for Washington's support.

"What is needed," Bunche bluntly told George Marshall dur- ing their August 6 meeting in the secretary's vast chambers, "is not numbers, but a token force to restore confidence that the Mediator has UN support. . . . In the Mediator's opinion," Bunche asserted, "the US has the deepest obligation to assist him in meeting these urgent needs. In accepting the principle that he would rely exclusively upon Truce Commission powers [i.e., US, France, and Belgium, and not the Soviet Union and/or Soviet bloc] he bowed to US wishes. As Mediator he cannot now accept the position that he must do without adequate assistance."

Bunche argued persuasively, but too late. On the very day Bernadotte returned to Rhodes, his mission's last scrap of credi- bility went up in smoke and ashes. During the night of August 15, three unarmed UN guards posted to the water-pumping sta- tion at Latrun withdrew to the nearby monastery, several hun- dred yards away, where they were bivouacked. Latrun was the primary source of Jewish Jerusalem's water supply and was under UN protection. The thunderclap of an explosion that shook the Judean Hills blasted the UN guards from their sleep several hours later. The men rushed to the pumping station and found only its smoldering remains. Expert Arab "irregulars" had placed explosives within and under the pumps. "Responsibility for the disaster," Colonel Albert L. Perry, the senior United Na- tions truce observer, later stated, "goes directly back to the UN's failure, after the most urgent requests, to supply armed guards."

The charred ruins of the Latrun water-pumping station pro- vided Israelis a handy metaphor for the world body's impotence. Bernadotte, too, grasped the meaning of this latest blow. "I had asked time and again for a month that the 40 armed police who were needed to guard Latrun should be sent. They had not yet come. And now the pumping station had been blown up. The consequences of this act were incalculable."

Now the shattered mediator clung to his imminent escape from the region as to a life raft. The means for getting away was the approach of his mid-August trip to Stockholm, to chair the International Red Cross Conference. "I had to consider now whether I ought not to cancel my journey. . . . If I went the Jewish Press might interpret it as showing a lack of sense of responsibility—even though there was nothing I could do if I stayed. On the other hand, to cancel my journey might easily give the impression that the situation in Palestine was more serious than it actually was."

Though the secretary-general had approved this trip as one of Bernadotte's conditions for accepting his post as mediator, Lie, who still refused to visit the troubled region, now had second thoughts. "Viewed from here it seems to me that there is very considerable danger that your absence from Palestine in near future may endanger remarkable results you have already achieved," Trygve Lie wired Bernadotte in early August. "I fully appreciate and remember original agreement that you should return to Stockholm for Red Cross Convention, but know that you would not wish to press this point if your absence endangers whole Palestine position."

Nothing would stop the exhausted, dispirited, fifty-three-year-old man from flying home on August 13. "To get away from my work for a short time might possibly be all to the good," he rationalized; ". . . perhaps it would be good for me to breathe a different atmosphere for a little while. . . ."

CHAPTER NINETEEN

WHAT WENT WRONG?

SUCCESS, THE SAYING GOES, HAS MANY FATHERS; FAILURE IS AN OR-
phan. And so it was with the Bernadotte mission, an orphan by
August 1948, with the once-proud midwives who had presided
at its birth now busily distancing themselves from the child. The
United Nations, and the State Department under George C.
Marshall, having presented the mediator with few guidelines but
an almost unlimited mandate to redraw the map of Palestine and
secure, as the Swede saw fit, their cherished dream of peace in
the region, failed to provide him the minimal support required
for the job. They were simply relieved the problem was out of
their hands.

By mid-August it was apparent that the Bernadotte mediation
had careened out of control. How did it happen? officials in
London, New York, and Washington now wondered out loud.
Where did Bernadotte go wrong? For in the State Department
and within the halls of the UN Secretariat, they had read the almost gleeful references in the *Palestine Post,* the voice of Israel's
moderate center, to another round of "useless discussions" between Bernadotte and Israeli leaders. "Count Bernadotte conferred for two hours yesterday with Dr. Dov Joseph, Military
Governor of Jerusalem," the *Post* reported. "The Foreign Minister, Mr. Shertok, arrived in the city while the talk was in
progress, but he did not attend. . . . Israeli sources are none too
confident that the supposedly indefinite truce will last long."
The *Post,* obviously unaware of the acrimonious secret session
held at the King David Hotel between the foreign minister and

the mediator, and witnessed by Baruch Nadel, recounted. The newspaper featured elaborate accounts of the count's fine time on the other side of the divide. "After holding a press conference, Count Bernadotte was the guest at lunch of Brigadier Glubb Pasha and Lt. Col. Abdullah el-Tel at the Rockefeller Museum [in Jerusalem]. He spent an hour at Ramallah where he was welcomed by the Mayor Khalil eff Saleh, and met Sir Raphael Cilento [the UN official charged with the refugee problem] who was touring Arab refugee districts."

Before leaving Israel for Stockholm, Bernadotte himself had been startled by Foreign Minister Shertok's offer of direct, unmediated peace talks with the Arabs, a suggestion unlikely to elicit a favorable response, but which spoke reams about Israel's contempt for the mediator's efforts. The wires between the UN Secretariat and the State Department burned with urgent and astonished queries. What went wrong? they wondered.

"Israel becoming increasingly intransigent with regard to Jerusalem, the Mediator, and observers," cabled Jessup to Marshall on August 9. And from the US consulate in Jerusalem to Secretary Marshall, three days later, this: "Mrs. Myerson's [Golda Meir's] attitude re Jerusalem is alarming as she is considered one of the most moderate of Jewish leaders."* On the heels of this cable, the consul followed with an attempt to explain the shift in Israeli posture to his chief, who had never set foot in the region. Based on a conversation with the director of Jerusalem's Hebrew University, Dr. Werner Senator, Consul MacDonald wired Marshall that the "great majority [of Israelis] now opposed to the internationalization of Jerusalem. He attributes shift in opinion basically *to loss of confidence in the United Nations and Bernadotte.* [Italics added.] [Dr. Senator] blames following factors for deterioration of United Nations influence: Bernadotte's proposal to turn Jerusalem over to Arabs, worldwide and particularly Christian disinterest in the fate of Jerusalem, a long list of incidents culminating in the blowing up of the Latrun water pumping station which indicate the UN's inability to enforce its decisions. [He] *felt the apparent impotence of the United Nations*

---

*Golda Meir, a member of Ben-Gurion's Labor Party and a close ally of the prime minister, had since 1948 been pursuing secret negotiations with King Abdullah regarding the future of Arab Palestine.

has given great impetus to elements who favor disregarding United Nations and relying on Jewish force." (Italics added.)

Now even Secretary Marshall dropped his glacial composure and interrupted President Truman's reelection campaign with a top-secret memorandum. There was trouble ahead, he warned, due to the *"hostility of Israelis . . . toward the military observers serving under Count Bernadotte . . . the refusal of the Israeli military governor in Jerusalem to cooperate with Count Bernadotte"* (italics added), as well as the Israeli refusal to accept the return of approximately 300,000 Arab refugees. But instead of proposing that the UN's meager presence in Palestine be shored up into something other than the "laughingstock" Dov Joseph had called it, Marshall had other ideas. Let us make good use of Israel's need for American dollars and diplomatic recognition as bargaining chips to modify the new state's conduct. "As a friend of Israel," Marshall wrote the president, "we deem it of paramount importance that this new republic not place itself before the bar of world opinion and the United Nations in the role of an aggressor."

Truman once described his personal decision-making process thus, "Once a decision was made I did not worry about it afterward. I had trained myself to look back into history for precedents, because instinctively I sought perspective in the span of history for the decisions I had to make." Truman had already made up his mind. The president's intimate knowledge of the Old Testament imbued him with a sense of the justice of the new state's self-assertion. Intertwined with this conviction were the imperatives of his party's domestic politics, which were strongly pro-Israel. With the presidential election only two and a half months away, Harry Truman could not ignore the growing force of the Jewish lobby.

Besides, in assuming Israel would respond well to the implicit threat of the judgment of "world opinion," Secretary Marshall had missed a very basic point. "Israel does not owe its existence to the sacrifice of others," Abba Eban maintained many years later. "The memory of having won birth and survival by a solitary decision has worked on Israeli attitudes ever since, giving us strength against outside pressures. Self-reliance has become our posture, since neither the UN nor anybody else has risked any blood when our destruction was imminent."

The paralyzing consequences of Secretary Marshall's tepid response to Bernadotte's many pleas for help made one fact of the UN's existence clear to the Swede. He could not operate without full and firm American and, to a somewhat lesser extent, British backing. Bernadotte, Bunche told the secretary of state in mid-August, "is not eager to offer suggestions until he is assured that the US and UK governments are in agreement" with his proposals. The mediator felt that "if UK and US are in agreement and if these governments can reach a general line in accord with his views (upon which he does not insist), chances are that both Jews and Arabs, although violently protesting, may quietly move along lines of eventual settlement."

In Stockholm, Folke Bernadotte savored "the change of air" and the soothing quiet of his hometown's streets as he prepared to chair the International Red Cross Conference. In Jerusalem, the truce was flagrantly violated by both sides. Mortar and artillery shells once more reverberated against ancient walls and in streets deserted by nearly all but the bravest or most desperate. Bernadotte and Bunche had picked the least-opportune moment to be absent from the region. "UN observers appear powerless to take effective action to bring about a cease-fire," the beleaguered American consul wired Secretary Marshall on August 17. "Their moral authority has practically evaporated. Jewish authorities are obstructing the work of the United Nations observers."

Alarm spread like an infection among the UN observers. One of the senior observers Bernadotte left behind in Israel, Henri Vigier of France, cabled Bunche, still in New York: "Much disturbed by last daily report from Jerusalem . . . greater number and sharper tone of accusations and counter accusations. . . . Jews today are openly challenging limitation on admission of men of military age and are skeptical about the United Nations . . . making difficulties for observers. . . . Arab popular excitement is growing, not only against Jews but against Observers, especially Americans, following alleged use of UN arm bands by Jews. . . . The Mediator's quick return might help. . . ."

In mid-August, Folke Bernadotte acquired yet another powerful adversary, this one all the more threatening because he had President Truman's ear. James G. McDonald, former professor of government, had served as the League of Nations high commissioner for refugees and later as a member of the 1946 Anglo-American committee on Palestine. As of the first of August, he was the president's special representative to Israel. McDonald was called a "professional Zionist" by State Department officials, who distrusted his outspoken support of the Zionist cause. Long before most, McDonald had concluded that the Jews of Europe were under sentence of death. It was 1933 and, as the League of Nations high commissioner for refugees, McDonald faced the man who had proclaimed the Third Reich just months before, across a conference table. "I have never forgotten what he [Hitler] said to me," McDonald recalled. " 'The world will yet thank me [Hitler said] for teaching it how to deal with the Jews.' Soon my fears were confirmed in my work," McDonald noted. "I had no difficulty in sharing Dr. Weizmann's pessimism about the future of European Jews and in sympathizing increasingly with the intense devotion to the task of building a Jewish haven in Palestine."

McDonald's many supporters in Tel Aviv and Jerusalem hailed as brilliant his appointment as America's first ambassador to Israel. Implicit in the selection was the fact that President Truman clearly shared McDonald's vision of a strong, secure homeland for world Jewry.

". . . I shall expect you to keep me personally informed," Truman wrote the new envoy, "on such matters as relate to the arms embargo, the appropriate time for full recognition, and the types of assistance as may be required and can properly be granted to the new States. Let me assure you that you have my fullest confidence and support."

After only three weeks in Israel, sidestepping the normal diplomatic channels, McDonald wrote a "Dear Clark" letter to the president's special assistant, Clark Clifford, "to explain more fully why from the point of view of the Provisional Government of Israel the seeming concentration by the US and the UN on the indefinite truce . . . is tantamount to taking sides with the Arabs against the Jews and . . . may finally force the Provisional Government [of Israel] to resume the war despite the possibility of US and UN sanctions.

"So long as the Arabs refuse peace negotiations either directly with the Jews or through the UN or other auspices, it should be perfectly clear Israel cannot demobilize. Until . . . the Arab states recognize the existence of an independent Israel, the Jewish authorities will know that the Arabs are continuing to prepare to destroy the Jewish State.

"Hence an indefinite truce is, from Israel's point of view, equivalent to a death sentence to be executed at the convenience of the Arabs.

"My own conclusion is that since the President and the Department want peace, they should concentrate on getting peace negotiations started. To reply that this is difficult or that the Arabs won't accept is to confess that the Arabs can indefinitely call the tune.

"*On this issue, I do not think that the US should be overly influenced by the views of either the Mediator or the British. The former, so far as I can judge, is almost completely discredited, not only among the Jews, but among the Arabs. His inability to enforce his decisions and his loquacious pronouncements have left him neither substantial moral authority nor dignity.*" (Italics added.)

Apart from Lehi's, the American envoy's was the most damning appraisal of the mediator. The charge came from a man who, though yet to set eyes on Folke Bernadotte, wielded considerable influence in Washington. An oblivious Bernadotte had become a pawn in a high-stakes power game between Secretary Marshall, who still backed the mediator, and James McDonald, who, without knowing him personally, did not. Each man vied for the president's support of his version of the truth. "Changed attitude of Jews in Jerusalem toward Bernadotte and UN," Marshall cabled the American consul in Jerusalem, John J. MacDonald (no relation to the president's special envoy), on August 18, "is due we feel perhaps not so much to intrinsic loss of prestige by Mediator and by UN, as to fact that Jews are seemingly lifting their sights and are campaigning to achieve new objectives, namely control of Jerusalem itself. It would seem natural, if this is the case, for them to deprecate UN and Mediator. . . . Israelis . . . will be making a great mistake if they seek to base [their] policy on the alleged decrease in UN prestige and the ability of the UN to carry out its decisions."

In a telegram marked "Top Secret," the secretary of state wired Ambassador McDonald in Tel Aviv that "I do not concur in your conclusion that 'Jewish emphasis on peace negotiations now is sounder than present US and UN emphasis on truce and demilitarization and refugees. . . . When you state that Jewish emphasis on peace negotiations is sound, do you mean that the Provisional Government of Israel has any assurance that there is any Arab government with which it can negotiate? Please telegraph on this point. . . . Leaders of Provisional Government of Israel should be quick to see that non-military sanction voted by the Security Council as, for example, a ban on any financial transactions with aggressor state or modification of arms embargo, would have immediate consequence in such a state as Israel. In fact, we are hopeful that wise counsels in Israel will perceive that new state cannot exist except by acceptance of international community and that PGI, of all new governments, should be most responsive to this fact.

"We believe that leaders of Israel stand at a moment of greatest opportunity for showing true statesmanship and thus to establish their republic on impregnable moral basis which will lead to sound political and economic development. US stands ready to give Israel its assistance to this end." The cable was signed George C. Marshall; in the margin were scrawled the initials HST.

The new ambassador replied to the secretary of state with another top-secret memorandum addressed to both Truman and Marshall: "I am convinced that neither Ben-Gurion nor Shertok in their talks with me exaggerated when they said in substance: 'On no matter adversely affecting our independence or our security will we yield to the threat of UN sanctions, even if these are backed by your Government, which we know to be our friend. *What we have won on the battlefield we will not sacrifice at the council table.*" (Italics added.) Closing ominously, McDonald pleaded that "our government guard zealously against permitting its good intentions and love of peace [to] betray it into supporting a UN policy which would mean armed conflict with Israel."

Abba Eban was not the only Israeli official who deemed Bernadotte's continued influence to be destructive for his country. The Israeli ambassador to London, Michael Comay, cabled his colleague in Johannesburg that the mediator had met with a complete lack of response from any quarter and "he now seems rather deflated and is concentrating on the truce plus a couple of other issues like the Arab refugees." "We would remove him from the scene altogether" —the ambassador to South Africa echoed Eban's earlier sentiments— "if we had the option. *His mere presence there is unsettling* [italics added], and he remains a potential instrument of pressure against us for territorial and other concessions."

If Bernadotte's "mere presence" was "unsettling" to Israelis, it was partly as a result of the way the high-profile mediator operated: his frequent press conferences, his flying trips around the region, more exceptional then than now, which called too much attention to the man and provided too handy a symbol for those who did not want an imposed settlement of the conflict. Israel's independence was too new, too frail, for it to submit so soon to outside pressure to clip its wings. What Bernadotte failed to grasp was that, from the Israeli perspective, the country had every right to territory won during the summer campaign. "Bernadotte simply didn't take into account the fact that Israel held these territories only as a result of her successful defense against Arab attack," Walter Eytan noted. "He didn't seem to think the Arabs owed Israel anything for the destruction they had caused. So he began to propose compromise proposals which would bedevil the issue for many years."

Obsessed with finding a just settlement, one that would deal fairly with both sides, unfamiliar with the notion of "no war, no peace" which we have come to associate with the region, Bernadotte still believed he could satisfy two essentially irreconcilable adversaries. Equally remarkable is that none of the more seasoned participants, not Secretary Marshall, Trygve Lie, Bunche, nor a slew of professional diplomats in the field, advised him otherwise.

Marshall and McDonald waged their memo wars throughout August and into September, with McDonald pressing for an end to the UN's mediation role and the start of direct US-sponsored Arab-Israeli negotiations. By late August, the secretary of state had finally realized that the mediator could not be left to his own devices. Bernadotte's original proposal, to give Jerusalem to the Arabs, had cost the effort incalculable damage in all but Abdullah's eyes. Ambassador Jessup alerted the secretary of state that, "to avoid a situation wherein the Mediator again makes proposals which are considered unrealistic by both sides and rejected by them," London and Washington should quietly reach an agreement and submit it to the mediator. Marshall now pushed for a joint Anglo-American proposal that would carry the label "Made in Sweden."

Away from Palestine for three weeks, the mediator failed to

grasp that, as the situation in the region deteriorated, the truce daily broken by both sides, so, too, did his stature diminish. As the deflation of his reputation proceeded, so did the inflation of Israel's hopes for a successful fall military offensive. The Israeli Defense Forces had nearly completed the groundwork for the new campaign.

Much to Marshall's chagrin, in late August, Bernadotte announced to the international press in Stockholm (there to cover the Red Cross Conference) that he would be presenting the UN General Assembly with a possible solution for Palestine when it met in Paris in late September. Marshall sent a sharply worded reproof to Stockholm, ordering the US ambassador there to "restrain Bernadotte" while the United States sought to adopt a common line on Palestine with Britain. Once we have that nailed down, Marshall promised, we shall discuss it with the mediator. "However, this last development seems far off, and meanwhile we feel that any approach to the General Assembly on so delicate a question should be most carefully weighed with respect to its timing."

Bernadotte's absence from the scene did not dampen the Israeli press's combative tone toward him. "Mediator Threatens to Report Jews as Violators," read the *Palestine Post*'s headline on August 27, over a story that quoted Colonel Moshe Dayan, commander of the Sixth Brigade, at a press conference. "The trend in recent events tends to undermine my faith in the effectiveness of the measures of the UN Observers to maintain the truce in Jerusalem."

Referring to reports that the UN had charged the Jews with a flagrant violation of the truce in Jerusalem, Colonel Dayan traced the events that preceded the occupation of parts of the city by Jewish and Arab forces. He revealed that for eleven days prior to the occupation of the Agricultural Training Farm and the Arab College by his troops he had warned the UN observers daily that Egyptian troops were closing in on the area from the south. He had suggested to Brigadier General William E. Riley, Count Bernadotte's representative in Jerusalem, that a meeting be called with the Egyptian commander, but the general had stated that "it was difficult to make contact with the Egyptians."

Bunche left New York with the uneasy feeling that "quite apart from the Arabs and Israelis, his own Secretary General was not very solidly behind Bernadotte and himself [Bunche]." He arrived at Stockholm on August 31 to brief Bernadotte on his own unsuccessful efforts in New York and Washington to obtain more political and material support for the mediator. "Everyone here seems to have a title," Bunche noted of Bernadotte's Swedish circle. He found the Swedes nervously preparing for a Red Army invasion of their country. Estelle Bernadotte had already sent some of the family valuables to New York. Bunche's visit had another purpose. "He made the trip to Stockholm," Mrs. Bernadotte noted, "to report that Folke must see Lie before the General Assembly meeting, which had been moved from New York to Paris because of the refusal of the Dominican Republic to attend if it was held in New York. Folke had convinced Lie that the question of the [Arab] refugees must be on the agenda. When Ralph checked, he found that someone had been to Lie and succeeded in having the subject crossed off the agenda. . . . Trygve Lie proved himself a yes man if ever there was one. . . . Ralph knew what importance Folke attached to that problem, so Folke returned to Rhodes by way of Paris, where he could contact Lie and succeeded in getting the problem back on the agenda."

On Wednesday, September 1, Bernadotte and Bunche boarded the mediator's white plane for the Middle East. The count had been away from Israel for three weeks, a long time in the life of the three-month-old state. The parting for Folke and Estelle Bernadotte was made the more difficult as the couple had managed very little time alone together during those weeks. "One of the few evenings during the Red Cross Conference that Folke and I were able to be alone at home," Estelle Bernadotte recalled, "we went through all the details involved in the possible return of his body from Jerusalem (where he intended making his future headquarters), and the funeral proceedings. One problem regarding which we decided to call an old scouting comrade—a minister—had to do with finding out whether a coffin had to be transported [to Israel] or if cremation could be possible. We found out that cremation was not customary [in Israel]."

So unafraid of death was Bernadotte that he could spend an evening with his well-loved wife calmly planning his own funeral. The couple said no goodbyes. "See you in three weeks," Bernadotte promised his wife, for they planned to meet in Paris on September 19, to celebrate her forty-fourth birthday.

"Not enthusiastic about seeing Rhodes again," Bunche, who had vowed not to return without his wife but had been forced to do so, groused upon arriving. "Same place, same weather, same faces." Bernadotte immediately shifted into high gear, plunging back into his frenetic shuttle diplomacy as if his mandate had not in the intervening weeks been whittled down to a fragment.

In Cairo, Bernadotte and Bunche met with Azzam Pasha, who no longer impressed the mediator with either his wisdom or his statesmanship. Nor could Bernadotte have any illusions left regarding the Israelis' view of his efforts. Azzam Pasha related to him efforts by "Jewish representatives in Paris" to initiate direct talks between the two sides. "I heard very much the same thing again at a later conversation with the Syrian Prime Minister," Bernadotte recounted in his memoirs. "He told me that he had had a letter from a Jewish agent urging that no further use should be made of my services, as I was a British and American agent. Azzam Pasha told me, however, that it would be a mistake to open direct negotiations with the Jews. If any discussions were to come about on a final proposal for a settlement, they should be conducted through me as Mediator."

It was no longer just Lehi or Irgun that referred to Bernadotte as a British or American agent; Israeli authorities in their official communications now routinely dubbed him as such. "Change in the atmosphere here," reads Bunche's diary note of their September 9 meeting with the Israeli foreign minister. "Shertok and all his advisers no longer in shirtsleeves. They are all dressed up with ties and jackets. Shertok has a secretary taking verbatim notes of everything he says. The military officers now all have epaulettes and rank insignia and wear proper uniforms."

Bernadotte was not the only man in the region who was in a hurry. Ironically, fear that the mediator would succeed in getting the General Assembly to reopen the subject of Palestine later that month was part of the impulse behind Ben-Gurion's drive to prepare for a new round of fighting. Israel must present the world with new "facts on the ground."

With equal haste, three comrades, so familiar with each other's ways they needed little discussion, met in a drab fourth-story apartment on Tel Aviv's Ben-Yehuda Street. Yalin-Mor, tall, spectacled, running to fat after months of life as an armchair revolutionary, hosted the meeting of the Lehi high command. They all knew the purpose of the September 10 meeting, knew why Yehoshua Zetler sat restlessly waiting in the next room.

Time was running out. On September 5, the *Palestine Post*, in an article headlined "Mediator to Tour Capitals This Week," predicted, "This may be one of the last tours the Mediator makes through Arab and Jewish areas before he submits his report to the UN."

The barrel-chested man with the bushy eyebrows, "Michael," waited for the bellicose Eldad to release the gust of fury he had barely contained all summer. "If the world listens to Bernadotte and pressures our weakling government into making compromises, we will have lost our state!" Eldad thundered. "We cannot let this happen. We must show the world that it is just as futile for the United Nations to interfere in our affairs as it was for the British. Demonstrations are not enough."

Yalin-Mor, harboring future political ambitions, was uneasy still. The quiet one of the three, as usual, held his peace. But Shamir had pondered the operational aspect of the decision long enough. Shamir, who eight years earlier had recruited new members to Stern's underground with the cry "Men! If you want to smell fire and powder, come with us!" was ready to set the machinery of the assassination in motion.

"All right," Yalin-Mor conceded, "but this time we must have a cover," he insisted on that hot and sticky September day that sealed a man's fate. "Lehi cannot take responsibility this time." Shamir and Eldad agreed. After all, they were operating under the laws of their own country now, no longer merely striking a blow against British injustice. Shamir and Eldad were equally aware that among other reasons for the need of cover were their comrade's political aspirations in the upcoming Knesset elections.

Later that week, Yalin-Mor summoned Baruch Nadel from Jerusalem to Tel Aviv, to the Lehi commander's home. "He asked me a very curious question, a question I would only understand later. 'What do you think about "Hazit Hamoledeth" as a name for a movement?' Hazit Hamoledeth means 'Fatherland Front,' and I had a very uneasy feeling about this. It sounded like a Communist movement, and of course Yalin-Mor was heading that way anyway. But I said, 'Well, it's OK with me.' Later, when I found out what they really had in mind, I learned that it was the name of the Bulgarian Communist underground during the Nazi occupation."

" 'Hazit Hamoledeth,' Yalin-Mor, the budding socialist, told Shamir and Eldad, 'will be our cover. Fatherland Front, after the wartime Bulgarian underground. And no one, not even within Lehi's ranks, must know any more than that. People might suspect that it is Lehi, but we cannot give Ben-Gurion the means to finish us off.' "

The day they passed Bernadotte's sentence, American Ambassador James G. McDonald finally met the man whose efforts he had worked hard to undermine. McDonald invited Bernadotte to lunch during the Swede's flying visit to Tel Aviv on September 9. "The Count struck me as charming, public-spirited, wholly devoted, but not unusually able or perceptive," McDonald wrote in his memoirs. "He had, however, surrounded himself with an excellent staff; it included men of exceptional intelligence and of marked practical ability. Dr. Bunche, it seemed to me, was unquestionably the intellectual leader of the group, widely informed, cogent in his arguments and withal extremely charming.

"Bernadotte, speaking here with such charm and such cheerfulness, was in truth a tragic figure. He was working with forces beyond his control, and whose violence he underestimated; with all his nobility of character, his complete devotion to duty and his desire to succeed, he was progressing slowly in the work to which he had been assigned with such high hopes. . . . When after lunch some of the Count's colleagues spoke of the possibility that he might move his headquarters from Rhodes to Jerusalem, I could not help sounding a demurrer. 'I have fears for your safety,' I said. 'Jerusalem is still an armed camp—in fact several armed camps.' "

Shamir, Yalin-Mor, and Eldad had no trouble deciding who would lead the commando unit charged with the Hazit Hamoledeth mission: Zetler, the zealot who had kept Lehi alive in Jerusalem, and Yehoshua Cohen, the fighter who four years earlier had trained Lord Moyne's assassins. This was to be an even more momentous deed, however. The count, after all, did not represent a single power, but the United Nations. "Bernadotte was a personality and he had the power," Eldad recounted. "And what was the Jewish Army in 1948? He had the United Nations behind him and maybe he would overcome Ben-Gurion. This was a weak country. By this act, all foreign elements would be put on notice."

Zetler, elated at his orders, immediately sped back to Jerusalem. At Lehi's Camp Dror, he and the twenty-five-year-old Yehoshua Cohen picked their team of gunmen. "The operation was not difficult or dangerous in my eyes: to attack someone who is unprepared, without fear of any particular surprises. The main problem was the need to keep secret the identity of those who carried it out. They had to be good fighters but also know how to keep their mouths shut."

Cohen had a proven record as a clandestine guerrilla. He chose three others he felt were equally adept in the trade of death and silence. Yitzhak Ben-Moshe, known as "Betzalely" in the underground, one of those nameless, faceless, nerveless killers, who later became the pillar of his kibbutz, Kivri. "Gingi" Zinger, described by his comrades as "quiet and serious," a man hardened by his time in a British prison in Africa, where he and Cohen first met. Meshulam Makover, "Tall Yoav," a lanky six-footer with a drooping reddish mustache, selected for the mission because, as a child of Jerusalem's Old City, he knew every crooked alley and side street. A former member of the Irgun, he also possessed an ability deemed exceptional in the mostly prison-bred underground: he was a skilled driver. Also in common with the others, Makover was a man uncomfortable with words, but committed body and soul to Lehi's fixation: Jerusalem as capital of the new state.

"One day Zetler came to my room at Camp Dror," Makover remembered, "and within a casual conversation asked: What is your opinion regarding the liquidation of Bernadotte? I did not hide my enthusiasm. Two or three days later, Zetler came back and said, 'We have decided to do it. You will be on the operations team. Begin to prepare yourself.' He mentioned the names of the other members of the team. And so we began to organize ourselves."

One part of their mandate the commandos could not fulfill: absolute secrecy. According to Nadel, there were too many clues that a major operation was under way for others in Lehi to ignore. "Zetler came back from Tel Aviv and started telling people he cared about to look for places to hide. A number went into hiding in Jerusalem. They would go to somebody and rent one of the hundreds of rooms left behind when thousands of people fled to Tel Aviv. He told some others to go join the Israeli Army. He didn't give a reason, he just said, 'There's nothing for you to do here.' Arms, handguns, submachine guns, rifles, light machine guns were taken from the camp and hidden around town. In a city which was pretty much abandoned, you could hide a hundred tanks and nobody would find them."

Nadel, who stayed on in Jerusalem, recalled the moment he knew the assassination was in motion. Early in September, a large Chrysler sedan rolled out of the camp. Behind the wheel was a UN officer wearing the insignia of a Canadian soldier. In the back sat a tall man, dressed like a Canadian colonel. The guard at the entrance of Dror found it a little strange that UN people were leaving, but he was used to keeping his mouth shut. The colonel told the soldier to drive to the YMCA. On a narrow street near the YMCA building, the Chrysler stalled. The agitated soldier worked up a sweat but failed to get the car to start up again. Finally, the colonel stepped out and peered under the hood. After a while, he told the soldier to move and got behind the wheel himself. The car started up. "Sorry," the Canadian colonel told the soldier, "but I will have to drive on the day. You don't know much about these cars." And that is how Makover, disguised as a Canadian colonel, was chosen as the driver of the jeep.

"This was an early experiment to see if we could kill Bernadotte at the entrance of the YMCA. But they decided against this plan. It was too risky, too close to the UN. We knew that if Bernadotte came to Jerusalem, he would go to the Government House and from there he must go back to the New City, to the Y. Two routes led there, so we began preparations for an ambush at both."

While Yehoshua Cohen and his three-man death squad selected their weapons from Lehi's well-stocked armory and practiced sharpshooting on a firing range in an abandoned field in West Jerusalem, Ambassador James McDonald was picking up disturbing rumors in Tel Aviv. The first call came from his namesake, American Consul General John J. MacDonald. "He was greatly disturbed. He had been in a Jerusalem café when a group of terrorists came up to him, threatened him openly and warned him that the United States 'would not be permitted to replace Britain and that this would soon be made unmistakably clear.' He also reported that there had been open threats made in Jerusalem against Bernadotte as allegedly a British agent.

"Cummings [Herbert J. Cummings, the ambassador's special assistant, released from the Department of Commerce for temporary duty to Tel Aviv], who had been frequenting Sternist haunts with his 'girlfriend,' also had disquieting news for me. Something was going on, he said. Somehow he had the impression that preparations were being made for a violent blow somewhere."

The ambassador summoned an Israeli police officer to his Tel Aviv residence to alert him to the rumors. "The officer gave us every assurance that he was perfectly informed and would know in advance of any terrorist plan for action. . . . Later, I had the opportunity to speak to Sharett [Shertok]. . . . I recounted the rumors . . . and I cited the experience of John J. MacDonald. Sharett was much concerned and told me in strictest confidence of the Cabinet's decision taken the previous Sunday to dissolve the terrorist organizations. However, a difference of opinion within the cabinet and a plea for delay had postponed formal action until the following Sunday [September 19].

"I learned today too that some members of the Cabinet, including some of the rabbis, had asked for the delay in the hope of persuading the terrorists to dissolve peacefully and thus avoid the use of force and consequent bloodshed."

The ambassador and his daughter, Bobby, dined with Foreign Minister Sharett on the evening following McDonald's meeting with the Israeli police officer. "The twelve guests included the Chief Inspector of Police, Yehezkiel Sachar, and his wife. Shortly before the party broke up, I took Sachar aside and repeated the warning about possible terrorist direct action which I had given the previous Tuesday night to Sharett. Sachar listened attentively but gave no indication that he thought there was any cause for alarm or for emergency precaution action, not even when I repeated what Cummings had said of the impressions he had gained among the Sternists that they were about to strike. Nor was Sachar impressed even when I warned that a single blow by the Sternists might do Israel irretrievable harm. He commented, 'When terrorists talk most they are least dangerous. We know what they are doing. There is nothing to fear.'"

CHAPTER TWENTY

THE END OF THE
MEDIATION

OBLIVIOUS TO THE GATHERING DARKNESS, FOLKE BERNADOTTE
spent his last week absorbed in efforts he was still convinced
would make a lasting contribution to peace in the Middle East.
Back in the dowdy familiarity of the Hôtel des Roses, he and
Bunche, pulled even closer by adversity, settled down to work on
the mediator's recommendations for a long-term solution to the
Arab-Israeli war, modestly entitled "Progress Report of the
United Nations Mediator on Palestine." Bernadotte was to personally present it to the General Assembly, about to be convened
in Paris.

Finally aware that if one of the two sides in the conflict refused to acknowledge the other's existence, the two could hardly
be expected to form a "union," Bernadotte dropped the notion
of an Israeli-Transjordanian merger. In his new plan, Jerusalem
would belong neither to Israel nor to the Arabs, but would be internationalized along the original UN proposal. All of the fertile
Galilee would go to Israel, while Ben-Gurion's beloved Negev,
would, in return, go to Transjordan. Bunche recalled how
Bernadotte reached this decision. "After a sleepless night,
Bernadotte called [Bunche] at 5 A.M. and said that while he had
previously considered giving the Arabs only the part of the
Negev south of the 31st parallel, he had now decided to win
them over by detaching the Negev in its entirety from the State
of Israel."

Bernadotte also insisted on including in his peace proposal a
strong statement on the right of the Arab refugees to return to

their homes, or to receive compensation for their loss. He wrote "finis" on his mission by proposing that a UN Conciliation Commission succeed him.

On paper, it read like a fair-minded solution to an essentially unsolvable problem. Bernadotte was asking a great deal of the new nation, however. This decent, if somewhat naive, man underestimated the anger and alienation of the people whose support his plan needed if it was to be more than just so many hopeful words on paper. He was asking those who had just reeled from the pitch black into the first daylight of sovereignty to be fair-minded and generous to people bent on their destruction. From Yitzhak Shamir to David Ben-Gurion, Israelis, though suddenly in a position of strength, were in no mood to take the world at its word again. So soon after its own near destruction, this was not a nation ready to trust in any force beyond its own strength. In Israeli eyes, Bernadotte was an essentially detached man from an uninvolved country. What did he know of a struggle for survival?

Bernadotte and Bunche, neither of whom normally seemed to require more than two or three hours of sleep per night, worked without a break for three days and nights, exhausting their assistants, Doreen Daughton and Barbro Wessel, who actually fell ill in the process. Thanks to Bunche's particular drafting genius, their forty-thousand-word report was well on its way to completion by September 12. On that day, Bernadotte's wish for more active Anglo-American backing seemed answered. A member of the British consulate to Rhodes arrived at the Hôtel des Roses to inform Bernadotte that the United Kingdom and the United States had worked out a common line on Palestine, to be communicated to him in a few days' time. What neither Bernadotte nor Bunche understood was that Washington and London planned henceforth to circumvent the world body, which they now treated as little more than a decorous debating society.

"Department believes we are now in general agreement with British," Secretary Marshall had cabled Ambassador Lewis Douglas in London on September 11. "Department's position is one of persistent hope that Palestine dispute may be kept out of UN debate at this juncture. However, British are correct in assuming . . . that it may be necessary to have UN General Assembly, or possibly Security Council, *give blessing* [italics added] to any suggested settlement [i.e., agreed between London and

Washington] in order to enable leaders on both sides to carry their public opinion to acquiesce in such settlement." In plainer words, the world body would serve as a giant rubber stamp for policy decided by the two players with real power, the United States and Great Britain.

On September 13, under the thickest cloak of secrecy, London and Washington each dispatched a troubleshooter to Bernadotte's side: Robert McClintock, Dean Rusk's thirty-seven-year-old assistant, known to the Swede from his days as second secretary to the Stockholm embassy, and fifty-six-year-old Sir John Troutbeck, of His Majesty's Middle Eastern Office in Cairo, were en route to Rhodes. McClintock and Troutbeck were two little-known bureaucrats, with modest reputations outside their respective departments, unlikely to call attention to their mission. Secrecy was essential, for the world must assume this to be the mediator's peace proposal, not that of the two Great Powers. Even US Ambassador to Israel James McDonald was kept in the dark.

"With utmost secrecy," the US State Department cabled the Cairo Embassy on September 9, "inform Bernadotte and Bunche [of] McClintock's impending arrival and nature [of] conversations he authorized to undertake. We reemphasize need for absolute secrecy. In response to chance inquiry from outsiders, it can be said that purpose McClintock's flight Near East is to study Arab refugee problem in which Secretary has expressed deep personal interest."

As is often the case, the State Department and the Foreign Office's insistence on the clandestine nature of the Rhodes mission ultimately backfired. The Middle East is simply not a place where secrets can be kept very long. Within days, rumors were rife of a dark Anglo-American conspiracy behind the mediator's latest proposals. Four and a half decades later, many Israelis are still convinced that the whole thing was dictated by Bevin and Marshall, with Bernadotte meekly doing their bidding. In reality, Bernadotte's proposals were largely his, but remarkably close to the new common Anglo-American line. In a region nourished on conspiracies, this confluence of circumstances could not be accepted as such.

"They are really taking it seriously," Bernadotte commented to Bunche upon receiving word of McClintock and Troutbeck's arrival. Bunche wrote in his diary, "Count elated." Bunche, whose request for 5,000 troops to enforce the "peace" in Jerusalem had been turned down by Marshall, saw this as compensation. "If this comes off, it is my greatest success," he noted.

By the time the two diplomats arrived at the Hôtel des Roses, Bernadotte had already prepared the first draft of his report dealing with mediation, truce, and refugees. The four men then concentrated on the territorial issues. The main bone of contention among them was the Negev. Bernadotte and the British diplomat maintained that giving Israel the whole of Galilee was much more important than "a sliver of worthless desert," thereby missing the symbolism of the Negev for many Israelis. To Ben-Gurion, for instance, who saw it as embodying the promise of rebirth, the Negev represented an open frontier, a sparsely inhabited space that Israel could turn into a flourishing agricultural area. It was also of strategic value as a barrier between Egypt and Jordan, as well as providing access to the Red Sea.

On September 15, McClintock wired Dean Rusk a cable marked "Top Secret": "Department will note general similarity of Bernadotte's conclusions with US and UK views. Our conversations were devoted more to perfection of Bernadotte's first draft of the conclusions than to matters of substance in which all were in agreement. *Neither Troutbeck nor I went over body of Bernadotte's report* [italics added]. . . . Principal matter of substance upon which views of Bernadotte and UK were at variance with our own was whether Israel should be given even a token salient into Negev, such as our suggestion for a projection of Israeli territory south to Beersheba–Gaza road. British proposed southern frontier terminate at latitude of Majdal and found firm support from Mediator. Bernadotte said the responsibility was to propose terms founded on *strict justice* [italics added]. If Jews were to receive all of rich Galilee in return for giving up Negev to Arabs, to whom it would ever remain a worthless desert, Jews should not in his opinion have any salient to that area. Bernadotte was also swayed by information that there are mixed councils in Tel Aviv, Shertok and the more moderate leaders tending to feel that Negev for Galilee is a good bargain, while Weizmann and Ben-Gurion looked with mystical tenacity toward holding Negev and Galilee too.

"I told Bernadotte that I would recommend that Department support his proposals in their entirety, including his suggestion of Majdal-Faluja line as southern boundary of Israel. I made it clear, however, that this recommendation was in no way binding on US Government, that Negev was a question of much political importance to Jews, and that it might eventually be a political good judgment to give Israel a token holding in that area. (I think, however, that *from the point of impartial equity that Bernadotte is right.*)" (Italics added.)

On September 16, Bernadotte roused Bunche at 5 A.M. to say goodbye. Bone-tired after only three hours of sleep, he was on his way to Jerusalem. He felt that between them he and Bunche had produced a high-caliber document, now powerfully backed. "See you in Jerusalem," he told his friend. Bunche was staying behind one day longer to put the finishing touches on their peace proposal. The mediator boarded his plane, whose first stop was Beirut and then Damascus, where he intended to inspect UN-supervised Arab refugee camps. His final destination was Jerusalem.

While the mediator's white Dakota streaked across the blue Mediterranean sky, the foreign minister of Israel called a news conference which, had he known about it, would have burst Folke Bernadotte's bubble of optimism regarding the prospects for peace in Palestine. The short, solemn Moshe Shertok strode into the briefing room in the Hakirya ministry flanked by two uniformed officers: Israeli Defense Forces Chief of Operations Yigal Yadin and Army Commander for Jerusalem Moshe Dayan. Shertok had enlisted the support of such heavy firepower with a purpose. He was throwing down the gauntlet to the mediator. War is in the air, Shertok announced; the Arabs are arming and nobody is trying to stop them, least of all the mediator. Striding up to a nest of microphones, his medals ablaze under the bright lights, the legendary former Haganah commander, now supreme commander of all Israeli forces, Colonel Yadin, spoke. The Army had solid information that the enemy had been bringing up reinforcements on a conspicuous scale. "We thought it better that the world know. The days of truce may come to an end in the very near future."

Preparations for war, Shertok interjected, had been necessitated "by the futility of the truce-observing machinery. It was inconceivable that the 55 UN observers in the Arab countries have things under control." Shertok solemnly noted, "While I do not wish to impute ill will, bias, or intent to discriminate on the part of the truce-observing organization, nevertheless there is discrimination. The Mediator's staff appear to labor under a political theory that it is necessary to show firmness towards Israel, and be a little more lenient and patient with the other side." Quick decisions were made, the foreign minister charged, with respect to charges against the Jews, while there was procrastination with respect to Arab truce violations. There was, for example, no firm reaction after the demolition of the Latrun pumping station, which the mediator called a "grave violation."

The polite euphemisms and lubricating smiles of diplomacy had no place in this news conference, which crackled with belligerence. "General Lundström himself"—Yadin added to the Israeli list of indictments—"told me privately he lacked the manpower to do a proper job of truce observing. Why does he not declare publicly that he cannot perform the task, instead of saying he has everything under control?"

Foreign Minister Shertok concluded by saying, "The truce regime cannot go on." Flanking the foreign minister, the youthful Colonel Dayan added that it was obvious who was doing all the sniping in the area around the YMCA, in the center of Jewish Jerusalem. "Yet the UN does not denounce the violators, but seeks to make concessions with them." Are Israeli forces stronger or weaker than the Arabs since the beginning of the cease-fire? a correspondent asked. The minister hastily replied, "Weaker," but the commander of the Army interrupted him: "A clear answer will be given in the future."

By the time Folke Bernadotte's white plane with the Red Cross markings touched down at Kalandia airstrip near Jerusalem, at ten-thirty on the morning of September 17, the newspaper headlines had picked up the war fever. "Shertok and Army Warn War May Start Soon—Charge Mediator with Truce Discrimination," the *Palestine Post* screamed.

CHAPTER TWENTY-ONE

A MAN CALLED NIMRY

IN THE END, IT WAS BY CHANCE THAT LEHI SUCCEEDED IN KILLING Bernadotte. The assassination should have been aborted by the British mole inside Lehi. "The fact that we got Bernadotte is a historical joke, it was really by mistake," claims Baruch Nadel. That mole, according to Nadel and a handful of other former terrorists who worked with him, was a silken-smooth operator, a self-confessed double agent known by both the British and the underground as "Nimry," Hebrew for "leopard." Legend had it that the agent had slain such an animal while living with a tribe of desert Bedouins. One of the few hard facts about his past that the still-debonair, seventy-plus Nimry will confirm is that he was born Nahum Chachkes, in Haifa.

Talking with Nimry now, it is easy to understand why the British deemed him, in his own words, "a reasonable Jew." In his navy blue blazer, with a polka-dotted ascot tucked inside a white shirt, his thinning gray hair brushed neatly back, in appearance, style, and manner he seems the antithesis of the zealot. Nimry does not deny having been in the employ of the colonial power, but insists the intelligence he provided London was of a "low-grade" variety. His heart, he insists, was always with Lehi's cause.

In the forties as editor of a scholarly periodical, the *Journal of the Middle East Society,* Nimry claims he found the perfect cover for spying on the enemy. "They knew me as a respectable editor. It never occurred to them I was in Lehi." Both Abba Eban and former Israeli President Chaim Herzog were members of

Nimry's academic society and regular contributors to his journal. From 1946 through 1948, Nimry led seminars on the politics and history of the region in his German Colony villa, which was abandoned by its Arab owners. A number of British officers, diplomats, and journalists looking for a chance to while away the long nights of colonial service and for an opportunity to mix with select "natives," were regulars. It was at these gatherings, Nimry claims, that he gathered useful information for the underground. "I passed on information [to Lehi] regarding where [British] arsenals were kept. I found out when they were about to hang two Irgun boys on terrorist charges and alerted the underground, so it could plan to retaliate. The British trusted me. I had lived with Englishmen and learned some of their tricks. I thought we could apply some of these tricks the same way they applied them to us. They were the grand masters of the imperial game, after all. They ran the Empire with a handful of men. I learned from them that giving in, and being the good boy, doesn't play in politics. There is a tribe of Arabs in northern Iraq, devil worshipers. They believe a good god exists and doesn't do much harm. But they offer sacrifices to the bad god. And this is how the British operated vis-à-vis the Arabs. They curried their favor, created the Arab League for them, thinking they could win them over. But of course they couldn't. The whole Arabist line of the British was a failure as a result."

In the hot-wired Lehi camp during the summer of 1948, Nimry was seen by some as a valuable asset and by others as dangerous to deal with. Zetler, a rough man imbued mostly with animal instincts and a finely honed rage against the outside world, was impressed by the suave agent. "Nimry didn't try to hide he was working for the British, but he'd tell us, 'I work for you. I deceive British intelligence,' " recalled Nadel. "From the beginning of June, Nimry and his South African–born partner, Stanley Goldfoot, began playing an important role in the murder of Bernadotte. Zetler put them in charge of intelligence in the case."

Today, Nimry maintains absolute silence on Bernadotte. "I will not enter into discussions of Bernadotte's murder," he flatly states. Another of his comrades in the underground, Y. S. Brenner noted, "I could never free myself of the suspicion that Nimry actually worked for them, not us. But I haven't got the slightest evidence to prove this. Just a gut feeling that something wasn't quite right with him and Goldfoot. But he impressed Zetler and he let them run strategy. Nimry struck me as dangerous."

To Nadel, Nimry is a man "who makes a snake seem like a clumsy creature." Nadel says he alerted Shamir to his suspicions about Nimry. " 'Don't worry,' Shamir replied, 'we keep him at arm's length. We get information from him and feed him harmless material. Sometimes we give him misinformation. We know he's on the British payroll.' " Nimry himself admits he reported to a British intelligence officer named Charteris who was in charge of the Middle East Intelligence Desk in the War Department. "I still see some of my former commanders from those days, and we have very pleasant conversations. They respected me. Of course, they were furious when they found out that I was working for Lehi. But those who had a certain level of intellect and civilization accepted it. I miss those friendly meetings we used to have."

In an official document dated January 1949, an MI-5 (British Internal Security Service) officer mentions that both Nimry and his sidekick Goldfoot "worked for us for a while." Nadel says it was Zetler who gradually allowed Nimry into Lehi's inner circle. "He trusted Nimry one hundred percent. One day during the cease-fire, Nimry told Zetler he'd been with the British consul and knew the consul planned on going to a concert that night. Nimry said, 'This is a good time for you to go to the consulate and rob their food stores.' And Zetler sent Nimry and a few of our boys with a jeep and they cleaned out the British stores. And after that as far as Zetler was concerned, Nimry was a great guy."

Which is why Zetler relied on Nimry, with his impeccable manners and connections to the hated British, to track Bernadotte's movements on September 17. According to General Aage Lundström's sworn statement, Bernadotte only decided during lunch at the YMCA that day that he would go from Government House back to the New City for his meeting with Dov Joseph. "During lunch, the programme for the afternoon was arranged. Normally on Folke Bernadotte's journeys the programme was always arranged in advance. That was not the case on this visit to Jerusalem." How, then, within two to three hours, were his assassins able to organize an ambush at the precise time and place of the passage of the mediator's convoy?

"Nimry told Zetler the mediator will come through Kata-mon," Nadel asserted, "which is why we had the jeep waiting there, and not at Abu Tor, the other possible route to the New City. Nimry told Zetler this to mislead him. He was told by British intelligence to give Lehi the wrong information. It was no secret at all that we wanted to kill Bernadotte. The British were trying to protect him through their agent, Nimry. They expected him to go through Abu Tor, the more direct way to the New City. But Bernadotte changed his mind, as Lundström said, in the last possible minute. I'm sure of this because of how Nimry behaved when he found out Bernadotte had passed through Katamon, where we shot him. Nimry was at our Talbiya camp afterwards and said out loud, 'He really went through Kata-mon?' He repeated this several times—'He really went through Katamon?'—as if he just couldn't take it in, or hide his astonish-ment. And of course he was scared to death about what British intelligence would do to him, for leading Lehi right to its prey."

Nimry denies this and claims his partner Stanley Goldfoot tipped off Zetler regarding Bernadotte's route. "Goldfoot picked it up at the Jerusalem Press Club," Nimry claims, and Zetler confirms this version. But according to Nadel, "The Press Club didn't know anything about Bernadotte's itinerary, only Berna-dotte's own party knew this—that was the point."

At four o'clock on the afternoon of September 17, the four-man hit team sat in the well-tuned jeep, unprotected from the bleach-bright sunshine, waiting for the convoy to pass. For one hour of unrelieved tension, the four men in the jeep could do nothing but hope Bernadotte would not change his route at the very last minute. Earlier, the four had hauled three steel gasoline barrels filled with stones to the roadside. They now rolled the barrels onto the narrow road, leaving just enough room for one jeep, theirs, to pass.

One thing they had not counted on during the weeks of target practice in West Jerusalem were the children. The small dairy, or the Tnuva Shop, as it is locally known, located where Palmach Street rises toward Talbiya, was a magnet for kids after school. It also obscured the assassins' clear view of the road below.

Twelve-year-old Yoram Katz and his friend Uri Scharf were on their way to the Tnuva Shop for a snack when they spotted the spanking new jeep sitting idly by the deserted road. "I approached the jeep," Yoram later told police. "I saw four men in it, all in uniform. I wanted to ask them about their firearms. I thought they were tommy guns, but they told me they were Czechoslovakian Stens. They all spoke Hebrew. From the position of the spring and the cocking handle, I noticed that the letters IZL [Irgun Zvai Leumi—the Irgun] were written on the butt. One of them . . . told me, 'If you don't want to get a kick, be off,' . . . I returned home and the men remained there. . . . I stood outside waiting for Uri to come with his bicycle. After about five minutes, I suddenly heard shots, one long burst of shots from an automatic machine gun from the direction of the jeep . . . and saw two young men from the jeep running on the left side of the road toward the UN cars, which were flying the UN flags and which had stopped behind the jeep that was . . . blocking the way. The first two men of the jeep fired in the direction of the wheels of the first and second cars, and at the same time the third man from the jeep who had jumped to the right side of the road fired into the second or third car . . . through the window of the car. . . . I heard in all about thirty, forty shots and as soon as they stopped, the two young men on the left side of the road jumped into the jeep, which had already begun to move away at top speed in the direction of Kiryat Shmuel, and I also saw that the man who was on the right side of the road tried to reach the escaping jeep but failed, and then he dropped his weapon on the road . . . and disappeared, and I did not see him anymore. . . . The jeep passed by me and disappeared on the road leading to Rehavia and soon afterward the UN cars passed by me in the same direction to town. . . . I hurried to the scene of the shooting and found on the road many empty cartridge cases of a Sten gun. I lifted up two of them and gave them to my father. Meanwhile, many people gathered at the place of the shooting."

Meticulously planned, the murder climaxed in disarray. The killer himself, Yehoshua Cohen, a legend in the underground, had taken too long to finish the job. His orders, as those of his comrades, had been: Whoever first recognizes the mediator must shoot to kill. But only Bernadotte. Colonel Sérot's sudden forward lurch cost him his life. It also threw the assassin off-balance. So did the Red Cross car's unexpected presence between the two UN cars. Cohen thus took longer than the few seconds allotted for the entire operation. He took two minutes.

Cohen looked up and saw that Meshulam Makover, the jeep's driver, was nosing the car north toward Talbiya. The two other men, Gingi Zinger and Yitzhak Ben-Moshe, had already jumped aboard the moving jeep. Cohen heard Makover floor the vehicle, turning left over the deserted dirt road. He sprinted in the same direction, dropping the barrel and the magazine of his submachine gun as he raced to catch up to the accelerating jeep.

Though Cohen knew his fingerprints were smeared all over the gun parts, he had no time to bend down and pick the parts up as he raced in the direction of the moving jeep. What Cohen had no way of knowing was that the driver, Makover, had his own reason for panic. Of the four, Makover had the most distinct features. Even under his visored cap, a gift to the Israeli Army from the American Yiddish Hatmakers Association, his large, bulbous nose and thick red mustache were conspicuous. Though Makover never left the jeep while his three comrades performed their task, he saw that Israeli Army Captain Moshe Hillman, riding in the UN convoy's first car, had recognized him.

Among those who gathered at the site of the shooting moments after the jeep sped away was Nissam Assar, a garage mechanic. Feeling something underfoot, Assar bent down to discover two gun parts lying in the dust. The mechanic picked up Yehoshua Cohen's gun barrel and magazine. After silently examining the gray metal objects he held in his hand, Assar decided they were too important to be left on the road. Rather than turn them over to the authorities, however, he handed the incriminating evidence to his boss, Yitzhak Meyuhas. Meyuhas was not sure what to do with them and kept the parts until Sunday. The next day, he handed them to "a friend in the Police." By then, all fingerprints had been wiped off the gun parts, though it was determined that the cartridges the local kids had so eagerly scooped up at the scene of the crime had all come from that gun. Yoram, his friend Uri, and an eleven-year-old named Dalia Igra, all of whom had observed the murder of the mediator like silent spectators at a play, maintained they could not identify any member of the hit team.

Captain Hillman spent a very anxious twenty-four hours after the assassination. He had recognized the driver of the jeep, a fellow Jerusalemite, Meshulam Makover. He figured Makover had spotted him as well. Makover was no less uneasy about Hillman. "Moshe Hillman knows me," Makover told Zetler when the death squad reached its Jerusalem hiding place. "We have common friends who work with him at the electric company. I am almost positive he won't say anything, but just in case, let's warn him." So the day after the assassination, a small note was pinned to Hillman's door. The message contained two words in Hebrew meaning "Hillman watch out."

"I showed the note to my commanding officer, Moshe Dayan," Hillman recalled. "He asked me, 'What do you want us to do? Should we send you abroad?' 'No,' I answered. 'Don't send me abroad. I am an officer, you are my commander. I take orders from you.' "

"Look," Dayan advised the young captain, "just forget about it. Nothing will come of it. We didn't hear anything. We didn't see anything."

And so Hillman did. "I shut up. Makover would watch me from a distance. He did some work for my son. I would look at him and not say a word, and he would look at me in silence. And we would see each other on Yom Kippur next to the Western Wall, where the underground meets. We never said a word."

Hillman, assigned by the Israeli Army to guide Bernadotte safely through Jerusalem, said he has no regrets about his role in the case. "I was the first to give the police my account, but they didn't publish it [in Bernadotte's posthumously published account, *To Jerusalem,* in which Lundström and the others in the convoy described their versions of the assassination]. Lundström said I would get a decoration from Sweden for bravery, but I never did. Besides, nobody asked me to identify the men. Makover was only the driver, why should I pick him out?"

In the official police report, Captain Hillman claimed, "It was the first time that I saw these young men [in the jeep] and I am doubtful whether I shall be able to recognize them."

Among the most contemptible words in the Hebrew language is *mosser,* or "informer." "In those days in Jerusalem, you simply didn't turn in a Jew," says former Palmach commander Chaim Hefer. "We just weren't used to having a Jewish government. There was this underlying feeling that a government can't be

Jewish, can't be ours! Besides, everybody was afraid of underground reprisals."

They laid the mediator's body in the same ornately painted room in the YMCA where the Swede had held discussions with Jewish leaders throughout that summer of rising, then falling, hopes. Two armed Israeli soldiers stood at attention beside the UN-flag-draped coffins. The mediator's visored Boy Scout hat and his baton, a hated symbol of oppression to many Israelis, a harmless affectation for the count, lay atop his coffin. "I fell apart when I saw that," Barbro Wessel recalled. "The strength I had found to carry him from the car to the hospital, I lost it all then."

"We picked up a Negro," Hillman, standing outside the Y, heard on his two-way radio from Israeli Army Headquarters, Jerusalem. The "Negro" turned out to be Dr. Ralph Bunche, who finally landed in Jerusalem later that day, September 17, after a long delay in Haifa caused by the passport troubles with Israeli authorities of his British secretary, Doreen Daughton. Bunche was already airborne, on his way to join Bernadotte in Jerusalem, when one of the US Marines attached to the Haifa UN Truce Supervision Headquarters picked up the rapid tap-tap of an urgent Morse-coded message from Jerusalem: "Bernadotte has been shot." William Mashler was in the room. "We fell absolutely dead silent. It was such a shock. We somehow never expected it. We assumed that the UN was too important an international body to be felled by a bullet. Death is something we didn't think would happen to one of us. Sure, we knew about the underground in Jerusalem, but surely they wouldn't go for the mediator."

As Bunche crossed into the Jewish sector, at Mandelbaum Gate, an Israeli officer whispered the news of his friend's murder. General Lundström was there, too, still in shock, still wearing his bloodstained white uniform. After the initial shock of the news, Bunche was struck by the pointlessness of this crime. Bunche understood the Swede's need to give something back, as payment for the too-good hand he had been dealt. He knew the Swede had no capacity to hate, no capacity to hold a man's origins against him. A good man was dead, for what crime? That he lacked the suppleness of mind for the task assigned him, that he had been in too great a rush for a solution, that he had tried to simplify a conflict that did not lend itself to simplicity? Those around Bunche recall he never lost his composure but went straight to the YMCA and stayed alone in the room with the flag-draped coffins. Then he reached for his typewriter and poured all of his rage and hurt into his message to the secretary-general of the United Nations.

Minutes later, Bunche received a cable from Arkady A. Sobolev, the Russian who, in the absence of the vacationing Trygve Lie, was acting secretary-general. The cable informed him that he was to assume Bernadotte's position. Bunche's first task was to arrange for the homeward journey of Bernadotte's remains. The UN Secretariat, despite Estelle Bernadotte's express wishes to the contrary, decided that Bernadotte's final journey home would be through Haifa, Rome, Geneva, and Paris, before returning to Stockholm.

"He dies as the first conspicuous martyr to the ideal of the United Nations," the *New York Times* hailed Folke Bernadotte on its next day's editorial page. "He should live in history as one who did more for humanity than the Marshal [Bernadotte] who merely won battles. We can only hope that his death under such circumstances will discredit the men of blood on both sides in Palestine—that it will be, in its effect, a final act of mediation."

In the somnolent midwestern town of Crestline, Ohio, President Harry Truman, whistle-stopping across America in a desperate attempt to overcome Thomas E. Dewey's huge lead in the presidential race, raised his hands to quiet a raucous crowd of 3,500 citizens, come to cheer his arrival. "I have just been officially notified of Count Bernadotte's death," the president, standing on the back platform of his westbound train, told a crowd that fell suddenly silent. "I am shocked and deeply saddened by it."

Flags all over the world flew at half-mast. On the Swedish-American liner *Stockholm*, 402 passengers held a wake in memory of their countryman. Mats Berg, the ocean liner's young bartender, tried to explain to an American reporter the reason for the spontaneous shipboard mourning. "He was like Babe Ruth was to American youth," the bartender said.

Sven Grafström, the Swedish diplomat who had vehemently

opposed the appointment of the mediator "with more heart than brains," noted the "terrible news" in his diary of September 18, 1948: "I have not been able to think of anything else but this dreadful event during the whole day. The opinion is that it is the work of Stern's terrorist gang. How do these people look inside, who commit such awful acts and conduct themselves thus— cruel, meaningless, and stupid. Folke Bernadotte, who ought to be a hero to Jews all over the world based on his rescue mission . . . which happened in his name during the final stages of the war, murdered by Jews, when he is in the midst of trying to bring peace to the so called 'Holy Land.' Mark my words, a beautiful picture of today's world! One would have thought that precisely because the Jews, who suffered so much at the hands of gangsters, should seek to build new bridges to other oppressed peoples.

"Maybe the sacrificial death of Bernadotte will help the situation in Palestine. . . ."

Judah Magnes, the rector of Jerusalem's Hebrew University who had tried too late to alert Bernadotte to the dangerously charged issue of Jerusalem, wrote in the *New York Times*: "Count Bernadotte had come closer than any other man to bringing Jews and Arabs to an understanding. In a press statement issued August 23 I stated that he had 'done more to advance the cause of peace and conciliation in Palestine than all other persons put together.' "

Striking a tougher note, the eminent scholar who had once played mentor to a bright student named Avraham Stern warned: "It is very easy to join in the cry that Jewish terrorists are responsible for this atrocious crime. But who has been responsible for the terrorists? We all bear some responsibility. Certainly the large number of American supporters of Palestine do—the Senators and Congressmen, the newspaper publishers and writers and the large numbers of Jews and others who have supported terrorists morally and financially. . . .

"A large share of the blame is to be attributed to the recklessness of the charges made in Palestine and elsewhere against Bernadotte's honesty and good faith, charges which accused him of acting as the prejudiced agent of 'the British' or of 'British-American imperialism' or of the 'oil interests.' "

Taking time out of a special UN session in Paris, many members of the United Nations General Assembly traveled to Orly

Airport on September 21 to pay their last respects to the man they had dispatched to Palestine four months earlier. "At exactly 11 A.M.," Sven Grafström noted, "three white Dakotas with Red Cross and UN insignia landed in perfect formation. On a concrete platform stood two catafalques against a background of Swedish and French flags. French National Guard troops in their uniforms from the 1850s formed an honor guard, sounded drums, and presented arms. Bernadotte and his French aide's coffins were carried forward and were placed on catafalques. The French government and most of the UN delegations had assembled. Secretary Marshall and Foreign Minister Bevin were present, but no Russians. I exchanged a few words with the American, Begley, who was driving Bernadotte's car at the time of the attack. He said that there was no hope whatsoever of saving Bernadotte.

"Short speeches were given by the French Foreign Minister Schuman, President of the Security Council Sir Alexander Cadogan. . . . Thereafter, General Lundström thanked France with a few words, whereupon the very dignified ceremony ended with the immediate departure of Bernadotte's plane . . . in the direction of Stockholm."

Later, amid the massive splendor of the Palais de Chaillot, a dark mood settled over the General Assembly's opening session. Many of the delegates, including the entire Swedish delegation, were dressed in black. Secretary-General Lie, who had been so close-fisted in his support of the mediator, now proposed to honor Bernadotte's death in the line of United Nations service in a tangible way, by the creation of a guard force—a permanent UN peacekeeping force—made up of 300 to 3,000 men, recruited from member states. Its members would be able to carry sidearms and their chief role would be to protect United Nations personnel throughout the world.*

Several hours later, thousands of Stockholm residents ignored a sudden cold snap and waited for the white plane to land for

---

*Forty-five years later, in 1993, in the wake of UN peacekeeping operations in Bosnia, Cambodia, and Somalia, Lie's proposal would be dusted off again, debated—and again set aside.

the final time, at Bromma Airport. A heavily veiled Estelle Bernadotte, flanked by her two young sons and Folke Bernadotte's eighty-nine-year-old father, Prince Oscar, stood in the flower-decked hanger. Bernadotte's aides—Bunche, Lundström, Begley, and Barbro Wessel—whose plane landed minutes before the count's, lined up on either side of the widow and her sons. The aged father, who had outlived his youngest child, leaned in their direction and whispered, "Thank you for what you have done for my son."

When the doors of the count's plane opened to reveal the coffin, Swedish Boy Scouts and Red Cross workers sang Bernadotte's favorite hymn, "A Mighty Fortress Is Our God." Night had fallen by the time the hearse reached Folke Bernadotte's house in Djurgården. More Boy Scouts carrying torches lined the road leading to the house that Folke and Estelle had converted from his regimental mess into their home many years before.

On September 26, in the Gustav Vasa, the Church of Kings, Swedes took their final leave of Bernadotte. "We were seated in the sanctuary in front of the royal family," Grafström noted in his diary. "His Majesty's (the ninety-year-old King Gustav) continual coughing resounded throughout the church vaults. The ceremony was dignified and gripping. Trygve Lie and myself also followed along to the crematorium. . . . The bearing of Countess Bernadotte and her two sons in the church, as well as during the ceremonies outside at the crematorium, went beyond all praise. These figures, as if part of an antique tragedy, could not have fulfilled their painful parts in a more dignified and more exemplary manner than they did."

CHAPTER TWENTY-TWO

ESCAPE

AT TWO IN THE AFTERNOON OF THE DAY AFTER THE MURDER, Prime Minister David Ben-Gurion imposed a tight curfew on the jittery city of Jerusalem. Under Colonel Moshe Dayan's command, Israeli Defense Forces armored cars patrolled the deserted streets. Ports and airfields throughout Israel were closed. In newspapers and on handbills, the Israeli government called for public support, "as one man against the enemy within our midst," and every citizen was urged to give "active and unhesitating assistance" to the Army and police "in expunging the stain of terrorism from the soil of our country."

From his office in Tel Aviv, Ben-Gurion called for action "against an organization which uses murder as a political tool." In his diary he wrote, "This evening, I will raise these matters with the government."

Ben-Gurion's voice trembled with anger when he addressed Israel's first elected body on September 23. "I deeply regret that I have to begin with a tragic deed . . . horrible and shameful, that a gang of rogues, cowards, and low schemers murdered the UN envoy and his assistant Sérot . . . This despicable crime is all the more horrible because it is aimed at the supreme human institution of our time, the UN. . . . While the crime wore the mask of so-called patriotism, which is false, corrupt, and despicable, it assaults the honor of young Israel as an independent state still struggling for its existence and it stains Jerusalem, the Holy City, with the blood of innocents. . . .

"Disagreements between us and Count Bernadotte were considerable," the prime minister admitted, ". . . but in no way can they lessen the deep respect we felt for his personality and his mission and the chagrin and sorrow that we feel in his . . . tragic and heroic death."

Another fear also nagged at the agitated prime minister. What if the world body chose to honor the fallen mediator by adopting his final recommendations for the resolution of the Palestine conflict, recommendations he knew by now (for the outline of Bernadotte's final report did not remain secret for long) meant giving his cherished Negev to the Arabs.

The man who had been alerted to the possibility of Bernadotte's assassination, and had tried in vain to rouse Israeli officials to the danger, now felt betrayed. Ambassador James McDonald warned Prime Minister Ben-Gurion and Foreign Minister Shertok again that, if they did not crack down on the terrorists, Israel stood to lose gains purchased in lives. "In my dispatches to Washington," McDonald reminded Shertok, "I had denied this instability. I had insisted that the Provisional Government of Israel was a functioning institution capable of maintaining internal security. I don't want to be proved a liar."

The same day, Ben-Gurion proposed a "Law To Prevent Terrorism," declaring Lehi an illegal terrorist organization. The new law was passed unanimously by the State Council. Affiliation with Lehi or any other terrorist organization was made a crime punishable by imprisonment. It is supremely ironic that the law was frequently enforced later, during the seven-year leadership of Prime Minister Yitzhak Shamir, to prosecute Israelis meeting with members of the Palestine Liberation Organization.

But the prime minister's angry words were otherwise not backed up by deeds. Only one of Lehi's Jerusalem bases, Camp Dror, was actually surrounded by troops, and that only the following day. The Palmach's Har El Brigade was dispatched under the command of Schmuel Glinka to Camp Dror. Only 40 of the original 150 terrorists were still there. "The truth is," recalls Baruch Nadel, "that the Palmach didn't really want to do battle against Lehi. All morning, the Palmach regiments stood around the camp talking to the guys as they passed, and around noontime they decided to go inside. Glinka's lieutenant in the Palmach, a man named Morris, later told me he waited until noon so that everybody who wanted to leave could leave."

Jerusalem Consul MacDonald, however, seemed satisfied, cabling Washington on September 20: "Following up promise to use 'all force at its command' to track down Bernadotte's assassins, Israeli government imposed curfew in Jerusalem. . . . All Stern bases . . . surrounded and searched, Stern arms dump seized in Talbieh, and approximately 200 suspects arrested. In effort to identify murderers, suspects will be paraded before United Nations witnesses to crime."

Hardly. The four men in the jeep, as well as the three who had sent them, were not rounded up, scarcely even pursued. Moving fast, they were going back to that environment in which they thrived—underground.

Minutes after Bernadotte's body was ripped apart, the driver, Meshulam Makover, dropped off Yitzhak Ben-Moshe, "Betzalely," in the center of Jerusalem. By now, the gunman, Yehoshua Cohen, had caught up to them. "I'll be OK," Ben-Moshe told the other three as he jumped out. They knew better than to ask what arrangements he had made for himself. Ben-Moshe had reason to feel confident. He was headed to the home of a Jerusalem military policeman, where he spent his first night in hiding. The other three men drove to the Lehi camp for Orthodox Jews in Lifta. None among the Orthodox had heard of the murder. "It was Friday evening and they were already praying," Nadel recounted. "Of course, with the Shabbat they couldn't listen to the radio. On Saturday, after their last prayer, they turned on the radio and heard that Bernadotte had been assassinated and that Lehi was now an illegal organization. So they dropped their arms and grabbed their prayer shawls and disappeared into the Orthodox neighborhoods. Who would find them there?"

"No one there paid any attention to us," Makover recalled. "They were busy preparing for the Shabbat. We parked the jeep and walked off across the Sharei Pina quarter, where an apartment had been prepared for us." Makover, Cohen, and Zinger arrived at the apartment of Lehi sympathizer Yosef Amir (the brother of Eliezer Juravin, who today heads a well-known Israeli public-relations firm) just in time to celebrate the Shabbat.

The next day, September 18, the four men (Ben-Moshe had joined them again) moved to the house of Shmuel Rosenblum, a Lehi sympathizer who was also a member of the ruling Mapai Party. Located in Mea Shearim, Jerusalem's ultra-Orthodox religious quarter, Rosenblum's house was also considered safe. The death squad spent four peaceful days there, waiting to be rescued, while Jerusalem was under curfew and armored cars rumbled uselessly through its ancient streets. On the fourth day, a truck loaded with furniture backed up to Rosenblum's house. Cohen, Ben-Moshe, Zinger, and Makover slipped into massive wardrobes that were then covered with tarpaulin and tightly fastened with ropes. Thus hidden, they passed through several Palmach checkpoints before arriving safely in Tel Aviv, where they quickly disappeared into the crowded metropolis.

Lehi's three-man leadership were less quick to go underground. Baruch Nadel, assistant editor of *Mivrak,* was worried. His editor, Eliahu Amikam, had been caught in a roundup of Lehi members that Nadel himself had escaped. "I decided to go see Eldad's wife. Maybe she would know how to contact Eldad, so I could ask him, should I try to keep publishing the newspaper, should I hide, what should I do? I knocked at their apartment door on Dizengoff Street at six-thirty on a Saturday morning. I couldn't believe my eyes. Eldad came out in pajamas, with a towel around his neck. 'Well, did you hear the radio?' he asked me. 'All they do is talk about us all day,' he said, 'about Bernadotte's assassination.' He looked so pleased with himself. I said, 'Eldad, how come you're still here? You must hide immediately.' He just dismissed this with his hand. But his wife, Batya, was standing nearby and said to him, 'I told you that you have to go! And anyway, what did this Bernadotte ever do to you?' she asked her husband in a very exasperated tone. She was not in Lehi, she was not politically minded at all. And very quickly she threw some things into a small bag. 'Out, out!' she shouted, and off we went into the street.

"It was early, there were not many people out, though it was one of Tel Aviv's busiest streets. As we walked, Eldad said, 'This was a great act. The whole world is shocked. This will be the end of Bernadotte's plan.' So we went to Shamir's house, number 8 Gissin Street. It was so quiet, we could tell Shamir and his wife were still asleep. I waited outside while Eldad went in to get him. They came out in a few minutes. Shamir had also packed a small suitcase. We walked together for a few blocks and then the two of them went off on their own to a safe apartment. In the underground, you don't ask questions, so I don't know where they went. Six hours later, the police came looking for both of them, but too late. Shamir, who knew something about going underground, stayed in hiding until early spring, when things had calmed down."

Forty-eight hours after the assassination, Nadel shared a bench with Makover on the roof of a four-story safe house on Tel Aviv's Jobbins Street. "That's when he told me about the murder. But not everything. The four men were sworn to secrecy by Shamir, so he kept a lot to himself for many years. In the seventies, he was still worried about what might happen to him."

The audacious Nadel continued to move from safe house to safe house, foiling the authorities as long as he could. "A week after Bernadotte's murder, a man named Morris, a regiment commander in the Palmach who was married to someone from Kibbutz Hepzibah where I grew up, dropped in on my mother Miriam and gave her a key. 'It's to a small shack that belongs to my wife Havah and me, on the edge of Tel Aviv near the Yarkon River,' he told my mother. In those days, that was almost outside the city limits. Morris said, 'If somebody needs a rest or just to get away for a little while . . .' My mother understood Morris was thinking about me, and she told him, 'I don't want you to get in trouble.' And she refused the key. You see, Morris was one of the officers sent to finish off Lehi in Jerusalem."

But Nadel was eventually picked up and spent several months with other Lehi members in various loosely guarded prisons from Jaffa to Acre. In captivity as in freedom, Nadel and his fellow terrorists showed their mettle, baiting and taunting their easily intimidated prison guards until Ben-Gurion declared an amnesty and released the entire irritating lot of them in February 1949.

Equally laconic in the face of possible danger was the third member of the Lehi command, Natan Yalin-Mor. "At the time of the murder, Yalin-Mor and I were sitting in the Café Eldorado, in Haifa," Samuel Merlin recalled. "He had just arrived from Tel Aviv. We ordered some coffee, when Yalin-Mor asked to be excused. 'I have to make a phone call,' he said. He came back in a couple of minutes, jubilant. 'Bernadotte has been assassinated,' he said. And I was both surprised and impressed because Bernadotte was considered a great enemy and a very important personage in the United Nations. Bernadotte never traveled alone. It was an incredible feat. I was never an extremist, but this deed was more important than defeating a whole division of the

British Army. Israel was very frail then, and he proposed giving the Negev to the Arabs and demilitarizing Jerusalem and making it international, including the Jewish City. Bernadotte was a danger to Israel."

Yalin-Mor, burning to forge ties between Lehi and the East Bloc, was on his way to Czechoslovakia. Picked up by police at his Haifa hideout, along with another notorious Sternist, Mattiyahu Shmulovitz, he never made the flight to Prague. As the sole ranking members of Lehi to fall into official hands, on December 5, 1948, Yalin-Mor and Shmulovitz were tried on charges, not of murder, but of belonging to Lehi. No eyewitnesses stepped forward to identify the killers; the police descriptions of the hit men were so general as to be useless.

Yalin-Mor, the most reluctant of the three who had pronounced the death sentence on Bernadotte, was the only person involved in Bernadotte's assassination to suffer any consequences for the murder. In court, he denied any involvement at all with the crime, and made fine use of the trial to condemn the government's new antiterrorist law, claiming it placed collective responsibility on a group for the actions of one or two members. The Special Military Court, pronouncing judgment on Shmulovitz and Yalin-Mor, stated that "it is unable to establish with any degree of certainty that the murder of Count Bernadotte was carried out by order of Lehi."

At the same time, Yalin-Mor and Shmulovitz were found guilty of "terrorist activities" and sentenced to eight- and five-year prison terms respectively. Yalin-Mor denied Lehi's part in Bernadotte's death forever after, for which he earned the lifelong contempt of Yitzhak Shamir and Israel Eldad. "I don't know why Yalin-Mor denies this fact known to everyone," former Prime Minister Shamir scornfully noted in 1977. Shamir refuses even now to discuss the planning or the execution of the crime, but in his 1994 memoirs he writes: "On 17 September 1948 he [Bernadotte] was shot and killed in Jerusalem, the city he was ready to give away. Lehi took no responsibility for the deed; the idea was conceived in Jerusalem by Lehi members operating there more or less independently. Our opinion was asked and we offered no opposition."

On February 24, 1949, two weeks after Yalin-Mor and Shmulovitz were sentenced, Ben-Gurion ordered both terrorists freed, using the elections as the pretext for a general amnesty for terrorists. With a comfortable majority of the voters behind his Mapai Party, Ben-Gurion felt the time was ripe for the new nation to begin to heal its self-inflicted wounds. "We hoped to educate Lehi, rather than punish them" was the explanation Isser Harel, chief of Ben-Gurion's Secret Service, provided for this extraordinary largesse. There was very little outrage from the rest of the world, preoccupied by the Cold War that winter of 1949. Lehi's Fighters List, with its radical ideology mixing supernationalism with a socialist orientation, received 5,363 votes in the Knesset elections. It thus won one seat in the new parliament, which went to Yalin-Mor. The terrorist leader marched straight from prison to the Knesset.

A few months after Natan Yalin-Mor was freed from his brief prison term, he and Eldad met for a cup of coffee in Tel Aviv. "Suddenly, he said to me, 'Eldad, I don't remember that we decided about Bernadotte.' 'What are you talking about?' I asked him. 'It's just the two of us here, no one can hear our conversation.' But Yalin-Mor continued to insist, 'There was never a decision by the leadership of Lehi on Bernadotte.' I got up and left the café and never spoke to him again. At his funeral, many years later, friends were surprised that I came to pay my respects. 'You're right,' I told them. 'For me Natan Yalin-Mor died thirty years ago. We are only burying him today.' "

One by one, other Sternists emerged from their hiding places. At the same time, Lehi mocked Israeli authority once more, turning the prison fortress of Jaffa, where two hundred members of Lehi were being held, into a summer camp for rowdy youths. The Lehi prisoners, including the forty arrested in the Jerusalem camp, ripped the steel bars out of their windows and broke through the ancient walls separating them from one another. Satisfied with their work, Sternist men and women sat with their legs dangling out their windows, laughing at prison guards too intimidated to make a move against their hotheaded captives. When, as punishment for beating up a guard, the prison warden canceled family visits, the Sternists threw mattresses over the barbed wire surrounding the fortress and leapt across it to freedom. Bullets, fired carefully over their heads by prison guards, whistled past the escaping prisoners, who rushed toward Jaffa's cafés. By nightfall, most of the prisoners had streamed back to jail on their own. They had made their point. The only law they obeyed was their own.

As early as the day after Bernadotte's shooting, Ben-Gurion had a fairly clear idea of who was behind it. Already on September 19, the prime minister was on the cusp of the conspiracy, noting in his diary, "They are looking for the top guys: Friedmann-Yellin [i.e., Yalin-Mor], Eldad, Yezernitsky [Shamir] . . . the dangerous group is Yehoshua Cohen, Pinchas Cohen (his brother), Nehama Cohen (Yehoshua's wife). . . . Isser Harel [Ben-Gurion's security chief] believes they committed the murder." Ben-Gurion even knew the location of the hiding place of one of the plotters. Late in October, the prime minister dispatched one of his trusted lieutenants, Shaul Avigur, to Eldad's safe house. Avigur extracted a promise from Eldad. Lehi, Eldad agreed, would come aboveground, and join Israeli society. Ben-Gurion wrote in his diary on October 29, 1948: "Eldad swore he did not know who killed Bernadotte. He is a fool if he thinks that we believe him."

In his memoirs, Shamir recalls another meeting with Avigur, then deputy minister of defense, whom he contacted from his hiding place. "What worried me most were continuing reports of discrimination in the army against Lehi members. I felt that this had to end; there had to be a point after which conspiracy ceased and that cessation had to be recognized by the Government too. I asked a well-placed colleague to arrange a secret meeting for me with a spokesman for the Government, someone in whom Ben-Gurion had complete confidence; a meeting was arranged, but it was no ordinary emissary who was sent to talk to me. . . . I had been promised that I would not be followed or arrested and the man who drove to the private house in which Avigur and I met was Yair's brother-in-law, so I felt secure.

" 'Lehi is through with its former role,' I said to Avigur. 'We may perhaps go into politics. Or not. Whatever happens, a new chapter will open. The decree of illegality must be annulled and Lehi members must be released from jail. If not, we shall never feel completely safe and the underground will never totally die.'

" 'I understand,' Avigur replied, 'but guarantees must be mutual. How do I know that this is not a trick so that Lehi can stay in business, protected by the government of Israel?'

" 'Look,' I answered. 'Underground organizations can hide everything, conceal people, arms, safe houses, but not their very existence. An underground movement that does nothing, de facto, does not exist, does it?'

"He listened, without comment, then asked me to give him the names of Count Bernadotte's assailants. Nothing would happen to them, he said, but he wanted their names on file. I said 'No.' "

The assassination presented the prime minister with a real dilemma. "He was furious," noted his biographer, Shabtai Teveth. "It was his ideology that we are a nation ruled by the majority. This was his lifework. Lehi was endangering that. But this was not England. Rounding up so many Lehi people was an act of great personal courage. Ben-Gurion wanted a clean slate. He knew Israel could not go on like that. He did not take Bernadotte's murder as a simple criminal act. He thought they were misguided, misled, and misbegotten. But he also wanted to make his peace with the underground."

Yehoshua Zetler, Lehi's zealous military commander in Jerusalem, later took some credit for Ben-Gurion's lenient treatment of the assassins, claiming that he had called on the minister of the interior, Yitzhak Gruenbaum, a few weeks following the murder, to pass on a message from Ben-Gurion. "It would not be good if our people were sentenced," Zetler reportedly informed the startled Gruenbaum. "We don't want to take action against Jews if we don't have to."

The interior minister reportedly assured the terrorist not to worry. "They'll be sentenced to a few years in prison," he said. "Then we'll release them quite soon." Smiling, Zetler replied, "That's fair enough. Anything to satisfy world opinion."

The prime minister had other worries. Israeli forces were once more engaged in war. On September 26, Ben-Gurion proposed to the cabinet that Israel conquer the strip of land bordered by Latrun, Ramallah, Jericho, and the Dead Sea, and then move on to Bethlehem and Hebron. Given the strong international reaction against Israel following the mediator's assassination, only a few of his ministers backed the prime minister's ambitious battle plan.

The Israeli Defense Forces finally moved against the Egyptian Army on the southern front, seen as the more immediate threat to the country.

Though the Israeli government did not pronounce the Bernadotte case closed, not one of the hit team would ever spend a night in jail or face a court of justice.

Before disbanding in 1949, the underground held its first and final parade. "We had never all been together before," Shamir said, recalling the day. "Now people exchanged real names and addresses, openly dispensing with the safeguards of conspiratorial life, with the underground. . . . I remember the way men and women, with whom I had worked and been in danger, whom I had commanded and utterly trusted, looked at me that day, half disbelieving that I was the 'legendary' Michael, peering with the same curiosity at the men who had for so long called themselves Gera [Yalin Mor] and Eldad. . . . The mood was quiet, a little sad; there was a sense of vulnerability, maybe even of fear. How would it be above ground, without the shields, without the discipline, without the bonds of that singular comradeship?"

CHAPTER TWENTY-THREE

"UNO, SCHMUNO"

LEHI WAS RIGHT ON ONE IMPORTANT POINT: WITHOUT BERNA-
dotte, the Bernadotte Plan was dead. Despite the solemn words
hailing the man and his mission, the silent mourners who lined
roads from Haifa to Stockholm, and the flags at half-mast, the
plan Bernadotte hoped would be his lasting contribution to
peace died with him. Ralph Bunche, his successor, who, in defer-
ence to Bernadotte's memory, never assumed his title, made a
final, emotional plea to endorse a plan purchased at such cost.

"It is with a heavy heart," Ralph Bunche told the First Committee of the United Nations in October 1948,

> that I make this statement. But for that crime in Jerusalem com-
> mitted by a band of despicable gangsters, it would be Count
> Bernadotte himself who would be speaking to you now. The late
> Mediator was not only my Chief, but a treasured friend. In these
> months since the end of May I had come to know him well; to re-
> spect and admire him. He was an utterly honest and fearless
> man, completely independent in his thinking, and thoroughly de-
> voted to the effort to bring peace to Palestine. He had no axe to
> grind, no vested interest to serve. The Progress Report of the late
> Mediator which is before you . . . sets forth quite clearly in Part
> One the views of Count Bernadotte on the main issues of the
> Palestine conflict today. I need not repeat these views, and the
> more so since I am in full accord with them. . . .
>
> It is unthinkable that Arabs and Jews should be permitted to
> resume hostilities in Palestine. The threat to the peace of the
> Middle East generally, and even to the world, from conflict in
> Palestine, is far too great. . . . the Mediator, through four months

of negotiations of unprecedented intensity, strove by trial and error through reason and persuasion and every other honorable means, to find a common ground upon which the conflicting parties might meet.

"This common ground," Bunche admitted, "was never found . . . due entirely to the intransigence of the parties. On the fundamental issues, each side remained adamant."

Bunche pointed out how much more modest in scope the mediator's peace proposal was in September than it had been in June: "these conclusions were designed to suggest 'certain steps which . . . might be taken in the direction of settlement and conciliation of the differences between the two parties. . . .' He was convinced, as I am convinced, that the voice of the United Nations speaks with considerable authority in Palestine."

If the United Nations spoke with "considerable authority" early that summer, by fall its voice was barely above a whisper in Palestine. Unwilling or unable to enforce its own decisions, the UN became, for many Israelis, in Ben-Gurion's memorable putdown, "UNO, schmuno." As determined as Bunche was to salvage Bernadotte's mission, the Israeli government was equally determined to erase its traces. A memorandum in the Israeli Foreign Ministry Archives, dated September 28, 1948, states bluntly that the mediator's plan is "nothing more than a shopworn British plan which Bevin and his alter ego Harold Beeley have been peddling in Washington and at Lake Success for almost a year." The unsigned twelve-page document, which closely echoes Lehi's own theory of an Anglo-Bernadotte conspiracy, states:

> The shocking assassination of Count Bernadotte has been seized as the opportune moment to glorify that plan as a new Magna Carta for the Middle East. The author of the plan is not Count Bernadotte but Ernest Bevin. . . . Under the Bernadotte Plan, with Arab Palestine joined to Transjordan, the latter immediately becomes the legatee to ports at Gaza and Aqaba, both in the Negev. . . . The Bernadotte scheme, if adopted, means bases for British troops and new lifelines by land, air and sea to a rapidly disappearing empire. . . . It is obscure with respect to Jerusalem which, under the November 29 resolution of the United Nations, was to have been internationalized. It makes no

provisions whatsoever for direct access by the 90,000 Jews of Jerusalem to the Jewish state. It reduces the viability of the Jewish state by removing the largest land area assigned to that state, and by making impossible for a long time plans for the reestablishment of the survivors of Hitler's extermination program to be settled, as planned, in the Negev area.

... In addition, the Bernadotte Plan calls for the return to the Jewish state of some 300,000 Arab refugees who left the country voluntarily when the Arabs opened the war on Palestine. This would saddle the Jewish state with an impossible economic burden ... at the very moment when the Jewish state would be strangled in its efforts to rescue and rehabilitate Hitler's survivors.

But in the solemn figure of Secretary of State George C. Marshall, Bernadotte's proposals still had an ally. "My Government is of the opinion," Marshall announced from Paris on September 21, 1948, "that the conclusions are sound and strongly urges the parties and the General Assembly to accept them in their entirety."

Marshall's support, however, was not sufficient. For, on the subject of Israel, the State Department and the White House had resumed their wrestling match of the previous spring. As in the spring, Chaim Weizmann enlisted the aid of the president's friend Eddie Jacobson to persuade the president to repudiate Marshall's endorsement of the Bernadotte Plan. On October 5, Shertok told Marshall that Israel wanted both the Negev and western Galilee. Clark Clifford, aboard the Truman campaign train, suggested that perhaps the secretary of state was changing White House policy without checking with the president. Truman, desperately trying to catch up to Thomas E. Dewey, his Republican challenger, authorized a White House statement saying the US government had backed the UN resolution for partition of Palestine and the Democratic Party platform had done the same. Period. Rabbi Hillel Silver, head of the American section of the World Zionist Organization (who earlier pronounced Ralph Bunche's "usefulness as acting mediator ended" because of Bunche's heated reaction to the mediator's murder), now declared that not Folke Bernadotte, but State Department officials, had written the Bernadotte Plan. In some quarters, the charge stuck. "The State Department dictated the Bernadotte Plan,"

Baruch Nadel, among many others, still vehemently insists—inaccurately. "You will find a copy somewhere in the basement of the State Department."

On October 30, President Truman directed the American delegation to the Paris General Assembly session not to take a position on Palestine until after the elections on November 3. Though Marshall continued to stand behind Bernadotte's proposals "in their entirety," the Israelis knew they had won another round over the secretary of state. Israel's chief delegate, Abba Eban, attributes the demise of the plan to a piece of very good political fortune. President Truman summoned Marshall home from Paris to deal with the Berlin crisis, leaving John Foster Dulles in charge of the American delegation.* Dulles was not an enthusiastic supporter of the Bernadotte Plan. He told Eban that "Israel's military victory had proved something about the character of the Jewish people and therefore had strong moral and spiritual implications. He disagreed with Secretary Marshall so vehemently on this and other questions that he had stopped attending delegation meetings."

Eban, who also had the support of Clark Clifford in the White House, labored mightily to press his advantage during Marshall's absence. On November 20, he telegraphed Ben-Gurion that he "had a meeting with Jack Ross [a member of the American delegation to the UN] and he informed me confidentially that America does not support the British . . . regarding the acceptance of the Bernadotte Plan, but is choosing negotiations with the assistance of a mediating council."

In his diary on December 9, David Ben-Gurion wrote, "[Eliahu] Sasson summarizes the discussion at the UN: 'We entered the UN with the Bernadotte Plan—we left without Bernadotte and the Negev and the Galilee in our hands. Our military activities in the Negev and the Galilee shine in everyone's eyes.' "

By now, however, the Israeli prime minister had heard from one of his most trusted advisors that he had perhaps misjudged the dead mediator. In his diary, Ben-Gurion notes an October 7 visit from David Horowitz, a tireless Israeli envoy to New York

---

*This was in itself curious. Dulles, who would later become President Dwight D. Eisenhower's secretary of state, was simultaneously acting as Marshall's assistant in Paris and Dewey's campaign advisor during the campaign.

and London. "[Horowitz] claims that our conception of Bernadotte is incorrect. Bernadotte was not brilliant, but fair. He had no ties with the English. He met them four times, on his own initiative, to prove to them that the State of Israel existed as a fact which could not be challenged. He did not do this from love of Israel but because he wanted his mission to succeed, and he knew that he could not succeed otherwise." The prime minister then added this line to explain his own misjudgment of the mediator, "Blame the English. They made themselves hateful to the Jews and to the Arabs."

With Dulles in charge, the United States and Great Britain sponsored a "Conciliation Resolution," which proposed to accept Israel as an existing nation and to set up a United Nations committee to help work out its problems with its neighbors. On December 11, by a vote of 35 to 15, this amended resolution passed the General Assembly. It did not even mention the thirty-five-thousand-word plan for peace in Palestine that had cost a man his life. Before the end of the session, the US delegation proposed the admission of Israel as a member of the United Nations. France's and Canada's abstentions prevented immediate approval. By the following spring, however, Israel had the votes in the Security Council, and joined the world body as a full-fledged member on May 11, 1949.

Among those nine members who abstained in the spring vote on Israeli membership was the fallen mediator's own country. On June 3, 1949, Stockholm announced that it was fed up with Israel's lack of results in the hunt for Bernadotte's killers. Sweden decided that henceforth it would take matters into its own hands. A committee headed by Sweden's chief public prosecutor, Maths Heuman, along with the superintendent of the country's Criminal Police and several other outstanding criminologists as members, arrived to examine the Tel Aviv police files on the case. Nine months later, the Swedes' own findings were ready. The result was a tough-minded look at the often lax behavior, sometimes almost criminal negligence of the Israeli murder investigation. In particular, the Swedes faulted Israeli authorities for failure to arrange for an armed escort to accompany Bernadotte in Jewish Jerusalem. The Swedes further charged that the police inquiry revealed "such obvious and serious shortcomings" as to cast doubt on the seriousness of Israeli authorities.

To deal with the Swedish charges, the Israelis appointed a blue-ribbon committee of their own. The Israeli Committee of Inquiry consisted of District Judge Shimon Agranat, Walter Eytan of the Foreign Office, and Chief Prosecutor Chaim Cohen. The committee produced a sixty-seven-page reply to the Swedish charges. No escort was provided for the count based on the fact that no danger was foreseen. ". . . [I]t was natural for the authorities to believe that neither IZL (Irgun) nor Lehi would go so far as to plot his actual assassination, having regard for the great personal prestige of the man who represented the Supreme International Organization . . . and for the man to whom the Jewish people in particular were under so heavy an obligation for his great assistance in many spheres. . . . Even the staff of the Mediator was not convinced that the Mediator was in mortal danger, that is to say danger against which his own personality was not sufficient protection."

The Agranat Committee also defended the lack of armed escort on the basis of "the particular attitude adopted by Count Bernadotte in regard to the whole problem . . . that he and his personnel, the observers, had the right to go wherever they wanted unarmed and without protection."

The Agranat Committee raised no strong objection to the Swedish charge of police negligence in the investigation, saying, "The facts established by the Swedish Chief Prosecutor were for the greater part correct. . . . There is no doubt that on the day in question, September 17, 1948, the Jerusalem Police after the assassination . . . took no real step to discover or apprehend the culprits."

After attributing some of the investigation's shortcomings to the lack of a special criminal unit in the newly formed Jerusalem Police, the Israeli investigators paint a picture of ineptitude worthy of the Keystone Kops. "The Police could and should have taken certain preliminary steps for the apprehension of the culprits and [should] have opened a proper inquiry—steps which any police force knows how to take as a matter of routine . . . clues and details, even if superficial, about the description of the assailants and the identity of the jeep, from eyewitnesses, such as the inhabitants of the neighborhood in which the crime was perpetrated. . . . Mr. Rabinovitch, Chief Investigation Officer in Jerusalem . . . took no steps whatsoever on that evening in order to open the investigation. He was also unable to furnish the

Committee with any convincing explanation for his inaction. It is clear to the Committee that, had he troubled himself to go into the houses nearest the scene of the crime . . . he would have found among the tenants some eyewitnesses, and he might have been able to gather other facts from them. . . . The Police should obviously have cordoned off the site as quickly as possible in order to ensure that a subsequent examination of the site would be effective. . . . Had Rabinovitch cordoned off the scene of the crime, he would have prevented, at all events after his arrival there and during the night, strange persons or even persons connected with the crime, from removing bullets and cartridge cases, or other objects which might have been dropped by the assailants during their flight. . . ."

The Agranat Committee's harshest indictment against the police was for its bungled handling of the most important clues: the submachine gun barrel and magazine Yehoshua Cohen dropped in flight. By the time the police had retrieved them, both had been wiped clean of all fingerprints. "Police Sgt. Lowenstein demanded the portion of the weapon which had been found on the scene of the crime from the man who had picked it up, Private Yitzhak Meyuhas, an army driver . . . [who] refused to hand it over. . . . After Private Meyuhas returned to his base, he telephoned to a military policeman to come and take the weapon from him. The military policeman came and took the weapon . . . and handed the weapon over to the Orderly Sergeant [of the military police] and this latter gave it, possibly through the intermediary of a runner, to 2nd Lt. Ben Arie, who, acting on the orders of Col. Blum, put it in the safe. . . . From all this it follows that, had Mr. Rabinovitch acted with the maximum alacrity to obtain the weapon from the possession of the military police, he still would not have managed to prevent the destruction of the murderer's fingerprints on the said portion of the weapons."

As to the car, riddled with Cohen's bullets and smeared with Bernadotte's blood, according to the Israeli report, "this investigation took place only after the vehicle had in the meantime been repaired in a private garage. . . . Details such as these justify the conclusion that the police carried out a thorough examination of the Mediator's vehicle only after undue delay and without taking enough precautions to ensure that pending such investigation the vehicle would remain under its exclusive control and that unauthorized persons would have no access to it."

The Agranat Committee again agreed with the Swedish prosecutor in charging the police with failure to trace the "assailants'
jeep." "It is clear," the Israeli report concludes, "that during the
first hours after the perpetration of the outrage, no step was
taken to search for the jeep around the city. . . . A number of eye
witnesses including Hillman, Katz, Meyuhas . . . had given different descriptions of the jeep. Some of them even thought that
they would have been able to recognize the machine were they to
see it again. It would only have been expected that the police
would have enabled these witnesses to try to identify the jeep
from among the various machines taken by the army from the
Stern Gang bases. This did not happen. Here, too, as in the case
of the weapons, no arrangements were made to enable the police
to have access to the said vehicles for the purpose of the investigation."

The Israeli Committee of Inquiry minces no words in condemning the police's lackadaisical manner in dealing with eyewitnesses. "Failure to take the testimony of certain persons in
Count Bernadotte's party, including Gen. Lundström, Lt. de
Geer, Miss Wessel, and Col. Begley is a serious flaw in the conduct of the police investigation. Responsibility for this in the first
place lies upon the Jerusalem police who failed to take such testimony before [the witnesses] left Jerusalem on 18 September, on
their way overseas. . . ." The fact that no police lineup of members of the Stern Gang was ever organized, the committee attributes to the "general state of unrest which existed in the military
prisons at that time . . . which meant that it would be impossible
to hold such a parade without the use of force."

The committee attributes part of the gross negligence of the
police investigation to the "general atmosphere of terror" in
Jerusalem. An unnamed spokesman of the General Security Service asserted: "The dissidents, IZL and the Stern Group controlled Jerusalem and held the City by brute terror. Even the
police were afraid of them. The general public would under no
circumstances cooperate against them, not out of sympathy toward them but out of fear."

The committee also points out that the chief preoccupation
of the Israeli government and military police during the week of
September 17 was disarming the terrorists, not finding Bernadotte's killers. "It is clear beyond all doubt," the Israeli report
states, "that the plan to liquidate the Stern Group attracted most

attention during the course of the 18th and overshadowed the professional investigation into the murder. The successful conclusion of such an operation was regarded as a most . . . dangerous task. No one could have foreseen that the persons inside the Stern Group bases would surrender without bloodshed. It was necessary to carry out the arrests in private houses with the assistance of the civil police whose capabilities were not at the time overrated. It is easy to understand," the report concludes, "that in such an atmosphere of tension as prevailed on 18 September, no one thought about the necessity and importance of setting aside, for the purpose of investigation, the arms and vehicles to be taken from the . . . bases."

Though the inspector general of police told the Agranat Committee that "it was a fatal mistake that nothing was done during the first twenty-four hours," the three-man committee stopped short of condemning the police for negligence. For, the blue-ribbon team stated, the Israeli government was "sincere in its measures for bringing the murderers to justice." Nor did the committee recommend that the inquiry be reopened. Instead, it urged the Israeli government to simply admit "the existence of shortcomings and to express its apologies to the persons and institutions injured . . . while pointing out the sincere efforts taken by the Israeli Government to trace the assailants and bring them to trial."

Walter Eytan, one of the three men responsible for this report, later pointed out one fundamental reason for the investigation's startling lack of results. "There is a sort of tribal solidarity which acted to keep the murderers' secret. Bernadotte had become unpopular. A lot of the people, especially those who came from the European ghettos, especially after the Holocaust, but also among the Oriental Jews who used to live in Morocco and Iraq, felt, maybe still feel, that all the world is against us. There was this feeling that Bernadotte was against us. And so we closed ranks when we faced the outside world. This was not my own feeling, but many people shared this, based on centuries of persecution, inquisition, and the Holocaust. It has been a source of strength in a way, it has made our people draw close to each other. I don't entirely share this view myself, but it exists."

Eytan, a courtly, Oxford-educated diplomat, was charged with delivering the sixty-seven-page report to Stockholm in 1950. "I presented it to Östen Unden, the foreign minister, a dour sort of fellow. Dag Hammarskjöld was my official host, as my Swedish counterpart, and he gave a big lunch in my honor. We got on very well. Our report was accepted by Sweden, and as a result Stockholm opened diplomatic relations with us."

From a combination of embarrassment and unease, Israel, Sweden, and the UN proceeded to erase Folke Bernadotte's memory as thoroughly as the fingerprints on the barrel of Yehoshua Cohen's submachine gun had been erased. In their subsequent dealings with Israel, Swedish officials rarely ever brought up Bernadotte's name.

In the spring of 1990, President Chaim Herzog was invited by the Swedish government to Stockholm for a state visit. In his carefully worded toast to the visiting head of state, Folke Bernadotte's godson, King Karl XVI Gustav pronounced the murdered man's name for the first time in the presence of an Israeli head of state. The king referred to his fallen kinsman as one who had done much to strengthen Israeli-Swedish ties through his humanitarian work and "his mission to the concentration camps in 1945." As a protest, it was not much of a statement. But it was all the politicians who hold real power in Sweden would permit the monarch. Both the king and Queen Sylvia had pressed for the right to make a bolder statement. "We should ask for an apology," the queen insisted. "But, madam," the Foreign Office official informed the royal couple, "it all happened such a long time ago." "Perhaps," the queen answered, "you do not realize he was the king's godfather, and we take these things very seriously."

CHAPTER TWENTY-FOUR

"ROGUES, COWARDS, AND LOW SCHEMERS"

ONE MONTH AFTER THE MURDER OF BERNADOTTE, BARUCH Nadel met Eldad, who, though still in hiding, was becoming bolder, venturing out more frequently. The two met on a barren patch of land outside the Tel Aviv city limits, where the Municipal Building stands today. "I was shocked by his appearance," Nadel remarked forty years later. "He had transformed himself into Leon Trotsky. The same hair, the mustache, the little goatee, everything. I said to him, 'Eldad, what is our strategy now? The government has forced us underground; we pretend that we didn't kill Bernadotte. So what are we going to do?' He answered, 'Don't worry, the Red Army will soon take the whole Middle East. Then we will form a government under Mikunis [the secretary-general of the [Israeli] Communist Party] and Yalin-Mor, and they will decide.' "

Groping for some future role in the new society, Yitzhak Shamir had also turned sharply leftward in his politics. Shamir almost never committed his thoughts to paper, thus his recorded speech to Lehi members, gathered, early in the summer of 1949, at the Ramah Cinema in Ramat Gan, is significant. The little man still dreamed of revolution. From Avraham Stern's messianic right-wing militarism, Shamir slipped steeply toward communism. "Already now, Western imperialism is trying to take advantage of our economic weakness, to wring concessions out of us, whose meaning is surrender and complete subjugation," he told the audience, adopting the Cominform's jargon as his own.

...the dangers of imperialism and the fruits of its alliance threatening new attacks on our independence and the fact of our existence. To chase away these dangers, revolutionary steps are essential and justified ... if one particular economic circle continues to see its main function as defending its advantages, won from unceasing effort at avoiding giving its share to the general good. ... As an example of a public body which ... has successfully achieved its task, we can point to the Communist Party in the Soviet Union and in the Popular Democratic States [of Europe]. One cannot describe the enormous economic efforts which have been carried out in those countries, in agriculture and industry, without the loyal and fanatical cadres of party members.

Shamir's and Eldad's seduction by the Communist ideal (Yalin-Mor had been the first to convert; it had been his idea to use the name of a Communist underground organization as cover for Bernadotte's murder) was almost as irrational as their mentor Avraham Stern's embrace of the Third Reich. For whereas Hitler decimated a rich Jewish culture, Stalin outlawed its existence. By the time Shamir praised this new religion, Stalin had banned all Jewish religious learning and jailed Jewish writers and cultural figures. The most outspoken among Jewish intellectuals he murdered. But to Shamir totalitarianism had its attractions.

This paean to Communist ideals was Shamir's final "public" appearance for several decades. The former guerrilla spent years performing inconsequential jobs, including running unsuccessfully a chain of cinemas. He ceased to be a public figure. But in 1955 when the man called Michael was allowed to come in from the cold, Isser Harel, the head of Mossad, and Ben-Gurion's former security chief, recruited Shamir as a spy.

It was an inspired choice. The underground proved to have been a perfect training ground for the layered life of espionage. "In the underground," noted Professor Joseph Heller, "you learn not only terror, but how to lie as well." "I felt at home very soon," the new Mossad recruit recalled. "I had returned to an atmosphere, behavior, incentive, and points of view that were, in many ways, familiar to me." Shamir rose rapidly in Mossad's ranks before joining Menachem Begin's Herut Party. "While in Mossad," Seymour Hersh wrote in *The Samson Option,* "Shamir was known for his efforts to improve relationships with his KGB counterparts. ... He worked diligently to develop new ties with the Soviet Union, which he envisioned as a means for balancing or offsetting Israel's traditional reliance on the US." Shamir's fondness for the Soviet Union and distrust of the British and Americans would endure. As prime minister between 1983 and 1992 Shamir opened new channels to the Soviet Union, even sharing heretofore classified materials with the KGB.

In 1954, while on an inspection tour of the Negev, David Ben-Gurion spotted something new in the desert, a kibbutz that had not been there on his previous visit. The old man sprang out of the jeep to survey the gardens and newly constructed buildings of Kibbutz Sde Boker. The prime minister was introduced to one of the kibbutz's founders, a lean man, then in his thirties, fit and tan from days spent working the sandy soil. It was Yehoshua Cohen. He looked ordinary enough at first glance. Only the eyes, disconcerting for the calm way they fixed on people, sometimes caught one off guard.

The prime minister returned several times to the kibbutz, and each time saw Cohen, who, says Ben-Gurion's biographer, Shabtai Teveth, told the prime minister right away about his past in the underground. Ben-Gurion had, according to Teveth, looked up Cohen in his diary entry of September 18, 1948, and realized that, in Ben-Gurion's own words, the kibbutznik was one of the "gang of rogues, cowards, and low schemers" responsible for the murder of the mediator.

In 1956, when he retired from public life, Ben-Gurion moved into a small house in Cohen's kibbutz, hoping "to share the life of the simple people." Thus began the strange twilight relationship between the prime minister and the assassin. Unlike many other Israelis, Cohen seemed unintimidated by "the Old Man." To Ben-Gurion, Cohen embodied the rugged pioneer type, a Zionist of the old school, willing to spend his days in the scorched Negev, so the next generation might have an easier time. Cohen became not only his confidant, but his bodyguard as well. Each nightfall, the wiry younger man and the short, stooped figure with the extraordinary flaring white hair could be seen strolling through the gardens and orchards of Sde Boker. The two could easily be mistaken for father and son.

"I took a walk with Yehoshua," Ben-Gurion wrote in his diary on August 29, 1960, "and asked him if he knew that his

Lehi friends conducted negotiations with Hitler in 1941. . . . He said that all of his friends knew about that . . . this was the policy of Stern, that whoever opposed the British could become our ally."

A year later, the prime minister, increasingly isolated by his position as the country's venerated founding father, told a group of visiting academics that "among the few close friends I have, I count one from Lehi and one from Mapam (the United Workers Party), Yehoshua Cohen and Veronchik Cohen . . . because the other young people vacillate, but they are still tied down, glued to the land of Sde Boker, and they are the closest to me."

Ben-Gurion was no longer alive when the man who shot Folke Bernadotte admitted the murder had been a mistake. "I know we killed the wrong man," Yehoshua Cohen confessed to Joseph Heller. "The black man [Ralph Bunche] was the right man. He was the man with the ideas."

Yitzhak Ben-Moshe, another of the four men in the jeep, also chose a pioneer kibbutz after he retired from the underground, in his case Kibbutz Kivri. There, on September 15, 1984, his former colleagues gathered for his funeral. He was the first member of the death squad to die. Inevitably, the old warriors, having said goodbye to the man they called "Betzalely," started to swap stories about the old days. Yehoshua Cohen, left alone for a moment with the dead fighter's son, whispered, "You know, Yair, until now it was not possible to say anything, for fear it would hurt your father. But he is safe now." The son looked puzzled. "It is important that you know," Cohen pressed on. "Your father was one of those who carried out that feat of bravery, the liquidation of Bernadotte." After several moments of silence, the thirty-eight-year-old shook his head and said, "He never even hinted that this was the case. I didn't know anything." Nor did the gunman's wife, who, upon hearing Cohen's story, remarked: "I remember that he was suspected of involvement in Bernadotte's death. I thought then perhaps he had taken part. But he never said a word."

Two years later, the aging former terrorists again assembled to bury one of their own: Yehoshua Cohen, the farmer's son born in British-Mandated Palestine who had fashioned himself into one of the new state's most fanatical warriors. In the August 19, 1986, obituary marking Cohen's death, *Yediot Aharonot* asked, "What did Ben-Gurion find in Yehoshua Cohen? Loneliness . . .

and concern for the people. [Cohen] was unable to change his political views, but ready for any sacrifice."

Approached by reporters at Yehoshua Cohen's funeral, Yitzhak Shamir, then deputy prime minister, brushed off their questions about the still-unsolved murder of the United Nations mediator: "In the underground we have made a vow . . . which obliges us to this very day: names and details connected with personal assassinations must remain secret until the end. They will never be disclosed."

But the electric Eldad had no intention of fading quietly into the night. Age had not tempered his combustible zeal. He was too contentious and unruly a figure for a successful political life. Instead, "the Doctor," as the diminutive Eldad is called by his followers, has made a career as a highly quotable supernationalist demagogue. He still regards the murder of Bernadotte as one of Lehi's greatest achievements. In his view, it saved Jerusalem from the Arabs. He wanted not to remain silent, but to achieve greater recognition. In 1960, Eldad approached Israel's then attorney general, Gideon Hausner, and told him he was going to publish the truth about Lehi's responsibility for the murder. "God forbid!" The attorney general sprang to his feet in horror at the prospect. "Do you know the problems you will create for your country?" Eldad was persuaded to keep still for a while longer.

By 1988, the surviving conspirators, with the notable exception of the former terrorist who held his country's highest elected office, could no longer contain their secret. Zetler, Makover, Eldad, and Hillman gave interviews to Israel's leading newspapers regarding their roles in the murder, as well as who was behind it. Only Gingi Zinger, retired and living in Haifa, has still refused to acknowledge any role as one of the four gunmen in the jeep. (His comrades no longer deny Zinger's role in the assassination, however.) Following the former terrorists' revelations, the lead editorial in Israel's respected daily, Ha'aretz, was entitled "Murder Is Murder."

Let's assume a man gets up one morning and finds an exclusive interview in a newspaper more or less as follows, "Do you remember twenty-three years ago three young girls were cruelly raped and murdered in Israel and the murderer was never caught? Well, gentlemen, I am willing to confess: I am that murderer. Not only me, but I had two partners, one of them a minister and an important public figure!"

Let's assume that a sensational confession like this was published—what would happen? You certainly assume that the police would arrest the bunch in a twinkle of an eye? Wrong! According to the criminal code, the statute of limitations on crimes is twenty years. Otherwise this past week the police would have had to arrest a list of people who admitted that they killed Count Folke Bernadotte on September 17, 1948. And among them, according to their own testimony, one is today prime minister of Israel.

But the law is the law, even if it is idiotic (and how else to call a law which recognizes a statute of limitations on murder?). But murder is also murder. And unlike wine, murder does not become any more refined with the passage of years. It still remains murder. From this perspective, there is no difference between he who murders for political reasons and he who just murders. . . . The worst of all . . . that the decision to assassinate Bernadotte . . . was taken at a meeting of the Lehi Central Committee in which Yitzhak Shamir, former Lehi commander, participated. Who pulled the trigger is less important, [Shamir] said in another place, what is important is that it was the Lehi Central Committee which decided on the assassination.

I have not read anywhere that Shamir is suing for slander. Nor does he deny any of this. He says, "It is of no interest to me now." Moreover, he is not even upset that he is accused in this public and collective fashion for his participation in the decision. But he is also misleading. The murder was not carried out in the days of the underground, as he says, but four months after the establishment of the State of Israel—a state whose processes of justice would have been capable of sentencing them to life imprisonment had this information been available at the time.

Perhaps we will never hear Shamir's own account of the murder of Folke Bernadotte. (Now that he has been returned by Israeli voters to private life, it is a supreme irony that the fugitive/terrorist-turned-politician, Yezernitsky/Michael/Shamir, has lived to enjoy a peaceful pensioner's life, while the privileged aristocrat, mowed down in a hail of gunfire, did not survive to see his grandchildren.) But those Israelis who have studied both the case and the man in the context of their country's history insist Shamir was the key player. "It takes a strong man to give such an order," says Shabtai Teveth. "This was no longer fighting the British. Under the Mandate, they had a lot of justification for terror. That was war. But with Bernadotte, we had a State of Israel by then. I don't see Eldad as an important part of this. I see him as a very good propaganda minister. But there is milk in his veins. Shamir was responsible for other such acts. It takes a certain kind of man to assume such responsibility. Shamir is such a man."

Not only has Yitzhak Shamir, who held the office of prime minister of Israel longer than any other, never disavowed his role in the murder of the mediator; he has frequently stated that his time as Lehi commander was the best time of his life. On his seventy-fifth birthday, Prime Minister Shamir said the world leader he would most have liked to meet was Mao Zedong.

For Abba Eban, Lehi's mystical nationalism and its various far-right offshoots in present Israeli life have done great damage to the country. "Their idea is to depend on nobody outside the State of Israel, which is absurd. That is really the end of a state, a kind of Masada-style self-destruction. There is a distinct suicidal element in Lehi, or else why would they try to negotiate with Hitler?"

In late 1991, former Palmach Commander Chaim Hefer watched with horror as the conspirators—Eldad, Makover, Zetler, and their accessory, former Haganah Captain Moshe Hillman—regaled the audience of a live television broadcast with details of how Lehi's guns cut down the United Nations' first Middle East mediator. "Lehi had a weakness for the aristocracy," Eldad volunteered, to the appreciative laughter of a studio audience of Lehi veterans and their families.

"You really should have seen how he would stand with his baton under his arm," Zetler interjected, giving a burlesque imitation of Bernadotte's military posture, "just like the British used to. . . ."

"You got a warning at home?" The television show host, Amos Ettinger, turned to Captain Moshe Hillman. "Did you tell anyone about the incident [i.e., Hillman's recognition of Makover, the jeep's driver]?"

"For forty years, no!" Hillman answered, to the exuberant applause and laughter of the studio audience.

"It made me ashamed," Chaim Hefer, today a respected Israeli commentator, ruefully noted. "The way they laughed and carried on about a murder. Sometimes in the Army you have to kill. Before independence, in the Haganah we shot a Nazi posing as a Jew named Wagner, a British plant. We had to kill him to save lives. But we never laughed about it afterwards. We wanted to forget about it."

At twilight on a fresh spring evening in 1992, the memorial park atop Jerusalem's Mount Herzl, commemorating the founder of modern Zionism, Theodor Herzl, is very still. Golda Meir, Levi Eshkol, and others who have served the state with distinction are buried here, near the monument to the state's spiritual founder. The country's military cemetery adjoins part of the neatly landscaped park and is a powerful sight. Row upon row of marble slabs thrust out of the dry Judean hill; the white tombstones of fallen Israeli soldiers glow pink and apricot in the sunset.

The quiet is suddenly broken by the crunch of gravel underfoot. A knot of old men climb the slope with heavy steps, men in their sixties and seventies, their bodies compact and close to the ground. Their faces are broad, their features large and blurred by the years. Some of them look East European, others of Mediterranean bloodline. They have the look of first-generation immigrants. Though they are mostly short, squat figures, one among them stands out, a gangly, loose-jointed man, well over six feet tall, with a thick mustache which, though mostly gray now, is still mixed with a few reddish strands. This is Meshulam Makover, the driver of the assassins' jeep that vanished without a trace forty-four years earlier.

Wives follow a respectful distance behind them, as was the custom in their youth. Though the women's waistlines are thick, they, too, look sturdy, resilient; they, too, played their part in the underground. Many of these men, like the prime minister of the day, who is expected by them, following a cabinet meeting, married the only women they came in contact with, their couriers in the underground. Some of them carry flowers. Though respectful of the solemn place, all of them look comfortable, unintimidated by their surroundings. They are among their own, among people they have known most of their lives. There are a few children and even a handful of denim-clad grandchildren among

them. It is very quiet. The rumble of the Holy City below is muf-
fled by the hills. Somewhere, an owl hoots.

Slowly, the group forms a semicircle around the twin tombstones. They are here to mark the forty-seventh anniversary of
the death by hanging of their comrades: two young men, ages
seventeen and twenty-two, who were executed by the British
colonial government in Egypt. The two Eliahus, as they are always referred to in the underground, shot and killed Lord
Moyne, the British minister of state for the Middle East. Like the
assassins of Bernadotte, Hakim and Bet-Zouri were members of
Lehi.

A rabbi in military fatigues, wearing a skullcap and prayer
shawl, begins a service the members of the group know as
well as their own names: the Kaddish, the Hebrew prayer for the
dead. The religious nod their heads more vigorously than the others as they murmur the prayer. Then their voices rise to the
melancholy hymn of the underground, "Anonymous Soldiers,"
composed by their founder, Avraham Stern.

> We are men without name, without kin,
> Who forever face terror and death,
> Who serve our cause for the length of our lives—
> A service that ends with our breath.
>
> In the days that are red with the flow of our blood,
> In the nights of blackest despair,
> Through the length and breadth of our land
> We shall raise our banner of strength without fear—
> Not driven like slaves at the master's command,
> Forced to die at the stranger's behest,
> We dream of the time when our people and land
> By freedom and peace will be blessed.

EPILOGUE

*"I have been thinking a lot about Folke
Bernadotte. . . . I would like to fly to Stockholm in his
former plane . . . for one day . . . just to place some
flowers on his grave."*

RALPH BUNCHE

FOR ISRAEL, SWEDEN, AND THE UNITED STATES, THE MURDER OF
Folke Bernadotte was something to forget as quickly as possible.
Sir Brian Urquhart, who later became the head of the UN's
peacekeeping operations, claims a "conspiracy of silence" was
thrown like a blanket over the assassination. "I've had difficulty
ever since Bernadotte's murder in joining the hue and cry over
'terrorism' when the subject comes up at the UN."

So muted was the world body's reaction, so lacking in any
real sanctions against the Jewish state for its failure to pursue the
murderers of the United Nations' mediator, that for Israel,
"world opinion" became an empty phrase. In the words of historian J. Bowyer Bell, Bernadotte's murder "immunized Israel to
international pressure and United Nations' interference." The
New York Times editorial that said the event would "discredit
the men of blood on both sides in Palestine" was unfortunately
wrong, as the next four decades would show.

As to the killers' claim of having saved their country from dis-
memberment by Bernadotte, given President Truman's unwillingness to press Israel too hard in 1948, and given the fact of
Washington's clear dominance of the world body, it seems un-

likely that Israel would have been forced to give up the Negev or to accept an internationalized Jerusalem had Bernadotte lived. Seen through the assassins' distorted lens, Folke Bernadotte appeared a much more powerful figure than he really was.

In many ways, Bernadotte served the role of scapegoat for both the United Nations and Washington. Both needed to *seem* to be doing the right thing by the Jews and the Arabs. Acting in haste, the UN perhaps chose the wrong man to fill this sensitive post. But could any man have done the job at that feverish time in the Middle East, with both sides hell-bent on combat and with the Great Powers as distracted as they were in the summer of 1948? How could Bernadotte, with his positive, can-do spirit and his almost total lack of a philosophical or historical background, understand the bruised, Dostoyevskian spirits who clung to Jerusalem as to a raft? His aristocratic self-assurance, his ramrod-straight military bearing, and his fatal rush for a settlement—none of this could inspire trust in people whose parents, sisters, and brothers had been grabbed in ghettos and died in the death camps only three years before. A man with no love for books, a near-total absence of a tragic dimension, should not have been sent to deal with the people of the Book.

Bernadotte was by no means alone in his failure to comprehend the aftershock of the survivors' brush with genocide. But there was a tragic arrogance to the Swede who really thought he could achieve what none could before and for many decades after him have been unable to accomplish: to make Jews and Palestinians accept each other's legitimate rights and live together on the same sliver of land.

Stung by the failure of Bernadotte's mission, the UN abandoned the effort to negotiate a comprehensive settlement between Arabs and Jews. The lesson the world body ought to have gleaned from Bernadotte's assassination was that words, even when uttered by the world's highest council, are not enough—if not backed by action and the willingness to use force if necessary. But the lesson was lost, and Palestine was to be only the first of many quagmires where the UN appeared impotent because of its failure to enforce rulings with muscle in the field.

In early 1949, Ralph Bunche, back at the Hôtel des Roses, gradually maneuvered the Israeli and Arab belligerents into signing an armistice. Bunche was well served by the fact that by then all parties were sick of war, ready for a face-saving way out. Bunche's job was made simpler by the military realities. Israel had dealt Egyptian forces a humiliating defeat in the Negev. Bunche's two goals were to get a cease-fire agreement and to persuade the two sides to withdraw their forces from the battlefield. Israelis from Weizmann to Ben-Gurion had made clear that no power on earth could force them to relinquish their hard-won claim on the Negev, as the Israeli military representative at the discussions on the Negev, a young officer named Yitzhak Rabin, made clear during the Rhodes talks.

It was not in search of a comprehensive peace plan that Bunche had summoned the belligerents to the Hôtel des Roses. They came to forge an armistice, drawn along then-existing military lines, banning the use of force by either party for an indefinite period. Even the physical arrangements at the Hôtel des Roses served Bunche's agenda. "For the first and only time, Arabs and Israelis were living in the same hotel and eating in the same dining room," Brian Urquhart noted, "on a remote island where there were no alternatives and no distractions. . . . The main recreation in the Hôtel des Roses was Ping-Pong and billiards, at which Bunche excelled. Rhodes presented no incentives for dallying or staying a moment longer than was necessary."

Bunche's task, even within the narrow confines of the Rhodes agenda, was Sisyphean. "I haven't been out of the hotel for two weeks now," he said. "I talk, argue, coax and threaten these stubborn people day and night, in the effort to reach agreement. I make a bit of progress here and another bit there, but it is so slow and so arduous. Sometimes I feel that I should just tell them to go home and forget about an armistice. This is killing work."

Once Egypt, the Arab power of the greatest consequence, and Israel had agreed to a disengagement, on February 24, 1949, Bunche invited Jordan, Lebanon, and Syria to Rhodes to participate in armistice negotiations. Within a few weeks, these countries, exhausted from the nearly year-long war, agreed to the terms of the troop withdrawal and armistice.

A weary Bunche wrote his wife: "I have been thinking a lot about poor Folke Bernadotte. . . . When my work is ended here in a week or two I would like to fly to Stockholm in his former plane . . . for one day . . . just to place some flowers on his grave. . . ."

The Rhodes Agreement, which would earn Bunche a Nobel Peace Prize, contained the conflict until the outbreak of a series of wars beginning in 1956. Though Ralph Bunche had been the architect behind many of Folke Bernadotte's proposals, he was always held in affectionate regard by the Israelis.

When Bunche died in 1971, Golda Meir waited in the rain until the doors of the funeral home in New York opened, determined that she would be the first to pay a final tribute to Bunche. Fairly or not, more for stylistic reasons than policy, Bunche evoked a different set of emotions among Israelis than the Swedish king's nephew.

Several years after Bernadotte's death, his character was subjected to an astonishing assault from a surprising source. In 1953, the eminent Oxford historian Hugh Trevor-Roper, the foremost British authority on the closing months of the Nazi regime, burnished the legend of Felix Kersten, Himmler's paradoxical masseur, and, at the same time, attacked Bernadotte's reputation as a skillful negotiator with the Nazis for prisoners of war and concentration-camp victims. In an article entitled "Kersten, Himmler, and Count Bernadotte," published in the *Atlantic Monthly* in February 1953, Trevor-Roper added his own credibility to Kersten's claim that he had rescued 3 million Dutchmen in 1941, explaining, "Fortunately, Himmler was at that time in a low state of health and particularly dependent on Kersten. Consequently, the move [to deport the Dutch en masse] was postponed until after the war. Himmler afterwards regretted his weakness in this matter. The Führer's decision, he sadly admitted, had been right; its postponement 'was all the fault of my wretched health, and my good Dr. Kersten.' "

Trevor-Roper went on to extol Kersten's heroics: "These and numerous other achievements of Kersten have long been known and are well authenticated. Why is it that after the war the knowledge of them was apparently suppressed and Kersten himself widely denounced as a Nazi? The answer to this question is to be found . . . in Sweden." The blame, he said, for Kersten's "mistreatment" lay with Folke Bernadotte. The historian dismissed Bernadotte's contribution to the rescue mission. "Of Count Bernadotte's activities in these negotiations," he said, "little need be said, for he was simply an agent—a 'transport offi-cer,' no more."

Trevor-Roper went even further in his attack on the Swede, dead for five years by then and thus unable to mount a defense of his record, claiming that Bernadotte had refused to take Jews with him to Sweden. "Count Bernadotte understands the Jewish peril," Trevor-Roper quoted Heinrich Himmler as having told Felix Kersten; "he refuses to take any Jews to Sweden; and now you [i.e., Kersten] speak for them and say that Sweden will take them! Which of you am I to believe?" The British historian quoted the SS general as having told his masseur, "Think of it! What a surprise! Count Bernadotte refused to take the Jews! You see how Nordic people think! They understand the Jewish prob-lem. However, I have promised my good Dr. Kersten, and I must keep my promise: Count Bernadotte must take the Jews whether he likes it or not. . . ."

Trevor-Roper's tone toward Bernadotte is grudging and re-sentful: "[Bernadotte] was overwhelmed with honors, decora-tions, degrees. He alone, it was declared, by facing Himmler in his den, had rescued Jews and Gentiles from death in the concen-tration camps. He was even credited with having ended the war. He was hailed as the 'Prince of Peace,' the Savior, and after his death the martyr of humanity."

From Stockholm to Tel Aviv, the charges leveled against a dead man by an esteemed historian provoked an international storm. On February 3, 1953, the Swedish Foreign Ministry is-sued an official response:

> The information according to which Bernadotte was to have refused to bring Jewish prisoners to Sweden is quite senseless. In fact, Bernadotte was working in close collaboration with the Government in Stockholm on including non-Scandinavian pris-oners—among them Jews—in the transports to Sweden. The req-uisite permission was eventually obtained from the German authorities, as Bernadotte was to learn during his last meeting with Himmler on the 24th of April 1945. . . . Those Swedish of-ficials who were present at the negotiations between Bernadotte and the respective German authorities testify to his unremitting efforts to save as many Jews as possible by taking them away from Germany to Sweden. . . . Consequently Trevor-Roper's alle-gation that Bernadotte was only a transport officer is erroneous.

Even today, many other historians are baffled by Trevor-Roper's unsubstantiated attacks. Was it professional jealousy, resentment that an untrained aristocrat had gained such spectacular access to the very characters Trevor-Roper could only analyze from a distance? Bernadotte's secretary, Barbro Wessel, attributes the English historian's venom to a letter Folke Bernadotte wrote to him, criticizing Trevor-Roper's own version of the fall of the Third Reich, entitled *The Last Days of Hitler.*

Bernadotte's letter is either lost or lies, still unavailable to this writer, in Trevor-Roper's files. But in a letter he wrote the count dated May 23, 1948, just four months before Bernadotte's assassination, Trevor-Roper unctuously referred to Bernadotte's upcoming testimony on behalf of Walter Schellenberg at the Nuremberg War Crimes Tribunal. "It is so kind of you to write so promptly in the middle of your pressing (and apparently harrowing) business," Trevor-Roper wrote from Christ Church College, Oxford, to the newly named Palestine mediator.

> I hope your visit as a witness in Nuremberg will be successful. I am sure no one will criticize you—or at least have the grounds to do so. I think it is rather to be admired. From my knowledge of Schellenberg's activities, I cannot think of a criminal count on which he could be personally condemned (except for belonging to a criminal organization—the SS). I should like also to wish you success in the . . . historic task you assumed in Palestine.

At the time, few disputed the respected British historian's assessment of Bernadotte and Kersten. And Trevor-Roper did not let matters rest with a single article. Several years later, in his foreword to *The Kersten Memoirs,* Trevor-Roper resumed his attack on Bernadotte, still uncritically accepting the masseur's version of events. ". . . [S]uddenly Bernadotte (to the surprise of Himmler and the dismay of Kersten) refused to handle non-Scandinavian prisoners. In the end, however, after a visit by Kersten to [Swedish Foreign Minister] Günther in Stockholm, these difficulties were all overcome."

In his foreword, Trevor-Roper also referred to the single piece of "evidence" attesting to Bernadotte's "anti-Semitism": a letter allegedly written by Bernadotte and addressed to Heinrich Himmler, dated March 10, 1945. Though the historian admits to having seen only "a copy," he nonetheless published it.

Honorable Mr. Himmler!

The Jews are not wanted in Sweden just as they are not wanted in Germany. This is why I fully understand your approach to the Jewish question. I hear from the medical practitioner Kersten that you have freed 5000 Jews to go to Sweden. I do not like it, because I do not want to take any Jews. But since officially I cannot refuse to transport them, I ask you, Mr. Himmler, do it yourself! The medical practitioner Kersten has no authority to negotiate the release of Jews, and has done it privately. This is also my attitude about transportation of French, Dutch, and Belgians to Sweden.

I would be glad if, as long as possible, I could take to Sweden Norwegians, Danes, and even Poles in the Red Cross' White Buses. As the medical practitioner Kersten says, you, Mr. Himmler, are ready to release all the Scandinavians in a place called Neuengamme.

Your "V" weapon is not hitting London well. I leave you a sketch with English military targets.

General Schellenberg was kind enough and agreed to pass this letter to you personally, so that it would not fall into undesirable hands.

Yours with honour,

F. Bernadotte

No one has ever claimed to have seen the "original" of this apparent fabrication. Barbro Wessel, who typed all Bernadotte's correspondence, says simply, "Folke didn't write his own letters and this is not in his language anyway." Despite its almost absurdly scurrilous tone, mixing anti-Semitism with treachery on Bernadotte's part, giving the Nazis advice on how to improve their aim on British military targets, the letter has nonetheless been cited in a number of accounts of this episode.

However crude the attack on Bernadotte's character, some of the mud stuck since Trevor-Roper's views inevitably carried impressive weight. In 1956, future British cabinet minister R. H. S. Crossman reviewed *The Kersten Memoirs* for the *New Statesman and Nation,* and wrote, "I accept Mr. Trevor-Roper's judgment—based on a long, painstaking investigation—that Kersten is a completely reliable witness who has been scandalously treated by the Swedish Government in an effort to maintain the myth that Count Bernadotte was a man of honour. It now appears certain that Kersten did almost everything during the last days of the Third Reich for which the vain, incompetent and untruthful Bernadotte claimed credit."

It was not until after 1972 that Kersten's character assassination of Bernadotte was revealed in its true light. The same organization that gave the masseur its seal of approval in 1949, the Netherlands Institute for War Documentation, decided, twelve years after Kersten's death, to reexamine his claims to have saved 3 million Dutchmen from deportation. Under the supervision of historian Louis de Jong, Holland's foremost scholar of World War II, a thorough study of all available documents revealed that Kersten's "diary" was manufactured years after the fact, that the "deportation" plan never existed, that all "historical evidence" produced by Kersten was forged by Kersten himself.

"This does not mean," the Dutch study concluded, "that Kersten did not play a very positive role in other attempts at freeing people from concentration camps. . . . In fact, Kersten might have been driven to invent the deportation story because of his situation in Sweden in 1945 . . . a situation partly caused by Count Bernadotte" (i.e., for not supporting Kersten's bid for Swedish citizenship and not giving him full public credit for his role in the Red Cross rescue mission). The new investigation presented Kersten as "vain but good-natured," a man who did try to do his best to save some people, but wildly overstated his own contributions.

No serious historian of any nationality has found a shred of evidence to support Trevor-Roper's charge that Bernadotte was an anti-Semite. In 1983, in an ironically similar situation, Trevor-Roper (by then Lord Dacre) "authenticated" sixty volumes of "diaries" alleged to be the Führer's own. The fact that one of the most distinguished historians of the Hitler period put his imprimatur on these "documents" led several of the world's shrewdest and most respected publishers, including *Newsweek* and the London *Sunday Times,* to accept these forgeries as genuine, and to run excerpts in their pages. Following the exposé, Trevor-Roper's distinguished colleague at Oxford University, A. L. Rowse, penned an article entitled "The Trial of Lord Dacre," describing him, at the age of seventy, as "a young man in a hurry." Rowse wrote, "I have always had reservations about him, since he started writing at Oxford as my protégé." A limer-

ick composed by students at Cambridge University on the subject of the Hitler "diaries" might just as well apply to Trevor-
Roper's endorsement of Kersten's diaries:

> There was a fellow named Dacre
> Who was God in his own little acre,
> But in the matter of diaries,
> He was quite ultra vires,
> And unable to spot an old faker.

"I made a mistake," Trevor-Roper (who refused all requests
by this author to address the subject of Bernadotte) told Israeli
historian Dr. Amitsur Ilan many years after the fact. He blamed
others for his own lack of historical judgment. "Professor
Posthumus [the Dutch historian who originally authenticated
Kersten's documents] was somewhat naive and took Kersten's
claims too literally." In 1983, Trevor-Roper issued an embarrassed public apology regarding his conduct on the matter of the
Hitler diaries. Today Bernadotte's sons say they are still waiting
for a sign of remorse regarding the historian's treatment of their
father.

The murder of Folke Bernadotte left a deeper psychological
imprint on Israel. The halfhearted justice dispensed to killers
known by so many in such a small place underscored the ambivalence of the government's attitude toward terrorism and of
Israelis' attitudes toward government authority. It is a state,
unique in the region, whose major newspaper alleges that "murder is murder," and points the finger at the prime minister of the
day, and need pay no price for its courage. A people steeped in
profound skepticism, a natural result for those stateless and
powerless for too long, do not easily adjust to boundaries and
limitations imposed even by their own state.

If, as has often been stated, Israel's brief history is a tapestry
woven out of the twin strands of hope and fear, the remarkable
career of Yitzhak Shamir is the triumph of fear over hope. Ob-
sessively guarded about his life, private and professional, this
key player in Israel's young life has, to date, managed to avoid
the scrutiny of both English- and Hebrew-speaking biographers.
The only existing biography of Shamir is in French. The former

terrorist has expressed himself neither on the circumstances of his Polish childhood nor, except in the most terse fashion, on his life as a leader of the underground. He declined this author's requests for an interview, or even a meeting, once he knew the subject matter to be discussed.

Only the barest facts of his extraordinary career are known. In 1965, forced to retire from Mossad, he asked his old foe in the underground, Menachem Begin, for a job. Begin, head of the Herut Party, offered him a lackluster position as the party's immigration director. Shamir's two chief qualities, patience and caution, paid off in his new incarnation as politician. At age sixty, in 1973, he was elected to the Knesset for the first time. Then, by a series of uncanny circumstances that knocked his competitors out of the running, he became speaker of the Knesset, then foreign minister. Finally, in 1983 the man who had been the country's most feared terrorist was elected prime minister. Still faithful to the vision of his original mentor, Vladimir Jabotinsky, Shamir summed up the chief goal of his long tenure: "With my whole history and the way I perceive the state," he told *Le Monde* in 1991, "I will never abandon the territories. I wouldn't want to enter national memory as someone who sold off part of Israel cheaply."

Given the overwhelming odds against Israel's birth and survival, however, the wonder is the dominance of the thread of hopeful pragmatism, for which Ben-Gurion and his successors—including Prime Minister Yitzhak Rabin—stand. The tension between these tendencies, so obvious in 1948, has never been resolved, however. It is a dilemma to which few Israelis are oblivious. Israel's first native-born prime minister, Rabin has admonished his countrymen against the notion that "the whole world is against us." And yet Prime Minister Rabin has also warned that "we will learn to believe in a better world. But most important, we will not trust in others any longer, generous as they may be: only us, only ourselves. We will protect ourselves."

Many Israelis, in 1948 and on subsequent occasions over the years, have suspected that police work to catch homegrown terrorists has been less than vigorous. And once caught, Jewish terrorists are generally treated with latitude. A tendency to accept a separate justice for terrorists began with the assassination of Folke Bernadotte, and haunts Israelis still. In a poll taken after Israeli terrorists attacked three Palestinian mayors, 36.6 percent of a sample of about 1,200 Jewish adults answered yes to the question of whether terrorism should be used against Arabs in response to terrorism. Fifty-four percent answered no. "There is a feeling," then President Chaim Herzog noted, "that the only way you can deal with the Arabs is to pay them back in their own coin. There has been an undercurrent of this for a long time. It's something that cuts right across party lines and is based more on country of origin. [The Israeli] won't do it himself, but he doesn't mind if somebody else does."

Folke Bernadotte paid with his life for not grasping the reality to which Middle East peacemakers ever since him have had to adjust: The "facts on the ground," however shifting, cannot be ignored. Bernadotte also missed another fundamental point: it was not only the "extremists" who felt a tribal solidarity with their own kind, an innate suspicion of outsiders with plans for Jews, and a mystical attachment to Jerusalem. These deeply rooted feelings are widely held in Israeli society. Both the mediator and those who appointed him failed to see that a Swedish aristocrat, seemingly aloof and indifferent, would serve as a convenient symbol for all that was wrong with the world's treatment of Jews.

Avraham Stern's dream of reclaiming the whole of the Golden City as Zion's capital was not to be realized for another two decades. Upon reaching the Wailing Wall on the fourth day of the Six-Day War in 1967, Major General Moshe Dayan spoke for all Israelis: "We have returned to all that is holy in our land. We have returned never to be parted again." In the war's aftermath, Dayan presided over the reburial of the casualties of 1948 on Jerusalem's Mount of Olives. Addressing his fallen comrades, Dayan solemnly intoned: "We have not abandoned your dream and we have not forgotten your lesson. We have returned to the mountain, to the cradle of our people, to the inheritance of the Patriarch, the land of the Judges and the fortress of the Kingdom of the House of David. We have returned to Hebron and Shechem [Nablus], to Bethlehem and Anatot, to Jericho and the fords of the Jordan at Adam Hai'ir."

NOTES

INTRODUCTION

xi. "disobey any command": *New York Times,* April 19, 1994.

xii. "Peacekeeping by itself": *Foreign Affairs,* December 1992, p. 90.

xii. "to take such measures": Bernadotte's memoir, *To Jerusalem* (London: Hodder & Stoughton, 1951).

CHAPTER ONE

The author interviewed Barbro Wessel and Moshe Hillman for first-hand descriptions of Bernadotte's final day in Jerusalem. For background on Transjordan's role in the Israeli War of Independence, see *The British Empire in the Middle East, 1945–1951,* by William Roger Louis (New York: Oxford University Press), sec. IV, Palestine.

In addition to the accounts of Barbro Wessel and Moshe Hillman, the author relied on the eyewitness reconstructions of the mediator's final journey by Gen. Aage Lundström, Maj. Massart, Lt. Col. M. Flach, and Maj. Jan de Geer, as published in Bernadotte's memoir, *To Jerusalem* (London: Hodder & Stoughton, 1951).

The author interviewed Lehi members Nahum Chachkes (Nimry), Baruch Nadel, Israel Eldad, and Yaakov Heruti for the assassins' perspective on the murder.

5. For Bernadotte's lack of security, see Amitsur Ilan's *Bernadotte in Palestine, 1948* (London: Macmillan, 1989), pp. 166-95.

5. For the various subdivisions within Jerusalem, see Sydney Bailey, *Four Arab-Israeli Wars and the Peacekeeping Process* (New York: St. Martin's Press, 1982), p. 16.

CHAPTER TWO

The author relied on interviews with Barbro Wessel, Moshe Hillman, and Bertil Bernadotte, as well as Amitsur Ilan's interview with Estelle Bernadotte, for the scene regarding the murder's aftermath. Ben-Gurion's biographer, Shabtai Teveth, provided the description of the prime minister's reaction to the assassination. The author also drew on Ben-Gurion's diaries (September 17, 1948, entry) which are filed at Kibbutz Sde Boker, Israel.

18. "On the 17th": Lehi letter from the papers of Baruch Nadel.

19. Bertil Bernadotte related to the author the story of the radio announcement of his father's murder in Jerusalem.

CHAPTER THREE

Interviews with various former members of Lehi, including Y. S. Brenner, Baruch Nadel, Israel Eldad, and the Israeli scholar of Lehi, Dr. Joseph Heller, provided the background for much of this chapter.

20. "We had no instructions": Larry Collins and Dominique Lapierre, *O Jerusalem* (New York: Simon & Schuster, 1988), p. 321.

21. The author interviewed Dean Rusk for Marshall's reaction to the White House's recognition of Israel, and drew on the secret memorandum of May 17, 1948, from Robert Lovett to the White House, as published on p. 1005 of the *Foreign Relations of the United States*, (hereafter, *FRUS*) vol. V (1948).

21. "We have tried for years": For an account of Sir Alexander Cadogan's presentation of the Palestine question before the United Nations, see Trygve Lie's memoir, *In the Cause of Peace*, (New York: Macmillan, 1954), p. 160.

21. The author relied in part on Howard Sachar, *A History of Israel* (New York: Knopf, 1981), for material on Britain's noncooperation in Israel's transition to independence.

22. "If the Great Powers": *In the Cause of Peace*, p. 76.

22. "My primary concern": Lie's letter to Secretary of State Marshall is among the papers of Sir Brian Urquhart.

23. The descriptions of Lie are drawn from the author's interviews with Sir Brian Urquhart and A. M. Rosenthal.

24. The account of Washington's ambivalence toward the question of recognizing Israel is based on the author's interviews with Clark Clifford and Dean Rusk.

CHAPTER FOUR

Author's interviews with Dr. Joseph Heller and Prof. Y. S. Brenner are the sources for Lehi's vision of Jerusalem.

Uri Zvi Greenberg's unpublished translations are in the Israeli Institute for the Translation of Hebrew Literature in Tel Aviv.

Yaakov Heruti shared his view with the author during interviews in Tel Aviv.

25. See Sachar, *A History of Israel,* for more on the UN's 1947 decision.

26. "The [Westerners] were attracted": Sachar, *A History of Israel,* p. 295.

26. Author's interviews with Shabtai Teveth and Abba Eban provided the material regarding Ben-Gurion's and Weizmann's views on history and on Jerusalem.

28. Baruch Nadel related the information regarding Yehoshua Zetler to the author.

29. The author learned about Deir Yassin from Baruch Nadel, Moshe Hillman, and Prof. Joseph Heller; there is relevant material on the subject in Larry Collins and Dominique Lapierre, *O Jerusalem,* pp. 284–85.

30. Baruch Nadel described Lehi's post–Deir Yassin situation to the author.

CHAPTER FIVE

31. For a description of Sir Alexander Cadogan, the author interviewed Abba Eban.

32. Sir Brian Urquhart related to the author how Bernadotte was selected. See also UN Archives (New York), DAG 13.3.3, Box 43, for material on this subject, including Secretary Marshall's letter to the Stockholm embassy.

32. Grafström's diaries, in the possession of Count Bertil Bernadotte, were the source for the material regarding Bernadotte's reaction to his new position.

34. *Ma'ariv,* September 13, 1968, p. 16, describes Shamir's escape from African captivity.

CHAPTER SIX

36. For Shamir's early life, the author relied on interviews with Lenni Brenner, a scholar of the Israeli underground (see *The Iron Wall: Zionist Revisionism from Jabotinsky to Shamir* [London: Zed Books, 1984]), with Shamir's former comrades Baruch Nadel and Israel Eldad, as well as on Charles Enderlin's *Shamir* (in French) (Paris: Olivier Orban, 1991). Enderlin's is the sole existing biography (to date) of the former terrorist and prime minister.

38. Jabotinsky's quotations are from Enderlin, *Shamir,* p. 24, and from Brenner, *The Iron Wall,* pp. 73–74.

39. Natan Yalin-Mor's memoirs (in Hebrew), p. 121, contain the material regarding Shamir's time in the Revisionist Youth Movement (Y. S. Brenner Papers).

40. "One more cow": Enderlin, *Shamir,* p. 26.

41. See Brenner, *The Iron Wall,* pp. 102–3, for a description of Jabotinsky's negotiations for transporting Jews to Palestine.

41. "I have the right": Enderlin, *Shamir,* p. 26.

41. At Warsaw University: Y. Shamir, *Summing Up* (London: Weidenfeld & Nicolson, 1994), p. 7.

43. "The Strange Career of Yitzhak Shamir," *Village Voice,* July 3, 1984, describes Shamir's time in the underground. The author also interviewed various members of the underground (i.e., Baruch Nadel, Y. S. Brenner, Yaakov Heruti, Israel Eldad) regarding their initiation rites.

CHAPTER SEVEN

45. Uri Avnery's article "Around Us Only Terror and Fear," *Der Spiegel* 86 (1986), recounts the Irgun's terrorist activities in 1938.

45. Six months after: Chamberlain's announcement is reprinted in Sachar, *A History of Israel,* p. 222.

46. "That he could do this!": Sachar, *A History of Israel,* pp. 222–25.

46. Debate in the House of Commons, April 26–27, 1939, quoted by Arthur Koestler in *Promise and Fulfillment* (New York: Macmillan, 1949), p. 58.

46. "created a vacuum": Sachar, *A History of Israel,* pp. 224–25.

46. "their war is our war," Sachar, *A History of Israel,* pp. 222–25.

47. This was the opposite of Jabotinsky's belief: Nicholas Bethell, *The Palestine Triangle: The Struggle Between the British, the Jews, and the Arabs 1935–48* (London: André Deutsch, 1979), p. 162.

47. "The Jewish Agency reacted to this": Yalin-Mor's memoirs, p. 60 (Y. S. Brenner Papers).

47. The underground launched full-scale warfare: Gerold Frank, *The Deed* (New York: Berkley Publishers, 1963), pp. 73–74, as well as the author's interviews with Yaakov Heruti and Prof. Joseph Heller.

47. Palestine thus began its transformation: Based in part on J. Bowyer Bell, *Terror out of Zion* (New York: St. Martin's Press, 1979), p. 153.

48. Avraham Stern's youth education was described to the author by Prof. Joseph Heller and is also depicted in Yalin-Mor's memoirs, including the quote "We knew that our people's freedom," from pp. 55–56.

49. "the world's first truly free Jew": E. Katz, "The Person in the Attic," *He Hazit* 1 (Tammuz 5703; 1943), reprinted in *Lehi Writings* (Tel Aviv, 1959), p. 125.

49. "His Zionism was not": Yalin-Mor memoirs, p. 56.

49. The author interviewed Samuel Merlin for his memories of Stern.

49. "a pure, enlightened soul": Frank, *The Deed,* p. 98.

50. He taught courses: Samuel Katz, *Days of Fire* (Garden City, N.Y.: Doubleday, 1968), p. 17.

50. "Stern's origins are in European fascism": Author's interview in Jerusalem with Prof. Joseph Heller, Hebrew University, Jerusalem.

51. "Try to put yourself in the place of a Jew": *New Statesman and Nation,* August 1947.

51. "I heard a lot about him": Dan Margalit's interview with the prime minister about the fiftieth anniversary of Stern's murder, *Ma'ariv,* January 31, 1992, Shabbat supplement, p. 3.

52. "The Irgun were only attacking buildings": Bethell, *The Palestine Triangle,* p. 161.

52. Yezernitsky/Shamir later defended the strategy: Ibid.

52. In his recently published: Excerpted from *Yediot Aharonot,* January 14, 1994.

52. In a matter of months: Tsvi Tsameret's interview with Yehoshua Cohen, July 8, 1972, on file at the Hebrew University Institute for Contemporary Jewry, Oral Testimony Division.

52. Yezernitsky's first task was: Tsvi Tsamaret's interview with Shamir, 1973, Hebrew University Institute for Contemporary Jewry, Oral Testimony Division.

53. "We were of diverse mentality": Author's interview with Y. S. Brenner.

53. "For a moment": Author's interview with Baruch Nadel.

53. "That period in the underground": Yossi Melman, in *Ha'aretz,* August 27, 1991.

53. For background on Stern's attempt to contact Hitler, the author interviewed historians Joseph Heller and Lenni Brenner and used Brenner's study, *The Iron Wall,* pp. 194–95. Stern's letter to von Papen is in the files of the German Foreign Affairs Ministry in Bonn. The file is entitled the "Italian Arms Strike Committee" E234156, with a copy in the Central Zionist Archives, Jerusalem, File 43/14K. Joseph Heller also reproduced it in his book *Lehi: Ideology and Politics 1940–1949* (Jerusalem, 1989).

55. For more on Lubentchik's arrest by British agents, see Enderlin, *Shamir,* p. 78.

55. Brenner, *The Iron Wall,* p. 197, describes Yalin-Mor's arrest by British agents.

55. Barbara Tuchman, *Bible and Sword* (New York: New York University Press, 1956), p. 305, details Herzl's attempt to contact von Plehve.

55. "What was, was justified": Shamir, interviewed on Israeli Army Radio, September 4, 1991.

55. "I did not trust it": *Ma'ariv,* January 31, 1992, Shabbat supplement, p. 3.

56. But Shamir has never: Tsvi Tsameret's interview with Yehoshua Cohen, July 8, 1972.

56. "No shame": *Ma'ariv,* January 31, 1992.

56. Stern put the indelible: Shamir, *Summing Up,* pp. 33–34.

56. He churned out poetry: Frank, *The Deed,* p. 101.

57. "The Eighteen Principles": This document is contained in the Lehi Museum, Tel Aviv.

57. "I went about": Geulah Cohen to Nicholas Bethell, in Bethell, *The Palestine Triangle,* p. 127.

57. "Our headquarters": Ibid., p. 160.

58. Stern's murder was described to the author by several of his followers, including Y. S. Brenner and Baruch Nadel, and is also recounted in Yalin-Mor's memoirs. See p. 21 for Yalin-Mor's reaction to the murder.

58. "It was not a very good way": Bethell, *The Palestine Triangle,* p. 129.

58. "Captain Morton helped us": Ibid.

59. "I thought that my world": Shamir, interviewed on Israeli Army Radio, September 4, 1991.

CHAPTER EIGHT

60. "I am one of those": Folke Bernadotte, *Instead of Arms,* (Stockholm: Bonniers, 1948).

60. "I remember that my father": Ralph Hewins, *Count Folke Bernadotte: His Life and Work,* (London: Hutchinson, 1948), p. 21.

61. "the service, horses and pleasure": Bernadotte, *Instead of Arms,* p. 11.

61. "He had a feeling": Amitsur Ilan's interview with Estelle Bernadotte Ekstrand, December 1983.

62. "Life in a hospital": Hewins, *Count Folke Bernadotte,* p. 28.

62. "This was one of the most painful things": Author's interview with Count Bertil Bernadotte.

62. "With his usual methodical precision": Hewins, *Count Folke Bernadotte,* p. 42.

63. "I wondered to myself": Ibid., p. 45.

64. "The idea of making Dragongården": Estelle Bernadotte Ekstrand's 1983 interview with Amitsur Ilan. The author also relied on Count Bertil Bernadotte's recollections of his parents for this section.

65. "We liked it much better there": Author's interview with Count Bertil Bernadotte.

66. The passages from Sven Grafström are found in his diaries (in Swedish and covering the years 1938–44 and 1945–54), which were made available to the author by Count Bertil Bernadotte.

66. The radio scripts regarding Bernadotte's Red Cross work are in the Stockholm Red Cross Archives filed under "Bernadotte," mainly boxes 32–41.

68. "At his first of many": Hewins, *Count Folke Bernadotte,* p. 87.

68. "Beneath the hatred": Ibid.

69. "Even though the night": Bernadotte, *Instead of Arms,* p. 53.

69. By late 1944: For this section regarding Sweden's growing interest in some sort of a rescue operation, the author is indebted to Steven Kobelik's detailed study of the problem, *The Stones Cry Out: Sweden's Response to the Persecution of the Jews 1933–1945* (New York: Holocaust Library, 1988). The author also interviewed Judith Goldstein and Eleanor Storch for additional material regarding the Swedish rescue mission.

71. Since March 1939: Joseph Kessel, *The Man with the Miraculous Hands,* with an introduction by Hugh Trevor-Roper (New York: Farrar, Straus & Cudahy, 1961).

71. "Kersten massages a life": Felix Kersten, *The Kersten Memoirs,* with an introduction by H. R. Trevor-Roper (London: Hutchinson, 1956), p. 12.

71. In December 1944: H. R. Trevor-Roper, "Kersten, Himmler, and Count Bernadotte," *Atlantic Monthly,* February 1953.

72. The facilitator behind this: Ilan, *Bernadotte in Palestine,* p. 28.

72. By February 10, 1945: Red Cross Archives, Stockholm, Bernadotte File.

72. "It would be futile": Hewins, *Count Folke Bernadotte*, p. 112.

73. Thus, no direct negotiations: Red Cross Archives, Stockholm, Bernadotte File.

73. "Discussions were held": Grafström diaries (Count Bertil Bernadotte Papers).

CHAPTER NINE

74. For background on the Bernadotte mission to Germany, the author relied on Kobelik, *The Stones Cry Out,* chap. 2, "Sweden and the Jewish Problem 1933–1945," and chap. 4, "No Truck with Himmler."

74. But the Führer had proclaimed: Hewins, *Count Folke Bernadotte,* p. 110.

75. "From the start": Folke Bernadotte, *The Curtain Falls* (New York: Knopf, 1945), pp. 29, 30.

75. "When I suddenly saw him": Ibid., p. 42.

76. "He said there could be": Ibid., pp. 50–51.

76. Eager to change the subject: Ibid., pp. 56–57.

77. "Regarding the Bernadotte Mission": March 13 entry of Grafström diaries, (Count Bertil Bernadotte Papers).

77. "Swedish authorities": Bernadotte to Storch, February 26, 1945; Eleanor Storch to author.

78. At the same time: Bernadotte, *The Curtain Falls,* p. 69.

78. Drafted in Himmler's own hand: From the Netherlands Institute for War Documentation, Kersten File.

78. Back once more in Stockholm: Memorandum of March 27, 1945, Red Cross Archives, Stockholm, Bernadotte File; also reprinted in Kobelik, *The Stones Cry Out,* pp. 117–41.

79. Bernadotte, often trailed: Hewins; *Count Folke Bernadotte,* p. 148.

79. On March 30: Bernadotte, *The Curtain Falls,* p. 80.

79. Once Bernadotte was inside the factory: Ibid., p. 85.

79. The British continued to take a dim view: Eden to Churchill, April 5, 1945, FO 9554 23.

80. For background on this section, the author is indebted to Jon Bridgman's *The End of the Holocaust and the Liberation of the Camps* (Portland, OR.: Areopagitica Press, 1947), and Hugh Trevor-Roper's *The Last Days of Hitler* (New York: Macmillan, 1947).

80. By the end: Kobelik, *The Stones Cry Out,* chap. 4.

81. Bernadotte's message: Winston S. Churchill, *Triumph and Tragedy,* vol. VI (Boston: Houghton Mifflin, 1953), p. 466.

81. Churchill added: Ibid., pp. 467, 468.

82. Whatever the motive: Bernadotte, *The Curtain Falls,* p. 14.

83. "Schellenberg was an excellent actor": Estelle B. Ekstrand's interview with Amitsur Ilan, 1983.

83. Bertil Bernadotte remembers: Author's interview with Count Bertil Bernadotte.

83. Estelle Bernadotte kept: Estelle B. Ekstrand's interview with Amitsur Ilan.

84. "Kersten is known to me": Mallet to Foreign Office, February 25, 1945, FO 371 48026.

84. Folke Bernadotte was less enthusiastic: Estelle B. Ekstrand to Amitsur Ilan.

84. By late 1945: For material regarding Felix Kersten, the author drew on material in the Netherlands Institute for War Documentation, Amsterdam, Kersten Files, as well as the Stockholm Red Cross Bernadotte File.

85. N. W. Posthumus: Author's interview with David Barnouw of the Netherlands Institute for War Documentation.

86. "He liked to think well": Author's interview with Count Bertil Bernadotte.

86. "Because of his position": Folke Bernadotte to Irene Schellenberg, October 25, 1945, Red Cross Archives, Stockholm, Bernadotte File.

CHAPTER TEN

88. Michael, received: Enderlin, *Shamir,* p. 105.

88. Even among the inmates: Author's interviews with Y. S. Brenner and Matti Meged.

89. Shamir was a hunted man: Author's interview with Yossi Melman; and see also the London *Times,* October 14, 1986.

90. Before he could start recruiting: Yossi Melman, "Who Drew First?" *Ha'aretz,* February 2, 1991.

90. "His behavior towards other people": Tsvi Tsameret's interview with Yehoshua Cohen, 1973, Hebrew University Institute for Contemporary Jewry, Oral Testimony Division; also Melman, "Who Drew First?"

90. "Giladi," Shamir would recall: Shamir, *Summing Up,* p. 154.

91. Only after Giladi's elimination: Tsvi Tsameret's interview with Shamir, 1973.

91. "In large measure": Enderlin, *Shamir,* p. 99.

92. "With Giladi, it was really a tragedy": *Ma'ariv,* January 31, 1992, pp. 3, 6.

92. "The decision was difficult": Melman, "Who Drew First?"

92. Eldad, known as the Doctor: Author's interviews with Israel Eldad and Baruch Nadel.

93. "Lehi was logical": Author's interview with Y. S. Brenner.

94. On a steamy day in August: The author is indebted to Gerold Frank and his fine study of the Moyne killing, *The Deed* (New York: Berkley Books, 1963).

94. "He would take something": Amos Nevo, "Shamir," *Yediot Aharonot,* September 7, 1986.

94. "We knew, in spite of denials": Author's interview with Y. S. Brenner.

95. "My dear fellow": Author's interview with Joseph Heller; see also Frank, *The Deed,* pp. 4–5.

96. "What influenced [Bet-Zouri]": Frank, *The Deed,* p. 132.

96. The disaster "dumbfounded": Ibid., p. 180.

96. Yehoshua Cohen, Lehi's most valued fighter: Author's interview with Joseph Heller, who had spent time with the former terrorist prior to his death in 1986; and see Frank, *The Deed,* p. 25.

96. "Our attack on Moyne": Frank, *The Deed,* pp. 196, 197.

97. Of the 30,000: Ibid., p. 203.

98. "Since Zionism began": Ibid., p. 16.

98. Five decades later: Shamir, *Summing Up,* pp. 22–23.

99. The hard men: Yalin-Mor memoirs, p. 318 (Y. S. Brenner Papers).

100. "Four years have passed": Ned Temko, *To Win or to Die* (New York: Morrow, 1987), pp. 72–107; and Frank, *The Deed,* p. 157.

100. Teddy Kollek, chief of intelligence: Teddy Kollek, *For Jerusalem* (New York: Random House, 1992), pp. 58–59.

101. Still under deep cover: Yalin-Mor's memoirs, p. 484 (Y. S. Brenner Papers).

101. "We respected Shamir": Author's interview with Y. S. Brenner, Utrecht, 1991.

101. To avoid capture: Uri Avnery, "Around Us Only Terror and Fear," *Der Spiegel* 48 (1986).

101. "Eldad lectured on": Yalin-Mor memoirs, pp. 433, 434 (Y. S. Brenner Papers).

101. "Geulah's voice": Ibid., pp. 349, 350.

102. "I married clandestinely": *Ma'ariv,* September 13, 1968, p. 16.

102. At around the same time: Enderlin, *Shamir,* p. 122.

103. "Even within your cell": Author's interview with Y. S. Brenner.

103. Almost immediately: Conor Cruise O'Brien, *The Siege: The Story of Zionism and Israel* (London: Paladin Books, 1988), p. 259.

104. Natan Yalin Mor represented Lehi: Ned Temko, *To Win or to Die,* p. 87.

105. General Sir Evelyn Barker: Eric Silver, *Begin: The Haunted Prophet* (New York: Random House, 1984), p. 73.

105. "I was sure nothing would happen": "Interview of the Week," *Ma'ariv,* September 13, 1968, p. 16.

105. Yalin-Mor recalled: Yalin-Mor's memoirs, p. 409 (Y. S. Brenner Papers).

106. The circumstances of Shamir's imprisonment and the assassination of Sgt. Martin were related to the author by Israel Eldad.

CHAPTER ELEVEN

107. "One hundred thousand Englishmen": Samuel Katz, *Days of Fire* (Garden City, N.Y.: Doubleday, 1968), p. 127.

107. The author relied on Alan Bullock's *Ernest Bevin: Foreign Secretary 1945–1951* (New York: Norton, 1983), esp. pp. 219–59, on Palestine, and the chapter entitled "London, November-December, 1947," pp. 476–510. *The Politics of Partition* by Avi Shlaim (Oxford: Oxford University Press, 1990) also contains useful background on this subject.

108. In 1946, Samuel Merlin: Author's interview with Samuel Merlin, who could not recall the exact day in 1946 when his meeting with Duff Cooper occurred.

109. The appalling images: David Hirst, *The Gun and the Olive Branch* (London: Faber & Faber, 1977), pp. 118–19.

109. Some American Zionist extremists: *New York Herald Tribune,* May 15, 1947.

109. "the British are everywhere": Ralph Bunche's letter of June 20, 1947, is among the Urquhart Papers.

109. On UNSCOP's first working day: Brian Urquhart, *Ralph Bunche* (New York: Norton, 1993), p. 141.

110. "The longer we stay": Bunche to Ben Gerig, July 23, 1947 (Urquhart Papers).

110. In its report: Sachar, *A History of Israel,* p. 284.

110. On the critical issue: George Kirk, *The Middle East, 1945–1950* (London, 1954), pp. 245–46.

110. Once more, the British: William Roger Louis, *The British Empire in the Middle East* (London: Oxford University Press, 1984), p. 473.

110. Less than a month later: Arthur Koestler, *Promise and Fulfillment* (New York: Macmillan, 1949), p. 142.

111. To Arthur Koestler: Ibid., p. 143.

111. "So long as my Government": Author's interview with Abba Eban.

111. *Après moi le déluge:* Koestler, *Promise and Fulfillment,* p. 145.

111. "Maybe we were wrong": Beeley to Lord Nicholas Bethell, reproduced in O'Brien, *The Siege,* p. 278.

112. "The United Nations really mattered": Author's interview with A. M. Rosenthal.

112. "Nobody who lived that moment": Author's interview with Abba Eban.

113. Over cups of tea: Abba Eban, *Personal Witness* (New York: Putnam, 1992), p. 110.

114. By the end of that winter: Sachar, *A History of Israel,* pp. 198–99.

114. On February 28, 1948: FRUS, vol. V (1948), pp. 666–68.

114. It was Harry Truman's: Author's interview with Dean Rusk.

115. Secretary of Defense James Forrestal: David McCullough, *Truman* (New York: Simon & Schuster, 1992), pp. 598–603.

115. Perhaps no one: Robert D. Kaplan, *The Arabists* (New York: Free Press, 1993), pp. 92–99.

116. "It was one of the worst messes": Ibid., p. 612.

116. "It was my hope": Harry S. Truman, *Years of Trial and Hope 1946–1952* (Garden City, N.Y.: Doubleday, 1966), p. 166.

CHAPTER TWELVE

117. That same week: Author's interview with Matti Meged.

118. On May 24: Collins and Lapierre, *O Jerusalem,* p. 480.

118. "I found a seventeen-year-old Polish boy": Author's interview with Matti Meged.

119. The Haganah admitted: Author's interview with Matti Meged; and see also Collins and Lapierre, *O Jerusalem,* pp. 472–90.

119. "The Count is affable": Ralph Bunche to Ruth Bunche, May 25, 1948 (Urquhart Papers).

120. "They became fast friends": Estelle B. Ekstrand to Amitsur Ilan. (Barbro Wessel Papers).

120. "Ralph was a Negro": Ibid.

120. "My treasured friend": Ralph Bunche in a speech to the First Committee of the UN, October 1948 (undated manuscript among Urquhart Papers).

120. The following morning: From Bernadotte's own account in *To Jerusalem*, pp. 8–13.

122. However, since the Israelis: Sachar, *A History of Israel*, pp. 316–17.

123. "Instead of coming straight to Palestine": see Dov Joseph's *The Faithful City: The Siege of Jerusalem, 1948* (London: Hogarth Press, 1962), chap. XII, "Count Bernadotte," p. 290.

123. "As I stepped from my aircraft": Commander Robert Jackson's memory of Bernadotte is from the United Nations Staff Recreational Council's publication, *Journal of the Society of Writers*, December 1986, p. 61.

123. The description of Bernadotte's Cairo visit is drawn from Count Bernadotte's own account in *To Jerusalem*, pp. 17–36.

124. "I won't let them spy": Author's interview with Barbro Wessel.

124. Sir Alexander Cadogan's exchange with Abba Eban was related to the author during an interview with Mr. Eban.

125. Bernadotte was elated: Bernadotte, *To Jerusalem*, pp. 32–35.

127. Four Royal Air Force Tempest fighters: Ibid., p. 36.

CHAPTER THIRTEEN

The author relied on Ralph Bunche's notes (Brian Urquhart Papers) and Bernadotte's *To Jerusalem*, p. 38, for a description of Bernadotte's initial meeting with David Ben-Gurion.

128. "I remember standing": Author's interview with Walter Eytan.

129. Bunche called the meeting "unpleasant": Bunche memorandum re discussion with David Ben-Gurion, United Nations Archives, New York, DAG 13/3/0.

129. It is clear: David Ben-Gurion, *Israel: A Personal History* (New York: Funk & Wagnalls, 1971), p. 120.

130. The travel-weary Bernadotte's spirits: Bernadotte, *To Jerusalem*, p. 39.

130. The next day: Diaries of David Ben-Gurion, June 1, 1948, entry, Ben-Gurion Archives, Sde Boker, Israel.

130. "again the truce has failed": *Ha'aretz,* June 2, 1948.

130. He was joined by John Reedman: Author's interview with John Reedman.

131. The passage regarding King Abdullah is from Bernadotte, *To Jerusalem,* esp. p. 41.

131. Upon landing, Bernadotte's party: Foreign Office memorandum of February 18, 1946, in Public Records Office, 84/78, London.

131. Brigadier General Norman Lash: Sir John B. Glubb, *Soldier with the Arabs* (London: Hodder & Stoughton, 1957), chap. VIII, "The First Truce."

132. "I tried to express myself": Bernadotte, *To Jerusalem,* p. 42.

132. "Like myself you are of royal blood": Dan Kurzman, *Genesis 1948: The First Arab-Israeli War* (New York: World, 1970), p. 448.

132. The afternoon, spent in the company: Bernadotte, *To Jerusalem,* p. 41.

133. On May 27: Author's interviews with Dean Rusk and John Reedman; and as background, see also Glubb's memoirs, *Soldier with the Arabs.*

133. "Bernadotte represented everything": Author's interview with William Mashler.

134. "We would send a message": Bunche diary notes, p. 375 (Urquhart Papers).

134. Between June 3 and 7: Author's interviews with Barbro Wessel and John Reedman.

134. "Both sides love to haggle": Bunche diary notes, p. 375 (Urquhart Papers).

135. "These guys seem to believe": Ibid., pp. 303, 304.

135. "The Arabs living in Jerusalem": This is quoted in the original, unedited, unpublished version of *To Jerusalem,* pp. 42–57, and is cited by Sune Persson in his book *Mediation and Assassination: Count Bernadotte's Mission to Palestine* (London: Ithaca Press, 1979), p. 130.

135. "They had explained": Bernadotte, *To Jerusalem,* p. 55.

136. "His reaction was immediate": Ibid., p. 59.

136. Shertok seemed to realize: Author's interview with Amitsur Ilan.

136. Shertok knew that Israel: Ilan, *Bernadotte in Palestine,* p. 93.

136. "The Israeli view of Bernadotte": Author's interview with John Reedman.

137. "In Lake Success": Bernadotte, *To Jerusalem,* p. 73.

137. Was it not true: Author's interview with Joseph Heller.

138. For Israelis, the most sensitive: Bernadotte, *To Jerusalem,* pp. 63–68.

138. "The Count hugged me": Bunche diary notes, p. 311; and Persson, *Mediation and Assassination,* p. 132.

138. "Tell Bernadotte": FRUS, vol. V (1948), p. 1107; and Persson, *Mediation and Assassination,* p. 132.

138. Both sides needed the truce: Ilan, *Bernadotte in Palestine,* p. 93.

139. "This job was beyond": Author's interview with John Reedman.

139. Not all concerned parties: UN Archives, DAG 13/3/0, Box 22.

CHAPTER FOURTEEN

140. "Bernadotte's Camps": See various entries from Ben-Gurion diaries, summer of 1948, Kibbutz Sde Boker, Israel.

140. "These were British-built camps": Author's interview with Baruch Nadel.

140. "The Arabs have nothing to lose": Ben-Gurion, *Israel: A Personal History,* p. 141.

141. "Why does Bernadotte": Ben-Gurion's comment was quoted to the author by his biographer, Shabtai Teveth, in an interview in Tel Aviv.

141. A tiny staff: Author's interview with Brian Urquhart; and Bunche's diary notes, p. 373 (Urquhart Papers).

142. The New York Police Department: Author's interview with William Mashler.

142. John Reedman, an economist: Author's interview with John Reedman.

142. "The Security Council": Abba Eban, *My Country* (New York: Random House, 1968), p. 58.

143. They had to scrounge: Author's interviews with Brian Urquhart and William Mashler.

143. "I considered the humanitarian": Bernadotte, *To Jerusalem*, p. 99.

143. On a call to New York: Bunche diary notes, p. 337 (Urquhart Papers).

144. Arthur Koestler, in Palestine: Koestler, *Promise and Fulfillment*, p. 258.

144. The Israelis claimed: Bernadotte, *To Jerusalem*, p. 145.

144. From his Palmach unit headquarters: Author's interview with Chaim Hefer.

145. The mediator's widow recalled: Ilan's interview with Estelle Bernadotte Ekstrand.

145. During one of his calls: Author's interview with Brian Urquhart.

145. "Rhodes is a beautiful island": Ralph Bunche to Ruth Bunche (Urquhart Papers).

146. "The Count (Ha Rozen): Shabtai Teveth's private papers.

146. "I do not know what you foresee": Letter 179, *The Letters of Chaim Weizmann*, vol. XXIII, series A, August 1947–June 1952 (Jerusalem: Israel Press, 1980).

146. Back in Tel Aviv: Bernadotte, *To Jerusalem*, p. 105.

147. "Jerusalem," Eytan insists: Author's interview with Walter Eytan.

147. "On the flight from Tel Aviv": Bernadotte, *To Jerusalem*, p. 107.

148. As if to confirm: FRUS, vol. V (1948), p. 1122.

148. A week later: Ibid., p. 1139.

148. "I began to realize": Bernadotte, *To Jerusalem*, p. 107.

148. Others with more sensitive antennae: FRUS, vol. V (1948), p. 1141.

149. There is no record: Bernadotte, *To Jerusalem*, p. 12.

CHAPTER FIFTEEN

150. "Two important developments": Bernadotte, *To Jerusalem*, pp. 111, 113, 114–15.

151. "To the Secretary-General": UN Archives, DAG 13/3/0/1.

152. On June 18: Bunche diary notes, p. 337 (Urquhart Papers).

152. "The job couldn't": Author's interview with Brian Urquhart.

152. On June 27: Bernadotte, *To Jerusalem*, p. 126.

154. In his diary note for June 27: Bunche diary notes, p. 407 (Urquhart Papers).

154. "Count Bernadotte can't stand waiting": Ibid., p. 334.

154. Foreign Secretary Bevin: Louis, *The British Empire in the Middle East*, chap. 9.

155. The first portents from Israel: Bernadotte, *To Jerusalem*, p. 137.

155. "Count's suggestions utterly negative": Shabtai Teveth Papers.

155. On June 29: Ben-Gurion diaries, Sde Boker, Israel, pp. 38–39.

155. The reply expressed "surprise": UN Archives, DAG 13.3.3.0, Box 44.

156. With the barest trace of a bow: Author's interviews with William Mashler and John Reedman; and Bernadotte, *To Jerusalem*, pp. 152–58.

157. Ralph Bunche, the originator: Author's interview with Brian Urquhart.

158. Leaks to the press: UN Archives, Security Council document S/863, July 1948.

158. The Arabs were no more enthusiastic: Bunche diary notes, p. 408 (Urquhart Papers).

158. "Unfortunately," ran the Arab reply: Persson, *Mediation and Assassination*, p. 149.

158. Unmentioned in the official Arab reply: FRUS, vol. V (1948), p. 1159.

158. Rumors of the Swede's "friendship": Shabtai Teveth Papers.

159. Walter Eytan, who only a few weeks before: Author's interview with Eytan.

159. Judah Magnes's letter to Bernadotte is in the Swedish Red Cross Archives, Stockholm, Bernadotte File.

160. "I understand quite well": Bernadotte's letter to his brother is among Count Bertil Bernadotte's papers.

161. The CIA had picked up: CIA memorandum, July 27, 1948, FRUS, vol. V (1948), pp. 1240–48.

162. By late summer: Sachar, *A History of Israel,* p. 339; and Collins and Lapierre, *O Jerusalem,* p. 543.

162. An equally dramatic development: *Documents on the Foreign Policy of Israel* (hereafter, DFPI), vol. I (December 1947–May 1948), p. 163.

162. Prime Minister Yitzhak Rabin: *New York Times,* October 23, 1977; and David Shipler, *Arab and Jew* (New York: Times Books, 1986), p. 33.

163. Dr. Chaim Weizmann wrote a friend: Weizmann to Josef Cohn, June 29, 1948, *The Letters and Papers of Chaim Weizmann,* vol. XXIII (Jerusalem: Israel Universities Press, 1980).

164. Reuters Jerusalem correspondent: Jon Kimche, *Seven Fallen Pillars,* (London: Secker & Warburg, 1950), p. 248.

164. Among Lehi's three leaders: Author's interview with Israel Eldad.

CHAPTER SIXTEEN

166. Shertok privately assured him: DFPI, vol. I, pp. 279–90, 295–97.

166. Reuven Shiloah, later an armistice negotiator: Author's interview with Brian Urquhart; and Bunche diary notes (Urquhart Papers).

166. Bunche called Secretary-General Lie's aide: Bunche diary notes, p. 428. (Urquhart Papers).

166. "The Arab people": CIA memorandum, July 27, 1948, FRUS, vol. V (1948), pp. 1240–48.

167. "The decision": Glubb, *A Soldier with the Arabs,* pp. 149–50.

167. Abdullah cabled Bernadotte: Bernadotte, *To Jerusalem,* p. 163.

167. "Abdullah was very nervous": Unedited version of Bernadotte, *To Jerusalem,* deleted from the published account, reprinted in Persson, *Mediation and Assassination,* pp. 141–44.

168. Glubb Pasha provided the answer: Glubb, *Soldier with the Arabs,* p. 150.

169. Barbro Wessel recalled feeling sorry: Author's interview with Barbro Wessel.

169. The Cold War's chill winds: Author's interviews with Brian Urquhart, A. M. Rosenthal, Barbro Wessel; and see also Bernadotte, *To Jerusalem,* pp. 166–78.

171. In remarks certain to arouse: "Report of the Mediator on Palestine to the Security Council," SCOR Supplement for July 1948, pp. 47–63, UN Archives, New York.

171. "We all admired him": Author's interview with Brian Urquhart.

172. In a meeting with Philip Jessup: Jessup to Marshall, July 17, 1948, FRUS, vol. V (1948), p. 1228.

173. "We have had the best": DFPI, vol. I (1948), p. 364.

173. "What we resented": Author's interview with Abba Eban.

173. "Consider our interest": *Israel and Palestine,* Political Report no. 130, January 1987 (Paris: Magelan), p. 20.

CHAPTER SEVENTEEN

175. Around the end of June: Author's interview with Baruch Nadel.

178. "their dedication to their own programs": Dov Joseph, *The Faithful City* (New York: Simon & Schuster, 1960), p. 31.

178. While Lehi wavered: C. S. Sulzberger, *A Long Row of Candles* (New York: Macmillan, 1969), pp. 402–3.

179. "A man comes to you": Transcript of the Hebrew-language broadcast of "This Is Your Life," with Amos Ettinger, November 1991.

179. "In Jerusalem, in the summer": Author's interview with Y. S. Brenner.

180. "The room was packed": Bernadotte, *To Jerusalem,* p. 158.

180. The dynamic quality: Pablo de Azcárate, *Mission in Palestine, 1948–1952* (Washington, D.C.: Middle East Institute, 1966), pp. 93–95.

181. "Major Labarrière's death": Bernadotte, *To Jerusalem,* p. 160.

CHAPTER EIGHTEEN

182. "In June, July, and August": Author's interview with Baruch Nadel.

183. Shertok and Dov Joseph did not: Bernadotte, *To Jerusalem,* p. 189.

183. Bunche scribbled in his diary: Bunche diary notes, p. 441 (Urquhart Papers).

183. Two days later: UN Archives, DAG 13/3/0/1.

184. "Am still without reply": Bunche diary notes, p. 439 (Urquhart Papers).

184. Not surprisingly, Bunche noted: Ibid., p. 443.

184. "We know that the United Nations": Bernadotte, *To Jerusalem*, p. 193.

185. Secretary of State Marshall's attempt: FRUS, vol. V (1948), p. 1251.

185. "Yes, we certainly had a good laugh": Bernadotte, *To Jerusalem*, p. 194.

186. "At the present time": FRUS, vol. V (1948), p. 1242.

186. "Department has in mind": UN Archives, DAG 1/2 1.4.1, July 21, 1948.

186. "There is no assurance": FRUS, vol. V (1948), p. 1275.

186. "Our own opinion": Ibid., p. 1274.

186. On August 1: August 1 memorandum from John J. MacDonald to George C. Marshall, ibid., p. 1265.

186. "Two weeks have elapsed: Ibid.

187. But Secretary Marshall was too preoccupied: Forrest C. Pogue, *George C. Marshall,* vol. 4 (New York: Viking, 1987); pp. 336–78, and author's interview with Dean Rusk.

187. "To suggest that the settlement": DAG 1.2.1.4, Box 8, "Instruction to Senior US Military Observer."

187. Bernadotte was slowly learning: Bernadotte, *To Jerusalem*, pp. 193–94.

188. "We heard that Bernadotte": Ben-Gurion, *Israel: A Personal History,* p. 233.

188. It was as the most visible symbol: Bernadotte, *To Jerusalem*, p. 198.

189. An aloof Dov Joseph: Ibid., p. 199.

189. "It's become a laughingstock": MacDonald to Marshall, FRUS, vol. V (1948), p. 1276.

189. "He [Shertok] admitted": Bernadotte, *To Jerusalem*, p. 210.

189. "Israelis now swashbuckling": Bunche diary notes, p. 444 (Urquhart Papers).

189. "Nothing that I could propose": Bernadotte, *To Jerusalem,* p. 199.

189. British Foreign Secretary Bevin: FRUS, vol. V (1948), p. 1291.

190. "Shertok,"—the Swede recalled: Bernadotte, *To Jerusalem,* p. 212.

190. "Before we left Jerusalem": Ibid., p. 200.

190. Desperate for a sign: Commander Jackson's reflections are from the *United Nations Staff Journal,* December 1986, p. 61.

192. "He looked very good": Author's interviews with Baruch Nadel and Y. S. Brenner.

193. "I soon became aware": Bernadotte, *To Jerusalem* (London: Hodder & Stoughton, 1951), pp. 207–8.

194. "When we demonstrated": "This is Your Life," with Amos Ettinger, November 1991.

194. If the meaning: From Shabtai Teveth's papers on David Ben-Gurion.

194. Israeli Interior Minister: Ben-Gurion, *Israel, A Personal History,* p. 262.

194. An unaccustomed heaviness: Author's interview with Barbro Wessel.

195. "What is needed": Memorandum from Jessup to Marshall, August 6, 1948, National Archives, Washington, D.C., Diplomatic Files, Palestine series, 1948, RG 59 867N.

195. "Responsibility for the disaster": James G. McDonald, *My Mission in Israel* (London: Gollancz, 1951), pp. 43–44.

195. "I had asked time and again": Bernadotte, *To Jerusalem,* p. 217.

196. Nothing would stop: Ibid., p. 218.

CHAPTER NINETEEN

197. "Count Bernadotte conferred": *Palestine Post,* August 4, 1948.

198. "After holding a press conference": Ibid.

198. "Israel becoming increasingly intransigent": FRUS, vol. V (1948), p. 1298.

198. On the heels of this cable: Jerusalem to Secretary of State, August 16, 1948, National Archives, Diplomatic Files, Palestine, 1948.

199. "As a friend of Israel": Marshall to President Truman, August 16, 1948, National Archives, Diplomatic Files, Palestine, 1948.

199. Truman, once described: Harry S Truman, *Years of Trial and Hope 1946–1952* (Garden City, N.Y.: Doubleday, 1956), pp. 157–69; Robert J. Donovan, *Conflict and Crisis* (New York: Norton, 1977), pp. 369–87.

199. "Israel does not owe": Author's interview with Abba Eban.

200. Bernadotte, Bunche told: FRUS, vol. V (1948), pp. 1308–9.

200. "UN observers appear powerless": Ibid., p. 1317.

200. "Much disturbed by last": UN Archives, DAG 13/3/3/0:2.

200. The section on James G. McDonald is drawn from his memoirs, *My Mission in Israel,* and from an interview with Dean Rusk, as well as the relevant parts of C. S. Sulzberger's memoirs, *A Long Row of Candles.*

201. "I shall expect you": President Truman's letter of July 21, 1948, is reprinted in McDonald, *My Mission in Israel,* p. 12.

201. After only three weeks: FRUS, vol. V (1948), p. 1339.

202. In a telegram marked "Top Secret": Memorandum from Marshall to Tel Aviv, August 24, 1948, National Archives, Diplomatic Files, Palestine, 1948.

203. The new ambassador replied: Ibid.

203. Abba Eban was not: Urquhart notes, pp. 491, 492 (Urquhart Papers).

204. "Bernadotte simply didn't take": Author's interview with Walter Eytan.

204. Ambassador Jessup alerted: FRUS, vol. V (1948), p. 1289.

204. Marshall now pushed: Ibid., p. 1373.

205. "restrain Bernadotte": Urquhart notes, p. 463 (Urquhart Papers).

205. "Mediator Threatens to Report Jews": *Palestine Post,* August 27, 1948.

205. Bunche left New York: Brian Urquhart, *Ralph Bunche* (New York: Norton, 1993), p. 172.

206. "One of the few evenings": Estelle B. Ekstrand to Amitsur Ilan.

207. "Not enthusiastic about seeing Rhodes": Bunche diary notes (Urquhart Papers), p. 501.

207. In Cairo, Bernadotte and Bunche: Bernadotte, *To Jerusalem,* p. 229.

207. "Change in the atmosphere here": Bunche diary notes, p. 503 (Urquhart Papers).

208. The barrel-chested man: Author's interviews with Israel Eldad and Baruch Nadel. See also Kurzman, *Genesis,* p. 556; and J. Bowyer Bell, "Assassination in International Politics," *International Studies Quarterly* 16 (March 1972), p. 75.

208. Yalin-Mor, harboring future: Author's interviews with Joseph Heller and Baruch Nadel.

208. "Men! If you want to smell fire": Frank, *The Deed,* p. 88; and Yair Amikam, in *Yediot Aharonot,* February 28, 1977, pp. 1–7.

208. Later that week: Author's interview with Baruch Nadel.

209. The day they passed: McDonald, *My Mission in Israel,* pp. 65–66.

209. Shamir, Yalin-Mor, and Eldad: Author's interview with Dr. Israel Eldad.

210. Zetler, elated at his orders: Roni Shaked, in *Yediot Aharonot,* September 11, 1988. pp. 2–5.

210. Also in common with the others: Ibid.

210. One part of their mandate: Author's interview with Baruch Nadel.

211. While Yehoshua Cohen: McDonald, *My Mission in Israel,* pp. 68–70.

212. The ambassador and his daughter: Ibid.

CHAPTER TWENTY

213. "After a sleepless night": Bunche's diary notes, p. 500 (Urquhart Papers).

214. "Department believes we are now": Memorandum of Secretary

Marshall to Ambassador Douglas in London, National Archives, Diplomatic Files, Palestine, 1948.

215. Even US Ambassador to Israel: Ilan, *Bernadotte in Palestine,* p. 186.

215. "With utmost secrecy": FRUS, vol. V (1948), p. 1387.

215. "They are really taking it seriously": Bunche diary notes, p. 503 (Urquhart Papers).

216. Bernadotte and the British diplomat: Ibid., p. 464.

216. On September 15: FRUS, vol. V (1948), p. 1398.

217. While the mediator's white Dakota: *Palestine Post,* September 17, 1948, p. 1.

CHAPTER TWENTY-ONE

219. In the end: Author's interviews with Baruch Nadel and Nahum Chachkes, aka Nimry.

221. In an official document: Minutes by Thirkel, January 1949, Foreign Office 371/61735; see also Foreign Office 371/75266 185964 for another reference to Nimry as a British intelligence agent (Public Records Office, Kew Gardens, London).

221. "During lunch, the programme":Bernadotte, *To Jerusalem,* p. 253.

222. At four o'clock: Statements of Yoram Katz and Uri Scharf taken by Jerusalem Police on September 18, 1948, in the Israeli Foreign Ministry Archives, Jerusalem, Bernadotte File.

223. Meticulously planned: Author's interviews with Moshe Hillman, Barbro Wessel, Israel Eldad, and Baruch Nadel.

224. Among those who gathered: Statement of Nissam Assar taken by Jerusalem Police, in the Israeli Foreign Ministry Archives, Jerusalem, Bernadotte File.

225. Captain Hillman spent: Author's interview with Moshe Hillman.

225. Among the most contemptible words: Author's interview with Chaim Hefer.

226. "We picked up a Negro": Author's interview with William Mashler.

226. Bunche understood the Swede's need: Author's interview with Brian Urquhart.

227. Flags all over the world: *New York Times,* September 21, 1948, p. 55.

227. Sven Grafstrom the Swedish diplomat: From Grafström's diaries among Count Bertil Bernadotte's Papers.

228. Judah Magnes, the rector: *New York Times,* September 24, 1948, p. 24.

228. Taken time out: The description is drawn from Grafström's diaries, which form part of Count Bertil Bernadotte's Papers, as well as from a *New York Times* dispatch of September 21, 1948, p. 3.

CHAPTER TWENTY-TWO

231. At two in the afternoon: *New York Times,* September 19, 1948, p. 1.

231. From his office: Author's interview with Shabtai Teveth. The author also wishes to thank Mr. Teveth for providing a copy of Ben-Gurion's Knesset speech.

232. The man who had been alerted: McDonald, *My Mission in Israel,* p. 77.

232. The new law: Author's interview with Israeli political activist Abie Natan.

232. Jerusalem Consul MacDonald: MacDonald to Marshall, September 20, 1948, National Archives, Diplomatic Files, Palestine, 1948.

233. The four men in the jeep: *Yediot Aharonot,* September 11, 1988.

233. "It was Friday evening": Author's interview with Baruch Nadel.

233. "No one there paid any attention": *Yediot Aharonot,* September 11, 1988; and author's interviews with Israel Eldad and Baruch Nadel.

234. Lehi's three-man leadership: Author's interview with Baruch Nadel.

235. Equally laconic: Author's interview with Samuel Merlin.

236. The Special Military Court: UN Archives, May 3, 1949, p. 2. DAG 13/3..3.0

236. "I don't know why": Shamir to reporter Yair Amikam as quoted in *Yediot Aharonot,* February 28, 1977, pp. 1, 7.

KATI MARTON

236. Shamir refuses even now: Dan Margalit, in *Ma'ariv*, January 31, 1992.

236. "On 17 September": Shamir *Summing Up*, p. 75.

237. "We hoped to educate": Bar Zohar's interview with Isser Harel in *Hamemune* (Tel Aviv), 1978, p. 49. Harel, who later became the head of Mossad (Israeli Intelligence), proceeded to recruit several former Lehi members, including Shamir, to his service.

237. A few months after: Author's interview with Israel Eldad.

238. As early as the day: Ben-Gurion's diary entries of September 19 and October 29, 1948, Kibbutz Sde Boker.

238. In his memoirs: Shamir, *Summing Up*, p. 75–76.

239. The interior minister reportedly: Kurtzman, *Genesis*, p. 567.

240. Before disbanding: Shamir, *Summing Up*, p. 76.

CHAPTER TWENTY-THREE

241. "It is with a heavy heart": Ralph Bunche's speech to the United Nations First Committee, October (undated manuscript) 1948, found in the UN Archives, DAG 13/3.3.0.

243. But in the solemn figure: FRUS, vol. V (1948), pp. 1415–16.

243. Marshall's support, however: Pogue, *George C. Marshall,* p. 375.

243. Rabbi Hillel Silver: *New York Times,* September 20, 1948, p. 6; and Pogue, *George C. Marshall,* p. 375.

244. On October 30: Pogue, *George C. Marshall,* p. 376.

244. He told Eban: Author's interview with Abba Eban; see also Eban's memoir, *Personal Witness,* p. 178.

244. On November 20: Ben-Gurion diary entries of November 20 and December 9, 1948, Kibbutz Sde Boker.

245. Among those nine members: "Finding of an Examination of a Report Submitted by the Israeli Government on the Assassination of Count Bernadotte," Israeli Foreign Ministry Archives, Jerusalem, Bernadotte File.

246. To deal with the Swedish charges: Author's interview with Walter Eytan.

247. The Agranat Committee's harshest indictment: "Finding of an Examination of a Report . . . ," p. 22.

247. As to the car: Ibid., p. 24.

248. The Agranat Committee again agreed: Ibid., p. 29.

248. The Israeli Committee of Inquiry: Ibid., p. 34.

248. "The committee attributes part: Ibid., p. 47.

248. "It is clear beyond all doubt": Ibid., p. 51.

249. Though the inspector general: Ibid., p. 60.

249. "There is a sort": Author's interview with Walter Eytan.

250. From a combination: Author's interview with Count Bertil Bernadotte.

CHAPTER TWENTY-FOUR

251. "I was shocked": Author's interview with Baruch Nadel.

252. "In the underground": Author's interview with Joseph Heller.

252. "I felt at home": Shamir, Summing Up, p. 79.

252. "While in Mossad": Seymour Hersh, The Samson Option (New York: Vintage, 1993), pp. 286, 297, 298.

253. In 1956, when he retired: Author's interview with Shabtai Teveth.

253. "I took a walk": David Ben-Gurion's diary (Shabtai Teveth Papers).

254. "I know we killed the wrong man": Author's interview with Joseph Heller.

254. Yitzhak Ben-Moshe, another: Yediot Aharonot, September 11, 1988.

254. Two years later: Yediot Aharonot, September 19, 1986.

255. Approached by reporters: Ma'ariv, August 15, 1986.

255. But the electric Eldad: Author's interview with Eldad. See also Ilan, Bernadotte in Palestine, pp. 205, 241; and Yediot Aharonot, February 28, 1977.

255. By 1988: Author's interviews with Moshe Hillman, Israel Eldad, Yaakov Heruti.

255. "Murder Is Murder": Yoel Marcus, in Ha'aretz, September 20, 1988, p. 13.

257. "It takes a strong man": Author's interview with Shabtai Teveth.

257. Not only has Yitzhak Shamir: Author's interviews with Yossi Melman and Joseph Heller.

257. For Abba Eban: Author's interview with Abba Eban.

257. In late 1991: Transcript (translated for the author from the original Hebrew) of "This Is Your Life," with Amos Ettinger, November 1991.

257. "It made me ashamed": Author's interview with Chaim Hefer.

259. "We are men without name": Abraham Stern, "Anonymous Soldiers," quoted by Gerold Frank in *The Deed,* p. 645.

EPILOGUE

260. "I've had difficulty": Author's interview with Brian Urquhart; see also Brian Urquhart, *A Life in Peace and War,* (New York: Norton, 1987).

260. In the words of historian J. Bowyer Bell: J. Bowyer Bell, "Assassination in International Politics," *International Studies Quarterly* 16 (March 1972).

263. In an article: *Atlantic Monthly,* February 1953.

265. But in a letter: Trevor-Roper's letter to Count Bernadotte is among the Bernadotte Papers on file in the Red Cross Archives in Stockholm.

265. Several years later: Kersten, *The Kersten Memoirs,* p. 15.

266. In 1956: *New Statesman,* April 7, 1957.

267. "This does not mean": Hans Heinrich Wilhelm and Louis de Jong, "Zwei Legenden aus dem Dritten Reich," article published by Dutch Institute for War Documentation, Amsterdam, 1972, pp. 79–142.

268. "There was a fellow named Dacre": Robert Harris, *Selling Hitler* (New York: Pantheon, 1986), p. 326.

268. "Professor Posthumus": Ilan, *Bernadotte in Palestine,* p. 262, n. 45.

269. The tension between these tendencies: "For Israel's Aged Survivors, a Day of Particular Anguish," *New York Times,* April 19, 1993.

270. "There is a feeling": David Shipler, *Arab and Jew* (New York: Times Books, 1986), p. 123.

270. "We have not abandoned": Ehud Sprinzak, *The Ascendance of Israel's Radical Right* (New York: Oxford University Press, 1991), p. 40.

ACKNOWLEDGMENTS

Much of the material for this book was gathered during trips to Israel, Sweden, Great Britain, and Holland. I am once again indebted to the Freedom Forum Media Studies Center at Columbia University and, in particular, to Everette E. Dennis for providing me with access to the university's remarkable collection of books and periodicals as well as a year's sanctuary to pursue my research as a Visiting Scholar.

I am first of all grateful to Count Bertil Bernadotte, the son of the murdered mediator, for the many hours of his time, for his vivid recollections of his father and his generosity in allowing me access to the Bernadotte family's letters and other historic documents in both London and Stockholm. In Sweden, Barbro Wessel, Bernadotte's secretary, was of invaluable help in reconstructing the mediator's final hours, as well as the drama of Bernadotte's four-month-long Middle East peace effort. I thank James Cavallie, Jan Lindroth, and Per Gunnar Ottoson of the Swedish Royal Archives for allowing me to spend days freely studying the Bernadotte family papers. I am also grateful to Gunnar Nyby for permitting me access to material on Count Bernadotte's work with the Swedish Red Cross. Lena Biörck Kaplan provided me with hospitality and friendship during my Swedish stay as well as introductions to key members of the Swedish Foreign Ministry.

In the United States, a great many people provided information and editorial guidance. Foremost among those who gave of their time and wisdom in helping me to understand the thorny issues of the Middle East were Lenni Brenner, Arthur Hertzberg,

Peter Osnos, Dean Rusk, A. M. Rosenthal, Samuel Merlin, Seth Lipsky, Gerold Frank, Marilyn Berger, Felix and Elizabeth Rohatyn, Peter Jennings, Richard Bernstein, Suzanne Braun Levine, Judith Goldstein, Eric Breindel, and William Mashler. Josh Freidman, *Newsday*'s Pulitzer Prize–winning former Middle East correspondent, also gave unstinting support to this project and made many helpful suggestions regarding the manuscript. I thank him from the bottom of my heart.

Sir Brian Urquhart, as the United Nations chief peacekeeper over several decades, understands the issues raised in this book more than anyone else, and was generous with his time and memories. I cannot thank him enough for his support and his boundless generosity in allowing me to use his files on his former chief and longtime friend, Ralph Bunche.

Marilla Guptil, librarian of the United Nations Archives, was of invaluable help in retrieving critical UN documents for my research. Michael Kettle performed the same task in retrieving material from the British Public Records Office in London.

In Israel, I am grateful to the people who run the Jerusalem haven for writers and artists known as Mishkenot Sha Ananim; they made my stay in their country memorable. Also in Israel, I thank Chaim Hefer, Dr. Amitsur Ilan, Leah Van Leer, Professor Joseph Heller, the Honorable Walter Eytan, Ambassador Abba Eban, Uri Savir, Yossi Olmert, Shabtai Teveth, Yossi Melman, Dan Pattir, Moshe Hillman, Israel Eldad, and Yaakov Heruti for their time and contribution to my research.

In particular, I owe a debt to Baruch Nadel, a former Sternist who agreed to cooperate with this project. It would not have been possible for me to breathe life into a forty-five-year-old murder without Nadel's vivid and painstakingly rendered memories of his years in the underground. He provided an unvarnished account of his role in laying the groundwork for the assassination of Folke Bernadotte. Nadel has repented neither his part in Bernadotte's murder nor his participation in the terrorist underground. Though I do not share his unshakable conviction that assassination is a legitimate tool of politics, I thank him for helping me to understand the mind of a fanatic.

In Holland, I had the invaluable assistance of David Barnouw, archivist at Amsterdam's Institute for War Documentation, in piecing together the baffling role Felix Kersten played in damaging Folke Bernadotte's reputation as a humanitarian. Also in Holland, I am grateful for the time and hospitality of Professor and Mrs. Y. S. Brenner in Utrecht. Professor Brenner, a former Sternist, was brilliant in his analysis of why Avraham Stern's way might have seemed a logical option for some Holocaust survivors.

I could not have written this book without the translations from Hebrew to English provided by my friend and research assistant Sarinah Kalb. Sibylle M. Fischer did yeoman's work translating German documents, as did my father, Endre Marton, who spent many hours making sense out of barely legible German letters and memoranda. Lena Biörck Kaplan and Kristina Friberg translated Swedish documents into English. I thank them all.

For believing in this project—and in me—from the very beginning, I thank my agent and friend, Amanda Urban.

I am grateful to my indomitable editor, Linda Healey, who has worked her usual magic on this manuscript.

For providing sound historical and editorial guidance, and emotional support, I thank Richard Holbrooke.

ILLUSTRATION
CREDITS

P. 1 of insert: top, courtesy of the Central Zionist Archives; p. 1 bottom, courtesy of the Bettmann Archive; p. 2 top, courtesy of the Bettmann Archive; p. 2 bottom, courtesy of AP/Wide World Photos; p. 3 top and bottom, courtesy of the Central Zionist Archives; p. 4 top and bottom, courtesy of AP/Wide World Photos; p. 5 top, center, and bottom, p. 6 top and bottom and p. 7 top, courtesy of Count Bertil Bernadotte; p. 7 center, Dokumentationsarchiv des Osterreichischen Wilderstandes, courtesy of USHMM; p. 7 bottom, courtesy of Count Bertil Bernadotte; p. 8 top and center, courtesy of AP/Wide World Photos; p. 8 bottom, courtesy of the Central Zionist Archives; p. 9 top, courtesy of Count Bertil Bernadotte; p. 9 bottom, courtesy of AP/Wide World Photos; p. 10 top and center, courtesy of the United Nations; p. 10 bottom, courtesy of the Bettmann Archive; p. 11 top, courtesy of Count Bertil Bernadotte; p. 11 bottom, courtesy of AP/Wide World Photos; p. 12 top, center, and bottom, courtesy of Count Bertil Bernadotte; p. 13 top, courtesy of AP/Wide World Photos; p. 13 center and bottom, courtesy of Count Bertil Bernadotte; p. 14 top and center, courtesy of AP/Wide World Photos; p. 14 bottom and p. 15, courtesy of Count Bertil Bernadotte; p. 16, courtesy of Israel GPO/ASAP.

Photograph research by Carousel Research, Inc./Laurie Platt Winfry and Beth Krumholz.

INDEX

as Israeli capital, 148–49, 183,
    210, 270
Jewish ambivalence about, 27
Jewish sector of, 4, 5–6, 25, 129,
    135, 136, 157–58, 218
Jewish underground in, 25, 28,
    57, 149, 194, 233–38, 248
Katamon quarter of, 12
Mandelbaum Gate of, 4
New City of, 10, 25
Old City of, 9–10, 25, 26, 28,
    129, 144, 188, 210
Red Cross in, 6, 9, 11
Sharei Pina quarter of, 233–34
snipers in, 5, 9, 12, 33, 188
Talbiya section of, 12, 149
UN observers in, 4, 7n, 185–89,
    191, 195
"zone of sanctuary" in, 6
Jerusalem-Tel Aviv road, 17, 33,
    147, 148
Jessup, Philip, 148, 172, 186, 198,
    204
Jewish Agency, 43, 47, 117, 120n
Jews:
    Diaspora of, 25, 53
    Jews vs., 25–30, 100
    Orthodox, 25, 27, 101, 176,
        233
    Sephardic, 176
    victimization of, xii, 25, 26–27
Joseph, Dov, 9, 123, 147, 149, 178,
    182–83, 189, 194n, 197, 199,
    221
Journal of the Middle East Society,
    219–20
Juravin, Eliezer, 233

kacha, 91
Kahane, Meir, ix–x
Kalanit, SS, 117, 118
Karl, Prince of Sweden, 9, 61, 66
Karl XVI Gustav, King of Sweden,
    250
Katz, Yoram, 222–23, 224, 248
Keitel, Wilhelm, 87
Kennan, George, 114–15
Kersten, Felix:

Bernadotte and, 71, 82, 84–86,
    263–68
diaries of, 267, 268
Himmler influenced by, 70–71,
    73, 78, 80, 85–86
Swedish citizenship requested by,
    71, 84–85, 267
Kersten Memoirs, The (Kersten),
    86, 265
Kesselring, Albert, 87
Khachaba Pasha, 124
Khouri, Faris el-, 136
Kimche, Jon, 164
King David Hotel, 6, 176–78,
    182–83, 197–98
    bombing of, 104–5
Kirkbride, Alec, 132, 133
Kissinger, Henry, x
Koestler, Arthur, 46–47, 51, 111,
    144
Kollek, Teddy, 100–101
Kollontai, Alexandra, 68

Labarrière, Major, 181
Labor Party (Israel), 145–46
Labour Party (England), 103–4
Lash, Norman, 3, 4, 131
Last Days of Hitler, The (Trevor-
    Roper), 265
Latrun, battle of, 118–19
Latrun pumping station, 191, 195,
    198, 218
League of Nations, 3–4, 21, 43,
    123, 138, 200–201
Lebanon, 55
    in Arab-Israeli War (1948), 20,
        137, 262
Lehi (Lohmey Heruth Israel):
    Ben-Gurion opposed by, 16–17,
        25, 26–27, 90, 99, 100,
        140–41, 144
    Bernadotte Plan opposed by,
        164–65, 175–76
    Bernadotte's assassination linked
        to, 18, 208–9, 228, 236, 246,
        248–49, 252, 255–58
    British as targets of, 51, 57, 93,
        94–99, 107